CAREER OPPORTUNITIES IN HEALTH CARE

Second Edition

SHELLY FIELD

Foreword by

ARTHUR E. WEINTRAUB
President, Northern Metropolitan Hospital Association

Checkmark Books®
An imprint of Facts On File, Inc.

CAREER OPPORTUNITIES IN HEALTH CARE, SECOND EDITION

Checkmark Books
An imprint of Facts On File, Inc.
132 West 31st Street
New York NY 10001

Library of Congress Cataloging-in-Publication data

Field, Shelly.
   Career opportunities in health care / Shelly Field.—2nd ed.
      p. cm.
   Includes bibliographical references and index.
   ISBN 0-8160-4816-9 (hc : alk. paper)—ISBN 0-8160-4817-7 (pbk : alk. paper)
   1. Medicine—Vocational guidance. 2. Allied health personnel—Vocational guidance. I.
Title.
R690 .F54 2002
610.69—dc21   2002021650

Checkmark Books are available at special discounts when purchased in bulk quantities for businesses, associations, institutions, or sales promotions. Please call our Special Sales Department in New York at (212) 967-8800 or (800) 322-8755.

You can find Facts On File on the World Wide Web at http://www.factsonfile.com

Cover design by Nora Wertz

Printed in the United States of America

VB Hermitage 10 9 8 7 6 5 4 3 2 1

This book is printed on acid-free paper.

This book is dedicated with gratitude to Henry Williams, M.D.,
a brilliant, compassionate, and caring physician who is loved and
respected by patients and colleagues throughout the world.
Thank you for taking care of us!

CONTENTS

FOREWORD

Most Americans today receive a highly sophisticated range of health services under a variety of private health insurance systems and under governmental programs such as Medicare or Medicaid. These services are carried out in many different settings: in general and specialty hospitals, community health centers, nursing homes, home care, mental health centers, ambulatory health facilities, diagnostic and treatment centers, and via public health agencies.

The public demand for comprehensive, quality health care will continue to grow dramatically. Present pressures will intensify due to changing demographics and an aging population, advances in medical technology and new drug therapies, escalating costs, a growing number of uninsured, heightened concern for quality and value, new managed care arrangements, and consolidation of services.

At the same time, the nation faces shortages of key health care personnel, particularly in the area of nursing, but also in other important positions, such as radiology, laboratory personnel, pharmacists, physical and occupational therapists, nursing aides, and medical records staff.

These dynamics present many exciting challenges and rewarding opportunities for men and women seeking careers in health care. Those who are dedicated to the care and betterment of others will find few fields as attractive and fulfilling as health care.

The exploding health care industry and the advancing technology that goes along with it have generated a wealth of employment opportunities throughout the country and the world. Wherever you live, there are opportunities in this field.

I have personally experienced the health care industry's expansion while working as the president of the Northern Metropolitan Hospital Association (NorMet) for the past 20 years. NorMet is one of several associations representing hospitals within New York State. The NorMet hospitals, in addition to delivering essential health services, provide more than 30,000 jobs in health care within their communities. These include direct patient care, administration, social services, therapy, marketing, public relations, planning, development, geriatrics, pharmacy, and many technical specialties.

The expansion of the industry has resulted in myriad employment opportunities in all facets of health care. There has long been a need for a comprehensive guide detailing these career opportunities. Shelly Field, a nationwide human resources consultant, career expert, and stress management specialist, has done a remarkable job of researching these opportunities and detailing them in this volume.

Career Opportunities in Health Care is an excellent source for those just starting in this exciting field. It also offers food for thought for professionals who aspire to move into other parts of the industry. The book gives people at all levels of their careers an opportunity to match their skills, talents, and interests to the vast arena of the health care industry.

If you're seeking a career with no limits—one offering future growth opportunities—I can think of no better industry in the world providing the opportunity and ability to make a difference in the lives of others than health care. I urge everyone looking for a great career to read this book to learn more about the possibilities.

Arthur E. Weintraub
President, Northern Metropolitan Hospital Association

ACKNOWLEDGMENTS

I thank every individual, company, corporation, agency, association, and union that provided information, assistance, and encouragement for this book.

I acknowledge with appreciation my editor, James Chambers, for his continuous help and encouragement. I also gratefully acknowledge Ed and Selma Field for their ongoing support in this and every other project.

Others whose help was invaluable include: Ellen Ackerman; Aerobics and Fitness Association of American (AFAA), Aerobics Center; Harrison Allen; Julie Allen; American Association for Counseling and Development: American Association of Advertising Agencies; American Association for Music Therapy; American Dance Therapy Association; American Dental Assistants Association; American Dental Association; American Dental Hygienists Association; American Geriatrics Society; American Health Care Association; American Hospital Association; American Optometric Association; American Physical Therapy Association; American Society for Hospital Marketing and Public Relations; Dan Barrett; Lloyd Barriger, Barriger and Barriger; Allan Barrish: Bio-Chemical Dependency Unit, Community General Hospital, Sullivan County, N.Y.; Joyce Blackman; Steve Blackman; Albee Bockman, Mobilemedic Emergency Medical Service Katrina Bull; Theresa Bull; Earl "Speedo" Carroll; Eileen Casey, Superintendent, Monticello Central Schools; Catskill Development; Anthony Cellini, Town of Thompson Supervisor; Brandi Cesario; Patricia Claghorn; Andy Cohen; Bernard Cohen; Dr. Jessica L. Cohen; Lorraine Cohen; Norman Cohen; Commission on Opticianry Accreditation; Community General Hospital, Harris, N.Y.; Jan Cornelius; Crawford Memorial Library staff; Margaret Crossley, Nevada Society of Certified Public Accountants; Meike Cryan; Daniel Dayton; W. Lynne Dayton; Carrie Dean; Charlie Devine, Devine Realty, Inc.; Direct Mail/Marketing Association, Inc.; Direct Marketing Educational Foundation, Inc.; Jane Donohue; Michelle Edwards; Scott Edwards; Ernest Evans; Field Asso-

ciates, Ltd.; Deborah K. Field, Esq.: Edwin M. Field; Greg Field; Lillian (Cookie) Field; Mike Field; Robert Field; Selma G. Field; Gale Findling, R.N.; Finkelstein Memorial Library staff; Greg Fotiades; John Gatto; Sheila Gatto; Gerontological Society of America; Kaytee Glantzis; Sam Goldych; Gail Haberle; Joyce Harrington, Harris Home Health; Harris Services; Hermann Memorial Library staff; Terry Hooks; Jan Hopkins, R.N.; Patricia Hopkins, Joan Howard; Jimmy "Handyman" Jones; Margo Jones; Bruce Kohl, Boston Herald.com; Karen Leever; Liberty Public Library staff; Ginger Maher; Robert Masters, Esq.; Werner Mendel, New Age Health Spa; Phillip Mestman; Rima Mestman; Beverly Michaels; Martin Michaels, Esq.; Monticello Central High School Guidance Department; Monticello Central School High School Library staff; Monticello Central School Middle School Library staff; Jennifer Morganti, Nevada Society of Certified Public Accountants; Cindy Moorhead; David Morris; National Association For Music Therapy; National Association of Alcoholism and Drug Abuse Counselors; National Resource Center on Health Promotion and Aging; Earl Nesmith; New York State Employment Service; New York State Nurses Association; Ellis Norman, UNLV; Peter Notarstefano; Joy F. Pierce; Public Relations Society of America; Radiology Department of Community General Hospital, Sullivan County, N.Y.; Ramapo Catskill Library System; Doug Richards; Martin Richman; Genice Ruiz; Diane Ruud, Nevada Society of Certified Public Accountants; Society of Illustrators; Debbie Springield; Matthew E. Strong; Sullivan County Community College; Thrall Library staff; Anne Thum, R.N.; Marie Tremper; U.S. Department of Labor; Brian Vargas; Carol Williams; John Williams; John Wolfe; Johnny World; WSUL Radio; and WVOS Radio.

My thanks also to the many people, associations, companies, and organizations that provided material for this book and wish to remain anonymous.

HOW TO USE THIS BOOK

Purpose

The health care industry has evolved tremendously since 1997, when the first edition of *Career Opportunities in Health Care* was published. With today's new technology, amazing things can be accomplished. An operation might be performed in one location with other medical teams around the world watching via an Internet hookup. Mechanical hearts have been implanted into humans. Cloning is now a reality.

Health care continues to be one the fastest growing sectors in the economy. The industry includes careers in a vast array of areas; health care services and medical technology are only two. Thousands of people currently work in the health care industry. There is a need for many more due to the increase of both the elderly population and the use of advanced medical technology.

This book was written for everyone who aspires to work in the expanding health care industry, but is not sure how to enter. The 80 jobs discussed in this book, including eight new to this edition, encompass careers in health services and medical technology as well as health care administration.

If you are considering a job in the expanding industry of health care, this is the book for you. This new edition of *Career Opportunities in Health Care* helps you determine what you might want to do in health care and in what sector you might want to be involved. It offers career opportunities, describes where to locate them, how to train for each position, and most importantly, how to be successful in your quest.

The health care field requires a great variety of people with many different talents and skills. It needs physicians, nurses, administrators, marketing and public relations specialists, many different types of therapists, technologists and technicians, educators, office personnel, and more. The trick in locating a job is to get the right training, develop your skills and use them to get in the door. Once you have your foot in the door, you have a good chance of climbing the career ladder into other positions.

Read through the book and determine what you are qualified for, or how you can obtain training in the field of your interest. You can then work towards getting into a lucrative, exciting, and rewarding career in health care.

Sources of Information

Information for this book was obtained through interviews, questionnaires, and a wide variety of books, magazines, newsletters, television and radio programs, college cata-logs, and so on. Some information came from people with experience working in the industry. Other data were obtained from friends and business associates in various areas of health care.

Among the people interviewed were men and women in all aspects of health care, including individuals working in the business and administration end of the industry, hospitals, clinics, health maintenance organizations (HMOs), nursing homes, extended care facilities, labs, colleges, private physician's offices, schools, colleges, social service agencies, nonprofit organizations, public relations and publicity firms, newspapers, magazines, radio and television personnel, placement companies, human resources departments, and so on. Also interviewed were physicians, nurses, human resource directors, lab personnel, therapists, social workers, alcohol and drug counselors, technologists, technicians, administrators, public relations directors, volunteer directors, geriatric specialists, and planning directors. Professionals were contacted, as were schools, colleges, universities, personnel offices, unions, trade associations, and the like.

Organization of Material

Career Opportunities in Health Care is divided into 18 general employment sections. These sections are: Medicine; Dentistry; Vision Care; Nursing; Social Services; Health Care Administration; Health Care Marketing, Public Relations, Planning, and Development; Clinical Laboratory Services; Therapy; Geriatrics and Long-term Care; Dietetics and Nutrition; Pharmaceuticals; Medical Records; Radiology and Biotechnology; Technicians and Technologists; Counseling; Speech and Hearing; and Miscellaneous Career Opportunities. Within each of these sections are descriptions of individual careers.

There are two parts to each job classification. The first part offers job information in a chart form. The second part explains the job more thoroughly.

Appendixes offer information you might need to get started looking for a job. Names, addresses, phone numbers, fax numbers, websites, and e-mail addresses have been included where possible. You might want to send resumes for job possibilities or check out the availability of internships.

The appendixes include educational programs for those interested in health services administration, pre-med, music therapy, physician assistants, and health services public relations and marketing. Also included are a listing of trade associations and unions, a bibliography of books and periodicals related to the health care industry, and a glossary.

Whether you choose to be a doctor or nurse, social worker, therapist, technician or technologist, home health aide, marketing director, public relations assistant, admitting officer, health services administrator, nurse's aide, optometrist, physician's assistant, emergency medical technician, health promotion coordinator, sonographer, medical illustrator, geriatric assessment coordinator, nursing home activities director, medical records transcriptionist, or pharmacist, your job can be both exciting, fulfilling, and rewarding. Your career in health care is out there waiting. You just have to go after it!

Shelly Field
www.shellyfield.com

INTRODUCTION

The health care industry . . . what other industry can make such a difference in other people's lives?

Those who choose a career in this field often have an avocation as well as a vocation. They want to help others and make a difference. In some situations, the work of someone in health care can mean the difference between a person living or dying.

The health care industry together with medical technology has turned into a multibillion-dollar business. Many thousands of people work in the various facets of this industry. One of them can be you.

For thousands of years, people who have helped others to heal have always been held in high regard. Those who work in health care today are still held in high esteem.

How do people decide on a career in health care? There are many paths. Some individuals, perhaps someone just like you, visited a doctor or had to go to the hospital, and at that moment decided what their life's vocation would be. Others might have realized that health care was a growing industry.

Almost any talent you have can be applied to obtaining a job in health care. You can be anything from a doctor or nurse, to a singer, dancer, or artist who works as a music, dance, or art therapist. You might be a pharmacist or pharmacist technician. You could decide that you want to work with the elderly and become a nursing home activities director, geriatric social worker, geriatric care manager, or geriatric assessment coordinator. You might aspire to be a doctor, dentist, dental hygienist, optician, lab assistant, technician, technologist, home health assistant, emergency medical technician (EMT), optometrist, optician, nurse-midwife, or physician assistant.

You might want to work in complementary health care and become a homeopathic physician. Perhaps you want to use your skills as a secretary, receptionist, fund-raiser or personnel manager to work in the administration of a hospital or health care facility. There are creative positions in medical writing, publicity jobs for public relations and marketing people, and positions in the business end of the industry as accountants, auditors, union negotiators, and human resources personnel. Those who want to work in education can become school health or public health educators.

As you read the various sections in this book, searching to find the job of your dreams, keep in mind that there are many ways to get into the health care industry. I have provided you with the guidelines. You have to do the rest.

Within each section of this book you will find all the information necessary to acquaint you with most of the important jobs in the health care industry. A key to the organization of each entry follows:

Career Profile

At a quick glance, the Career Profile offers a brief description in chart form of job responsibilities and duties, possible alternate job titles, employment prospects, best geographical location, and any prerequisites necessary for the job.

Career Ladder

The career ladder illustrates the normal job progression. Remember, however, that there are often no hard-and-fast rules. Job progression may occur in almost any manner.

Position Description

Every effort has been made to give well-rounded job descriptions. Keep in mind that no two jobs are the same. Jobs might have various supervisors for the same type of position. Some organizations or companies might also eliminate some positions or add others.

Salaries

Salary ranges for the 80 job titles in the book are as accurate as possible. Salaries for jobs in health care vary greatly, due to such factors as the specific job an individual is working at, as well as his or her experience and responsibilities. Earnings also are dependent on the specific facility or company an individual is working in and its size, location, and prestige.

Employment Prospects

If you choose a job that has an EXCELLENT, GOOD, or FAIR rating, you are lucky. You should have an easier time finding a job. If, however, you would like to work at a job that has a POOR rating, don't despair. The rating only means that it is difficult to obtain a job—not totally impossible.

Advancement Prospects

Try to be as cooperative and helpful as possible in the workplace. Don't try to see how little work you can do. Be enthusiastic, energetic, and outgoing. Do that little extra that no one asked you to do. Learn as much as you can. When a job advancement possibility opens up make sure that you're prepared for it.

Education and Training

Although the book only gives the *minimum* training and educational requirements, this doesn't mean that's all you should have. Try to get the best training and education possible. A college degree does not guarantee a job in any aspect of health care, but it will help prepare you for life in the workplace. It may also be required for entry. Education and training also encompass courses, seminars, apprenticeships, programs, on-the-job training, internships, and learning from others.

Experience/Skills/Personality Traits

Experience, skills, and personality traits required will differ from job to job. Whichever job you select to work at, you will probably need a lot of perseverance and energy. You will also have to be articulate and pleasantly aggressive. Being outgoing also helps. Contacts are important in all facets of business, so make as many as you can. These people will be helpful in advancing your career and helping you network. Do not burn bridges. When you make a friend in this industry, it is likely you will see him or her again in your career. If you make an enemy, the same will happen.

Best Geographic Location

The good news is that health care jobs are available throughout the country. Large metropolitan areas may offer more opportunities because there are more facilities. This does not mean that they are the only locations to look for employment. Smaller metropolitan areas often host smaller or less prestigious facilities. These may offer easier entry, especially if you do not have prior experience.

Unions/Associations

Unions and trade associations offer valuable help in getting into many of the jobs in health care as well as making con-

tacts. They may also offer scholarships, fellowships, seminars, and other beneficial programs.

Tips for Entry

Use this section for ideas on how to get a job and gain entry into the areas that interest you. When applying for any job always be as professional as possible. Dress neatly and conservatively. Don't wear sneakers. Don't chew gum. Don't smoke. Don't wear heavy perfume or cologne. Always have a few copies of your resume with you. These too, should look neat and professional. Don't forget to check and recheck your resume for proper grammar, spelling, and content.

Use every contact you have. Don't get hung up on the idea that you want to get a job without anyone's help. If you are lucky enough to know someone who can help you obtain a job you want, take him or her up on it. You will have to prove yourself at the interview and on the job. Nobody can do that for you.

The last piece of advice in this section is to be on time for everything. This includes job interviews, phone calls, work, meetings, sending letters, and so on. People will remember when you're habitually late and it will work against you in advancing your career.

Have fun reading this book. It will help you find a career you will truly love. Don't get discouraged. Don't give up. Every job you have teaches you something and is a stepping stone to the job of your dreams. Have faith and confidence in yourself. When you do get the job you have been dreaming about, become a mentor, share your knowledge and help others fulfill their dreams too.

We love to hear success stories about your career and how this book helped you. If you have one and you want to share it, go to www.shellyfield.com. I can't wait to hear from you!

Good luck!

Shelly Field

MEDICINE

MEDICAL DOCTOR, GENERAL

CAREER PROFILE

Duties: Helping patients attain and maintain good health; examining patients; diagnosing and treating patients' illnesses.

Alternate Titles: Doctor; M.D.; Physician

Salary Range: $75,000 to $350,000+

Employment Prospects: Excellent

Advancement Prospects: Good

Best Geographical Location(s) for Position: Positions are located throughout the country

Prerequisites:

Education or Training—Medical school, including internship; residency required to specialize

Experience—Internship

Special Skills and Personality Traits—Compassion; emotional stability; good judgment; caring; diagnostic skills

CAREER LADDER

```
┌─────────────────────────────────┐
│      Specialist or Physician     │
│      with a Larger Practice      │
└─────────────────────────────────┘

┌─────────────────────────────────┐
│          Medical Doctor          │
└─────────────────────────────────┘

┌─────────────────────────────────┐
│             Student              │
└─────────────────────────────────┘
```

Position Description

Medical Doctors have a large number of responsibilities and duties. Their main functions are helping patients attain and maintain good health.

Medical doctors are also referred to as physicians, doctors of medicine or M.D.'s. (doctors of osteopathy or D.O.'s are also physicians and are covered in another profile in this book.)

M.D.'s may specialize in a variety of fields. If the specialty is general or family practice, pediatrics or internal medicine, the M.D. will often be the patient's primary care physician.

Many medical doctors choose a specialty. Patients are often referred to these doctors by primary care physicians. Specialties include, but are not limited to, allergies, cardiovascular medicine, dermatology, gastroenterology, pulmonary medicine, surgery, pathology, radiology, neurology, obstetrics and gynecology, plastic surgery, homeopathy, and emergency medicine. Some of these specialists are covered in other entries in this book.

A physician or medical doctor's responsibilities depend to a great extent on the individual's specialty. Similar duties exist among all specialties. For example, all physicians examine patients. They are also expected to talk to patients to determine what symptoms and problems exist. Individuals may recommend, order, and perform a variety of diagnostic tests. If the physician is a general practitioner, he or she may refer a patient to a specialist to diagnose or treat specific conditions. Specialists have more specific duties depending on their line of work.

After a patient's illness has been diagnosed, the physician must prescribe a course of treatment. This may include medication, surgery, or various therapies.

Physicians often help patients stay in good health with preventative medicine. This can include examinations, immunizations, or advice on exercise and diet.

As part of their job, physicians answer patients' questions regarding their health or a medical procedure. Medical doctors are also expected to answer questions of patients' family members when necessary.

Medical doctors usually work long hours. They may be on call for a variety of emergencies and are often involved in life-and-death situations.

While this type of work can be stressful, the ability to help others is very rewarding and fulfilling to most individuals in this profession.

Salaries

Medical doctors can earn $75,000 to $350,000 or more. Earnings vary greatly depending on a number of variables. These include the specific type of work setting and its geographic location. Other factors include the specialty, experience, responsibilities, and professional reputation of the individual.

Employment Prospects

Employment prospects for medical doctors are excellent. A doctor can start his or her own practice, become a partner, or be an employee in a hospital, health care facility, nursing home, prison, school, college, medical group, HMO, urgi-center, surgi-center, clinic or public health center. (See glossary for definitions of *urgi-center* and *surgi-center*.)

Advancement Prospects

Advancement prospects for medical doctors are based on the paths they take. Some physicians climb the career ladder by obtaining additional education and specializing. Others go into private practice. Some individuals build up their professional reputation and obtain a large roster of patients. This results in increased earnings.

Still others go into research or teaching as a method of advancing their careers. Physicians working in hospitals can also become medical directors.

Education and Training

It takes a great deal of education and time to become a medical doctor. Individuals must complete at least three years of college before entering medical school. The medical programs are four years long. There are schools throughout the country offering a combined medical school program which lasts only six years.

Competition for admittance into medical school is fierce. Individuals must take the Medical College Admission Test (MCAT). Selection criteria includes exam scores, college grades, letters of recommendation, interviews, and participation in extracurricular activities.

Individuals must also take and pass an exam offered by the National Board of Medical Examiners while still in school.

Even more training is required for those who want to specialize or be board certified in a specialty. This training can take up to five years in a residency program. Those aspiring to be board certified must also take and pass another exam.

M.D.'s must be licensed. Requirements include graduating from an accredited medical school, completing an internship, and taking and passing the licensing exam.

Experience/Skills/Personality Traits

M.D.'s must be very compassionate, caring people. Successful doctors have a good "bedside manner." As they will often be dealing with life-and-death situations, individuals should have excellent judgment and the ability to work under stress and pressure. Emotional stability is essential. Stamina is mandatory when working long hours.

Physicians must have good diagnostic skills. Scientific aptitude is necessary. Individuals should be organized and detail oriented. Communications skills are also needed.

Unions/Associations

Aspiring physicians can obtain additional career information by contacting the American Medical Association (AMA) or the American Medical College (AMC).

Tips for Entry

1. If you are beginning to build a practice, consider participating at local health fairs. This is a good way for people in the community to get to know you.
2. Offer to speak to local civic groups and nonprofit organizations. This is another way people in the area can get to know you.
3. Many schools contract out for physicians.
4. Rural areas needing doctors will often help pay for medical school if you make a contract to return to the area and work for a certain number of years.
5. It is easier to build a practice in less populated areas that do not have a great many physicians.

OSTEOPATHIC DOCTOR

CAREER PROFILE

Duties: Helping patients attain and maintain good health; examining patients; diagnosing and treating patients' illnesses.

Alternate Titles: Doctor; O.D., Doctor of Osteopathy; Physician; Osteopath

Salary Range: $75,000 to $350,000+

Employment Prospects: Excellent

Advancement Prospects: Good

Best Geographical Location(s) for Position: Positions may be located throughout the country

Prerequisites:
Education or Training—Osteopathic school including internship
Experience—Rotating internship required
Special Skills and Personality Traits—Compassion; emotional stability; good judgment; caring; diagnostic skills

CAREER LADDER

```
┌─────────────────────────────┐
│   Specialist or Physician    │
│   with a Larger Practice     │
└─────────────────────────────┘

┌─────────────────────────────┐
│     Osteopathic Doctor       │
└─────────────────────────────┘

┌─────────────────────────────┐
│          Student             │
└─────────────────────────────┘
```

Position Description

Osteopathic doctors have a large number of responsibilities and duties. Their main functions are helping patients attain and maintain good health.

Osteopathic doctors are also referred to as physicians, Doctors of osteopathy, or D.O.s. Medical doctors or M.D.'s are also physicians and covered in another profile in this book.

Doctors of osteopathy (D.O.s) and medical doctors (M.D.'s) both utilize all accepted methods of treatment when caring for patients. These may include drugs and surgery. However, when treating patients, D.O.s place an emphasis on the body's musculoskeletal system. Their beliefs note that a person requires the proper alignment of bones, muscles, ligaments, and nerves in order to reach optimum health.

In many cases, the D.O. is a patient's primary care physician. Doctors of osteopathy may also specialize in a variety of fields including family practice, pediatrics, internal medicine, emergency medicine, cardiovascular medicine, surgery, obstetrics and gynecology, homeopathy, and so on. Some of these specialties are covered in other entries in this book.

A doctor of osteopathy's responsibilities depend to a great extent on his or her specialty. Similar duties exist among all physicians. For example, all doctors examine patients, all and they are also expected to talk to patients to determine what symptoms and problems exist. They may recommend, order, and perform a variety of diagnostic tests. If the D.O. is a general practitioner, he or she may refer a patient to a specialist to diagnose or treat specific conditions. Specialists have more specific duties depending on their line of work.

After a patient's illness has been diagnosed, the physician must prescribe a course of treatment. This may include medication, surgery, or various therapies.

Osteopathic physicians often perform body work or body manipulations as part of their patient's healing regime. This process may have an effect on various body parts, including the patient's bone structure, ligaments, and nerve structure. This is helpful in treating the "whole patient." O.D.s believe that if the body is aligned, patients will heal faster and be healthier.

Physicians often help patients stay in good health with preventive medicine. This can include examinations, immunizations, or advice on exercise and diet.

As part of their job, physicians answer patients' questions regarding their health or a medical procedure. Osteopathic doctors are also expected to answer the questions of patients' family members when necessary.

Osteopathic doctors usually work long hours. They may be on call for a variety of emergencies and are often involved in life-and-death situations.

While this type of work can be stressful, the ability to help others is very rewarding and fulfilling to most individuals in this profession.

Salaries

Osteopathic doctors can earn $75,000 to $350,000 or more. Earnings vary greatly depending on the specific type of work setting and its geographic location. Other factors include the specialty, experience, responsibilities, and professional reputation of the individual.

Employment Prospects

Employment prospects for osteopathic doctors are excellent. An individual can either start his or her own practice, become a partner or be an employee in a hospital, health care facility, nursing home, prison, school, college, medical group, HMO, urgi-center, surgi-center, clinic or public health center. (See glossary for definitions of *urgi-center* and *surgi-center.*)

Advancement Prospects

Advancement prospects for osteopathic doctors are based on the career paths they take. Some climb the career ladder by obtaining additional education and specializing. Others go into private practice. Some individuals build up their professional reputation and obtain a large roster of patients. This results in increased earnings.

Still others go into research or teaching as a method of advancing their careers. Osteopathic physicians working in hospitals can also become medical directors.

Education and Training

It takes a great deal of education and time to become an osteopathic doctor. Individuals must complete at least three years of college before entering osteopathic school. The osteopathic programs are four years long.

Competition for admittance into osteopathic school is fierce. There are a limited number of schools in the country. Individuals must take an admission exam prior to being accepted. Selection criteria includes the scores of the exam, college grades, letters of recommendation, interviews, and participation in extracurricular activities.

Individuals must also take and pass an exam offered by the National Board of Osteopathic Medical Examiners while still in school.

After finishing osteopathic school, O.D.s go through 12 months of rotating internships.

Even more training is required for those who want to specialize or be board certified in a specialty. This training can take up to five years in a residency program. Those aspiring to be board certified must also take and pass another exam.

O.D.s must be licensed. Requirements include graduation from an accredited osteopathic school, taking and passing the licensing exam, and completing an internship.

Experience/Skills/Personality Traits

Osteopaths must be very compassionate, caring people. Successful doctors have a good "bedside manner." As they may be dealing with life-and-death situations, individuals should have excellent judgment and the ability to work under stress and pressure. Emotional stability is essential. Stamina is mandatory when working long hours.

Osteopathic physicians must have good diagnostic skills. Scientific aptitude is necessary. Individuals should be organized and detail oriented. Communication skills are also needed. The ability to perform manipulations is mandatory.

Unions/Associations

Aspiring osteopathic doctors can obtain additional career information by contacting the American Osteopathic Association (AOA) and the Association of Colleges of Osteopathic Medicine.

Tips for Entry

1. If you are beginning to build a practice, consider participating at local health fairs. This is a good way for people in the community to get to know you.
2. Offer to speak to local civic groups and nonprofit organizations. This is another way to get and keep yourself in the public eye.
3. Many schools contract out for physicians.
4. Rural areas needing doctors will often help pay for medical school if you make a contract to return to the area and work for a certain number of years.
5. It is easier to build a practice in less populated areas that do not have a great many physicians.

HOMEOPATHIC PHYSICIAN

CAREER PROFILE

Duties: Helping patients attain and maintain good health; examining patients; diagnosing and treating patients' illnesses using homeopathic medicines.

Alternate Titles: Homeopath; Doctor; M.D.; Physician; O.D., Doctor of Osteopathy; Osteopath

Salary Range: $75,000 to $350,000+

Employment Prospects: Excellent

Advancement Prospects: Good

Best Geographical Location(s) for Position: Positions may be located throughout the country

Prerequisites:

Education or Training—Medical school or osteopathic school; advanced schooling in homeopathy and/or study with practicing homeopathic physician

Experience—Internship and study with practicing homeopathic physician

Special Skills and Personality Traits—Compassion; emotional stability; good judgment; caring; diagnostic skills; excellent memory

CAREER LADDER

```
┌─────────────────────────────┐
│   Homeopathic Physician     │
│    with a Larger Practice   │
└─────────────────────────────┘

┌─────────────────────────────┐
│   Homeopathic Physician     │
└─────────────────────────────┘

┌─────────────────────────────┐
│    General Practitioner     │
└─────────────────────────────┘
```

Position Description

Homeopathic Physicians are doctors who specialize in the field of homeopathy. They may be either M.D.s (doctors of medicine) or D.O.s (doctors of osteopathy).

Homeopathy is a branch of medicine based on the principles developed by Samuel Hahnemann in the late 1700s. Very popular in the 1800s and early 1900s, homeopathy is once again becoming popular, as many Americans want a more natural and holistic approach to medicine and healing.

Homeopathic physicians, like most other complementary physicians, treat the patient as a whole rather than treating one specific symptom. In order to do this, homeopathic physicians select remedies that most closely match the broad range of symptoms unique to the patient.

To do this, in addition to physical examinations, homeopathic physicians usually take extensive case histories from patients. By doing this, the physician will have a better sense of a patient's physical, mental, and emotional symptoms, which is necessary to make a proper diagnosis.

Homeopathic medicine and remedies are based on the principles of a minimum dosage and prepared in a special manner by homeopathic pharmacists. There are literally thousands of different remedies, each prepared with different potencies, which a homeopathic physician may prescribe.

Homeopathic physicians, like all other physicians, may further specialize in a variety of fields. If the specialty is general or family practice, pediatrics, or internal medicine, the physician may also be the patient's primary care physician.

Homeopathic physicians examine patients. Individuals may recommend, order, and perform a variety of diagnostic tests. In some cases, the homeopathic physician may refer a patient to another specialist to diagnose or treat specific conditions. Depending on a patient's condition, the homeopathic physician may prescribe homeopathic remedies or various other therapies.

Homeopathic physicians may see patients with chronic or acute illnesses as well as those seeking preventive health care. They often offer advice on healthy living habits including diet and exercise.

As part of their job, homeopathic physicians answer patients' questions regarding their health or medical procedures. They are also expected to answer questions of patients' family members when necessary.

Homeopathic doctors usually work long hours. They may be on call for a variety of emergencies, and like most other doctors, they are often involved in life-and-death situations. However, the ability to help patients interested in being treated in a complementary manner is very rewarding.

Salaries

While there are exceptions, homeopathic physicians generally work as sole practitioners. There are also a number of complementary care clinics which employ homeopaths.

Individuals may earn $75,000 to $350,000 or more depending on their experience and professional reputation.

Employment Prospects

Employment prospects for homeopathic physicians are excellent as homeopathy becomes more popular.

Advancement Prospects

Homeopathic physicians advance their career by building a good professional reputation and obtaining a large roster of patients. Some individuals also teach as a method of advancing their careers.

Education and Training

It takes a great deal of education and time to become any type of physician, and homeopaths are no exception. At least three years of college must be completed before entering either medical or osteopathic school. Both the medical and osteopathic programs are four years long. There are schools throughout the country offering a combined medical school program which lasts only six years.

Competition for admittance into medical and osteopathic school is fierce. Individuals must take the Medical College Admission Test (MCAT). Selection criteria includes the scores of the exams, college grades, letters of recommendation, interviews, and participation in extracurricular activities.

M.D.s must also take and pass an exam offered by the National Board of Medical Examiners or, for D.O.s the National Board of Osteopathic Medical Examiners while still in school, as well as completing an internship.

Individuals seeking to practice homeopathy may take postgraduate training programs and/or preceptorships with experienced homeopaths. This means that, like an apprentice, they study and learn from a practicing homeopath. Most homeopathic physicians continue their education in homeopathy through lectures, seminars, or correspondence courses. The Council on Homeopathic Education (CHE) has recently begun certifying content and structure of homeopathic courses.

Homeopaths, like other physicians, may want to specialize or be board certified in a variety of other specialties. In these cases, even more training is required, which can take up to five years in a residency program in the specialty. Those aspiring to be board certified must also take and pass another exam.

M.D.s and D.O.s must be licensed. Requirements include graduating from an accredited medical or osteopathic school, completing an internship, and taking and passing the licensing exam.

Certification is voluntary for homeopathic physicians, and there are a number of certifying agencies. It should be noted that while most states consider homeopathy to be a practice of medicine, legal requirements vary by state.

Experience/Skills/Personality Traits

Homeopathic physicians must be very compassionate, caring people with a good "bedside manner." They should have excellent judgment and the ability to work under stress and pressure. Emotional stability is mandatory.

Homeopaths must have good diagnostic skills. The ability to really hear what a patient is saying is imperative in selecting an appropriate remedy. Scientific aptitude is necessary. Individuals should be organized, detail oriented, and have an excellent memory. Communication skills are also needed.

Unions/Associations

Those interested in learning more about becoming a homeopathic physician should contact the Council on Homeopathic Education (CHE), the North American Society of Homeopaths (NASH), the American Institute of Homeopathy (AIH), or the National Center for Homeopathy (NCH).

Tips for Entry

1. If you are beginning to build a practice, consider participating in local health fairs. This is a good way for people in the community to get to know you.
2. Offer to speak to local civic groups and nonprofit organizations. This is another way people in the area can get to know you.
3. Contact homeopathic organizations. Many know where homeopathic physicians are needed.
4. Network, network, network. The more people who know what you do, the bigger your practice will be.
5. Continue your education. Even if you have not completed medical school, you can still take classes to learn about homeopathy.

CARDIOLOGIST

Duties: Providing preventive care for patients with potential heart problems; examining, diagnosing, and treating patients; educating people about heart disease

Alternate Titles: Doctor; M.D., Medical Doctor; O.D., Osteopathic Doctor; Osteopathic Physician

Salary Range: $75,000 to $350,000+

Employment Prospects: Excellent

Advancement Prospects: Good

Best Geographical Location(s) for Position: Positions may be located throughout the country

Prerequisites:

Education or Training—Medical school plus internship and residency

Experience—Internship and residency required

Special Skills and Personality Traits—Ability to deal well with people; compassion; emotional stability; good judgment; caring; diagnostic skills

```
┌─────────────────────────────────────┐
│ Cardiologist Specialist or Surgeon or│
│ Cardiologist with a Larger Practice  │
└─────────────────────────────────────┘

┌─────────────────────────────────────┐
│            Cardiologist              │
└─────────────────────────────────────┘

┌─────────────────────────────────────┐
│        General Practitioner          │
│        or Family Practice            │
└─────────────────────────────────────┘
```

Position Description

Heart disease is one of the leading killers in the United States. Physicians who specialize in prevention and treatment of heart disease are called cardiologists.

While many cardiac patients are middle aged and older, cardiologists also may treat people of all ages.

Cardiologists may be doctors of medicine (M.D.s) or doctors of osteopathy (D.O.s). Doctors of medicine and doctors of osteopathy both utilize all accepted methods of treatment when caring for patients. These may include drugs and surgery.

Cardiologists, like all other physicians, have a great many responsibilities. They must obtain a medical history from patients, including any family history of heart disease. This is important because some heart disease is hereditary. It is also helpful for the cardiologist to know if a patient has experienced any pains, prior high blood pressure, or high cholesterol.

For many, the first visit to a cardiologist is either right before or right after a heart attack. The cardiologist is expected to examine patients, order tests, and determine if there is heart disease or damage, and if so, the extent.

If heart disease is present, the cardiologist must prescribe a course of treatment. This may include medication, surgery, or various therapies. Sometimes special procedures may be recommended, such as an angioplasty to clean the plaque out of blood vessels. Depending on qualifications, the cardiologist will either perform this procedure him or herself or refer the patient to a cardiologist who specializes in heart surgery.

Patients who have heart disease often visit the cardiologist at regular intervals to check the progression of the disease and monitor their treatment. Cardiologists counsel patients on healthier ways to live, including exercise, stress management, and diet.

Studies have shown that patients who follow certain dietary and exercise regimes can stop and even reverse heart disease. With this in mind, one of the important functions of cardiologists is educating people about heart disease and its prevention. This is important for both those who have heart disease and to prevent those who don't from possibly getting it.

Cardiologists often must deal with life-or-death situations. Some heart attack victims survive. Others do not. One of the responsibilities cardiologists have is informing family members that a patient has died. This is a very difficult job.

It is common for patients with heart disease and their relatives to be frightened and need reassurance. Cardiologists must be compassionate and reassuring, not only to patients, but to frightened family members. Cardiologists are expected to answer the questions of patients and their families.

Some cardiologists specialize in additional fields. These might include surgery, geriatrics, or pediatrics, among others. Whatever the specialty, cardiologists usually work long hours and may be on call for a variety of emergencies.

Salaries

Cardiologists can earn $75,000 to $350,000 or more. Earnings vary greatly depending on the specific type of work setting and its geographic location. Other factors include the experience, responsibilities, and professional reputation of the individual.

Employment Prospects

Employment prospects for cardiologists are excellent. A cardiologist can start his or her own practice, become a partner with a group, or be an employee in a hospital, health care facility, nursing home, prison, medical group, HMO, urgi-center, surgi-center, clinic, or public health center. (See glossary for definitions of *urgi-center* and *surgi-center*.)

Advancement Prospects

Advancement prospects for cardiologists are based on their career paths. Some climb the career ladder by obtaining additional education and specializing even further. For example, some cardiologists also become cardiac surgeons.

Cardiologists may also advance their careers by going into private practice. Some individuals build up their professional reputation and obtain a large roster of patients. This results in increased earnings.

Still others go into research or teaching as a method of advancing their careers. Cardiologists working in hospitals can also become medical directors.

Education and Training

It takes a great deal of education and time to become a cardiologist. Whether the cardiologist is an M.D. or D.O., he or she must complete at least three years of college before entering medical school or osteopathic school. The medical and osteopathic programs are both four years long. There are schools throughout the country offering a combined college degree/medical school program which lasts only six years.

Competition for admittance into medical school and osteopathic school is fierce. Individuals must take the Medical College Admission Test (MCAT). Selection criteria include exam scores, college grades, letters of recommendation, interviews, and participation in extracurricular activities.

Students must also take and pass an exam offered by the National Board of Medical Examiners or the National Board of Osteopathic Medical Examiners.

As part of their training, individuals complete an internship. They then go through three or more years of graduate medical education, called a residency, to become a cardiologist. Those who want to be board certified in cardiology also must take and pass another exam.

Cardiologists must be licensed. Requirements include graduating from an accredited medical or osteopathic school, taking and passing the licensing exam and completing an internship and residency.

Experience/Skills/Personality Traits

Many people who are in need of cardiac care are frightened of what lies ahead. It therefore helps for cardiologists to be very compassionate, caring people with good communication skills. A good "bedside manner" is essential to success. As cardiologists may be dealing with life-and-death situations, individuals should have excellent judgment and the ability to work under stress and pressure. Emotional stability is mandatory. Stamina is also necessary when working long hours. Cardiologists need good diagnostic skills and scientific aptitude.

Unions/Associations

Individuals interested in becoming cardiologists can obtain additional career information by contacting the American College of Cardiology (ACC), American Association of Cardiovascular and Pulmonary Rehabilitation (AACVPR), the Cardiology Association or other cardiac specialty associations. Other helpful associations might include the American Medical Association (AMA), the American Medical College (AMC), the American Osteopathic Association (AOA), and the American Association of Colleges of Osteopathic Medicine (AACOM).

Tips for Entry

1. If you are beginning to build a practice, consider participating at local health fairs. This is a good way for people in the community to get to know you.
2. Offer to speak to local civic groups and nonprofit organizations. This is a good method for educating people on heart disease prevention as well as getting your name and specialty in the public eye.
3. Job openings in hospitals and health care facilities are often advertised in special health care sections of the classifieds.
4. It is easier to build a practice in less populated areas that do not have a great many cardiologists.
5. Areas of the country with a large senior population may have a higher need for cardiologists.

OBSTETRICIAN/GYNECOLOGIST

CAREER PROFILE

Duties: Diagnosing and treating diseases and disorders of female patients; handling preventive health care for female patients; giving prenatal, natal, and postnatal care to women

Alternate Titles: OB/GYN; M.D, Medical Doctor; O.D., Osteopathic Doctor; Osteopathic Physician

Salary Range: $100,000 to $350,000+

Employment Prospects: Excellent

Advancement Prospects: Good

Best Geographical Location(s) for Position: Positions may be located throughout the country

Prerequisites:

Education or Training—Medical school plus internship and surgical residency

Experience—Internship and residency required

Special Skills and Personality Traits—Good manual dexterity; ability to deal well with people; compassion; emotional stability; good judgment; diagnostic skills; stamina

CAREER LADDER

```
┌─────────────────────────────┐
│   Obstetrician/Gynecologist  │
│      with a Larger Practice  │
└─────────────────────────────┘

┌─────────────────────────────┐
│   Obstetrician/Gynecologist  │
└─────────────────────────────┘

┌─────────────────────────────┐
│     General Practitioner     │
│       or Family Practice     │
└─────────────────────────────┘
```

Position Description

Obstetricians and gynecologists are physicians who handle the special medical needs of women. Individuals in this line of work are often referred to as OB/GYNs.

Obstetricians and gynecologists may be doctors of medicine (M.D.s) or doctors of osteopathy (D.O.s). Doctors of medicine and doctors of osteopathy both utilize all accepted methods of treatment when caring for patients. These may include drugs and surgery.

OB/GYNs, like all other physicians, have a great many responsibilities. They are expected to obtain medical histories from patients so they can give them the very best medical care. This task is often done by a nurse before the exam.

OB/GYNs diagnose and treat diseases and disorders of the female reproductive system. They examine patients to determine medical problems, as well as utilizing a variety of lab and radiological tests as diagnostic aids. If a problem is found, an OB/GYN prescribes a course of treatment. This may include drugs, surgery, or other procedures.

A big function of OB/GYNs is handling preventive health care for women. Many patients visit OB/GYNs for annual exams as a part of this preventive medical care. OB/GYNs perform examinations as well as various tests to assure that patients are healthy. OB/GYNs help women decide what type of family planning and birth control is best for them.

OB/GYNs give prenatal, natal, and postnatal care to women. They examine women to determine their condition using a variety of lab tests as diagnostic aids. When the OB/GYN determines a woman is pregnant, he or she will usually offer diet, vitamin, and exercise recommendations so that the mother-to-be and baby will be as healthy as possible. During the course of a pregnancy, the OB/GYN is expected to examine the mother-to-be periodically to assure that the pregnancy is progressing normally.

OB/GYNs deliver babies as well as care for the mother and child for a time after childbirth. They may perform surgeries such as cesarean sections or other procedures to assure the mother's health and the infant's safety.

OB/GYNs usually work long hours. They may be on call for a variety of emergencies as well as patients giving birth.

Salaries

OB/GYNs can earn $100,000 to $350,000 or more. Earnings vary greatly depending on the specific type of work setting and its geographic location. Other factors include the experience, responsibilities, and professional reputation of the individual.

Employment Prospects

Employment prospects for OB/GYNs are excellent. An OB/GYN can either start his or her own practice, become a partner with a group, or be an employee in a hospital, health care facility, nursing home, prison, medical group, HMO, urgi-center, surgi-center, clinic, or public health center. (See glossary for definitions of *urgi-center* and *surgi-center*.)

Advancement Prospects

Advancement prospects for OB/GYNs are based on their career paths. Some climb the career ladder by obtaining additional education and specializing. Other individuals build up their professional reputation and obtain a large roster of patients. This results in increased earnings.

Still others go into research or teaching as a method of advancing their careers. OB/GYNs working in hospitals can also become medical directors.

Education and Training

It takes a great deal of education and time to become an OB/GYN. Whether the OB/GYN is an M.D. or D.O., he or she must complete at least three years of college before entering medical school or osteopathic school. The medical and osteopathic programs are both four years long. There are schools throughout the country offering a combined college degree/medical school program which lasts only six years.

Competition for admittance into medical school and osteopathic school is fierce. Individuals must take the Medical College Admission Test (MCAT). Selection criteria includes exam scores, college grades, letters of recommendation, interviews, and participation in extracurricular activities.

Individuals must also take and pass an exam offered by the National Board of Medical Examiners or the National Board of Osteopathic Medical Examiners while still in school.

As part of their training, individuals complete an internship. They then go through three or more years of graduate medical education (called a residency) to become an OB/GYN. Those who want to be board certified also must take and pass another exam.

OB/GYNs must be state licensed. Requirements include graduating from an accredited medical or osteopathic school, taking and passing the licensing exam, and completing an internship and residency.

Experience/Skills/Personality Traits

OB/GYNs should be compassionate people with good communication skills. A good "bedside manner" is essential to success. Excellent judgment and the ability to work under stress and pressure are needed. Emotional stability is mandatory. Stamina is also necessary. Manual dexterity is essential. Good diagnostic skills and scientific aptitude are also required.

Unions/Associations

Individuals interested in becoming OB/GYNs should contact the American College of Obstetricians and Gynecologists. Other helpful associations might include the American Medical Association (AMA), the American Medical College (AMC), the American Osteopathic Association (AOA), and the American Association of Colleges of Osteopathic Medicine (AACOM).

Tips for Entry

1. If you are beginning to build a practice, consider participating in local health fairs. This is a good way for people in the community to get to know you.
2. Offer to speak to local civic groups and nonprofit organizations. This is a good method for educating people on preventive health care as well as getting your name in the public eye.
3. Job openings in hospitals and health care facilities are often advertised in special health care sections of the classifieds.
4. It is easier to build a practice in less populated areas that do not have a great many OB/GYNs.

PEDIATRICIAN

CAREER PROFILE

Duties: Helping infants, children, and adolescents attain and maintain good health; examining patients; diagnosing and treating patients' illnesses

Alternate Titles: Doctor; M.D, Medical Doctor; O.D.; Osteopathic Doctor; Osteopathic Physician; Physician

Salary Range: $75,000 to $350,000+

Employment Prospects: Excellent

Advancement Prospects: Good

Best Geographical Location(s) for Position: Positions may be located throughout the country

Prerequisites:

Education or Training—Medical school plus internship and residency

Experience—Internship and residency required

Special Skills and Personality Traits—Ability to deal well with children; compassion; emotional stability; good judgment; diagnostic skills

CAREER LADDER

```
┌─────────────────────────────────────┐
│  Pediatric Specialist or Pediatric   │
│  Physician with a Larger Practice    │
└─────────────────────────────────────┘

┌─────────────────────────────────────┐
│             Pediatrician             │
└─────────────────────────────────────┘

┌─────────────────────────────────────┐
│       General Practitioner           │
│       or Family Practice             │
└─────────────────────────────────────┘
```

Position Description

Pediatricians are physicians who specialize in treating children. Their patients may include children of various ages ranging from infancy through adolescence.

Pediatricians may be doctors of medicine (M.D.s) or doctors of osteopathy (D.O.s). Doctors of medicine and doctors of osteopathy utilize all accepted methods of treatment when caring for patients. These may include drugs and surgery.

The difference between the two is that when treating patients, D.O.s place an emphasis on the body's musculoskeletal system. In their belief, a person requires the proper alignment of bones, muscles, ligaments, and nerves in order to reach optimum health.

Pediatricians, like all other physicians, have a great many responsibilities. Individuals often see the same child for a variety of ailments.

In some cases, parents bring their child to the pediatrician for annual checkups or immunizations. In other instances, parents may bring their child to a pediatrician for an acute or chronic illness.

Pediatricians are responsible for examining patients. They are also expected to determine what symptoms and problems exist. Individuals often obtain much of this information from the parents (or guardians) as well as the children. Pediatricians often must obtain medical history from parents or guardians.

Pediatricians must have a great deal of patience. It is not uncommon for children to be frightened of doctors. Many do not like the examination or the treatment. Parents of ill children may also be frightened and need reassurance.

After examining patients, pediatricians must diagnose any problems. In some cases, they will order tests. Once a diagnosis is obtained, pediatricians must prescribe a course of treatment. This may include medication, surgery, or various therapies. If a specialist is required, he or she is expected to refer the patient to the appropriate specialist.

A common responsibility of many pediatricians is administering routine immunizations. Individuals often counsel parents on immunizations which are recommended and needed.

Many pediatricians also counsel parents on preventive health care for their children, which might include diet, vitamins, exercise, and hygiene.

Parents may bring children to a pediatrician to make sure they are developing properly. The pediatrician will then check to see if the child is experiencing normal growth and development.

Some pediatricians specialize in additional fields. These might include surgery, communicable diseases, oncology, allergies, cardiovascular, and so on.

As part of their job, pediatricians answer patients' or parents' questions regarding health or a medical procedure.

Pediatricians usually work long hours. They may be on call for a variety of emergencies and are often involved in life-and-death situations.

While this type of existence can be stressful, the ability to help children can be very rewarding.

Salaries

Pediatricians can earn $75,000 to $350,000 or more. Earnings vary greatly depending on the specific type of work setting and its geographic location. Other factors include the experience, responsibilities, and professional reputation of the individual.

Employment Prospects

Employment prospects for pediatricians are excellent. A Pediatrician can either start his or her own practice, become a partner or be an employee in a hospital, health care facility, nursing home, prison, school, college, medical group, HMO, urgi-center, surgi-center, clinic, or public health center. (See glossary for definitions of *urgi-center* and *surgi-center.*)

Advancement Prospects

Advancement prospects for pediatricians are based on their career paths. Some climb the career ladder by obtaining additional education and specializing even more. Others go into private practice. Some individuals build up their professional reputation and obtain a large roster of patients. This results in increased earnings.

Still others go into research or teaching as a method of advancing their careers. Pediatricians working in hospitals can also become medical directors.

Education and Training

It takes a great deal of education and time to become a pediatrician. Whether the pediatrician is an M.D. or D.O., he or she must complete at least three years of college before entering medical school or osteopathic school. The medical and osteopathic programs are both four years long. There are schools throughout the country offering a combined medical school program which lasts only six years.

Competition for admittance into medical school and osteopathic school is fierce. Individuals must take the Medical College Admission Test (MCAT). Selection criteria includes the scores of the exams, college grades, letters of recommendation, interviews, and participation in extracurricular activities.

Individuals must also take and pass an exam offered by the National Board of Medical Examiners or the National Board of Osteopathic Medical Examiners while still in school.

As part of their training, individuals complete an internship. They then go through three or more years of graduate medical education (residency). Those who want to be board certified in pediatrics also must take and pass another exam.

Pediatricians must be licensed. Requirements include graduating from an accredited medical or osteopathic school, taking and passing the licensing exam, and completing an internship and residency.

Experience/Skills/Personality Traits

Pediatricians must be very compassionate people. The ability to deal well with children is essential. Communication skills are mandatory.

Successful pediatricians have a good "bedside manner." As they may be dealing with life-and-death situations, individuals should have excellent judgment and the ability to work under stress and pressure. Emotional stability is essential. Stamina is necessary when working long hours.

Pediatricians must have good diagnostic skills. Scientific aptitude is necessary. Individuals should be organized and detail oriented.

Unions/Associations

Aspiring pediatricians can obtain additional career information by contacting the American Medical Association (AMA), the American Medical College (AMC), the American Osteopathic Association (AOA), the American Association of Colleges of Osteopathic Medicine (AACOM), the American College of Osteopathic Pediatricians (ACOP), and the American Academy of Pediatrics (AAP).

Tips for Entry

1. If you are beginning to build a practice, consider participating at local health fairs. This is a good way for people in the community to get to know you.
2. Offer to speak to local civic groups and nonprofit organizations. This is another way people in the area can get to know you.
3. Many schools contract out for pediatricians.
4. Rural areas needing pediatricians will often help pay for medical school if you make a contract to return to the area and work for a certain number of years.
5. It is easier to build a practice in less populated areas that do not have a great many pediatricians.
6. Check out the Sunday paper's classified section for openings. Many hospitals and health care facilities advertise in a special health care section of the classified ads.

SURGEON

Duties: Examining patients; consulting with patients; operating on patients to repair injuries and treat diseases

Alternate Titles: Doctor; M.D, Medical Doctor; O.D., Osteopathic Doctor; Osteopathic Physician

Salary Range: $100,000 to $350,000+

Employment Prospects: Excellent

Advancement Prospects: Good

Best Geographical Location(s) for Position: Positions may be located throughout the country

Prerequisites:

Education or Training—Medical school plus internship and surgical residency

Experience—Internship and residency required

Special Skills and Personality Traits—Good manual dexterity; ability to deal well with people; compassion; emotional stability; good judgment; diagnostic skills; stamina

Surgeon with a Larger Practice

Surgeon

General Practitioner or Family Practice

Position Description

Surgeons are physicians who specialize in performing surgery on patients. Within this specialty are many subspecialties for treating a range of conditions requiring surgical intervention.

Neurosurgeons, for example, specialize in operations performed on the nervous system. Plastic surgeons specialize in repairing or restoring damaged, lost, or deformed parts of a patient's face or body, or perform cosmetic surgery. Cardiac Surgeons specialize in operations on the heart and vascular system.

Orthopedic surgeons specialize in skeletal problems. Oncology surgeons specialize in surgery for cancer patients. Surgeons may operate on patients to repair injuries, prevent disease, correct deformities, or improve functions in patients.

Surgeons may be doctors of medicine (M.D.s) or doctors of osteopathy (D.O.s). Doctors of medicine and doctors of osteopathy both utilize all accepted methods of treatment when caring for patients. These may include drugs and surgery.

Surgeons, like all other physicians, have a great many responsibilities. Individuals are expected to obtain medical histories from patients. This may include prior surgeries, allergies to drugs, anesthesia, and so on. It is imperative for the surgeon to have as much information as possible so that he or she can minimize the risk to patients going under anesthesia.

Surgeons examine patients to determine if they are candidates for surgery. They may review reports and tests from other specialists or the patient's primary care physician. In many cases, they may perform a physical to make sure the patient is healthy enough to go through a surgical procedure. In other instances, the physical may be performed by a primary care physician.

Once it has been determined that a patient needs surgery, the surgeon must explain to the patient the operation and any risks associated with it. He or she is expected to answer any questions and try to put the patient and his or her family at ease.

Surgeons consult with the anesthesiologists who will be in the operating room with them. They also give instructions to other staff on preparing patients and the operating room for the surgery.

Surgeons perform operations in antiseptic rooms using sterilized and antiseptic instruments and equipment. They may use a variety of instruments and techniques depending on the specific surgery. Surgeons must instruct staff on any care to be given to the patient after the operation.

The surgeon will often talk to the patient's family to inform them about the success of the operation. He or she will tell them what can be expected medically.

The surgeon checks on the progress of patients to assure that the patient is healing properly. He or she will do this soon after the procedure, as well as checking often with follow-up visits.

It is not uncommon for patients undergoing surgery to be frightened and need reassurance. Surgeons must be compassionate and reassuring not only to patients, but to frightened family members as well.

Surgeons usually work long hours. They may be on call for a variety of emergencies as well as scheduled procedures. Some operations are very long and require the surgeon to be on his or her feet for many hours.

Salaries
Surgeons can earn $100,000 to $350,000 or more. Earnings vary greatly depending on the specific type of work setting and its geographic location as well as the subspecialty. Other factors include the experience, responsibilities, and professional reputation of the individual.

Employment Prospects
Employment prospects for surgeons are excellent. A surgeon can either start his or her own practice, become a partner with a group, or be an employee in a hospital, health care facility, nursing home, prison, medical group, HMO, urgi-center, surgi-center, clinic, or public health center. (See glossary for definitions of *urgi-center* and *surgi-center.*)

Advancement Prospects
Advancement prospects for surgeons are based on their career paths. Some climb the career ladder by obtaining additional education and specializing even further. For example, some surgeons become neurosurgeons.

Some individuals build up their professional reputation and obtain a large roster of patients. This results in increased earnings.

Still others go into research or teaching as a method of advancing their careers. Surgeons working in hospitals can also become medical directors.

Education and Training
It takes a great deal of education and time to become a surgeon. Whether the surgeon is an M.D. or D.O., he or she must complete at least three years of college before entering medical school or osteopathic school. The medical and osteopathic programs are both four years long. There are schools throughout the country offering a combined college degree/medical school program which lasts only six years.

Competition for admittance into medical schools and osteopathic schools is fierce. Individuals must take the Medical College Admission Test (MCAT). Selection criteria includes the scores of the exams, college grades, letters of recommendation, interviews, and participation in extracurricular activities.

Individuals must also take and pass an exam offered by the National Board of Medical Examiners or the National Board of Osteopathic Medical Examiners while still in school.

As part of their training, individuals complete an internship. They then go through three or more years of graduate medical education (called a residency) to become a surgeon. Those who want to be board certified in surgery or a subspecialty also must take and pass another exam.

Surgeons must be state licensed. Requirements include graduating from an accredited medical or osteopathic school, taking and passing the licensing exam, and completing an internship and residency.

Experience/Skills/Personality Traits
Many people who are in need of surgical procedures are frightened of what lies ahead. It therefore helps for surgeons to be very compassionate people with good communication skills. A good "bedside manner" is essential to success. Surgeons may be dealing with life-and-death situations and therefore should have excellent judgment and the ability to work under stress and pressure. Emotional stability, stamina, and manual dexterity are essential. Good diagnostic skills and a scientific aptitude are also needed.

Unions/Associations
Individuals interested in becoming a surgeon should contact the American Surgical Association. Other helpful associations might include The American Medical Association (AMA), the American Medical College (AMC), the American Osteopathic Association (AOA) and the American Association of Colleges of Osteopathic Medicine (AACOM).

Tips for Entry
1. If you are beginning to build a practice, consider participating in local health fairs. This is a good way for people in the community to get to know you.
2. Offer to speak to local civic groups and nonprofit organizations. This is a good method for educating people about heart disease prevention as well as getting your name and specialty in the public eye.
3. Job openings in hospitals and health care facilities are often advertised in special health care sections of the classifieds.
4. It is easier to build a practice in less populated areas that do not have a great many physicians.

CHIROPRACTOR

CAREER PROFILE

Duties: Performing musculoskeletal manipulations; helping patients attain and maintain good health; examining patients; prescribing exercise and self-care

Alternate Titles: Doctor of Chiropractic; Chiropractic Physician

Salary Range: $45,000 to $200,000+

Employment Prospects: Good

Advancement Prospects: Fair

Best Geographical Location(s) for Position: Positions may be located throughout the country

Prerequisites:

Education or Training—two to four years of undergraduate college; four years of chiropractic college
Experience—experience in a medical setting helpful; business and managerial experience may also be useful
Special Skills and Personality Traits—manual dexterity; compassion; communication skills; good judgment

CAREER LADDER

```
┌─────────────────────────────┐
│   Chiropractor with Large    │
│      Roster of Patients      │
└─────────────────────────────┘

┌─────────────────────────────┐
│        Chiropractor          │
└─────────────────────────────┘

┌─────────────────────────────┐
│     Chiropractic Student     │
└─────────────────────────────┘
```

Position Description

Chiropractors are doctors of chiropractic. They deal mainly with patients' muscular, nervous, and skeletal systems. Chiropractors believe that when people have any type of interference with the normal flow of these systems, their immune system will be compromised.

While they deal with the body's structural and neurological systems, chiropractors also place a heavy emphasis on the spine and vertebrae believing that a problem or an imbalance in the spine and/or vertebrae can cause pain in the patient.

Patients visit chiropractors for a number of reasons. Some have acute problems such a pulled back or stiff neck. Others have chronic problems such as headaches, fatigue, backaches, and so on. Still others visit a chiropractor for preventive health care.

Whatever the reason, chiropractors generally have a holistic approach to health care. They try to treat the whole patient rather than just treating the immediate health problem.

Chiropractors are expected to take the patient's medical history. They may ask about previous illnesses, injuries, falls, accidents, and the like. They will inquire about current and past pains and problems to determine if the problem is chronic or acute. In some cases, a nurse or assistant handles this function and the chiropractor will review it.

After taking a medical history, the chiropractor performs an examination, which might include a postural and spinal analysis, visual, physical, neurological, and orthopedic exams and lab tests. In some cases the chiropractor will also utilize X rays or other diagnostic imaging techniques.

The major treatment used by chiropractors is manipulation and adjustment of the spine. Chiropractors may also use other physiological therapies for treatment, including water, light and ultrasound, massages, and electric and heat treatments. They may recommend the use of braces, straps, and other supports to help align the body.

Some chiropractors counsel patients on nutrition, diet, exercise, and stress management. Chiropractors do not prescribe drugs or perform surgery.

Individuals who run their own practice may also have managerial and administrative duties.

Salaries

Earnings for chiropractors can vary greatly depending on a number of factors. These can include the reputation, experience, and personality of the individual, as well as the geographic location. Earnings will also be determined by whether the chiropractor has his or her own practice or is an employee.

Salaried chiropractors may earn $40,000 to $75,000 or more. Individuals with their own practices may earn $35,000 to $200,000 or more.

Employment Prospects

Employment prospects for chiropractors are good. Individuals may find employment throughout the country in health care facilities, chiropractic clinics, alternative health and complementary care clinics, chiropractic offices, and health spas. Many chiropractors open their own practice or go into partnership with other chiropractors.

Advancement Prospects

Advancement prospects for chiropractors are based on their career paths. Some climb the career ladder by working for another chiropractor or in a clinic and then striking out on their own. Those who are in their own practice advance their careers by building up a large roster of patients. Still others go into research as a means of career advancement.

Education and Training

In order to become a chiropractor, individuals must complete two to four years (depending on the state) of undergraduate education and then a four-year chiropractic college program. When completed, individuals will receive a doctor of chiropractic degree.

Chiropractors must be licensed in the state in which they work. Licensure requirements vary by state but generally include taking and passing an examination administered by the National Board of Chiropractic Examiners.

Individuals must also complete continuing education programs annually to maintain licensure.

Experience/Skills/Personality Traits

Hand dexterity is necessary to perform adjustments. Acute observation skills are also needed to detect physical abnormalities. Individuals should be compassionate. Individuals should be detail oriented with good communication skills.

Unions/Associations

To obtain more information on chiropractic careers, individuals may contact American Chiropractic Association (ACA), the International Chiropractic Association (ICA), the Federation of Chiropractic Licensing Boards (FCLB), or the Council on Chiropractic Education (CCE).

Tips for Entry

1. If you are beginning to build a practice, consider participating in local health fairs. This is a good way for people in the community to get to know you.
2. Offer to speak to local civic groups and nonprofit organizations. This helps get your professional name in front of the public.
3. If you are still in school, look for a summer or part-time job in a chiropractic office or clinic.
4. It is easier to build a practice in less populated areas that do not have a great many chiropractors.

PHYSICIAN ASSISTANT

CAREER PROFILE

Duties: Assist physician with patient care; perform examinations; take medical histories; order medical tests

Alternate Title(s): PA

Salary Range: $32,000 to $100,000+

Employment Prospects: Excellent

Advancement Prospects: Good

Best Geographical Location(s) for Position: Positions may be located throughout the country

Prerequisites:

Education or Training—Completion of accredited degree program

Experience—Experience in health care necessary

Special Skills and Personality Traits—Compassion; emotional stability; communication skills; organization; self-confidence; leadership

CAREER LADDER

```
┌─────────────────────────────────────┐
│   Physician Assistant Specialist     │
│   (Emergency Medicine, Geriatrics,   │
│   Pediatrics, Surgery, Occupational  │
│   Medicine, etc.) or Physician       │
│   Assistant Supervisor               │
└─────────────────────────────────────┘

┌─────────────────────────────────────┐
│         Physician Assistant          │
└─────────────────────────────────────┘

┌─────────────────────────────────────┐
│   Nurse, Emergency Medical           │
│   Technician, Technologist,          │
│   Technician, or Student             │
└─────────────────────────────────────┘
```

Position Description

Physician assistants are responsible for handling many of the routine, time consuming duties of the physician. Physician assistants, also called PAs, are formally trained for this career.

Physician assistants provide a necessary service. In addition to taking care of routine tasks, individuals often handle minor medical emergencies when doctors are unavailable or consult with a physician by telephone when no doctor is at the scene.

While physician assistants always work under the supervision of a doctor, the extent of the supervision varies depending on the situation. In some settings, the physician assistant may work directly with a doctor performing routine tasks such as taking patients' medical histories, performing physical examinations, and ordering routine lab tests and or X rays.

In other settings the physician assistant might be responsible for handling more specific tasks. These may include treating cuts, lacerations, bruises, and burns, and setting broken bones. A great deal of the responsibilities of the physician assistant are determined by the amount and type of training the individual has had.

A physician assistant might interpret lab tests, treat minor medical injuries, make preliminary diagnoses, and prescribe treatments. In some states, physician assistants can prescribe medications.

Other responsibilities of the physician assistant might include management or administrative duties such as running a doctor's office or clinic, ordering supplies and equipment, and supervising other employees. An individual with surgical training may handle both pre- and postoperative patient care and work in operating rooms.

Specific duties of the individual are determined by the supervising physician and by the organization within which he or she is employed. The laws of each state also determine the duties that a PA may perform.

A physician assistant might work in a number of settings including doctors' offices, clinics, or hospitals. Some individuals opt to work in general medicine; others work in specialty areas such as emergency medicine, pediatrics, internal medicine, family medicine, or surgery.

In some situations, the PA is the primary source of health care in an area. This is often the case in very rural areas where doctors are not always available. Similarly, PAs often bear a great deal of responsibility for the care of patients in clinics where there simply are not enough physicians available to handle the high influx of people requiring medical attention.

The PA in these settings may consult with physicians by phone or work directly with doctors on days when they are available.

Salaries

Salaries for physician assistants vary depending on a number of factors including geographic location, specific employment setting, and specialty. Other factors affecting earnings include the training and experience level of the individual as well as qualifications and responsibilities.

Physician assistants will have earnings ranging from $32,000 to $100,000 or more.

Employment Prospects

Employment prospects are excellent for physician assistants. Individuals may work in a variety of employment settings including physicians' offices, hospitals, clinics, health maintenance organizations (HMOs), prisons, colleges, nursing homes, and rehabilitation centers. Physician assistants may find employment easily in rural communities, as well as urban and suburban areas.

Advancement Prospects

With additional training and experience, advancement prospects are good for physician assistants. Individuals can climb the career ladder by attaining a position in a larger or more prestigious employment setting. This can result in increased responsibilities and earnings. PAs may also secure additional education and go into a specialty such as surgery or emergency medicine.

Education and Training

Specific training requirements for physician assistants is mandated by individual states. Most require the completion of an accredited educational program. Depending on the particular program, students may attain either a master's, bachelor's, or associate's degree or certificate.

Depending on the specific state, individuals must usually also pass a certifying examination after graduation from an accredited program. Individuals are then certified as Physician Assistant-Certified (PA-C). In order to stay certified, most states also require approximately 100 hours of continuing education every two years as well as a recertification exam every six years.

Individuals may also go through post graduate residencies for training in specific specialties.

In order to be admitted into most programs, candidates are required to have two years of college in addition to some type of work experience in the health care field.

As a rule, physician assistant programs are approximately two years long. The programs include both classroom instruction and clinical experience. Courses include human anatomy, physiology, microbiology, biochemistry, nutrition, clinical pharmacology, and clinical medicine. Other subject matter includes geriatric and home health care, medical ethics, and disease prevention.

Students must go through clinical experience in a vast array of areas including family medicine, pediatrics, general surgery, inpatient and ambulatory medicine, obstetrics and gynecology, geriatrics, emergency medicine, internal medicine, and ambulatory psychiatry.

Experience/Skills/Personality Traits

Due to the nature of the job, it is essential that physician assistants be emotionally stable, compassionate, caring individuals who enjoy helping others. Good communication and leadership skills are necessary. Those considering a career in this field should be comfortable working around ill and injured people.

Unions/Associations

Individuals aspiring to become physician assistants can contact the American Academy of Physician Assistants (AAPA), the Association of Physician Assistant Programs (APAP), and the National Commission on Certification of Physician Assistants, Inc. (NCCPA).

Tips for Entry

1. Contact hospitals, clinics, nursing homes, etc. to see if you can qualify for a part-time job. Prior experience in the field is necessary to get into one of the accredited programs.
2. Join a volunteer ambulance corps. This experience and training will be invaluable.
3. Write to the Association of Physician Assistant Programs to obtain a list of accredited programs.
4. You might also want to contact the National Commission on Certification of Physician Assistants, Inc. to learn more about eligibility requirements for the Physician Assistant National Certifying Examination.
5. Create your own position. Send your resume and a short cover letter to physicians' offices, clinics, hospitals, etc. to see if they are interested in hiring a PA.
6. The more areas in which you have training, the more employable you will be in this field. Make time to continue your education.

EMERGENCY MEDICAL TECHNICIAN

CAREER PROFILE

Duties: Providing immediate care to patients requiring medical attention; transporting patients to hospital or other health care facility

Alternate Title(s): EMT; EMT-Basic; EMT-Ambulance; EMT-Intermediate; EMT-I; EMT-Paramedic; Paramedic

Salary Range: $20,000 to $50,000+

Employment Prospects: Excellent

Best Geographical Location(s) for Position: Positions may be located throughout the country

Prerequisites:

Education or Training—Formal training course; certification is necessary

Experience—Working in volunteer ambulance corps or training as a medic in the armed forces is helpful

Special Skills and Personality Traits—Compassion; emotional stability; ability to lift and carry heavy loads; physical fitness; levelheadedness

CAREER LADDER

```
┌─────────────────────────────────────┐
│   Emergency Medical Technician       │
│   Intermediate or Paramedic          │
└─────────────────────────────────────┘


┌─────────────────────────────────────┐
│   Emergency Medical Technician       │
└─────────────────────────────────────┘


┌─────────────────────────────────────┐
│            Student                   │
└─────────────────────────────────────┘
```

Position Description

Almost everyone has seen an ambulance zooming into a location and medical personnel jumping out to help someone in need of medical care. The individuals who do this job are called Emergency Medical Technicians or EMTs. The main function of Emergency Medical Technicians is to offer immediate care to patients requiring urgent medical attention.

Every work day can be different for EMTs depending on the types of calls they receive. EMTs may be called to help victims of automobile accidents or people experiencing a heart attack or stroke. They may be required to give medical care to victims of gunshot wounds, stabbings, overdoses, suicide attempts, poisonings, or drownings. They may even deliver babies in emergency situations. The EMT must give immediate care to patients and transport them to a hospital or other medical facility.

EMTs generally work in teams of two. Dispatchers tell the teams where they need to go, and the EMTs drive to the patient's location in specially equipped emergency vehicles.

Once at the scene, the EMTs are expected to assess the situation and determine the extent of a patient's injury or illness. The EMTs will then give the patient proper medical treatment. The level of training and certification of the EMT determines what procedures he or she can perform. All emergency medical technicians are trained and certified to perform basic emergency procedures, such as opening airways, restoring breathing, administering oxygen, immobilizing fractures, bandaging wounds, and controlling bleeding. All EMTs can also assist in childbirth, treat and assist heart attack victims, and offer initial care to both poison and burn victims.

With additional training, EMTs may perform other procedures such as administering intravenous fluids, using a defibrillator to shock a heart that has stopped, and assessing the condition of trauma victims. These EMTs are referred to as EMT-Intermediates or EMT-Is.

EMTs with the most training are known as EMT-Paramedics. EMT-Paramedics are allowed to administer drugs both orally and intravenously, interpret EKGs, use monitors, and insert breathing tubes.

In addition to treating patients, EMTs may be required to help free victims from vehicles in car, train, plane, bus, or boat accidents. Other responsibilities include transferring patients to the emergency department of the medical facility and reporting observations regarding patients' conditions and care provided. EMTs are also expected to replace used supplies, decontaminate the interior of the ambulance, and check equipment. EMT teams work together to treat patients, obtain and monitor vital signs, and transport the victim to a medical facility.

Individuals in this line of work are often exposed to contagious diseases including Hepatitis-B and AIDS. They also are often involved in life and death situations. While some may find this type of job stressful, most EMTs find it fulfilling and challenging.

Salaries

Earnings for EMTs can vary greatly depending on a number of variables including the specific job setting, geographic location, training, experience, and responsibilities. EMTs working full-time can earn between $20,000 and $50,000 or more. Generally EMTs working in fire departments earn more than those working in other settings. Those with the most training and certification will have higher earnings than those with basic training.

Employment Prospects

Employment prospects for EMTs are excellent. While positions may be located throughout the country, many local ambulance corps in smaller towns and villages are run by volunteers. Jobs will be more plentiful in larger metropolitan areas. Individuals may work for private ambulance services; fire, police, and rescue departments; and hospitals.

Advancement Prospects

Advancement prospects for EMTs are based to a great extent on training and experience. An individual can obtain additional training and move up to become an EMT-Intermediate or an EMT-Paramedic. An EMT who wants to advance past the paramedic level can become a supervisor, operations manager, administrative director, or executive director of emergency service. Individuals may also become EMT instructors. One of the drawbacks for many people who advance past the paramedic level is that they are no longer involved in fieldwork.

Education and Training

Aspiring emergency medical technicians must go through a formal training course. These courses are offered throughout the country in hospitals; vocational technical schools; police,

fire, and health departments; and in colleges and universities. It should be noted that these are nondegree programs.

The EMT-Basic training program includes approximately 150 hours or more of classroom work. In addition individuals must go through an internship in a hospital emergency room.

The next level of training, EMT-Intermediate, includes approximately 300–400 hours of additional instruction. Training to become an EMT-Paramedic can include from 1600 to 2,000 hours depending on the specific state requirements.

EMTs at all levels must usually go through refresher courses and continuing education to keep up on new procedures and equipment.

EMTs must be certified. To receive certification they must graduate from a training program and pass written and practical exams administered by either the specific state regulatory agency or the National Registry of Emergency Medical Technicians.

Experience/Skills/Personality Traits

EMTs must be compassionate people who like to help others. Due to the nature of the work, they need to be in good physical condition and have the ability to lift and carry heavy loads. EMTs must be emotionally stable, as they are often thrust into life-and-death situations.

In order to become an EMT an individual must be at least 18 years old and have either a high school diploma or the equivalent. A driver's license is necessary.

Unions/Associations

EMTs may belong to the National Association of Emergency Medical Technicians (NAEMT).

Tips for Entry

1. Look for an internship in a hospital emergency room. This will give you valuable experience.
2. Join your local volunteer ambulance corps. The training and experience will be invaluable.
3. Jobs may be advertised in the classified section of the newspaper under headings such as "EMTs," "Paramedics," "Health Care," "Emergency Medical Technician," or "Rescue Squad."
4. The more training you have, the more marketable you will be. Continue your training and advance your certification level.
5. If you are in the armed forces, training as a medic is good preparation and experience.

DENTISTRY

DENTIST

CAREER PROFILE

Duties: Examining, diagnosing, and treating patient's teeth and gums; performing surgery on gums and bones; extracting teeth

Alternate Title(s): None

Salary Range: $50,000 to $200,000+

Employment Prospects: Fair

Advancement Prospects: Fair

Best Geographical Location(s) for Position: Positions may be located throughout the country

Prerequisites:

Education or Training—Graduation from dental school
Experience—Practical and clinical experience obtained in dental school
Special Skills and Personality Traits—Manual dexterity; diagnostic skills; light touch; good visual memory; communication skills

CAREER LADDER

```
┌─────────────────────────────────┐
│   Dentist in Private Practice or │
│            Specialist            │
└─────────────────────────────────┘

┌─────────────────────────────────┐
│             Dentist             │
└─────────────────────────────────┘

┌─────────────────────────────────┐
│             Student             │
└─────────────────────────────────┘
```

Position Description

Almost everyone has been to the dentist at one time or another. People visit the dentist for a variety of reasons; some go for preventative care, and others need problems diagnosed or treated.

Patients visit a dentist to treat a wide array of problems that they may experience with their teeth or tissues of their mouth. Dentists may remove decay in a patient's teeth and then fill cavities. They also take X rays of a patient's teeth as well as reading these X rays to determine where potential problems exist. Dentists often visually examine a patient's teeth to see if and where tooth or gum problems are located.

Dentists can diagnose and treat problems such as gingivitis, impacted and infected roots, chipped or broken teeth, and tooth decay. Dentists are expected to instruct patients on preventative treatment. They may instruct patients on brushing, flossing, and the use of fluorides in dental care.

Dentists may also perform surgery on gums and supporting bones to treat gum disease. They may extract teeth that are decayed, impacted, or need to be removed for other reasons. In some situations they may make molds and take measurements to make caps, dentures, or plates to replace missing teeth.

Dentists may work in general practice or specialize in a number of different areas. These include orthodontics, which handles straightening teeth; surgery; periodontics, or the treatment of gums and bones which support teeth; prosthodontics, the making of artificial teeth and dentures; oral pathology; pediatric dentistry; endodontics, or root canal therapy; and dental public health.

Dentists who work in private practice may be required to handle a variety of duties such as overseeing dental hygienists, dental assistants, dental laboratory technicians, receptionists, and bookkeepers.

Salaries

Dentists can have annual earnings ranging from approximately $50,000 to $200,000 or more. Variables affecting earnings include the experience and professional reputation of the individual, his or her specialty, and geographic location. Other factors affecting earnings include the type of employment of the individual such as whether he or she is self-employed or works for another individual or institution.

As a rule, specialists have higher incomes than those in general practice.

Employment Prospects

Employment prospects are fair for dentists. Individuals may find full- or part-time employment opportunities throughout the country.

Dentists may be self-employed, work as an associate or partner, or be employed in a number of different settings. These include private dental offices, group practices, public clinics, schools, hospitals, and HMOs (health maintenance organizations).

Advancement Prospects

Advancement prospects are fair for dentists. Individuals may move up the career ladder by beginning their own practice. Some dentists advance their careers by specializing; this in turn results in increased earnings.

Education and Training

In order to become a dentist, an individual must attend a dental school that has been approved by the Commission on Dental Accreditation. This program usually takes four years. Individuals may finish with either a degree as a doctor of dental surgery (D.D.S.) or a doctor of dental medicine (D.D.M.).

Dental school curriculum includes classroom instruction as well as laboratory work and pre-clinical and practical experience.

To be accepted at dental school, individuals must first have three to four years of college. Some dental schools require a bachelor's degree. Aspiring dentists must also take and pass a national examination prior to acceptance at dental school.

Those who wish to practice in a speciality must usually obtain additional training.

Dentists must be licensed in the state in which they work. Licensing is obtained by graduating from dental school and passing a written and practical exam.

Experience/Skills/Personality Traits

Dentists usually obtain experience while in dental school by treating patients in clinics affiliated with the college or university.

Dentists need a wide array of skills. These include manual dexterity, a light touch, and a good visual memory. Diagnostic skills are also necessary as are a scientific aptitude and communications skills.

Unions/Associations

Individuals interested in pursuing a career as a dentist may obtain additional career information by contacting the American Dental Association (ADA) and the American Association of Dental Schools (AADS).

Tips for Entry

1. Many schools host annual career fairs. Visit these and speak to dentists to see if this is a career for you.
2. Once you graduate from dental school, join civic groups and organizations. These are good places to meet people, make contacts, and develop a practice.
3. You might also volunteer your services at a local clinic or school. This will help people get to know you in the community.
4. Positions in this field are often advertised in the classified section of newspapers under heading classifications such as "Health Care," "Dentistry," "Dentist," or "Clinic."

DENTAL ASSISTANT

CAREER PROFILE

Duties: Assisting dentist; preparing patients for treatment; sterilizing and disinfecting instruments; making patients comfortable; billing patients

Alternate Title(s): None

Salary Range: $16,000 to $28,000+

Employment Prospects: Good

Advancement Prospects: Fair

Best Geographical Location(s) for Position: Positions may be located throughout the country

Prerequisites:
 Education or Training—Either on-the-job training or a formal training program
 Experience—Entry level; no experience necessary
 Special Skills and Personality Traits—Ability to follow instruction; personality; manual dexterity; reliability

CAREER LADDER

```
┌─────────────────────────────────────────┐
│   Office Manager or Dental Hygienist     │
└─────────────────────────────────────────┘

┌─────────────────────────────────────────┐
│            Dental Assistant              │
└─────────────────────────────────────────┘

┌─────────────────────────────────────────┐
│         Entry Level or Student           │
└─────────────────────────────────────────┘
```

Position Description

For many people going to the dentist can be a stressful experience. The dental assistant works with the dentist to help make the patient as comfortable as possible. Dental assistants can have varied responsibilities depending on the job. Functions can run the gamut from working in patient care to working in the laboratory to managing the dental office.

For dental assistants who work in patient care, their duties begin before the patient arrives at the dentist's office. The dental assistant will obtain the correct dental records, prepare the tray setups for dental procedures, and sterilize and disinfect the instruments and equipment.

When the patient arrives, the dental assistant will escort the patient to the correct office. An important function of the job is making the patient comfortable in the dental chair. The dental assistant will then prepare the patient for treatment.

The dental assistant is expected to help the dentist during treatment by handing the dentist the correct instruments when requested and keeping the patient's mouth dry with a suctioning device. During this time the assistant will perform additional duties such as preparing mixtures and removing the excess dental cement used in filling teeth.

Many dental assistants are also expected to prepare materials used for making impressions of the teeth and to expose and process dental X-ray films. Depending on the specific job, dental assistants may be expected to handle a wide array of office activities including billing patients, receiving payments, arranging and confirming patient appointments, and ordering supplies.

Salaries

Earnings for dental assistants can range from approximately $16,000 to $28,000 or more depending on a number of variables, including the qualifications, experience, education, and responsibilities of the individual as well as the geographic location. Generally, dental assistants who have gone through formal educational programs and are certified will have higher salaries than others.

Employment Prospects

Employment prospects for dental assistants are good. Positions can be located throughout the country, with more opportunities in larger metropolitan areas. Individuals in this line of work may work full- or part-time. Some dental assistants work for more than one dentist.

Advancement Prospects

Advancement prospects for dental assistants depend on the career path of the individual. Some become office managers; those who obtain additional training may become dental hygienists.

Education and Training

There are a number of different training methods for dental assistants. Many learn on the job. Others are trained in dental assisting programs in vocational technical schools, community and junior colleges, or trade schools. Those interested in pursuing careers in this field should consider taking courses in chemistry, biology, health, and office practices.

There are over two hundred training programs approved by the American Dental Association's Commission on Dental Accreditation. These programs offer classroom, laboratory, and pre-clinical instruction in dental assisting skills. Programs are approximately one year or less in duration and lead to a certificate or diploma. Two-year programs offered in junior or community colleges may lead to an associate degree.

Dental assistants may be certified through the Dental Assisting National Board. Those wishing to be certified must graduate from an accredited training program or have two years of full-time experience working as a dental assistant.

Individuals must also pass a written certification exam and a course in CPR.

Experience/Skills/Personality Traits

Dental assistants need to be personable people with the ability to work well with others. Manual dexterity is essential to success in this type of position. Organization and reliability are also necessary, as is the ability to follow instructions.

Unions/Associations

Dental assistants can become members of the American Dental Assistant's Association. Other helpful organizations for those pursuing a career in this field include the Commission on Dental Accreditation (CDA), the American Dental Association (ADA), and the Dental Assisting National Board, Inc. (DANB).

Tips for Entry

1. Jobs may be advertised in the classified section of the newspaper under headings such as "Dental Assistant," "Dental Clinic," or "Dental Office."
2. If you go through an accredited training program, use its job placement service.
3. Contact dentists and dental clinics to see if they have openings.

DENTAL HYGIENIST

CAREER PROFILE

Duties: Providing preventative care; teaching patients how to practice good oral hygiene; examining patients' teeth and gums; cleaning teeth

Alternate Title(s): None

Salary Range: $19,000 to $40,000+

Employment Prospects: Good

Advancement Prospects: Fair

Best Geographical Location(s) for Position: Positions may be located throughout the country

Prerequisites:
    Education or Training—Graduation from an accredited school of dental hygiene
    Experience—Practical experience obtained in school
    Special Skills and Personality Traits—Manual dexterity; ability to work well with others; compassion; communication skills; ability to put people at ease

CAREER LADDER

```
┌─────────────────────────────────────┐
│   Dental Hygienist in large, more    │
│  prestigious office or in a Research, │
│   Teaching, or Clinical Practice in   │
│   Public or School Health Programs    │
└─────────────────────────────────────┘

┌─────────────────────────────────────┐
│          Dental Hygienist            │
└─────────────────────────────────────┘

┌─────────────────────────────────────┐
│               Student                │
└─────────────────────────────────────┘
```

Position Description

Most people identify dental hygienists as the professionals who clean patients' teeth. Dental hygienists perform this job as well as an array of other functions. Their main responsibilities are helping patients maintain oral health and providing preventative dental care. Hygienists work under the supervision of a dentist.

Dental hygienists teach patients how to practice good oral hygiene and keep their teeth and gums in the best health possible. To do this, they explain to patients how to select toothbrushes and demonstrate the proper methods of brushing and flossing teeth.

Dental hygienists are expected to examine patients' teeth and gums to detect cavities, diseases, and any possible abnormalities. They are also responsible for cleaning patients' teeth. This may involve removing calculus, stains, and plaque from teeth. Many dental hygienists also apply sealants or other protective agents to the teeth. After cleaning the teeth, hygienists polish them to make them look whiter.

As part of a dental exam, the hygienist may take and develop dental X rays. Other responsibilities may include applying temporary fillings and removing sutures. In certain states dental hygienists may also administer local anesthetics and nitrous oxide/oxygen analgesia.

Many dental hygienists develop and implement programs for young people or others in the community regarding dental health.

Salaries

Earnings for dental hygienists can range from approximately $19,000 to $40,000 or more. Variables affecting earnings include the specific job and geographic location as well as the individual's education, experience, and responsibilities. Generally, dental hygienists with more education working in larger cities will earn higher salaries than those in other situations.

Employment Prospects

Employment prospects for dental hygienists are excellent. While positions can be located throughout the country, increased opportunities will be found in larger metropolitan areas.

Dental hygienists can work in an array of settings including private dentist offices, clinics, group practices, schools, nursing homes, extended care facilities, and state or federal health departments. Dental hygienists may work full- or part-time. Flexible hours are often made available by employers.

Advancement Prospects
Dental hygienists may advance their careers by locating similar positions in larger or more prestigious offices. Some advance by obtaining additional training and locating jobs in research, teaching, or clinical practices or finding work in public or school health programs.

Education and Training
Dental hygienists must graduate from an accredited dental hygiene school, where they receive laboratory, clinical, and classroom instruction. There are over 200 programs accredited by the Commission on Dental Accreditation. Most programs lead to an associate's degree. These programs are usually sufficient for finding work in a private dental office. There are a limited number of programs leading to a bachelor's or master's degree. These are usually required for individuals interested in working in research or clinical practice for public or school health programs or teaching.

Requirements for applicants vary from school to school. Some prefer one or two years of college prior to entering the program. High school students aspiring to work as dental hygienists should take classes in biology, chemistry, and mathematics.

Experience/Skills/Personality Traits
Dental hygienists must be licensed by the state in which they practice. Licensing requirements include graduation from an accredited dental hygiene school and a written and clinical examination.

Manual dexterity is necessary for this type of job. Hygienists must also be compassionate and enjoy working with others. The ability to put people at ease is helpful. Communication skills are necessary.

Unions/Associations
Dental hygienists may belong to the American Dental Hygienists' Association (ADHA). Another association helpful to those interested in a career as a dental hygienist is the American Dental Association (ADA).

Tips for Entry
1. Jobs may be advertised in the classified section of the newspaper under headings such as "Dental Office," "Dental Clinic," "Dental Hygienist," or "Hygienist."
2. Just because a job is not advertised does not mean that there is not one available. Consider sending your resume and a short letter to dentists, clinics, hospitals, schools, geriatric centers, and extended care facilities. Remember to ask that your resume be kept on file if there are no current openings.
3. If you enjoy working with children you might consider trying to locate a pediatric dentist or dental clinic.
4. You might also consider sending your resume and a short cover letter to geriatric and long-term facilities. These settings may also be in need of more dental hygienists.

VISION CARE

OPTOMETRIST

CAREER PROFILE

Duties: Examining patients' eyes; diagnosing vision problems and eye disease; treating vision problems

Alternate Title(s): Doctor of Optometry; O.D.

Salary Range: $40,000 to $125,000+

Employment Prospects: Good

Advancement Prospects: Good

Best Geographical Location(s) for Position: Positions may be located throughout the country

Prerequisites:

Education or Training—Degree from an accredited school of optometry

Experience—Clinical experience provided in optometry program

Special Skills and Personality Traits—Ability to deal well with others; compassion; aptitude for science; business sense; communication skills

CAREER LADDER

```
┌─────────────────────────────────┐
│   Optometrist with Large,        │
│   Successful Practice            │
└─────────────────────────────────┘

┌─────────────────────────────────┐
│          Optometrist             │
└─────────────────────────────────┘

┌─────────────────────────────────┐
│           Student                │
└─────────────────────────────────┘
```

Position Description

Optometrists are health care professionals who provide primary vision care for people by examining their eyes and diagnosing vision problems and eye disease. While optometrists are not medical doctors, they do hold a doctor of optometry degree. Optometrists may also be called O.D.s.

Optometrists may use instruments and drugs to examine a patient's eyes. When conducting examinations, they test the patient's visual acuity, depth and color perception, and ability to focus and coordinate the eyes. After the exam, the optometrist is expected to analyze the test results and come up with a treatment plan if necessary. Treatments can include glasses, contact lenses, or vision therapy.

Optometrists in certain states are allowed to prescribe topical or oral drugs to treat eye diseases such as conjunctivitis and corneal infections. They may also provide postoperative care to patients who have had cataract operations.

Optometrists may be in general practice or may specialize in working with a specific group of people or patients with specific types of vision problems. They may be a private practitioner, operate a franchise optical store, or be an employee of another optometrist. Private practitioners or franchise optical store operators may also be responsible for running their office, developing a patient base, and keeping records.

Salaries

Earnings of optometrists can range from approximately $40,000 to $125,000 or more depending on a number of factors. Optometrists in private practice usually have higher earnings than salaried individuals. Other variables include the reputation, experience, and specialization of the O.D., as well as the specific geographic location.

Employment Prospects

Employment prospects for optometrists are good. Individuals may locate positions throughout the country. As noted previously, optometrists may operate franchise optical stores, be private practitioners, or be salaried employees of these individuals. Optometrists may also enter into partnerships or group practices or work for HMOs or hospitals.

Advancement Prospects

There are a number of methods of career advancement for optometrists. Private practitioners can develop a large customer base and have higher earnings. Some optometrists advance their careers by obtaining additional education and doing research or teaching.

Education and Training

Optometrists must complete a course of study at an accredited optometry school. This is a four-year program. Prior to admittance, students must attend at least three years of pre-optometric study at an accredited college or university.

Competition is fierce for students desiring to enter optometry school. They must take the Optometry Admissions Test (OAT). This examination, which measures a student's academic ability and scientific comprehension, is usually taken after the sophomore or junior year in college.

The optometry program includes classroom and laboratory study in addition to clinical training. Useful classes before optometry school include those in English, math, chemistry, biology, physics, and business.

Master's and Ph.D. degrees are available in visual science, physiological optics, neurophysiology, public health, health administration, health information and communication, or health education to optometrists seeking higher education. Graduates of optometry programs may also take advantage of one-year clinical residency programs in a variety of subjects such as pediatric optometry, geriatric optometry, low vision rehabilitation, vision therapy, contact lenses, hospital-based optometry, primary care optometry, or family practice optometry.

Experience/Skills/Personality Traits

Optometrists should be personable people who have the ability to deal well with others. A good business sense is essential to those in private practice. An aptitude for science is necessary.

Unions/Associations

Optometrists can become members of the American Optometric Association (AOA). This organization provides support and guidance to members.

Tips for Entry

1. Jobs may be advertised in the classified section of the newspaper under headings including "Eye Care," "Optometrist," and "Vision."
2. Prepare yourself to run a business by taking business management courses.
3. Contact franchise optical stores for job opportunities.
4. You might also consider sending your resume and a short cover letter to hospitals, HMOs, or extended care facilities. Be sure to ask that they keep your resume on file if no current openings are available.

DISPENSING OPTICIAN

CAREER PROFILE

Duties: Preparing and fitting glasses and contact lenses; filling prescriptions; helping customers choose frames; adjusting and fitting finished glasses

Alternate Title(s): None

Salary Range: $24,000 to $39,000+

Employment Prospects: Good

Advancement Prospects: Fair

Best Geographical Location(s) for Position: Positions may be located throughout the country

Prerequisites:

Education or Training—Training requirements vary from on-the-job training to apprenticeships to a college degree in ophthalmic dispensing or optometric technology

Experience—Experience requirements vary

Special Skills and Personality Traits—Ability to deal well with the public; communication skills; manual dexterity; math and science skills

CAREER LADDER

```
┌─────────────────────────────────────┐
│  Manager or Owner of Optical Store   │
└─────────────────────────────────────┘

┌─────────────────────────────────────┐
│         Dispensing Optician          │
└─────────────────────────────────────┘

┌─────────────────────────────────────┐
│  College Student, Ophthalmic Lab     │
│    Technician, or Apprentice         │
└─────────────────────────────────────┘
```

Position Description

Dispensing opticians are the people responsible for preparing and fitting glasses and contact lenses. They begin by examining prescriptions written by optometrists and ophthalmologists to determine the lens specifications.

A good dispensing optician has the ability to assist customers in choosing the most appropriate eyeglass frames, types of lenses, and lens coating. In order to do this the optician must consider customers' prescriptions as well as their occupation, facial features, coloring, habits, etc. If a customer is happy with the way a pair of glasses look, he or she is much more apt to wear them when needed.

In addition to helping with frame selection, the dispensing optician must measure customers to make sure the glasses will fit properly. The distance between the centers of the pupils is measured, as is the distance between the eye surface and the lens.

The dispensing optician prepares work orders for the ophthalmic laboratory technicians so that they can grind and insert lenses into the frames. The optician gives the lab technician the lens prescription and information on the lens size,

material, color, and style. There are some specially trained dispensing opticians who prepare, grind, and insert lenses themselves.

Once the lenses are in the frames, the dispensing optician checks lens power to make sure that the prescription has been filled correctly. The customer tries on the glasses to make sure they fit and are comfortable. During this process, the optician may have to reshape the frames.

Other responsibilities of the dispensing optician include repairing, adjusting, and refitting broken frames. In some cases, the dispensing optician is responsible for fitting contact lenses and showing customers how to insert, remove, and care for their contacts.

The dispensing optician will usually work Monday to Friday, 9 to 5, or hours fairly close to that. Individuals working in retailing may, however, work evenings and weekends.

Salaries

Dispensing opticians have earnings ranging from $24,000 to $39,000 or more depending on a number of variables. These might include the specific work environment as well as the geographical location where the individual works. Other factors include the amount of experience and certification of the dispensing optician.

Opticians who run their own retail stores will usually earn more than those in salaried positions. However, employees in retail stores may receive commissions, bonuses, and profit-sharing packages in addition to their salaries.

Employment Prospects

Employment prospects are good for dispensing opticians. They may work for ophthalmologists or optometrists or find employment in retail optical shops, one-stop optical super-stores, or the optical departments of drug or department stores. Some dispensing opticians open their own stores and become self-employed. There are also opportunities available to work on a part-time basis.

Advancement Prospects

Advancement prospects are fair for dispensing opticians. They can climb the career ladder by obtaining additional experience, training, or accreditation. Some might become managers of optical stores. Others prefer to become sales reps for either manufacturers or whole-salers of eyewear. Many dispensing opticians decide to open their own business.

Education and Training

Training requirements for dispensing opticians vary depending on the position. Formal opticianry training is primarily offered in community colleges although there are a number of colleges and universities with similar programs. Those that are accredited by the Commission on Opticianry Accreditation award two-year associate degrees in ophthalmic dispensing or optometric technology. There are also a number of shorter pro-grams spanning one year or less. Other training options include informal on-the-job training and apprenticeships.

Over twenty states license dispensing opticians. In these states, those who have no formal college training must usu-ally go through two- to four-year apprenticeships. Appren-ticeships involve technical training and experience in office management and sales.

Individuals still in school should take courses in physics, basic anatomy, algebra, geometry, and mechanical drawing.

Experience/Skills/Personality Traits

There are employers who hire dispensing opticians with no background in opticianry at all. Others prefer applicants who have worked as ophthalmic lab technicians or have gone through formal training.

As dispensing opticians will be dealing with the public, they should be personable people who get along well with others. Good communication skills and the ability to be tactful are imperative.

Working in retail requires good business skills, and sales-manship is helpful. Manual dexterity is necessary, as are math and science skills.

Voluntary certification or registration is available through the American Board of Opticianry and the National Contact Lens Examiners. Certification must be renewed every three years. In order to renew, opticians must take continuing education.

Unions/Associations

Dispensing opticians usually do not belong to a union. Indi-viduals may contact the National Academy of Opticianry (NAO) for educational guidance and support for those working in this field.

Tips for Entry

1. To be as marketable as possible, get the best educa-tion you can.
2. Contact the Commission on Opticianry Accreditation (COA) for a list of accredited training programs. (The address can be located in the appendix of this book.)
3. Large chains and one-stop optical superstores often offer structured apprenticeship programs.
4. Positions can often be located in the classified section of the newspaper under headings such as "Dispensing Optician," "Optician," "Optical," or "Opticianry."
5. Consider sending your resume to large drug and depart-ment stores with optical departments. Remember to ask that your resume be kept on file if there are no current openings.
6. If you are still in school or taking part in an accredited training program, contact the job placement office for job possibilities.

OPHTHALMIC LABORATORY TECHNICIAN

CAREER PROFILE

Duties: Cutting, grinding, and finishing prescription eyeglass lenses

Alternate Title(s):   Ophthalmic Lab Tech; Manufacturing Optician; Optical Mechanic; Optical Goods Worker

Salary Range: $19,000 to $34,000+

Employment Prospects: Good

Advancement Prospects: Fair

Best Geographical Location(s) for Position: Positions may be located throughout the country

Prerequisites:
   Education or Training:—On-the-job training
   Experience—No experience necessary for many positions
   Special Skills and Personality Traits—Manual dexterity; math and science skills; ability to do precision work

CAREER LADDER

```
┌─────────────────────────────────┐
│   Dispensing Optician or Lab     │
│   Manager or Supervisor          │
└─────────────────────────────────┘

┌─────────────────────────────────┐
│   Ophthalmic Laboratory Technician │
└─────────────────────────────────┘

┌─────────────────────────────────┐
│            Student               │
└─────────────────────────────────┘
```

Position Description

Ophthalmic laboratory technicians are responsible for physically making prescription eyeglass lenses. When people need glasses they usually first go to an optometrist or ophthalmologist, who will examine the person's eyes and write a prescription for eyeglasses. The patient will then go to a dispensing optician to choose frames and be fitted for glasses. The dispensing optician will give the prescription to the ophthalmic lab technician, who will grind the lenses according to specifications. In some cases, the dispensing optician also does the work of the ophthalmic laboratory technician.

Prescription glasses have curved lenses. Ophthalmic laboratory technicians cut, grind, edge, and finish lenses so that light is focused onto the retina of the wearer's eye. In this way, a person's vision can be improved dramatically.

In order to do their work, ophthalmic laboratory technicians mark the lenses to determine where the curves should be ground, according to the prescription. The lenses are placed into a machine which is set at the specifications necessary to grind them correctly. Other machines then smooth the rough edges and polish the glass.

Before the ophthalmic laboratory technician is finished, he or she must make sure that the lenses have been made correctly by putting them in an instrument called a lensometer, which determines that the degree and placement of the curve is perfect.

At that point, the lab technician cuts the lenses and finishes off the edges to fit the lenses into the frames and assembles the finished glasses.

The ophthalmic laboratory technician usually works Monday to Friday, 9 to 5, or hours fairly close to that, though they might be required to work weekends or evenings.

Salaries

Ophthalmic lab technicians may have annual earnings ranging from $19,000 to $34,000 or more depending on a number of variables, including the amount of training and experience the individual has and the specific job and its geographic location.

Employment Prospects

With the population of middle-aged and older people growing, more people than ever require glasses. Employment prospects are, therefore, good for ophthalmic lab technicians. Employment opportunities may be located throughout the country.

Individuals may find work in retail optical shops, one-stop optical superstores, or the optical departments of drug or department stores, among others. There are also opportunities available to work on a part-time basis.

Advancement Prospects

Advancement prospects for ophthalmic lab technicians are fair. Individuals can climb the career ladder by obtaining additional education or training and becoming dispensing opticians. With experience, some ophthalmic laboratory technicians become supervisors or managers of labs.

Education and Training

Training for ophthalmic lab technicians is usually obtained on the job. Complete training takes from six to eighteen months. Another training option is an optical technology program in a vocational or trade school. These programs usually award certificates or diplomas. Programs in this field, however, are few and far between. Training in this area is also available through programs offered in the armed forces.

Experience/Skills/Personality Traits

Many jobs in this field are entry level. Potential applicants should be high school graduates. Manual dexterity is necessary, as is the ability to do precision work.

Unions/Associations

There is no specific union for ophthalmic lab technicians. Individuals may receive educational support and guidance from either the Opticians Association of America (OAA) or the Commission on Opticianry Accreditation (COA).

Tips for Entry

1. Contact the Commission on Opticianry Accreditation (COA) for a list of accredited training programs. (The address can be located in Appendix II of this book.)
2. Send your resume and a short cover letter to one-stop optical superstores or large drug and department stores with optical departments. Ask that your resume be kept on file if there are no current openings.
3. Openings are often posted in the windows of optical stores.
4. Positions can often be located in the classified section of the newspaper under headings such as "Ophthalmic Lab Technician," "Optical," or "Opticianry."

NURSING

REGISTERED NURSE

CAREER PROFILE

Duties: Providing care for sick or injured patients; administering medications; supervising L.P.N.s, orderlies, and nurse's aides; recording symptoms

Alternate Title(s): R.N.

Salary Range: $30,000 to $95,000+

Employment Prospects: Good

Advancement Prospects: Excellent

Best Geographical Location(s) for Position: Positions may be located throughout the country

Prerequisites:

Education or Training—Graduation from accredited school of nursing

Experience—Clinical experience obtained in nursing school

Special Skills and Personality Traits—Compassion; empathy; communication skills; good judgment

CAREER LADDER

```
┌─────────────────────────────────────┐
│   Nursing Supervisor, Nurse          │
│   Practitioner, or Nurse Anesthetist │
└─────────────────────────────────────┘

┌─────────────────────────────────────┐
│          Registered Nurse            │
└─────────────────────────────────────┘

┌─────────────────────────────────────┐
│     Nursing Student or L.P.N.        │
└─────────────────────────────────────┘
```

Position Description

Registered nurses (R.N.s) provide care for sick and injured people. They also help those who are not sick stay well. R.N.s can have many different responsibilities, ranging from direct patient care to administration, depending on the specific setting in which they are working.

Registered nurses observe patients and assess and record their symptoms, reactions, and progress. R.N.s assist individuals in their recovery and rehabilitation. General responsibilities can include dressing wounds, providing emergency care, administering medications and injections, maintaining records, and offering health counseling.

Many nurses work in hospitals, providing bedside care. They are expected to carry out the medical regime prescribed by physicians. This may include administering medications, treatments, and therapies. Depending on the situation, R.N.s may be asked to supervise L.P.N.s (licenced practical nurses), orderlies, and nurses aides. R.N.s working in a hospital environment may be assigned to one area such as maternity, pediatrics, emergency, or intensive care, or may be expected to rotate among the various departments.

Individuals working in extended care facilities such as nursing homes may have similar duties. A great deal of their time is also spent on administrative and supervisory functions. Many R.N.s working in these types of facilities are expected to develop treatment plans.

R.N.s may become nursing supervisors or head nurses. These individuals plan the work schedules and duties of the nursing staff, including aides and orderlies. Nursing supervisors may also be responsble for training others in the nursing department and for maintaining records—such as schedule records, nursing records, and patient records—in a timely fashion.

Some R.N.s prefer to work as office nurses, assisting physicians in private practice or clinics. Other office nurses work in emergency medical centers, surgi-centers, and HMOs. Nurses in these settings are expected to prepare patients for exams and assist with the examination. Office nurses may also be required to maintain records.

R.N.s may work in occupational health or as industrial nurses at worksites providing nursing care to employees and customers. Others opt to work for private agencies, clinics, schools, prisons, or government settings. These jobs often require individuals to provide instruction on preventative health care, disease prevention, and nutrition. R.N.s in these settings may also be required to perform health screenings, tests, and procedures. Individuals may also opt for private duty—either in a patient's home or in a hospital—where patients need constant attention.

No matter what type of work setting R.N.s choose, they will be helping others. Hours for R.N.s vary depending on the specific setting and assigned shifts.

Salaries

Earnings for Registered nurses can vary greatly depending on the geographic location and specific job setting as well as the education and experience of the individual. R.N.s working full time may have earnings ranging from $30,000 to $95,000+ or more.

R.N.s with experience working in specialties or in supervisory positions earn more than those in other situations. In many settings, earnings for R.N.s are negotiated and set by bargaining unions.

Employment Prospects

Employment prospects for R.N.s are good. Individuals can find full- or part-time work throughout the country. Flex-time positions may also be available.

There are a vast array of opportunities in hospitals, health care facilities, and extended care facilities. Other job opportunities exist in schools, physician's offices, clinics, home health care agencies, and temporary agencies.

Advancement Prospects

Advancement prospects are excellent for R.N.s. Individuals with additional experience and training may move into supervisory or administrative positions. Others climb the career ladder by becoming clinical nurse specialists, nurse practitioners, or nurse anesthetists.

Education and Training

Educational requirements for registered nurses include a degree from an accredited school of nursing. Programs leading to an associate degree, or A.D.N., last approximately two years and are offered throughout the country in community and junior colleges. Aspiring R.N.s may also receive a bachelor's degree, or B.S.N, from a college or university. These programs take between four and five years. The last educational option for R.N.s is a two- to three-year diploma program offered at hospitals. Many nurses go through A.D.N. programs and then enter bachelor's programs for career advancement.

Nursing education includes classroom instruction as well as supervised training and clinical experience in hospitals and other health care facilities.

Experience/Skills/Personality Traits

Ill patients are often frightened. Some of the most important personality traits of a good R.N. are compassion, sympathy, empathy, and caring. R.N.s must also be responsible people with good judgment. Good communication skills and the ability to follow orders are necessary, as is the ability to work with ill and infirm people. A desire to help people is needed.

Unions/Associations

Depending on the specific employment setting, R.N.s may be members of a union which negotiates and sets salaries and work conditions.

The National Student Nurses' Association (NSNA), the National League for Nursing (NLN), and the American Nurses' Association (ANA) provide educational and professional support to members.

Tips for Entry

1. Consider volunteering in a hospital or other health care facility to make sure nursing is the vocation you want to pursue.
2. Visit career fairs in high schools, vocational schools, colleges, and hospitals to explore various career options in nursing.
3. Positions are often advertised in the classified section of newspapers under headings such as "Nursing," "Registered Nurse," "R.N.," "Health Care," "Hospitals," or "Extended Care Facilities."
4. Contact trade associations to obtain additional information on careers in nursing.
5. Send your resume and a short cover letter to the Directors of Human Resources departments at local hospitals and health care facilities.

NURSE-MIDWIFE

CAREER PROFILE

Duties: Caring for pregnant women; delivering babies; providing care after birth for mothers and babies

Alternate Title(s): Certified Nurse Midwife; CNM

Salary Range: $48,000 to $85,000+

Employment Prospects: Good

Advancement Prospects: Fair

Best Geographical Location(s) for Position: Positions may be located throughout the country

Prerequisites:

Education or Training—R.N. training plus one to two year certificate or master's program in nurse midwifery

Experience—Nursing experience in obstetrics and gynecology

Special Skills and Personality Traits—Ability to work under pressure; compassion; organization; attention to detail; interpersonal skills; communication skills; good judgment

CAREER LADDER

```
┌─────────────────────────────────────┐
│   Nurse-Midwife in Larger or More    │
│ Prestigious Facility, or Supervisory │
│      or Administrative Position      │
└─────────────────────────────────────┘

┌─────────────────────────────────────┐
│            Nurse-Midwife             │
└─────────────────────────────────────┘

┌─────────────────────────────────────┐
│           Registered Nurse           │
└─────────────────────────────────────┘
```

Position Description

Nurse-midwives are registered nurses who take care of pregnant women. They are certified professionals who work with other nurses and physicians in providing gynecologic and obstetric services to antepartum, intepartum, and postpartum patients. As a rule, nurse-midwives care only for low-risk, healthy patients.

Nurse-midwives may also be referred to as certified nurse midwives or CNMs. It should be noted that there is a great difference between nurse-midwives who are formally trained and midwives who are not required to receive any formal medical training.

Nurse-midwives have a number of responsibilities. They provide prenatal examinations and answer questions from the mother and father regarding the pregnancy, the baby, or related matters. They may also counsel the mother on nutrition and proper exercise during her pregnancy.

Nurse-midwives also care for women while they are in labor. Individuals check on the unborn child and the mother to make sure that there are no complications and everything is going smoothly. They ask the mother pertinent questions about her pregnancy, monitor the heart rate of the baby with special equipment, check the mother's dilation, and help her through labor.

When the mother is ready to deliver, the nurse-midwife will assist her in the delivery. The nurse-midwife may also be expected to care for both the mother and the child after the birth and often will teach the mother how to care for her newborn child.

It is essential that the nurse-midwife have good judgment. If any problems with the pregnancy or delivery are detected, a physician must be notified.

Some nurse-midwives also examine women who are not pregnant. They perform gynecological tests including pap smears, breast exams, pregnancy tests, or screenings for sexually transmitted diseases, and they may offer patients advice on birth control and family planning.

Nurse-midwives may work various hours and shifts including days, evenings, nights, and weekends. They may also be on call for emergencies and deliveries.

Salaries

Earnings for nurse-midwives begin at approximately $48,000 and can go up to $85,000 or more a year. Factors affecting earnings include the experience, education, responsibilities, and the professional reputation of the individual. Other variables include the specific job and geographic location.

Employment Prospects

Employment prospects are good for nurse-midwives. Many OB-GYNs are hiring CNMs to work in their offices. Other physicians, hospitals, clinics, medical centers, schools, and HMOs are also utilizing the services of nurse-midwives. Positions may be located throughout the country.

Advancement Prospects

Nurse-midwives who obtain experience and additional education may climb the career ladder in a number of ways. Some find similar positions in larger or more prestigious facilities or physicians' offices. This can result in increased earnings. Others who develop a good professional reputation often have patients flocking to them. Nurse-midwives can find administrative or supervisory positions, but many in this profession prefer taking care of patients.

Education and Training

In order to become a nurse-midwife, an individual must first graduate from an accredited school of nursing. Individuals may take a number of different educational routes to meet this requirement. These include attendance in a program leading to an associate degree or A.D.N. These programs, lasting approximately two years, are offered throughout the country in community and junior colleges. Aspiring R.N.s may also attend colleges or universities and go for a bachelor's degree or B.S.N. These programs take between four and five years. The last educational option for R.N.s is to participate in a two- to three-year diploma program offered at hospitals. Many individuals go through A.D.N. programs and then enter bachelor's programs for career advancement.

The R.N. must then complete a one- to two-year certificate or master's degree program in nurse midwifery. Certification is available through the American College of Nurse Midwives (ACNM).

Experience/Skills/Personality Traits

Successful nurse-midwives require compassion, understanding, and a desire to help others. They must be organized, detail-oriented people with strong interpersonal skills. Good judgment and the ability to work under pressure are essential in this job. Communication skills are also necessary.

Unions/Associations

Individuals aspiring to become nurse-midwives should contact the American College of Nurse Midwives (ACNM) for additional career information. Nurse-midwives may also be members of professional nursing trade associations including the National League for Nursing (NLN) or the American Nurses' Association (ANA). These groups provide educational and professional support to members.

Tips for Entry

1. Job openings are often advertised in the classified section of newspapers under headings such as "Nurse Midwife," "Certified Nurse Midwife," "Nursing," "Obstetrics," "Health Care," or "Clinics."
2. Send your resume and a cover letter to obstetricians and to personnel directors at hospitals and clinics. Remember to ask that your resume be kept on file if there are no current openings.
3. Register at your college placement office.
4. There are a number of employment agencies and search firms dealing specifically with jobs in health care.
5. Use the Internet to locate a job in this field. Search under health care jobs and hospitals.

NURSE PRACTITIONER

CAREER PROFILE

Duties: Performing nursing duties and many functions handled by physicians; giving physical exams; taking patients' health history; formulating plan of care

Alternate Title(s): NP

Salary Range: $48,000 to $85,000+

Employment Prospects: Good

Advancement Prospects: Good

Best Geographical Location(s) for Position: Positions may be located throughout the country

Prerequisites:

Education or Training—R.N. training plus completion of accredited program for nurse practitioners

Experience—Nursing experience necessary

Special Skills and Personality Traits—Decision-making skills; ability to work under pressure; compassion; organization; attention to detail; interpersonal skills; communication skills; good judgment

CAREER LADDER

```
┌─────────────────────────────────┐
│   Nurse Practitioner in Larger   │
│     or More Prestigious Facility │
└─────────────────────────────────┘

┌─────────────────────────────────┐
│        Nurse Practitioner        │
└─────────────────────────────────┘

┌─────────────────────────────────┐
│         Registered Nurse         │
└─────────────────────────────────┘
```

Position Description

Nurse practitioners are registered nurses with advanced training and education who work in conjunction with physicians in caring for patients. They handle nursing responsibilities as well as many functions normally handled by physicians.

Nurse practitioners have varied duties and functions depending on their specific jobs. They usually perform physical examinations and get a patient's health history from either the patient or his or her family. They may also perform certain preventative health measures within prescribed guidelines.

In order to diagnose a patient's illness, the nurse practitioner may order lab tests and/or X rays. He or she may then interpret and evaluate the diagnostic tests. In this manner the individual can identify and assess a patient's clinical problems and other health care needs.

The nurse practitioner accurately records all physical findings and may be expected to formulate a plan of care. The nurse practitioner may also recommend drugs or other forms of treatment, such as physical therapy. He or she may be asked to give a prognosis based on the patient's condition.

The nurse practitioner often takes care of minor illnesses including colds, sprains, and simple problems. Working under the supervision of a physician, the nurse practitioner may also treat hypertension, pneumonia, strokes, or congestive heart failure, or other illnesses that have specific treatments agreed upon by the physician.

The nurse practitioner is expected to discuss the patient's case with the physician and other health professionals to ensure that all normal medical practices have been observed. He or she is responsible for submitting health care plans and goals for each patient for periodic review and evaluation by a physician.

The nurse practitioner may refer patients to a physician or to another specialized health professional when consultations or referrals are needed.

Nurse practitioners may work various hours and shifts including days, evenings, nights, and weekends. They may also be on call for emergencies.

Salaries

Earnings for nurse practitioners begin at approximately $48,000 and can go up to $85,000 or more a year. Factors affecting earnings include the experience, education, responsibilities, and professional reputation of the individual. Other variables include the specific job and its geographic location.

Employment Prospects

Employment prospects are good for nurse practitioners. This is an emerging career which is expanding quickly. Individuals may find employment throughout the country in a variety of settings including hospitals, clinics, health centers, public health agencies, and health maintenance organizations (HMOs).

Advancement Prospects

Nurse practitioners who obtain experience and/or additional education may climb the career ladder in a number of ways. Some find similar positions in larger or more prestigious facilities or physicians' offices. This can result in increased earnings. In some states, nurse practitioners can work on their own.

Education and Training

In order to become a nurse practitioner, an individual must first graduate from an accredited school of nursing. Individuals may take a number of different educational routes to meet this requirement. These include attendance in a program leading to an associate degree or A.D.N. These programs, lasting approximately two years, are offered throughout the country in community and junior colleges. Aspiring R.N.s may also attend colleges or universities to obtain a bachelor's degree or B.S.N. These programs take between four and five years. Another educational option for R.N.s is to participate in a two- to three-year diploma program offered at hospitals. Many individuals go through A.D.N. programs and then enter bachelor's programs for career advancement.

R.N.s must then complete an accredited program for nurse practitioners. These programs may vary in length. This specialized education gives them extra skills in judgment and decision-making.

Registration and certification may be required by certain states and/or positions.

Experience/Skills/Personality Traits

Nurse practitioners should be compassionate, understanding people who enjoy helping others. They must be organized, detail-oriented and able to work under pressure. Good judgment and decision-making skills are mandatory in this career.

Nurse practitioners should have good interpersonal skills and get along well with others. Communication and supervisory skills are also needed for success in this field.

Unions/Associations

Nurse practitioners may be members of the American Academy of Nurse Practitioners (AANP) or professional nursing associations including the National League for Nursing (NLN) or the American Nurses' Association (ANA). These groups provide educational and professional support to members.

Tips for Entry

1. Job openings are often advertised in trade journals or in the classified section of newspapers under headings such as "Nurse Practitioner," "Nursing," "Nursing Specialties," "Health Care," or "Clinics."
2. Send your resume and a cover letter to the personnel directors at hospitals, clinics, and HMOs. Remember to ask that your resume be kept on file if there are no current openings.
3. Register at your college placement office.
4. There are a number of employment agencies and search firms dealing specifically with jobs in health care.
5. Use the Internet to locate a job in this field. Search under health care jobs and hospitals.

LICENSED PRACTICAL NURSE

CAREER PROFILE

Duties: Providing nursing care under supervision of physicians and registered nurses

Alternate Title(s): L.P.N.; Licensed Vocational Nurse; L.V.N.

Salary Range: $18,000 to $42,000+

Employment Prospects: Good

Advancement Prospects: Fair

Best Geographical Location(s) for Position: Positions may be located throughout the country

Prerequisites:

Education or Training—Completion of accredited licensed practical nursing program and state licensing exam

Experience—Clinical experience obtained in nursing school

Special Skills and Personality Traits—Compassion; caring; ability to follow instruction; communication skills

CAREER LADDER

```
┌─────────────────────────────┐
│      Registered Nurse       │
└─────────────────────────────┘

┌─────────────────────────────┐
│  Licensed Practical Nurse   │
└─────────────────────────────┘

┌─────────────────────────────┐
│      Nursing Student        │
└─────────────────────────────┘
```

Position Description

Licensed practical nurses (L.P.N.s) work under the supervision and direction of physicians and registered nurses, providing basic patient care. They assist in the care of patients who are injured, sick, convalescing, elderly, or handicapped. L.P.N.s also help care for newborns.

The duties of licensed practical nurses can vary greatly depending on the specific situation and working environment. Those who work in physicians' offices or clinics are responsible for preparing patients for exams and may assist physicians with exams.

L.P.N.s working in a hospital or health care facility will work more with patients' bedside care. They are expected to take patients' vital signs on a routine basis, monitoring their temperature, blood pressure, respiration, and pulse.

Licensed practical nurses also help patients become more comfortable by giving sponge baths, alcohol rubs, and massages, and treating bedsores. They often assist patients with personal hygiene such as bathing, brushing teeth, dressing, etc. If needed, L.P.N.s feed patients or help them feed themselves.

L.P.N.s are often required to insert catheters, prepare and give injections, administer routine lab tests, collect samples, and in some cases, record patients' food and liquid intake and output.

Depending on the state in which they work, L.P.N.s may be asked to administer medications prescribed by a physician or to start intravenous fluids. After patients are given medications and other treatments, L.P.N.s are responsible for observing patients and reporting any adverse reactions to physicians or other medical personnel.

Those working in nursing homes or other extended care facilities may be expected to work with other personnel on evaluating residents' needs and developing care plans.

Other responsibilities of L.P.N.s in certain employment situations might include keeping records, handling clerical duties, showing family members how to perform simple nursing duties, preparing simple meals for patients, assisting in the delivery of babies, and caring for and feeding infants or the elderly.

No matter the specific duties of L.P.N.s, one of their most important functions is to help patients be more comfortable not only physically but also emotionally. A caring, compassionate and understanding person often can make all the difference to an ill or infirm patient.

Work hours can vary depending on the specific job. L.P.N.s can work days, nights, evenings, weekdays, or weekends depending on the shift they are assigned.

Salaries

Earnings for L.P.N.s can vary depending on the geographic location and specific job setting as well as the education, experience, and responsibilities of the individual. Annual earnings can range from approximately $18,000 to $42,000 or more.

Employment Prospects

Employment prospects for L.P.N.s are good. Individuals can usually find employment throughout the country in a variety of health care settings. In addition to hospitals and other health care facilities, L.P.N.s often find work in rehabilitation centers, nursing homes, and extended care facilities. Others may work in private physicians' offices or clinics, work as private duty nurses, or find employment through temporary nursing agencies.

Advancement Prospects

Advancement prospects for L.P.N.s are dependent on the individual's interest and career direction. Many L.P.N.s are content with their work. Some obtain experience and become private duty nurses setting their own work hours. L.P.N.s can also climb the career ladder by obtaining additional education and becoming R.N.s.

Education and Training

Educational requirements for licensed practical nurses include completion of a state-approved practical nursing program. These are offered in trade, technical, and vocational schools as well as community and junior colleges. Other programs are offered in high schools, hospitals, four-year colleges and universities.

Practical nursing programs include classroom study as well as supervised clinical training. The course of study includes classes in basic nursing, patient care, anatomy, phys-

iology, administration of drugs, nutrition, first aid, and various nursing specialties. Practical nursing programs generally last approximately one year.

L.P.N.s must pass a licensing examination after completing the state-approved practical nursing program.

Experience/Skills/Personality Traits

Licensed practical nurses, like all others working in direct patient care, must be compassionate, caring people. They must be able to make others feel calm and comfortable.

Stamina and physical strength are helpful in caring for patients. Communication skills and the ability to follow directions are mandatory.

Unions/Associations

Depending on the specific employment setting, licensed practical nurses may be members of a union which negotiates and sets minimum earnings and work conditions.

Helpful associations for L.P.N.s include the National Federation of Licensed Practical Nurses, Inc. (NFLPN), the National League for Nursing (NLN), and the National Association for Practical Nurse Education and Service, Inc. (NAPNES).

Tips for Entry

1. Many hospitals have candy stripers or similar volunteer organizations. Volunteering in a hospital or other health care facility will help you to be sure nursing is the vocation you want to pursue.
2. Visit career fairs in high schools, vocational schools, colleges, and hospitals to explore various career options in nursing.
3. Positions are often advertised in the classified section of newspapers under headings such as "Nursing," "Licensed Practical Nurse," "L.P.N.," "Licensed Vocational Nurse," "L.V.N.," "Private Duty Nurse," "Health Care," "Hospitals," or "Extended Care Facilities."
4. Contact trade associations to obtain additional information on careers in nursing.
5. Send your resume and a short cover letter to the director of human resources at local hospitals and health care facilities. You might also consider contacting private physicians' offices or clinics.

NURSING ASSISTANT

CAREER PROFILE

Duties: Assisting nurses and other medical staff with patient care; taking vital signs; making patients comfortable; serving meals; keeping patients' rooms neat

Alternate Title(s): Nursing Aide; Nurse's Aide; Hospital Attendant; Psychiatric Aide

Salary Range: $15,000 to $30,000+

Employment Prospects: Good

Advancement Prospects: Fair

Best Geographical Location(s) for Position: Positions may be located throughout the country

Prerequisites:

Education or Training—Training requirements vary from on-the-job training to completion of a formal training program

Experience—No experience necessary

Special Skills and Personality Traits—Compassion; caring; personable; ability to follow orders; physical stamina and strength

CAREER LADDER

```
┌─────────────────────────────┐
│  Licensed Practical Nurse   │
└─────────────────────────────┘

┌─────────────────────────────┐
│     Nursing Assistant       │
└─────────────────────────────┘

┌─────────────────────────────┐
│        Entry Level          │
└─────────────────────────────┘
```

Position Description

Nursing assistants work under the supervision of nurses and physicians assisting them in patient care. They may also be called nurse's aides, hospital attendants, or nursing aides. They work with patients who are ill, injured, disabled, or infirm.

The duties of nursing assistants can be diverse depending on the specific work setting. Individuals may work with patients in hospitals, nursing homes, extended care facilities, or mental health settings.

Nursing assistants often perform many of the same duties as L.P.N.s. For example, they may be responsible for taking patients' vital signs. This includes monitoring their temperature, blood pressure, pulse, and respiration. Nurse's aides may also be expected to bathe patients and give massages, alcohol rubs, sponge baths, etc., to help them be more comfortable.

When patients call for help in hospitals, nursing assistants are responsible for answering the call bells. They also assist patients getting in and out of bed; help them into wheelchairs; escort them to the lab, operating room, or examining room; and walk with them for required exercise. Nursing assistants may deliver and serve meals and help patients eat when necessary. In most situations, they are also expected to keep patients' rooms neat, change linens, straighten beds, empty bedpans, etc.

Nursing assistants who work in nursing homes, psychiatric hospitals, and other extended care facilities often have more contact with patients than any other members of the staff. They therefore are more aware of physical, mental, and emotional conditions and changes that may develop in their patients. Nursing assistants in these situations help patients dress and attend to personal hygiene. They may also be expected to socialize with patients or lead them in recreational or educational activities. Good nursing assistants can often lift the spirits of depressed patients and positively influence their mental and emotional outlook.

Nursing assistants report to the nursing supervisor. Work hours vary depending on the specific job shift. Individuals may work days, nights, evenings, or weekends.

Salaries

Earnings for nursing assistants vary depending on the geographic location and specific job setting as well as the amount of training. Annual earnings can range from approximately $15,000 to $30,000 or more. Individuals who are certified and have gone through a training program will generally earn more than others.

Employment Prospects

Employment prospects for nursing assistants are good. Individuals can usually find employment throughout the country in a variety of health care settings including hospitals, extended care facilities, nursing homes, rehabilitation centers, and psychiatric hospitals. Many nurse's aides also work in private duty situations.

Advancement Prospects

In order for nursing assistants to advance their careers they must obtain additional training and become L.P.N.s.

Education and Training

Training requirements for nursing assistants vary. Jobs not requiring prior training usually offer either formal or informal on-the-job training programs. Formal training programs are offered in high schools, vocational-technical schools, nursing homes, hospitals, and community colleges. Those seeking to work in nursing homes may be required to complete a 75-hour training program and pass a competency evaluation. Psychiatric hospitals may require a similar formal training program.

Experience/Skills/Personality Traits

Many jobs do not require any experience at all in the health care field. Some may not even require the applicant hold a high school diploma.

Nursing assistants should be personable, compassionate, and caring people who like to help others. Stamina and physical strength are helpful in caring for patients. The ability to follow directions is essential.

Unions/Associations

Depending on the specific employment setting, Nursing assistants may be members of a union which negotiates minimum earnings and work conditions.

Tips for Entry

1. Job openings in this field are often advertised in the newspaper classified section under headings such as "Nurse's Aide," "Nursing Aide," "Nursing Assistant," "Psychiatric Aide," "Hospital Attendant," "Health Care," "Hospitals," "Long-Term Care," or "Extended Care Facilities."

2. Visit career fairs in high schools, vocational-technical schools, colleges, and hospitals to explore various career options in nursing.

3. As earnings may be determined by the amount of education and training you have, try to go through a formal training program. Contact local high schools, nursing homes, hospitals, and community colleges to see if they offer training programs.

5. Visit the personnel office of nursing homes, hospitals, psychiatric hospitals, and extended care facilities to locate available openings in this field.

PSYCHIATRIC AIDE

CAREER PROFILE

Duties: Assisting in caring for patients in mental health settings; helping patients dress, bathe, and groom themselves; leading patients in educational or recreational activities

Alternate Title(s): Psychiatric Nursing Assistant; Ward Attendant; Mental Health Assistant

Salary Range: $15,000 to $30,000+

Employment Prospects: Good

Advancement Prospects: Fair

Best Geographical Location(s) for Position: Positions may be located throughout the country

Prerequisites:

Education or Training—Training requirements vary from on-the job-training to completion of a formal training program

Experience—No experience necessary

Special Skills and Personality Traits—Ability to work with people who have emotional and mental problems; emotional stability; compassion; caring; personable; ability to follow instruction; physical stamina and strength

CAREER LADDER

```
┌─────────────────────────────┐
│   Psychiatric Technician     │
│     or Ward Supervisor       │
└─────────────────────────────┘

┌─────────────────────────────┐
│      Psychiatric Aide        │
└─────────────────────────────┘

┌─────────────────────────────┐
│        Entry Level           │
└─────────────────────────────┘
```

Position Description

Psychiatric aides assist in caring for mentally impaired or emotionally disturbed patients in mental health settings. They work under the supervision of physicians and nurses. Psychiatric aides are part of a team that often includes psychiatrists, psychologists, psychiatric nurses, social workers, and therapists.

A great deal of psychiatric aides' responsibilities involve the day-to-day care of patients. They help patients dress, bathe, and groom themselves. Psychiatric aides are also expected to socialize with their patients during the workday. This is an important feature of their job as it helps patients normalize their social skills. They may also lead patients in educational or recreational activities set up by others on the care team.

Activities may include playing board games or cards with patients on a one-on-one basis. Psychiatric aides may participate in quiet time activities such as watching television with patients. They are often expected to accompany patients on field trips such as picnics, sporting events, or shopping.

Psychiatric aides must observe patients, looking for and reporting symptoms, behavior, or emotions of which the professional staff should be aware.

Psychiatric aides may be asked to accompany patients to examinations, treatments, and other activities within the facility or off the grounds. They may also be required to restrain patients who become unruly.

Psychiatric aides have very close contact with patients. They, therefore, often have a positive influence on patients' mental and emotional outlook. As patients with emotional problems are often demanding, temperamental, or easily upset, this can often be a difficult job. However, many find this type of work rewarding.

Work hours will vary depending on the specific job shift. Individuals may work days, nights, evenings, or weekends.

Salaries

Earnings for psychiatric aides vary depending on the geographic location and specific job setting as well as the amount of training. Annual earnings can range from approximately $15,000 to $30,000 or more. Individuals who are certified and have gone through a training program will generally earn more than others.

Employment Prospects

Employment prospects for psychiatric aides are good. Individuals can usually find employment throughout the country in a variety of mental health care settings including hospitals, extended care facilities, and psychiatric hospitals.

Advancement Prospects

While advancement prospects are limited, psychiatric aides can obtain additional education and experience and become psychiatric technicians or ward supervisors.

Education and Training

Training requirements for psychiatric aides vary from job to job. Positions not requiring prior training usually offer either formal or informal on-the-job training programs. Some states require psychiatric aides to complete a formal training program. These programs are often offered in high schools, vocational-technical schools, psychiatric hospitals, and community colleges.

Experience/Skills/Personality Traits

Many jobs do not require any experience at all. Some may not even require the applicant hold a high school diploma.

Psychiatric aides should be able to work with people who have emotional and mental problems. They must be emotionally stable, personable, compassionate, and caring people. Stamina and physical strength are necessary in caring for patients. The ability to follow directions is essential.

Unions/Associations

Psychiatric Aides may be members of various unions including the American Federation of State, County, and Municipal Employees (AFSCME) or the Service Employees International Union (SEIU). Individuals may also belong to the National Association of Human Services Technologists (NAHST).

Tips for Entry

1. Job openings in this field are often advertised in the newspaper classified section under headings such as "Psychiatric Aide," "Mental Health Assistant," "Psychiatric Nursing Assistant," "Ward Attendant," or "Health Care."
2. Visit career fairs in high schools, vocational-technical schools, colleges, and hospitals to explore various career options in this field.
3. As earnings may be determined by the amount of education and training you have, try to go through a formal training program.
4. Contact local high schools, nursing homes, hospitals, community colleges, etc. to see if they offer training programs.
5. Visit the human resources office of psychiatric hospitals to see if there are any openings available in this field.
6. If you are still in high school, take classes in home nursing and first aid.

SOCIAL SERVICES

SOCIAL WORKER

CAREER PROFILE

Duties: Counseling clients; helping clients cope with social, personal, psychological, and economic problems; coordinating services of agencies; investigating abuse or neglect

Alternate Title(s): None

Salary Range: $28,000 to $60,000+

Employment Prospects: Good

Advancement Prospects: Good

Best Geographical Location(s) for Position: Positions may be located throughout the country

Prerequisites:

Education or Training—Educational requirements vary from bachelor's degree to master's degree

Experience—Experience through internships or supervised field instruction

Special Skills and Personality Traits—Interpersonal skills; compassion; emotional stability and maturity; communication skills

CAREER LADDER

```
┌─────────────────────────────────┐
│  Social Worker in Larger Agency  │
│        or Administrative         │
│      or Supervisory Position     │
└─────────────────────────────────┘

┌─────────────────────────────────┐
│          Social Worker           │
└─────────────────────────────────┘

┌─────────────────────────────────┐
│            Student               │
└─────────────────────────────────┘
```

Position Description

Social workers help people solve a wide array of problems by helping them identify their problems, assisting them in evaluating possible solutions, and finding useful resources.

Clients' problems can include an inability to find adequate housing, lack of job skills or employment, financial troubles, illness, disabilities, substance abuse, unwanted pregnancy, lack of child care, or antisocial behavior. Other problems might include family conflicts, child abuse, spousal abuse, or children who are out of control.

Social workers are expected to provide specific information and sources to help clients solve problems. They make sure clients are eligible for programs and services and help fill out forms and applications. They may help clients apply for public assistance such as welfare or food stamps, or they may help clients find proper child care, join rehabilitation programs for alcohol or drug addictions, or get counseling. Social workers visit clients on a regular basis to make sure proper services are being provided and that the services are useful to clients.

Social workers in some settings investigate reports of abuse and neglect. This is usually done by individuals working in child or adult protective services departments. It is up to the social worker to intervene when necessary. This may mean initiating legal action to remove children from homes and place them in foster care.

Other social workers assist single parents, arrange for adoptions, counsel socially dysfunctional children and youth, and help parents deal with caring for disabled children.

Social workers may specialize in a number of different fields. The majority of individuals specialize in clinical areas such as child welfare or family services. Others work in mental health, medical social work, or school social work.

Clinical social workers provide psychotherapy or counseling and other services in agencies, clinics, or private practice. They must keep accurate records and prepare reports on clients' problems, situations, and solutions. The job also involves coordinating the services of different agencies to help handle and solve clients' problems.

Social workers usually work a standard 40-hour week. They may, however, be expected to work weekends or evenings to meet with clients or handle emergencies when necessary.

Salaries
Earnings for social workers can range from approximately $28,000 to $60,000 or more annually. Factors affecting earnings include the education, experience, and responsibilities of the social worker. Other factors include the geographic area and specific employment setting. Generally, individuals with a master of social work degree (M.S.W.) earn more than those with a bachelor of social work degree (B.S.W.).

Employment Prospects
Employment prospects are good for social workers. Individuals may find employment throughout the country in a variety of employment settings including state, county, municipal, and federal government agencies; nursing homes; hospitals; non-profit social service agencies; and community and religious organizations. Social workers may often find part-time positions, work as consultants, or go into private practice.

Advancement Prospects
Social workers have good prospects for advancement. With additional experience and/or education, individuals can locate similar positions in larger agencies or more prestigious facilities, move into supervisory or administrative positions, consult, or go into private practice. Social workers may also teach in colleges or universities or do research.

Education and Training
Educational requirements vary from job to job for social workers. The minimum requirement for this position is a bachelor's degree. Good choices for majors include social work, sociology, or psychology.

Many positions require a master's degree in social work. Ph.D.s are often required for teaching and research.

Individuals graduating with a B.S.W. go through a 400-hour supervised field experience program that prepares them to work right after graduation. Those graduating with an M.S.W. go through 900 hours of supervised field instruction or an internship.

Certain states require social workers in any field to be licensed or registered. Voluntary certification is available through the National Association of Social Workers (NASW).

Experience/Skills/Personality Traits
Social workers often obtain experience volunteering or working part-time as social services aides. Others gain experience through internships or supervised field instruction in college.

Social workers must be emotionally mature, stable individuals who work well with others. They must be able to work independently and as part of a team. They should be caring, compassionate people with good judgment. Communication and counseling skills are necessary.

Unions/Associations
Social workers may be members of the Council on Social Work Education (CSWE), the National Association of Social Workers (NASW), or the National Network for Social Work Managers (NNFSWM).

Tips for Entry
1. If you aspire to work in the social work field, try to get either a B.S.W. or M.S.W. As noted above, these will prepare you to begin working right after graduation. Those who have degrees in other fields may have to get experience in other ways before finding a job as a social worker.
2. Send your resume and a cover letter to the personnel directors of hospices; home health agencies; schools; county, municipal, and federal government agencies; social service agencies; nursing homes; hospitals; and extended care facilities. Remember to ask that your resume be kept on file if there are no current openings.
3. Part-time positions may be available even if no full-time positions are open.
4. Jobs may be advertised in the classified section of newspapers under headings including "Social Worker," "School Social Worker," "Geriatric Social Worker," "Health Care," "Social Service Agencies," and "Clinical Social Worker."
5. Jobs in state, county, municipal, and federal government agencies may be civil service positions. Take civil service exams if they apply.
6. Look for classes, seminars, and workshops on various facets of social work. Additional education will make you more marketable.

SOCIAL SERVICES AIDE

CAREER PROFILE

Duties: Assisting social workers; helping clients fill out forms; referring clients to other agencies for assistance

Alternate Title(s): Case Aide; Community Aide; Social Service Assistant

Salary Range: $18,000 to $32,000+

Employment Prospects: Good

Advancement Prospects: Good

Best Geographical Location(s) for Position: Positions may be located throughout the country

Prerequisites:

Education or Training—On-the-job training

Experience—Volunteer work helpful, but not required

Special Skills and Personality Traits—Compassion; tact; emotional stability and maturity; communication skills

CAREER LADDER

```
┌─────────────────────────────────┐
│   Social Service Technician or  │
│          Social Worker          │
└─────────────────────────────────┘

┌─────────────────────────────────┐
│       Social Services Aide      │
└─────────────────────────────────┘

┌─────────────────────────────────┐
│           Entry Level           │
└─────────────────────────────────┘
```

Position Description

There are a great many social services available to people in need. Social services aides act as liaisons between social service agencies and those seeking assistance. Their main function is to enable agencies to help a greater number of people in a more effective manner. Social services aides work under the supervision of social workers.

Social services aides have a wide array of duties. When new applicants go to an agency for assistance, it is the job of the social services aide to greet them and describe the various services the agency offers.

The social services aide is responsible for gathering the necessary information from applicants to make sure that they are eligible for assistance. They must give applicants the appropriate forms and may help fill them out properly.

Social services aides may handle other duties such as counseling clients, offering them encouragement, and speaking for them when they can not speak up for themselves. They may also be required to provide emergency transportation to clients. Often they are expected to refer people to other public or private agencies for required assistance.

Social services aides may perform general duties or may specialize. Those who assist caseworkers are known as case aides. These individuals perform many of the same duties as caseworkers. For example, they may work with clients to help them locate employment. Other case aides may assist clients in finding affordable housing or necessary medical care. Case aides may also be responsible for helping clients find other appropriate resources and agencies.

Social services aides may specialize in the community worker field, investigating the problems of residents of certain neighborhoods. These aides may tell residents who are disadvantaged because of a variety of economic or personal handicaps about available services.

Social services aides may work solely in an office setting or may visit clients in their homes or other locations. Social services aides usually work a standard 40-hour week. Their work, however, like that of social workers, may include weekends or evenings.

Salaries

Earnings for social services aides can range from approximately $18,000 to $32,000 or more depending on the type of agency they work for and its geographic location. Other factors affecting earnings include the education, experience, and responsibilities of the individual.

Employment Prospects

Employment prospects are good for social services aides. Individuals may find employment throughout the country in a variety of employment settings including federal, state, county, and municipal government agencies; nursing homes; hospitals; nonprofit social service agencies; and community and religious organizations. Employment is expected to increase as a result of the growing number of people requiring social services. Both full-time and part-time jobs are available.

Advancement Prospects

Social services aides can advance their careers by obtaining additional experience, on-the-job training, and education. Individuals may locate better job opportunities in other agencies, resulting in increased responsibilities and earnings; become social services technicians; or, with additional education, become social workers.

Education and Training

Educational requirements vary from job to job. Most positions require on-the-job training. There are often programs offered in vocational-technical schools, or junior or community colleges that might be useful in this type of job.

Experience/Skills/Personality Traits

This is often an entry-level position. Individuals can obtain experience by volunteering in hospitals, agencies, or community outreach programs.

Social services aides should be compassionate, caring, mature, emotionally stable people who enjoy helping others. The ability to work well with others and as part of a team is essential. Good judgment is mandatory, and a fair amount of tact is often necessary. Communication skills, both verbal and written, are needed.

Unions/Associations

There is no union specific to social services aides. Individuals may contact the Council on Social Work Education (CSWE), the National Association of Social Workers (NASW), and the National Network for Social Work Managers, Inc. (NNFSWM) for additional career information.

Tips for Entry

1. If you aspire to work in this field and you are still in school, take classes in family living, psychology, English, and computers.
2. Jobs may be advertised in the classified section of newspapers under headings such as "Social Services Aide," "Case Aide," "Community Aides," and "Social Work."
3. Send your resume and a cover letter to the personnel directors of hospices; home health agencies; schools; county, municipal, and federal government agencies; social service agencies; nursing homes; hospitals; and extended care facilities. Remember to ask that your resume be kept on file if there are no current openings.
4. Part-time positions may be available even if no full-time positions are open.
5. Fluency in a second language often puts you one step ahead of other applicants.
6. Look for classes, seminars, and workshops on various facets of social work. Additional education will make you more marketable.

HEALTH CARE
ADMINISTRATION

HEALTH SERVICES ADMINISTRATOR

CAREER PROFILE

Duties: Managing health care facility; setting policies; assessing need for services; supervising assistant administrators and department heads

Alternate Title(s): Health Services Director

Salary Range: $45,000 to $250,000+

Employment Prospects: Good

Advancement Prospects: Good

Best Geographical Location(s) for Position: Positions may be located throughout the country

Prerequisites:

Education or Training—Master's degree in health services administration, hospital administration, or business administration

Experience—Administrative and supervisory experience necessary

Special Skills and Personality Traits—Decision-making skills; leadership skills; managerial skills; ability to work under pressure; organization; attention to detail; interpersonal skills; communication skills; good judgment; ability to deal with media

CAREER LADDER

```
┌─────────────────────────────────────┐
│  Health Services Administrator in    │
│  Larger or More Prestigious Facility │
└─────────────────────────────────────┘

┌─────────────────────────────────────┐
│    Health Services Administrator     │
└─────────────────────────────────────┘

┌─────────────────────────────────────┐
│    Assistant Health Services         │
│         Administrator                │
└─────────────────────────────────────┘
```

Position Description

Health care facilities and agencies require someone to oversee the management of the facility and its operations. The person in charge of this is called the health services administrator. He or she may also be referred to simply as the administrator or the chief executive officer, or CEO.

The health services administrator has many responsibilities and duties. He or she is in charge of making sure that the facility runs smoothly. Health services administrators plan, organize, coordinate, direct, and supervise the delivery of health care in the facility. Assistant administrators, department heads, and medical personnel assist in these functions. Specific responsibilities depend on the size and setup of the facility or organization.

The health services administrator is responsible for the entire operation of the facility. One of the main functions of the administrator is to set the overall direction of the institution; another is to oversee its financial management. In larger organizations, the administrator may have several assistant administrators to handle day-to-day decisions. Assistants may be responsible for certain clinical areas such as nursing, surgery, therapy, food service, and medical records. There may also be assistant or deputy administrators handling areas such as marketing, finance, housekeeping, human resources, public relations, and information management. The administrator is expected to supervise all assistants. He or she may meet with them regularly to discuss problems, situations, and activities.

The health services administrator is also involved in community outreach and planning. These services are imperative in the health care field. He or she will work closely with the marketing, public relations, and planning departments to try to develop programs that will reach the community and build a positive image for the facility.

The administrator is responsible for developing long-term plans for the institution. To do this he or she works with the assistant administrators to assess the need for additional services, equipment, or personnel, or larger facilities. When working on these projects, the administrator must develop ways to make them financially viable.

Other important functions of the health services administrator include making sure that the facility complies with all governmental regulations. This may entail working with groups who scrutinize the facility's performance, such as consumer groups, government agencies, insurance companies, third-party payers, and professional oversight bodies.

The administrator may be required to speak at meetings of local civic organizations and attend functions and conferences, etc. This is a job with a great deal of responsibility, and working hours are rarely nine to five. While assistant administrators may be on call at specified times, the top administrator is ultimately responsible for everything that happens and all problems at the institution. He or she is, therefore, on call 24 hours a day, seven days a week.

Salaries

Earnings for health services administrators can range from approximately $45,000 to $250,000 or more. Factors affecting earnings include the experience, education, and responsibilities of the individual. Other variables include the specific job, the size and prestige of the facility, and its geographic location. Generally, individuals working in larger, more prestigious facilities in metropolitan areas will earn the highest salaries.

Employment Prospects

Employment prospects are good for health services administrators. There are a variety of settings throughout the country in which individuals may find employment. These include hospitals, nursing homes, and extended care facilities. Many clinics, group practices, and health maintenance organizations (HMOs) also utilize the services of health services administrators.

Advancement Prospects

Health services administrators climb the career ladder by locating similar positions in larger or more prestigious facilities. This results in increased responsibilities and earnings. To advance, individuals must obtain a fair amount of experience and/or additional education.

Education and Training

Health services administrators must usually have a master's degree in hospital administration, public health, or health administration. Courses may include psychology, economics, human physiology, systems management in the health field,

medical terminology, institutional sanitation, administering medical care programs, geriatrics, purchasing and materials management, fiscal management, managerial accounting, and legal aspects of health care service. To be admitted into these programs, individuals must have a bachelor's degree. Good choices for majors include health administration, liberal arts, social sciences, or business administration. State licensing may be necessary for individuals working in long-term care facilities or nursing homes. Licensing is obtained by completing a state-approved training program and passing a licensing exam. Some states require continuing education in order to keep licenses current.

Experience/Skills/Personality Traits

Health services administrators should have leadership, management, and decision-making skills. The ability to deal with a vast array of people in different areas is necessary. Communication skills are essential.

Individuals must be organized and detail-oriented. The ability to speak in public is needed. Good judgment is mandatory.

Health services administrators should have good math skills and an understanding of statistics and budgets.

Unions/Associations

There are a number of associations to which health services administrators may belong. These include the Medical Group Management Association (MGMA). Individuals may obtain additional career information by contacting the Association of University Programs in Health Administration (AUPHA) or the American Association of Homes for the Aging (AAHA).

Tips for Entry

1. Job openings are often advertised in trade journals.
2. Other jobs are advertised in the classified section of newspapers under headings such as "Health Services," "Health Services Administrator," "Hospital Administrator," "Hospital Administration," "Nursing Homes," "Nursing Home Administration," "HMOs," "Health Care," and "Clinics."
3. Send your resume and a cover letter to the personnel directors of hospitals, nursing homes, extended care facilities, clinics, and HMOs. Remember to ask that your resume be kept on file if there are no current openings.
4. Register at your college placement office.
5. There are a number of employment agencies and search firms dealing specifically with jobs in health care.

ADMITTING OFFICER

CAREER PROFILE

Duties: Admitting patients to facility; obtaining admission information; explaining consent and insurance forms

Alternate Title(s): Admissions Clerk

Salary Range: $21,000 to $34,000+

Employment Prospects: Good

Advancement Prospects: Fair

Best Geographical Location(s) for Position: Positions available throughout the country

Prerequisites:
  Education or Training—On-the-job training
  Experience—No experience necessary
  Special Skills and Personality Traits—Personable, typing and word processing skills; communication skills

CAREER LADDER

```
┌─────────────────────────────────────┐
│    Chief Admitting Officer or        │
│  Director of Admitting Department    │
└─────────────────────────────────────┘

┌─────────────────────────────────────┐
│         Admitting Officer            │
└─────────────────────────────────────┘

┌─────────────────────────────────────┐
│           Entry Level                │
└─────────────────────────────────────┘
```

Position Description

When a patient enters a hospital or other health care facility, a procedure is initiated during which he or she is admitted. The person who handles this process is the admitting officer or admissions clerk.

Admitting officers are responsible for explaining the procedures of admittance to patients. They may interview patients and help them fill out consent forms and other paperwork. If a patient cannot speak for him- or herself, the admitting officer is responsible for interviewing a relative or friend to obtain information. This data may include the patient's name, address, age, health history, present medications, previous hospitalizations, and religion; the person to notify in case of emergency; the attending physician; and the individual or insurance company responsible for payment of the bill.

Admitting officers also explain the consent and insurance forms to patients or guardians and have them sign the forms.

Admitting officers are often called by physicians to coordinate appointments for elective surgery. They must work in conjunction with the O.R. staff to schedule elective surgery admissions. In these cases, admitting officers may be asked to send pre-admission forms and other information to patients. In other cases patients are admitted on an emergency basis and admitting officers must alert the appropriate departments of the emergency admission.

Other functions of admitting officers include preparing hospital identification bracelets, arranging for the safe keeping of patients' valuables, and assigning beds. Once a patient is assigned to a location, the admitting officer will arrange for the patient to be transported to the correct room or area.

Admitting officers are responsible for compiling information regarding each patient's insurance, financial status, and other personal data. He or she may be expected to provide forms to the billing or other departments.

Admitting officers work with the director of the admitting department in compiling a daily census. They may also be responsible for maintaining death records as well as preparing and filing birth certificates.

Admitting officers usually work a normal 40-hour week. They may work various shifts including days, evenings, nights, and weekends.

Salaries

Annual earnings for admitting officers in health care facilities can range from $21,000 to $34,000 or more depending on a number of variables. These include the size and location of the facility as well as the experience, education, and responsibilities of the individual.

Employment Prospects

Employment prospects are good for admitting officers interested in working in health care facilities. Individuals may find employment throughout the country in hospitals, extended care facilities, nursing homes, etc. Most facilities have a number of admitting officers on staff.

Advancement Prospects

Admitting officers can advance their careers in a number of ways. Individuals may find similar positions in larger, more prestigious facilities resulting in increased responsibilities and earnings. Others obtain additional experience and/or education and go on to become the chief admitting officer or the director of admitting.

Education and Training

Admitting officers usually are required to have a minimum of a high school diploma or its equivalent. On-the-job training is provided in most positions. Those seeking advancement may need a college degree.

Experience/Skills/Personality Traits

Admitting officers should be pleasant people who enjoy interacting with others. They should be courteous and efficient. Many people are frightened at the prospect of entering a hospital, so the ability to calm people down is a plus.

Typing and word processing skills are necessary. The ability to use a computer is also needed. Communication skills are mandatory.

Unions/Associations

Admitting officers may belong to a union in the health care facility in which they work.

Tips for Entry

1. If you are planning on advancing your career, try to get a college degree.
2. Send your resume with a short cover letter to the personnel offices of hospitals, nursing homes, extended care facilities, etc. Ask that your resume be kept on file if there are no current openings.
3. Jobs are often advertised in the classified section of the newspaper. Look under headings including "Admitting Officer," "Admissions Clerk," "Hospitals," and "Health Care."
4. If you are still in school, you might consider volunteering in the admitting department of a hospital or seeing if there is an internship available. This will give you valuable experience and help you make important contacts.

PATIENT ADVOCATE

CAREER PROFILE

Duties: Handling patient problems and concerns; acting as liaison between patients and hospital administration and staff; making staff aware of patients' perception of problems

Alternate Title(s): Patient Ombudsman; Patient Representative

Salary Range: $24,000 to $37,000+

Employment Prospects: Good

Advancement Prospects: Fair

Best Geographical Location(s) for Position: Positions available throughout the country

Prerequisites:

Education or Training—Educational requirements vary from on-the-job training to bachelor's degree

Experience—Experience in hospital environment necessary

Special Skills and Personality Traits—Knowledge of hospital policies and procedures; interest in working with people; compassion; understanding; communication skills; understanding of human relations

CAREER LADDER

```
┌─────────────────────────────────────┐
│   Director of Patient Advocates or   │
│  Administrative Position in Public   │
│        Relations Department          │
└─────────────────────────────────────┘

┌─────────────────────────────────────┐
│          Patient Advocate            │
└─────────────────────────────────────┘

┌─────────────────────────────────────┐
│    Volunteer Patient Advocate or     │
│           College Student            │
└─────────────────────────────────────┘
```

Position Description

Sometimes in hospitals and other health care facilities patients or their families have concerns, are unhappy for some reason, or feel that they have not been treated properly. Patient advocates (also called patient representatives or patient ombudsmen) are responsible for helping patients with problems and concerns. They must make the hospital administration and staff aware of the individual's perception of the situation and then try to find a solution to the problem.

In many situations, patients' concerns can be alleviated just by having someone listen to them. Patient advocates afford patients or their families an opportunity to voice their problems. Patient advocates must try to explain the situation or come up with a viable solution. They may explain the policies of the facility and the reasons behind them, or they may need to speak to administrators about the problem. The important thing is for patients to feel they are not being ignored.

It is essential that patient advocates be able to identify and assess what the real problem is. Often when people are upset, the actual problem is masked, so advocates are expected to investigate the allegations fully. They may question hospital staff to determine what really happened. The problems may involve anything from patient care or billing to something relatively simple such as not having a working television or phone in the patient's room.

Patient advocates are responsible for either responding to the problem or making sure that the appropriate personnel do so. In some instances a timely and well thought out response can prevent patients from taking legal action or going to the press about a concern. Patient advocates, in effect, must act as mediators between the hospital administration and a patient and/or his or her family.

Additional responsibilities of patient advocates may include collecting information regarding patient care problems and the satisfaction of patients with their hospital experience. This may be accomplished through questionnaires, surveys, and interviews. Patient advocates must not only collect the information but use it to better the services of the hospital and its staff. They may also help patients and the staff understand the facility's policies on patients' rights. Patient advocates may work with the staff of the hospital's public relations department in an effort to alleviate patient problems or concerns.

Depending on the specific facility, patient advocates may work a normal 40-hour week or may work varying shifts. They may be required to put in overtime when special situations or emergencies occur. Patient advocates may be expected to attend meetings or represent the hospital at functions for staff or the community.

Salaries

Salaries for patient advocates vary greatly depending on the specific job. In smaller hospitals, they may only work part time and be paid an hourly wage. Individuals who work full time may earn between $24,000 and $37,000 or more. Other variables affecting earnings include the specific facility size, prestige, and location as well as the experience, education, and responsibilities of the individual. Generally patient advocates with more education and experience or those working at larger facilities in metropolitan areas will have earnings at the higher end of the pay scale.

Employment Prospects

Employment prospects for patient advocates are good. Jobs in this area are increasing. Most hospitals and other health care facilities have at least one patient advocate. Larger facilities usually have more advocates on staff.

Individuals may find employment throughout the country in hospitals, nursing homes, extended care facilities, and other health care institutions. Individuals seeking this type of position might have to relocate to find a job.

Advancement Prospects

Advancement prospects are fair for individuals with experience. A patient advocate can climb the career ladder by locating a similar position in a larger or more prestigious facility. This will result in increased responsibilities and earnings. Individuals may also advance their careers by becoming the director of patient advocates. This position, however, is usually only found in larger facilities. Some patient advocates move on to supervisory positions in the hospital public relations department.

Education and Training

This is a relatively new type of career, so there are not established educational requirements. Some people who hold this job have received on-the-job training and only have a high school diploma. Others hold a two-year associate's degree. However, it is recommended that individuals interested in pursuing a career as a patient advocate have a bachelor's degree. Good majors for this type of job include social work, sociology, psychology, communications, public relations, English, nursing, and liberal arts.

Experience/Skills/Personality Traits

Patient advocates should have some type of experience in a hospital environment. This may be gained by working or volunteering in a health care institution. Some patient advocates began their careers as volunteers in this field.

A knowledge and understanding of patient care and patient problems is essential. Patient advocates should be people persons. They must enjoy working with and helping others, and they should be compassionate, understanding, and empathetic.

Good communication skills, both verbal and written are needed. An understanding of human relations is also necessary. The ability to listen and define problems is mandatory.

Unions/Associations

There are no major trade associations for patient advocates.

Tips for Entry

1. Volunteer as a patient advocate in a hospital or nursing home. Many facilities have auxiliaries or volunteer organizations.
2. Send your resume with a short cover letter to hospitals in your area. If they don't have a job open, request that your resume be kept on file.
3. Look for internships in hospitals or other health care facilities. They are a good way to get you foot in the door.
4. The Internet has a number of areas advertising jobs in health care. Look for a position in this field in one of the career resource centers on the World Wide Web.
5. There are agencies that deal specifically in health care. If you consider one, make sure you check to see who will pay the fee when you get a job, you or the employer.
6. Jobs are often advertised in the classified section of the newspaper. Look under headings including "Patient Advocate," "Patient Representative," "Patient Ombudsman," "Health Care," and "Hospitals."

DIRECTOR OF VOLUNTEER SERVICES

CAREER PROFILE

Duties: Coordinating activities of volunteers; recruiting, interviewing, and placing volunteers

Alternate Title(s): Volunteer Services Director; Volunteer Services Coordinator

Salary Range: $24,000 to $65,000+

Employment Prospects: Fair

Advancement Prospects: Fair

Best Geographical Location(s) for Position: Positions available throughout the country

Prerequisites:

Education or Training—Bachelor's degree or volunteer experience with supervisory and administrative responsibilities

Experience—Volunteer experience helpful

Special Skills and Personality Traits—Personable, written and verbal communication skills; responsible; tact; attention to detail; organization

CAREER LADDER

```
┌─────────────────────────────────────┐
│  Director of Volunteer Services in   │
│  Larger, More Prestigious Facility   │
└─────────────────────────────────────┘

┌─────────────────────────────────────┐
│    Director of Volunteer Services    │
└─────────────────────────────────────┘

┌─────────────────────────────────────┐
│      Assistant Director of           │
│      Volunteer Services              │
└─────────────────────────────────────┘
```

Position Description

Hospitals and other health care facilities often utilize volunteers in various areas and departments to augment the activities of hospital staff. The person in charge of coordinating the activities of a facility's volunteers is the director of volunteer services.

Volunteers may provide an array of nonclinical services to patients. They may also help hospital staff in a wide variety of ways. Volunteers may, for example, perform the duties of a receptionist in an emergency room, admitting office, or waiting room. They may calm the families of patients in surgery or explain the patients' status. Many hospital volunteers bring patients books and magazines or work in hospital-based businesses including gift and coffee shops. Volunteers may also handle a variety of clerical duties. Many volunteers keep patients company or play with children in pediatrics.

The director of volunteer services is in charge of placing all volunteers. In order for volunteers to be effective, the director of volunteer services must take into account each volunteer's interests, skills, and personality as well as the

facility's needs. It is essential that the director of volunteers interview potential volunteers to take advantage of each person's specific skills. Some people, for example, are good at fund-raising while others might excel in the skilled nursing unit for the aging.

The director of volunteer services works with the hospital's auxiliary. These individuals often provide additional fund-raising efforts as well as other services for the facility.

Recruitment is a large part of this job. The director of volunteer services is expected to go out into the community and find people willing to volunteer and to train them if necessary for their service. In addition to working with adults, in many hospitals, the director of volunteers must develop a program for teenage volunteers. Recruiting volunteers might require attending community group meetings and visiting schools. The director also develops programs designed to keep volunteers in the system. This might include organizing and providing recognition ceremonies, luncheons, or dinners.

Depending on the specific facility, the director of volunteers may be responsible for managing the hospital gift shop or coffee shop or for overseeing their management by either a volunteer or employee. The director may additionally be responsible for negotiating contracts for outside vendors and services related to the hospital gift or coffee shop.

The director of volunteers must develop objectives for the volunteer department and then find ways to implement these goals. The director is responsible for the compilation and maintenance of records about the volunteers, the number of hours each volunteer works, and the services performed by each volunteer.

The director of volunteers works closely with other departments within the hospital, including fund-raising and development, public relations, marketing, planning, administration, and nursing.

The director of volunteer services in a hospital or other health care facility generally works regular hours. He or she may be asked to work overtime to attend meetings, functions, or special events or to handle timely projects.

Salaries

Annual earnings for the director of volunteer services in a hospital can range from $24,000 to $65,000 or more depending on the experience, education, and responsibilities of the individual. Other factors affecting salaries include the size, location, and prestige of the facility.

Salaries can start for beginners at $24,000 and go to $30,000. Those with more experience, or those working at larger facilities in metropolitan areas, can expect earnings between the middle and high end of the salary scale.

Employment Prospects

Employment prospects for those interested in working as the director of volunteer services in a hospital or other health care facility are fair. Positions are available throughout the country.

Advancement Prospects

The director of volunteer services in a health care facility can advance his or her career by obtaining a similar position in a larger or more prestigious facility. This will result in increased responsibilities and earnings.

Education and Training

Educational requirements for this position vary. Generally, a bachelor's degree is required. Experience working in other areas of health care or even volunteer experience with supervisory and administrative responsibilities is necessary.

Experience/Skills/Personality Traits

In many instances, the director of volunteers has received experience as an assistant director of volunteers or has volunteer experience in health care or other areas in the community.

A director of volunteers must be a people person. He or she must get along well with others and generally like working with people. Supervisory and administrative skills are needed.

Individuals should be detail-oriented, organized, and responsible. Both verbal and written communication skills are necessary. Public speaking ability may be required because the position often entails speaking in front of groups. Good judgment and common sense are also important.

Unions/Associations

The director of volunteers of a hospital may be a member of many of the civic organizations in the area. This is important to make contacts in the community.

Tips for Entry

1. Join a hospital auxiliary and become a hospital volunteer.
2. Look for an internship in the volunteer department of a hospital or health care facility. This will give you valuable experience.
3. There are employment agencies dealing specifically with jobs in hospitals and other health care facilities. These might be useful in helping to locate a position.
4. This type of position is often advertised in the classified section of newspapers. Look under headings such as "Director of Volunteers," "Volunteer Director," "Director of Volunteer Services," "Health Care," and "Hospitals."

ASSISTANT DIRECTOR OF VOLUNTEER SERVICES

CAREER PROFILE

Duties: Assisting the director of volunteer services to coordinate activities of volunteers; recruiting and interviewing volunteers

Alternate Title(s): Assistant Volunteer Services Director; Volunteer Services Assistant Coordinator

Salary Range: $21,000 to $39,000+

Employment Prospects: Fair

Advancement Prospects: Good

Best Geographical Location(s) for Position: Positions available throughout the country

Prerequisites:

Education or Training—Bachelor's degree or volunteer experience with supervisory and administrative responsibilities

Experience—Experience volunteering helpful

Special Skills and Personality Traits—Ability to follow instruction; personable; written and verbal communication skills; responsible; tact; attention to detail; organization

CAREER LADDER

```
┌─────────────────────────────────┐
│  Director of Volunteer Services  │
└─────────────────────────────────┘

┌─────────────────────────────────┐
│     Assistant Director of        │
│      Volunteer Services          │
└─────────────────────────────────┘

┌─────────────────────────────────┐
│      Student or Volunteer        │
└─────────────────────────────────┘
```

Position Description

The director of volunteer services in a hospital is in charge of coordinating the activities of the volunteers at the facility. The assistant director of volunteer services is responsible for assisting the director of the department in this task.

The assistant director may have varied duties depending on the specific facility and size. The assistant is often responsible for coordinating the volunteer assignments and their time schedules. In the event that scheduled volunteers cannot be where they have been scheduled, the assistant is responsible for finding substitutes. He or she is also responsible for keeping attendance records for each volunteer.

The assistant director might also be responsible for supervising groups of volunteers. For example, he or she may oversee teenage candy stripers. The assistant will then be in charge of recruiting these junior volunteers. This may involve going to local high schools or career fairs in the area.

The assistant director of volunteer services may be assigned the task of conducting orientation or training sessions for new volunteers. He or she is responsible for handling problems or situations that may develop regarding volunteers. If the situation cannot be rectified, the individual is expected to discuss it with the director of the department.

The assistant director works closely with the director in placing volunteers. He or she might be responsible for interviewing volunteers to make sure they are utilized in the best manner.

The assistant may attend meetings with the director or on behalf of the department. He or she might also be responsible for acting as a liaison between the hospitals' auxiliary and the volunteer department. In this capacity, the individual might be expected to handle or supervise specific projects with the auxiliary.

The assistant director of volunteer services might help the director coordinate, organize, and conduct volunteer recognition ceremonies. These are necessary in order to help make volunteers feel appreciated and keep them motivated. Ceremonies may include luncheons, dinners, or other events. The assistant may be responsible for handling decorations, coordinating food service, finding appropriate speakers, and locating certificates, ribbons, etc. He or she may also be asked to handle administrative tasks, such as keeping records and writing reports.

The assistant director of volunteer services in a hospital or other health care facility will generally work regular hours. He or she may be expected to work overtime to attend meetings, functions, or special events or to handle timely projects.

Salaries

Annual earnings for the assistant director of volunteer services in a hospital can range from $21,000 to $39,000 or more depending on the experience, education, and responsibilities of the individual. Other factors affecting salaries include the size, location, and prestige of the facility.

Employment Prospects

Employment prospects for individuals interested in working as the assistant director of volunteer services are fair. Individuals may find employment in hospitals, extended care facilities, or other health care facilities throughout the country. Some facilities, however, have only a director on staff.

Advancement Prospects

The assistant director of volunteer services can advance his or her career by obtaining additional experience and/or education. Her or she can then become the director of volunteer services.

Education and Training

Educational requirements for this position vary. Generally, a bachelor's degree is required. However, sometimes experience working in other areas of health care or even volunteer experience with supervisory and administrative responsibilities will be accepted.

Experience/Skills/Personality Traits

The assistant director of volunteers must have administrative and supervisory skills. The ability to get along well with a variety of people is necessary. The individual must be personable and pleasant and have the ability to motivate others and make them feel needed. Verbal and written communications skills are needed for this position. Additionally, applicants should be extremely organized and detail-oriented.

Unions/Associations

The assistant director of volunteers working in a hospital may be a member of a number of civic and nonprofit groups in the area. This is important to make contacts in the community.

Tips for Entry

1. Experience volunteering is always helpful.
2. If you are still in school, consider becoming a candy striper.
3. If you are in college, try to find an internship in your local hospital's volunteer department.
4. Openings may be advertised in the classified section of newspapers. Look under headings including "Assistant Director of Volunteer Services," "Volunteer Services," or "Health Care."
5. Send your resume and a short cover letter to the personnel directors of hospitals in your area. Remember to ask that your resume be kept on file if there are no current openings.

QUALITY ASSURANCE DIRECTOR

CAREER PROFILE

Duties: Monitoring patient care; developing and implementing programs to enhance patient care; supervising staff; developing budgets

Alternate Title(s): Quality Assurance Manager; Director of Quality Assurance

Salary Range: $35,000 to $75,000+

Employment Prospects: Fair

Advancement Prospects: Fair

Best Geographical Location(s) for Position: Positions may be found throughout the country

Prerequisites:
Education or Training—Nursing degree or medical records training
Experience—Experience working in quality assurance department
Special Skills and Personality Traits—Organization; attention to detail; supervisory and management skills; understanding of hospitals and health care facilities

CAREER LADDER

```
┌─────────────────────────────┐
│   Quality Assurance/Risk    │
│    Management Director      │
└─────────────────────────────┘

┌─────────────────────────────┐
│  Quality Assurance Director │
└─────────────────────────────┘

┌─────────────────────────────┐
│ Quality Assurance Department│
│       Staff Member          │
└─────────────────────────────┘
```

Position Description

The quality assurance department of a health care facility is responsible for monitoring and improving the quality of patient care. Quality assurance also deals with the risk to the facility. The quality assurance department is expected to minimize any exposure and risk to the facility which might lead to potential loss.

The quality assurance director is in charge of developing a program to enchance the quality of patient care in the facility. The individual is also responsible for implementing and managing the program.

It is necessary for the director of quality assurance to understand the needs of the hospital so that he or she can plan the most effective quality assurance program. The quality assurance director must first evaluate programs that are already in place in the hospital. He or she can then make changes, when necessary, to improve the standards of care.

Quality assurance relates to a number of different services within the hospital, including utilization review, evaluation of medical care, risk management, and staff reviews. It

is mandatory to keep the standards of these services up to par in order to assure quality patient care. It is also important because many services in a hospital are governed by various regulatory agencies. These might include federal and state agencies, the Joint Commission on the Accreditation of Healthcare Organizations (JCAH), and third party payors. These agencies often order quality assurance reviews.

The quality assurance director selects and trains the department staff. This might include providing inservice education. The quality assurance director is also responsible for preparing, implementing, and monitoring the budget for the department.

The quality assurance director must keep up to date on all regulatory agency requirements associated with health care facilities. He or she may develop and coordinate programs to check the quality of the various programs within the hospital. The director will then tabulate results and write reports of findings. The quality assurance director also examines reviews conducted by outside agencies regarding the quality of care in the hospital and recommends changes when necessary.

In some facilities, the quality assurance director may also be responsible for handling risk management, that is, malpractice suits. In others, he or she will work with the risk management director to reduce claims and other losses.

The quality assurance director works normal hours. He or she may be expected to work overtime, evenings, or on weekends to prepare for a quality assurance review or to handle emergencies.

Salaries

Annual earnings for quality assurance directors can range from $35,000 to $75,000 or more depending on a number of factors. These include the education, experience, and responsibilities of the individual as well as the size, prestige, and geographic location of the facility.

Employment Prospects

Employment prospects are fair for quality assurance directors. All health care facilities require this position. Individuals may locate jobs throughout the country in hospitals, extended care facilities, and nursing homes.

Advancement Prospects

Quality assurance directors may advance their careers by obtaining additional experience and/or education. They may then find similar positions in larger or more prestigious facilities resulting in increased responsibilities and earnings. Individuals may also be promoted to the position of director of quality assurance and risk management.

Education and Training

Individuals interested in pursuing a career as a quality assurance director may have different types of educational backgrounds. They may be graduates of nursing school or related clinical health care programs or they may have received training in medical records.

Experience/Skills/Personality Traits

This position requires a fair amount of previous experience working in health care, specifically in the quality assurance department. Individuals may obtain this experience working as staff members in quality assurance or risk management.

Quality assurance directors must be organized, detail-oriented individuals. Supervisory and management skills are needed. The ability to prepare budgets is also necessary. An understanding of the inner workings of health care facilities is mandatory.

Unions/Associations

Quality assurance directors working in health care facilities may be members of the National Association of Hospital Development (NAHD).

Tips for Entry

1. There are a number of search and employment agencies dealing specifically with careers in the health care industry.
2. Look in the classified sections of newspapers under "Health Care," "Hospitals," "Quality Assurance," "Quality Assurance Director," or "Quality Assurance/Risk Management."
3. Join trade associations in fields you are interested in working in. Subscribe to their journals and attend their seminars and conventions.
4. Consider working in a smaller facility. These positions are often easier to locate.
5. Send your resume and a short cover letter to hospitals, nursing homes, and extended care facilities.

HEALTH PROMOTION AND WELLNESS COORDINATOR

CAREER PROFILE

Duties: Developing and implementing health education and wellness activities in a facility and the surrounding community

Alternate Title(s): Health Wellness and Promotion Coordinator

Salary Range: $25,000 to $60,000+

Employment Prospects: Fair

Advancement Prospects: Good

Best Geographical Location(s) for Position: Positions may be located throughout the country

Prerequisites:

Education or Training—Bachelor's degree in nursing, health care, public relations, marketing, or communications

Experience—Experience in publicity or marketing helpful

Special Skills and Personality Traits—Attention to detail; organization; oral and written communication skills; personable; good judgment

CAREER LADDER

```
┌─────────────────────────────────────┐
│  Health Promotion and Wellness       │
│  Director or Director of Public      │
│  Relations, Marketing, or Staff      │
│  Development                         │
└─────────────────────────────────────┘

┌─────────────────────────────────────┐
│  Health Promotion and Wellness       │
│  Coordinator                         │
└─────────────────────────────────────┘

┌─────────────────────────────────────┐
│  Student or Public Relations,        │
│  Community Relations, or Marketing   │
│  Assistant, or Staff Development Nurse│
└─────────────────────────────────────┘
```

Position Description

The health promotion and wellness coordinator is a professional who assists the director of public relations, marketing, and/or program development in the design, implementation, coordination, and promotion of health education and wellness activities.

The health promotion and wellness coordinator is responsible for promoting the health of the people within the community served by the hospital, including the hospital staff. To accomplish this, the individual must conduct research to determine the needs of the community and develop and implement programs that will be beneficial to the people in the community.

Programs may include health fairs in the facility or in other locations such as shopping centers, schools, or community centers. The coordinator may put together support groups for people who are suffering from anorexia, cancer, alcoholism, or drug abuse. Or he or she may find that there is a need for programs for teen mothers or that the community would benefit from testing for lyme disease, cholesterol, or prostate cancer. The coordinator is expected to determine the effectiveness of these programs through questionnaires and surveys. Programs can then be changed when necessary to meet needs and expectations.

The health promotion and wellness coordinator is often expected to attend meetings, functions, and conferences. He or she may be asked to speak to groups about programs that the hospital is implementing.

Depending on the specific facility, the health promotion and wellness coordinator may be responsible to the director of marketing, public relations, or program development. He or she works normal hours, but may sometimes have to work evenings or weekends to attend meetings, functions, or special events or to handle projects that must be completed in a timely manner.

Salaries

Annual earnings for a health promotion and wellness coordinator can range from $25,000 to $60,000 or more depending on the experience, education, and responsibilities of the individual. Other factors affecting salaries include the size, location, and prestige of the facility.

Employment Prospects

Employment prospects for individuals interested in working as a health promotion and wellness coordinator are fair. This position exists in hospitals and other health care facilities throughout the country. In smaller hospitals, the public relations or marketing director or staff development nurse may be responsible for handling the functions of the health promotion and wellness coordinator.

Advancement Prospects

There are a number of paths a health promotion and wellness coordinator can take toward advancement. The individual can find a similar position in a larger or more pretigious facility resulting in increased responsibilities and earnings. He or she might also become the health promotion and wellness director or director of either the marketing, public relations, or staff development department, depending on his or her education and experience.

Education and Training

A bachelor's degree is required for this position. Majors can be in nursing or other areas of the health care field or may be in marketing, public relations, or communications. Seminars and workshops in a variety of subjects including writing, promotion, and health care are useful.

Experience/Skills/Personality Traits

The health promotion and wellness coordinator of a hospital must be extremely organized and detail oriented. He or she will be running a variety of programs and must be able to keep track of everything. The ability to organize activities and time in a productive manner of essential.

The individual must also have excellent oral and written communication skills. He or she must be personable and pleasant. Good judgment and common sense are mandatory to this position. The ability to deal with the hospital staff and members of the community in a pleasant, efficient, and productive manner is needed.

Unions/Associations

The health promotion and wellness coordinator of a hospital or health care facility may be a member of a number of organizations including the Academy of Hospital Public Relations (AHPR), the National Association of Hospital Development (NAHD), or the American Society for Hospital Public Relations (ASHPR).

Tips for Entry

1. There are agencies throughout the country dealing specifically with jobs in the health care industry.
2. Join trade associations. Go to their meetings and network.
3. If you are in college, try to find an internship in your local hospital's health promotion or public relations department.
4. Openings may be advertised in the classified section of newspapers. Look under headings including "Health Promotion," "Health Promotion and Wellness Coordinator," "Wellness Coordinator," "Health Care," and "Hospitals."
5. Send your resume and a short cover letter to the personnel directors of hospitals in your area. Remember to ask that your resume be kept on file if there are no current openings.

HEALTH CARE MARKETING, PUBLIC RELATIONS, PLANNING, AND DEVELOPMENT

DIRECTOR OF HOSPITAL MARKETING

CAREER PROFILE

Duties: Developing and implementing programs to increase use of hospital; developing profit-making programs in facility; performing research

Alternate Title(s): Marketing Director; Director of Marketing

Salary Range: $28,000 to $150,000+

Employment Prospects: Fair

Advancement Prospects: Fair

Best Geographical Location(s) for Position: Positions available throughout the country

Prerequisites:

Education or Training—Bachelor's degree in marketing, public relations, communications, journalism, advertising, business, or health care planning

Experience—Marketing and writing experience helpful

Special Skills and Personality Traits—Communication skills; supervisory and management skills; writing skills; creativity; public speaking ability

CAREER LADDER

```
┌─────────────────────────────────┐
│   Director of Hospital Marketing │
│   in Larger or More Prestigious  │
│  Facility, Hospital Administrator,│
│     or Marketing Consultant      │
└─────────────────────────────────┘

┌─────────────────────────────────┐
│   Director of Hospital Marketing │
└─────────────────────────────────┘

┌─────────────────────────────────┐
│      Assistant Director of       │
│       Hospital Marketing         │
└─────────────────────────────────┘
```

Position Description

The director of hospital marketing is responsible for the development and implementation of programs used to increase the use of the facility. The individual is also responsible for developing reimbursable and/or profit-making programs and activities in the facility.

The director of marketing is expected to come up with both long- and short-term marketing objectives and strategies. These might include planning special campaigns or other programs. For example, the director of marketing may develop a special geriatric program designed to attract older individuals in the area. The marketing director might also develop a special program designed to attract women to the facility. The individual might suggest new services for the facility or recommend other ways to open new markets for the hospital.

In order to develop programs that will be well received, the marketing director must do a great deal of research. He or she must evaluate the trends in hospital usage as well as the services that are utilized. The individual may also do research regarding the needs of the community. This may be done through surveys, interviews, and studies in the community and with physicians in the area. In some cases, market research companies are hired to conduct this research. After research is completed, the marketing director must review and evaluate the information and make necessary changes in the marketing strategies being used.

In some facilities, the director of marketing may be expected to develop brochures, posters, press releases, flyers, and radio, television, and print ads to publicize services in the hospital. In other job settings, he or she may work with the development, public relations, and advertising departments to create an advertising campaign. The marketing director may also be expected to determine the viability of hospital services and determine the selling points of the facility. He or she must then formulate advertising themes, slogans, and logos.

Other responsibilities of the hospital marketing director may include preparing department budgets, developing presentations for administration and/or the hospital board, and making sure the staff is aware of hospital services.

The director of hospital marketing works long hours. This is not usually a nine-to-five job. He or she may be expected to attend meetings and represent the hospital at functions for staff or the community. There are always extra projects that must be attended to, deadlines to meet, or emergencies that must be handled. However, for many in this position, watching a facility grow and flourish is very rewarding.

Salaries

Salaries for the director of hospital marketing can vary greatly depending on the size, location, and prestige of the hospital as well as the experience, education, and responsibilities of the individual.

Annual earnings can begin at $28,000 and go up to $150,000 or more. Generally, individuals with more experience or those working at larger facilities in metropolitan areas will have earnings at the higher end of the scale.

Employment Prospects

Employment prospects for directors of hospital marketing are fair. Individuals may find employment throughout the country in hospitals or other health care facilities. Individuals seeking this type of position might have to relocate to find a job.

Advancement Prospects

Advancement prospects are fair for individuals with experience. The director of hospital marketing can climb the career ladder by locating a similar position in a larger or more prestigious facility. This will result in increased responsibilities and earnings. Some individuals advance their careers by striking out on their own and doing consulting in the field of marketing.

Education and Training

Individuals seeking a position in the marketing department of a hospital or other health care facility are usually required to have at least a bachelor's degree. Majors should be in marketing, public relations, communications, journalism, advertising, business, or health care planning. An advanced degree is often helpful. Seminars and workshops in marketing, public relations, health care planning, and writing are also beneficial.

Experience/Skills/Personality Traits

The director of hospital marketing often has experience as an assistant in marketing, public relations, or planning prior to obtaining this position. Any marketing experience will be useful.

The director of hospital marketing needs excellent communication skills, both verbal and written. Supervisory and management skills are needed as well. The ability to define and analyze problems in a logical, clear, and concise manner and perform research is essential. Public speaking ability is often required.

Creativity is necessary to be successful in this field. A knowledge of graphics, typography, photography, and layout is also necessary for the development of advertising materials.

Unions/Associations

The director of hospital marketing may belong to the American Marketing Association (AMA), the Public Relations Society of America (PRSA), the National Association of Hospital Development (NAHD), and the American Society for Hospital Public Relations (ASHPR). These groups all provide career guidance and professional support.

Tips for Entry

1. Join trade associations. They are useful in making contacts, networking, and finding jobs. Their trade journals often have job listings. Associations also may know of internships.
2. Look for internships in hospitals or other health care facilities.
3. There are a number of employment agencies and search firms dealing specifically with marketing and other communications positions. Consider using one to help you locate a job.
4. There are also agencies dealing specifically in health care. Whichever type of agency you consider, make sure you check to see who will pay the fee when you get a job, you or the employer.
5. Jobs are often advertised in the classified section of the newspaper. Look under "Marketing," "Hospitals," "Director of Hospital Marketing," "Health Care," etc.

DIRECTOR OF HOSPITAL FUND-RAISING AND DEVELOPMENT

CAREER PROFILE

Duties: Directing, planning, and implementing fund-raising efforts for hospital

Alternate Title(s): Director of Development; Director of Fund-Raising; Fund-Raising Director

Salary Range: $28,000 to $100,000+

Employment Prospects: Fair

Advancement Prospects: Fair

Best Geographical Location(s) for Position: Positions may be located throughout the country

Prerequisites:

Education or Training—Bachelor's degree in marketing, advertising, communications, journalism, or liberal arts required; M.B.A. helpful in advancement

Experience—Publicity, public relations, and fund-raising experience useful

Special Skills and Personality Traits—Aggressiveness; organization; attention to detail; writing and communication skills; computer competency; interpersonal skills

CAREER LADDER

```
┌────────────────────────────────────────┐
│   Director of Fund-Raising and          │
│   Development in Larger or More         │
│   Prestigious Facility or Director of   │
│   Public Relations, Marketing,          │
│   or Planning                           │
└────────────────────────────────────────┘

┌────────────────────────────────────────┐
│       Director of Fund-Raising          │
│          and Development                 │
└────────────────────────────────────────┘

┌────────────────────────────────────────┐
│   Assistant Director of Fund-Raising    │
│          and Development                 │
└────────────────────────────────────────┘
```

Position Description

Running a nonprofit hospital is expensive. There are a number of ways institutions attempt to sustain themselves. They charge patients for services or are reimbursed by insurance companies or third party providers. Most nonprofit facilities augment these monies with fund-raising efforts. The director of hospital fund-raising and development is expected to develop programs and campaigns to raise money to cover both non-reimbursed costs of the hospital and capital expenditures of the institution.

Programs to raise money may run the gamut from huge fund-raising dinners and balls to auctions, dances, benefits, telethons, and entertainment shows. Other campaigns and programs may include annual giving programs, sustaining campaigns, and trusts. The director of fund-raising must also develop ways to obtain gifts from corporations and individuals.

The director of hospital fund-raising and development often creates other types of campaigns designed to bring in needed monies. These might include direct mail solicitation programs or personal solicitation. Other types of programs may bring in money through planned giving, estate planning, bequests, and trusts.

There is a great deal of writing involved in this type of job. The director is responsible for developing direct mail letters, written appeals for bequests, brochures, press releases, advertisement copy, flier copy, fund-raising letters, invitations, and speeches.

The director of fund-raising and development often works with other departments in the facility such as public relations and marketing. The director may also work with volunteers, who often help implement many of the fund-raising programs, or board members, who cultivate potential donors within the community.

The director is responsible for supervising and training the development department staff. Depending on the size and structure of the facility this may include an assistant director and one or more staffers.

The director of fund-raising and development may often be required to attend luncheons, dinners, meetings, parties, and other affairs on behalf of the institution. He or she may speak to groups regarding fund-raising functions or the hospital's programs. The individual may also lead tours personally to show donors the building and the people being helped by the facility and illustrate how programs are working.

Another way of raising monies is to seek out grants. These might be offered by the government or private foundations. The director may handle this task or may assign an assistant to both seek out sources of grants and write the grant proposals.

The director of fund-raising and development is responsible for keeping records of donor management and resource development. He or she is also expected to make sure that each donation is acknowledged with a letter of appreciation. Other responsibilities include preparing budgets for the department and developing reports tracking the progress and success of varied fund-raising projects.

Salaries

Annual earnings for the director of fund-raising in a hospital can vary from approximately $28,000 to $100,000 or more depending on a number of factors. These include the individual's experience, education, and responsibilities as well as the size, prestige, and geographic location of the facility.

Individuals might also supplement income by receiving fringe benefit packages.

Employment Prospects

Employment prospects are fair for those seeking the position of director of fund-raising and development. There are numerous positions throughout the country in hospitals, extended care facilities, nursing homes, and other health care organizations.

Advancement Prospects

There are a number of paths for career advancement for the director of fund-raising and development. The individual may locate a similar position in a larger or more prestigious facility. This will result in increased responsibilities and earnings. Another possibility is promotion to the position of director or public relations and marketing. A great deal of the advancement possibilities depends on the structure of the specific facility. The position is often combined with public relations, planning, or marketing.

Education and Training

Generally, the director of fund-raising must have a bachelor's degree. Good choices for majors include public relations, marketing, advertising, journalism, liberal arts, and communications. A master's degree will help in career advancement.

Experience/Skills/Personality Traits

The director of fund-raising and development should be fairly aggressive, organized, and detail oriented. Interpersonal skills and the ability to deal with people in a variety of areas are essential. Excellent writing and communication skills are necessary. Computer competency is also mandatory. Experience in public relations, marketing, or implementing special events and fund-raising is a plus.

Unions/Associations

The director of fund-raising and development may belong to trade associations which will provide useful contacts and offer seminars and courses to hone skills in this field. Associations include the National Society of Fund Raising Executives (NSFRE), Direct Marketing Association, Inc. (DMA), National Association of Hospital Development (NAHD), and the Council for the Advancement and Support of Education (CASE), to name a few.

Tips for Entry

1. Seminars on fund-raising, development, marketing, or grant writing are helpful in honing skills and making important contacts.
2. Get experience in this area by volunteering to be on the fund-raising committee of a nonprofit organization. This service offers useful experience and is useful for your resume.
3. Look in the classified sections of newspapers under "Fund-Raising," "Public Relations," "Health Care," "Director of Fund-Raising," or "Director of Development."
4. Look for an internship in this field. Internships are often offered through colleges or nonprofit organizations.

ASSISTANT DIRECTOR OF HOSPITAL FUND-RAISING AND DEVELOPMENT

CAREER PROFILE

Duties: Assisting director of department with fund-raising programs

Alternate Title(s): Assistant Director of Development; Assistant Director of Fund-Raising; Fund-Raising Assistant Director

Salary Range: $23,000 to $40,000+

Employment Prospects: Fair

Advancement Prospects: Fair

Best Geographical Location(s) for Position: Positions may be found throughout the country

Prerequisites:

Education or Training—Bachelor's degree in marketing, advertising, communications, journalism, or liberal arts required; MBA helpful in advancement

Experience—Publicity, public relations, and fund-raising experience useful

Special Skills and Personality Traits—Aggressiveness; organization; writing and communication skills; computer competency; interpersonal skills

CAREER LADDER

```
┌─────────────────────────────────────┐
│  Director of Fund-Raising and        │
│  Development or Director of Public    │
│  Relations or Marketing               │
└─────────────────────────────────────┘

┌─────────────────────────────────────┐
│  Assistant Director of Fund-Raising   │
│  and Development                      │
└─────────────────────────────────────┘

┌─────────────────────────────────────┐
│  Trainee Position, Entry Level, or    │
│  Fund-Raising Staff Member            │
└─────────────────────────────────────┘
```

Position Description

The main duty of the assistant director of fund-raising and development working in a nonprofit hospital or health care facility is to assist the director of the fund-raising and development program raise monies for the facility. This is not an easy job because so many organizations are vying for funds donated by the public.

Responsibilities in this type of job will vary from position to position. However, there are a number of duties which remain the same no matter the setting.

The assistant director of fund-raising and development is responsible for assisting the head of the department with developing programs designed to raise funds for the institution. The individual will help raise the money not only for large capital campaigns but also for some of the smaller programs of the organization. After the creation or development of these programs, he or she will assist in their implementation. Programs to raise money can differ. They run from special event shows to creating huge annual fund-raising dinners, auctions, dances, telethons, and entertainment events. Other types of programs the assistant might help develop and implement could include century clubs and other annual giving or sustaining campaigns.

The individual's duties might involve working with or supervising other staff members in the department. He or she might also work with the public relations or marketing departments. Depending on the structure of the organization, the assistant may act as the assistant to the public relations, publicity, or marketing director.

Much of the fund-raising accomplished in nonprofit organizations is made possible by volunteers who do a lot of the "leg work," or the running around. In his or her job, the assistant will be responsible for working with the volunteers who help implement many of the programs. In order to get things done the individual must have the ability to make people feel wanted, needed, and useful. He or she might also be responsible for helping to locate volunteers who will assist on the varied projects.

The assistant director of fund-raising and development may be asked by the director to cultivate potential donors. To do this, the individual might attend luncheons, dinners, meetings, parties, and other affairs on behalf of the organization. At times, the assistant will be asked to speak to groups of people about fund-raising functions. At other times, to illustrate how programs are working, he or she may lead tours in order to show visitors the building and the people being helped by the facility.

The assistant might seek out grants offered by the government and private foundations. Depending on the circumstances, he or she may just locate these grants or may be responsible for writing proposals to attempt to secure them. The assistant director could also be responsible for seeking annual gifts from individuals and corporations and locating sponsorship for various projects the organization has undertaken.

The assistant will be responsible for writing reports for the director of the department as well as to describe progress of varied fund-raising projects to the board of directors. At times, he or she might write press releases or perform other publicity functions to promote fund-raising and development programs which are being undertaken.

Other writing responsibilities may include writing direct mail pieces, advertisement copy, flier copy, fund-raising letters, invitations, speeches, brochures, etc.

Part of the job of the assistant director of fund-raising and development will be to help the director run special events to raise money. Responsibilities might encompass doing anything which needs to get done in order to run a successful and effective program. These might include finding locations to run dinner dances, planning menus, making phone calls to assure good attendance at an event, locating individuals and businesses to donate door prizes, conducting phone-a-thons, locating guest speakers and chairpeople, keeping records of monies, soliciting donations, and more.

The assistant director of fund-raising and development may be responsible for keeping records of donor management and resource development as well as sending acknowledgments and thank you letters to donors.

The assistant director of fund-raising and development is responsible to the director of the department. The individual will also usually work closely with a board of directors as well as the executive director of the organization.

Salaries

Salaries for assistant directors of fund-raising and development who work for nonprofit organizations will vary greatly depending on many factors including the experience of the individual and the organization's type, size, location, and prestige.

Salaries for this position can range from $23,000 to $40,000 annually. Individuals might also supplement income by receiving fringe benefit packages.

Employment Prospects

Employment prospects are fair for those seeking the position of assistant director of fund-raising and development. There are numerous possibilities for work such as hospitals, health care facilities, and health care organizations.

Individuals can usually find employment for this type of position in any location in the country. Larger cities will offer more job possibilities.

There are also a fair number of part-time positions available in this field.

Advancement Prospects

Advancement prospects for the assistant director of fund-raising working in a nonprofit organization are fair. The individual can advance by becoming the director of fund-raising and development or the director of public relations or marketing in the same organization. He or she might advance by moving to a position in a larger hospital or other nonprofit group outside the health care industry. This can result in an increase in earnings.

Education and Training

The educational requirement for this position is a college degree. Important majors might include marketing, public relations, English, journalism, liberal arts, and communications. A master's degree will help in career advancement.

Any seminar on fund-raising, development, marketing, or grant writing will be useful.

Experience/Skills/Personality Traits

The assistant director of fund-raising and development should be fairly aggressive and have good organizational skills. He or she should have excellent writing and communication skills. Computer competency is essential. The individual in this position must also have good interpersonal skills, and the ability to deal well with volunteers.

Any experience in public relations, publicity, running of special events, and fund-raising is a plus.

Unions/Associations

The assistant director of fund-raising and development may belong to trade associations which will provide useful contacts as well as offering seminars and courses to hone skills in this field. Associations could include National Society of Fund Raising Executives (NSFRE), Direct Mail Association,

Inc. (DMA), National Association of Hospital Development (NAHD), and the Council for the Advancement and Support of Education (CASE) to name a few.

Tips for Entry

1. Join one or two nonprofit organizations which have causes you are interested in. Volunteer to be on the fund-raising committee. This will provide useful experience as well as an important addition to your resume.

2. Look in the classified sections of Sunday newspapers under "Fund-Raising," "Public Relations," "Health Care," and "Grant Writing" headings. This type of position may also be located in the display advertising section of Sunday newspapers.

3. Join trade associations in fields you are interested in working in. Subscribe to their journals and attend their seminars and conventions.

4. Many colleges and nonprofit organizations offer internship and trainee programs in this field.

PLANNING DIRECTOR

Duties: Developing strategic goals; implementing contracts and programs; writing grants

Alternate Title(s): Director of Planning

Salary Range: $42,000 to $125,000+

Employment Prospects: Fair

Advancement Prospects: Fair

Best Geographical Location(s) for Position: Positions may be available throughout the country

Prerequisites:

Education or Training—Master's degree in hospital or business administration

Experience—Experience in health care, planning, development marketing, etc.

Special Skills and Personality Traits—Written and verbal communication skills; analytical mind; organization; attention to detail

```
┌─────────────────────────────────┐
│   Planning Director in Larger or │
│    More Prestigious Facility or  │
│   Health Services Administrator  │
└─────────────────────────────────┘

┌─────────────────────────────────┐
│         Planning Director        │
└─────────────────────────────────┘

┌─────────────────────────────────┐
│        Assistant Planning,       │
│     Fund-Raising/Development,     │
│       or Marketing Director      │
└─────────────────────────────────┘
```

Position Description

In order for hospitals and other health care facilities to plan for the future of health care as it relates to their institution, they must develop strategic goals and objectives. The planning director is in charge of this massive responsibility. Depending on the size and budget of the facility, the planning director may also be responsible for other departments including marketing, public relations, and/or fund-raising.

The planning director develops programs for growth by identifying and evaluating current trends in health care. The individual takes into account the national economy as well as the needs of the community. He or she must also be aware of competing health care institutions in the region. The planning director must be knowledgeable about and keep up with all governmental legislation affecting hospitals and health care.

A great deal of the work of the planning director involves developing and writing papers and letters to define goals. In many situations, the planning director is responsible for either writing or assisting in the writing of grant applications for the funding of projects to help meet goals. He or she also negotiates and implements contracts, acquisitions, and programs needed to support and implement the goals.

The planning director meets with other departments in the hospital on a regular basis to see if they have ideas that may be helpful to achieving the planning goals. He or she also meets with the administration and staff of the hospital to explain strategic goals.

The planning director often takes part in efforts to establish or move along legislation that may help the facility. He or she is sometimes asked to serve on committees or community boards as a representative of the hospital.

Depending on the situation, the planning director may work with other members of the hospital staff or with consultants to handle research necessary for planning activities.

The planning director usually works a 40-hour week. He or she may be asked to work at night or on weekends to finish projects, attend meetings, or handle other responsibilities.

Salaries

Annual earnings for planning directors can range from $42,000 to $125,000+ or more depending on a number of factors. These include the size, prestige, and geographic location of the facility as well as the education, experience, and responsibilities of the individual. Generally, those working in larger facilities in metropolitan areas will have earnings at the higher end of the scale.

Employment Prospects

Employment prospects are fair for planning directors of hospitals and health care facilities. However, it should be noted that many facilities combine the functions of public relations, marketing, fund-raising, and development with this position. Those seeking positions may have to relocate to find a job.

Advancement Prospects

The director of planning can advance his or her career by locating a position in a larger, more prestigious facility. Another path toward career advancement is obtaining more experience and/or education and locating a position as a health services administrator.

Education and Training

Educational requirements for the director of planning of a hospital or health care facility are a master's degree in either hospital or business administration. Individuals with the best education will be most marketable in this area.

Experience/Skills/Personality Traits

Planning directors for health care facilities must have experience working in planning, health care, marketing, development, or a related field. Individuals should have the ability to think in an analytic manner to determine problems and solutions. Excellent communication skills, both verbal and written, are necessary to the success of this type of position. The individual must also be extremely organized and detail-oriented.

Unions/Associations

Planning Directors may be members of the National Association of Hospital Development (NAHD).

Tips for Entry

1. There are a number of search firms and agencies specializing in careers in the health care industry.
2. Send your resume with a short cover letter to the personnel office of hospitals, nursing homes, extended care facilities, etc. Ask that your resume be kept on file if there are no current openings.
3. Jobs are often advertised in the classified section of the newspaper. Look under headings including "Planning Director," "Planning," "Health Care," or "Hospitals."
4. Many people move into this position from areas including marketing, development, or public relations.

DIRECTOR OF HOSPITAL PUBLIC RELATIONS

CAREER PROFILE

Duties: Handling patient and public information; developing internal and external communications; promoting positive public image for facility

Alternate Title(s): Public Relations Director

Salary Range: $28,000 to $100,000+

Employment Prospects: Fair

Advancement Prospects: Fair

Best Geographical Location(s) for Position: Positions available throughout the country

Prerequisites:

Education or Training—Bachelor's degree in public relations, communications, journalism, advertising, business, or English required

Experience—Writing experience necessary; graphic experience helpful

Special Skills and Personality Traits—Supervisory and administrative skills; writing and communication skills; creativity; knowledge of graphics, typography, photography, and layout; computer skills

CAREER LADDER

```
┌─────────────────────────────────────┐
│ Director of Hospital Public Relations │
│    in Larger or More Prestigious      │
│    Facility or Marketing Director     │
└─────────────────────────────────────┘

┌─────────────────────────────────────┐
│       Director of Hospital            │
│        Public Relations               │
└─────────────────────────────────────┘

┌─────────────────────────────────────┐
│        Assistant Director of          │
│      Hospital Public Relations        │
└─────────────────────────────────────┘
```

Position Description

The director of hospital public relations has a great deal of responsibility. He or she is in charge of handling patient and public information, creating a positive image for the health care facility, and enhancing its reputation as a health care center.

Specific responsibilities vary depending on the job and the size of the hospital. Larger facilities usually have a public relations department in which there are a number of employees. In these situations, the director of the department is responsible for supervising a staff. In small hospitals, the public relations director may work alone.

The director of public relations handles the press, promotion, and public relations activities of the entire facility. This includes internal and external communications for the hospital. In facilities that have a public relations staff, the PR director might assign assistants and writers to specific projects. In small facilities, the PR director is responsible for developing and writing all internal and external communications.

The public relations director may obtain publicity for the facility by promoting special activities and programs that it has planned. These may include health fairs, women's wellness days, men's wellness days, baby fairs, career fairs, etc.

The director of hospital PR writes press releases to notify the media about the facility's activities. Press releases are also issued to announce the hiring of new physicians or other staff members, new equipment, or the achievements of staff members. Once press releases are sent out, the PR director may follow up by calling editors to ask if they need more information, photographs, etc. The press, in turn, will hopefully write articles regarding the events and activities in their newspapers and magazines and talk about them during radio and television programs.

The PR director is expected to understand and carry out hospital policies and procedures regarding patients, the media, and confidentiality.

It is essential for the PR director to maintain a professional, honest relationship with the media. When he or she sends out press releases or calendar events, a friendly business relationship can mean the difference between getting the story in the paper or on the air and not obtaining any exposure.

The hospital public relations director and his or her staff is expected to produce news releases, feature stories, and special request articles for the news and other media sources. The director must be sure that all information is correct and may be asked to take pictures or arrange to have them taken to enhance an article.

The hospital PR director may be expected to prepare internal hospital communications such as staff newspapers, program and promotional materials, letters, and internal memos. He or she is often responsible for developing, writing, designing, and printing publications used for promotion, education, or fund-raising as well as annual reports. Other writing projects may include patient information kits or questionnaires for quality assessment.

The public relations director works with other departments in the facility including the medical staff, fund-raising and development, and marketing. In some situations, the PR director will also handle fund-raising, development, and marketing responsibilities.

In some facilities, the PR director is responsible for placing advertising for the facility or its programs in the various media. In others, he or she works with either the advertising director or an advertising agency.

The director of hospital PR must develop and implement special events designed to enhance the hospital's image, raise funds, or increase the utilization of hospital services and contributions.

The public relations director can represent the hospital at official functions or meetings of civic clubs and other groups, or serve as the management representative for the hospital's auxiliary.

Salaries

Salaries for directors of hospital public relations vary greatly depending on the individual's experience and the size and location of the health care facility.

Salaries can start at $28,000 and go up to $100,000 or more. Those with more experience or those working at larger facilities in metropolitan areas will have earnings at the higher end of the scale.

Employment Prospects

Employment prospects for directors of public relations are fair. Positions are available throughout the country in hospi-

tals or other health care facilities. Individuals seeking this type of position might have to relocate to find a job.

Advancement Prospects

The director of hospital public relations can advance his or her career in a number of ways. Some individuals may find similar positions in larger, more prestigious facilities resulting in increased responsibilities and earnings. Others may become the director of marketing of a health care facility.

Education and Training

Those seeking a position in the public relations department of a hospital or other heath care facility are usually required to have at least a bachelor's degree. Course work should emphasize public relations, communications, journalism, advertising, business, psychology, or English. Seminars and workshops in public relations and writing are also helpful.

Experience/Skills/Personality Traits

The director of hospital public relations must have supervisory and management skills. The individual should have the ability to define and analyze problems in a logical, clear, and concise manner. Both written and verbal communication skills are essential. Public speaking ability is required in most positions, as are good phone skills.

A knowledge of graphics, typography, photography, and layout is needed. Computer skills are required. The ability to tolerate a hospital/health care atmosphere is needed to be successful in this field.

Unions/Associations

The director of hospital PR may belong to the Public Relations Society of America (PRSA), or the National Association of Hospital Development (NAHD).

Tips for Entry

1. There are a number of employment agencies and search firms dealing specifically with public relations and other communications positions. Consider using one to help you locate a job.
2. Jobs are often advertised in the classified section of the newspaper. Look under headings such as "Public Relations," "Public Relations Director," "Hospital PR Director," and "Health Care."
3. Join trade associations. In addition to providing professional support, their trade journals often advertise job openings.
4. Network. Go to association events. You can never tell when you might run into a potential employer.

ASSISTANT DIRECTOR OF HOSPITAL PUBLIC RELATIONS

CAREER PROFILE

Duties: Assist director of department in fulfilling responsibilities for patient and public information; help with internal and external communications for facility; promote hospital's image

Alternate Title(s): PR Assistant; Assistant PR Director

Salary Range: $23,000 to $47,000+

Employment Prospects: Good

Advancement Prospects: Fair

Best Geographical Location(s) for Position: Positions available throughout the country

Prerequisites:

Education or Training—Bachelor's degree in public relations, communications, journalism, advertising, business, or English required

Experience—Writing experience necessary; graphic experience helpful

Special Skills and Personality Traits—Excellent writing and communication skills; knowledge of graphics, typography, photography, and layout; computer skills

CAREER LADDER

```
┌─────────────────────────────────────┐
│  Director of Hospital Public Relations │
└─────────────────────────────────────┘

┌─────────────────────────────────────┐
│      Assistant Director of Hospital   │
│           Public Relations            │
└─────────────────────────────────────┘

┌─────────────────────────────────────┐
│      Public Relations Trainee or      │
│          Entry-Level Position         │
└─────────────────────────────────────┘
```

Position Description

The assistant director of hospital public relations assists the director of the department in fulfilling the responsibilities for patient, staff, and public information. He or she is also responsible for helping with internal and external communications for the hospital or health care facility. The assistant director of hospital public relations promotes the hospital's image and enhances its reputation as a health care center.

The PR assistant must understand hospital policies and procedures and be able to carry them out. For example, the facility might have a policy that states that no patient's condition can be given out. The individual must follow this policy when media calls come in. He or she must be able to relate this information to reporters without making them feel that they are being snubbed.

It is vital for the PR assistant to maintain a professional, honest relationship with the media. When he or she sends out press releases or calendar events, a friendly business relationship can mean the difference between getting the story in the paper or on the air and not obtaining any exposure. It is also important for the individual to maintain accurate media lists so he or she knows who to call or send information to.

The assistant director of public relations is often asked by the PR director to produce news releases, feature stories, and special request articles for the news and other media sources. He or she must have the ability to write in a clear, concise, and interesting manner. The assistant may obtain material for these releases by doing research or interviewing hospital staff, patients, volunteers, or other appropriate people in order to develop the story. At times, he or she may be required to take photographs of events or people in order to enhance a news story. At other times, he or she may arrange to have a photographer on hand to take pictures.

The assistant director of public relations may assist in the preparation of internal hospital communications such as staff newspapers, program and promotional materials, letters, internal memos, etc. He or she may be asked to design and/or write the copy for brochures, graphic materials, and special reports. The assistant may also develop patient information kits or questionnaires for quality assessment. The public relations assistant must have the ability to tabulate, review, and report responses.

Other writing responsibilities the assistant PR director may handle include preparing annual reports. He or she may also assist in the development, preparation, and placing of advertising.

Hospitals often hold special events to raise money, to increase the utilization of hospital services, and to enhance the image of the hospital. The assistant director of PR may be responsible for helping to develop and execute these types of events.

Depending on the size of the public relations department, the assistant PR director may also assist with hospital fund-raising, development, and marketing programs. The individual might be asked to serve as the management representative for the hospital's auxiliary, or may assist with any promotion of the hospital such as hospital tours and other in-hospital or community events.

The assistant director of public relations in a hospital or other health care facility generally works regular hours. He or she may work overtime to attend hospital meetings or special events or to meet a project deadline.

Salaries

Salaries for assistant directors of hospital public relations vary greatly depending on the individual's experience and the size and location of the health care facility.

Salaries for beginners range from $23,000 to $27,000. Those with more experience, or those working at larger facilities in metropolitan areas can expect earnings of $25,000 to $47,000 or more.

Employment Prospects

Employment prospects for those interested in becoming an assistant director of public relations in a health care facility are good. There are countless hospitals, mental health facilities, clinics, senior citizen homes, etc. located throughout the country. Each of these facilities usually has a public relations department. Individuals seeking this type of position might have to relocate, however, to find a job in their specific area of expertise.

Advancement Prospects

Advancement prospects are fair for assistant directors of public relations. Individuals can move up to the position of director of public relations, director of public information, or director of fund-raising. An assistant director of hospital public relations might obtain a position in a larger hospital where salaries would be higher.

Education and Training

Individuals seeking a position in the public relation department of a hospital or other heath care facility are usually required to have at least a bachelor's degree. Course work should emphasize public relations, communications, journalism, advertising, business, psychology, or English.

Experience/Skills/Personality Traits

People working in hospital and health care public relations should have the ability to define a problem logically, clearly, and concisely and to analyze it from all points of view.

Assistant directors of hospital/health care public relations should also have a knowledge of graphics, typography, photography, and layout. The ability to type and use word processors and computer equipment is essential.

A good writing style is necessary. Public speaking ability is required in most positions, as is the ability to communicate on the telephone in a polite, friendly, and effective manner.

Unions/Associations

Assistant directors of hospital public relations may belong to the Public Relations Society of America (PRSA) or the National Association of Hospital Development (NAHD).

Tips for Entry

1. Look for an internship in a hospital public relations, marketing, or fund-raising department. This will give you valuable experience.

2. Join a hospital or health care facility auxiliary and volunteer to do their publicity. This will help you become familiar with hospital policies and the duties of a PR assistant.

3. There are employment agencies dealing specifically with public relations positions. You might want to consider using one to help you find a job.

4. Public Relations positions in health care are advertised in the classified section of newspapers under headings such as "Health Care," "Public Relations," or "Marketing."

5. Join trade associations and get their monthly periodicals. Positions are often advertised in trade journals.

CLINICAL LABORATORY
SERVICES

MEDICAL LABORATORY TECHNICIAN

CAREER PROFILE

Duties: Collecting, receiving, separating, and storing specimens; preparing and analyzing specimens

Alternate Title(s): Medical Lab Technician; Lab Technician

Salary Range: $23,000 to $42,000+

Employment Prospects: Excellent

Advancement Prospects: Good

Best Geographical Location(s) for Position: Positions may be located throughout the country

Prerequisites:

Education or Training—Approved two-year certificate or associate degree program

Experience—Experience working in lab helpful, but not required

Special Skills and Personality Traits—Analytical skills; manual dexterity; ability to work under pressure; attention to detail; interpersonal skills; communication skills

CAREER LADDER

```
┌─────────────────────────────────┐
│     Medical Technologist        │
└─────────────────────────────────┘

┌─────────────────────────────────┐
│  Medical Laboratory Technician  │
└─────────────────────────────────┘

┌─────────────────────────────────┐
│            Student              │
└─────────────────────────────────┘
```

Position Description

Diseases are detected and diagnosed through medical testing. Medical laboratory technicians are responsible for collecting, receiving, separating, and storing specimens from medical tests. Individuals can work in general medical lab technology or specialize in assorted fields including clinical chemistry (the study of chemical substances in the blood); cytotechnology (the study of cells and their abnormalities); hematology (the study of blood); histology (the study of tissue structure); microbiology (the study of disease-producing organisms in the body); and virology (the study of viruses).

Medical laboratory technicians are responsible for obtaining specimens including blood, urine, or sputum from patients. Once specimens are collected, technicians perform tests on them using lab procedures. These tests are generally used to detect the presence of chemical substances or other problems in the blood or the presence of bacteria, fungi, or other disease-producing organisms in the body.

Medical lab technicians are responsible for preparing all specimens and setting up and operating the lab equipment necessary to perform the tests. Equipment may include microscopes, slides, and automatic analyzers.

Medical lab technicians are responsible for observing each specimen and noting its reaction. They then record the results on the patient's chart. Abnormal results must be reported immediately to a supervisor.

Medical lab technicians are responsible for maintaining all instruments and equipment. If anything is not working correctly, they are expected to report the problem to the supervisor. They are additionally responsible for preparing, storing, and labeling reagents and other supplies. It is essential that technicians adhere to all established safety measures.

Medical lab technicians work various shifts including daytime, evenings, nights, or weekends.

Salaries

Medical lab technicians may have annual earnings ranging from $23,000 to $42,000 or more. Variables include the experience, education, and responsibilities of the individual.

Other factors affecting earnings include the specific job and its geographic location.

Employment Prospects

Employment prospects are excellent for medical lab technicians. Individuals may find openings throughout the country in a variety of settings. These include hospitals, medical centers, independent labs, clinics, health maintenance organizations (HMOs), commercial labs, surgi-centers, urgi-centers, public health agencies, and private physicians' offices.

Advancement Prospects

Medical lab technicians can advance their careers by obtaining more education and experience. Some go on to earn a four-year degree and become medical technologists. Others find similar positions in facilities that afford them more responsibility and increased earnings.

Education and Training

Medical lab technicians generally must either have an associate's degree in medical technology or go through an approved certificate program in a hospital, vocational-technical school, or in the armed forces.

It is imperative that the program be recognized by the American Medical Associations Committee on Allied Health Education and Accreditation (CAHEA) or the Accrediting Bureau of Health Education Schools (ABHES).

Certain states require all lab personnel to be licensed or registered. Voluntary certification is also available.

Experience/Skills/Personality Traits

Medical Laboratory Technicians should have analytical judgment and problem solving skills. The ability to work under pressure is needed. Individuals should be detail-oriented and organized. Manual dexterity is necessary. Communication and computer skills are desirable.

Interpersonal skills and the ability to make people feel comfortable are helpful in this area.

Unions/Associations

Medical lab technicians may be members of the American Society for Clinical Laboratory Science (ASCLS). This organization provides guidance and support.

Tips for Entry

1. Positions may be advertised in the classified section of newspapers under headings such as "Medical Lab Technician," "Lab Technician," "Labs," "Health Care," or "Hospitals."
2. Send your resume and a cover letter to the personnel directors at hospitals, clinics, and labs. Remember to ask that your resume be kept on file if there are no current openings.
3. Jobs are often available in veteran's hospitals and medical centers. Information about employment is available from the Department of Veterans Affairs, Title 38 Employment Division (054D), 810 Vermont Avenue NW, Washington, DC 20420.
4. Other federal jobs may be available through the National Institutes of Health.

CLINICAL LABORATORY TECHNOLOGIST

CAREER PROFILE

Duties: Performing lab tests; preparing and making cultures; typing blood samples; examining blood and tissue samples

Alternate Title(s): Medical Technologist; Clinical Lab Technologist

Salary Range: $24,000 to $48,000+

Employment Prospects: Good

Advancement Prospects: Good

Best Geographical Location(s) for Position: Positions may be located throughout the country

Prerequisites:

Education or Training—Bachelor's degree with major in medical technology or life sciences

Experience—Experience working in lab helpful, but not required

Special Skills and Personality Traits—Analytical and problem solving skills; manual dexterity; ability to work under pressure; attention to detail; computer skills

CAREER LADDER

```
┌─────────────────────────────────────────┐
│  Supervisory or Administrative Position   │
└─────────────────────────────────────────┘

┌─────────────────────────────────────────┐
│     Clinical Laboratory Technologist      │
└─────────────────────────────────────────┘

┌─────────────────────────────────────────┐
│             College Student               │
└─────────────────────────────────────────┘
```

Position Description

Many diseases can be detected and diagnosed through chemical, biological, hematological, microscopic, immunologic, and bacteriological lab tests. Clinical laboratory technologists are the individuals responsible for performing many of these complex tests. They may have a number of different responsibilities depending on their experience and training.

Testing is utilized for a number of reasons. Some tests can determine if a patient has a certain disease or illness. Other tests may indicate the degree of an infection. The testing process is done through the examination and analysis of body fluids, tissues, and cells.

Clinical laboratory technologists draw blood from patients and may collect samples of body tissues or other subtances. In some situations, clinical laboratory technologists must make cultures of body fluids or tissue samples. These are then examined under a microscope to see if there are bacteria, fungi, parasites, or other types of microorganisms present.

Clinical laboratory technologists may also be responsible for examining samples to determine the chemical content or reaction to various test substances. Sometimes clinical laboratory technologists check blood to determine a patient's cholesterol or blood glucose levels. Other duties include typing and cross-matching blood samples for transfusions.

Technologists may work various hours including evenings, nights, and weekends. Individuals may also be on call for emergencies.

Salaries

Clinical laboratory technologists may have annual earnings ranging from $24,000 to $48,000 or more depending on a number of variables, including the experience, education, and responsibilities of the individual. Other factors affecting earnings include the specific job and geographic location.

Clinical laboratory technologists just beginning their careers earn between $24,000 and $34,000. Those with more experience working in metropolitan areas will earn salaries at the higher end of the scale.

Employment Prospects

Employment prospects are good for clinical laboratory technologists. Individuals with the most training will be more marketable. Clinical laboratory technologists may find positions throughout the country in a variety of settings. These include hospitals, medical centers, independent labs, clinics, health maintenance organizations (HMOs), commercial labs, public health agencies, and private physicians' offices.

Advancement Prospects

Advancement prospects are good for clinical laboratory technologists who obtain experience and continue their education. Individuals may locate similar jobs in larger facilities resulting in increased earnings and responsibilities. Others may be promoted to supervisory or administrative positions including chief medical technologist or lab manager.

Education and Training

While some facilities accept applicants who have a combination of on-the-job and specialized training, most require that clinical laboratory technologists have at least a bachelor's degree with a major in medical technology or in life sciences. These programs are offered in universities and hospitals throughout the country. Course work includes chemistry, biological sciences, microbiology, math, and clinical lab skills. Make sure that the college, university, or hospital program you are attending is accredited by the Committee on Allied Health Education and Accreditation in cooperation with the National Accrediting Agency for Clinical Laboratory Sciences.

Some states require clinical laboratory technologists to be licensed. Certain positions require certification. This may be obtained through a number of organizations including the Board of Registry of the American Society of Clinical Pathologists in conjunction with the American Association of Blood Banks, the International Society for Clinical Laboratory Technology, the American Medical Technologists, or the National Certification Agency for Medical Laboratory Personnel.

Experience/Skills/Personality Traits

Clinical laboratory technologists need to have good analytical and problem solving skills. Individuals should be detail-oriented and have the ability to work under pressure. Manual dexterity is necessary. Communication and computer skills are needed.

Clinical laboratory technologists should also have good interpersonal skills with the ability to make people feel comfortable.

Unions/Associations

There are a number of associations that clinical laboratory technologists can join, including the American Society of Clinical Pathologists (ASCP), the American Medical Technologists (AMT), and the American Association for Clinical Chemistry (AACC).

Tips for Entry

1. Jobs are often available in veterans' hospitals and medical centers. Information about employment is available from the Department of Veterans Affairs, Title 38 Employment Division (054D), 810 Vermont Avenue NW, Washington, DC 20420.
2. Other federal jobs may be available through the National Institute of Health.
3. Positions may be advertised in the classified section of newspapers under headings such as "Clinical Laboratory Technologist," "Labs," "Lab Technologist," "Health Care," and "Hospitals."
4. Send your resume and a cover letter to the personnel directors at hospitals, clinics, and labs. Remember to ask that your resume be kept on file if there are no current openings.

MEDICAL TECHNOLOGIST

CAREER PROFILE

Duties: Performing tests; obtaining specimens; analyzing cell and tissue specimens, blood, etc.; recording test results

Alternate Title(s): Medical Lab Technologist

Salary Range: $26,000 to $49,000+

Employment Prospects: Good

Advancement Prospects: Good

Best Geographical Location(s) for Position: Positions may be located throughout the country

Prerequisites:

Education or Training—Bachelor's degree in medical technology

Experience—Experience working in lab helpful, but not required

Special Skills and Personality Traits—Analytical skills; manual dexterity; ability to work under pressure; attention to detail; organization; communication skills

CAREER LADDER

```
┌─────────────────────────────┐
│   Chief Medical Technologist │
│      or Lab Manager          │
└─────────────────────────────┘

┌─────────────────────────────┐
│                             │
│   Medical Technologist      │
│                             │
└─────────────────────────────┘

┌─────────────────────────────┐
│     Student or Medical      │
│   Laboratory Technician     │
└─────────────────────────────┘
```

Position Description

Medical technologists perform an array of tests and procedures used to obtain data to treat and diagnose diseases in patients. They may perform chemical, bacteriologic, or microscopic tests on various cell and tissue specimens in order to locate abnormalities or identify disease-causing agents.

Individuals can specialize in a number of areas. These include blood bank technology; clinical chemistry (the study of chemical substances in the blood); cytotechnology (the study of cells and their abnormalities); hematology (the study of blood); histology (the study of tissue structure); microbiology (the study of disease-producing organisims in the body); and virology (the study of viruses). Specific duties will depend on the specialization.

Medical technologists are responsible for assembling any supplies and equipment that will be needed for tests. They must also make sure that each piece of equipment is functioning correctly. It is essential that the work area and equipment be kept spotless in order for tests to be accurate.

Medical technologists may draw blood or collect swabs from the nose, ear, throat, rectum, etc. of patients. In some instances, medical technologists obtain specimens of feces, sputum, pus, urine, or other fluids. These may be obtained directly from patients, from physicians or other health care workers diagnosing cases, or from autopsies.

Medical technologists then identify and label all specimens that have been obtained.

Medical technologists are responsible for cultivating and identifying any microorganisms located in the specimens. They may make smears on slides, stain specimens for examination, and observe cultures.

Medical technologists working in blood banks are responsible for collecting blood from donors. Technologists in this area may also test and store blood. They are responsible for maintaining records of blood donors and for typing and cross matching blood for transfusions.

Medical technologists working in other areas may be responsible for performing chemical tests on body fluids. Information collected from these tests may, for example, reveal sugar, blood, or drugs in the urine. Technologists may also perform serological tests on blood. These may detect syphilis, mononucleosis, and other diseases. Medical technologists may also perform immunological tests to determine allergies.

Medical technologists accurately record test results and findings and may be responsible for mailing or calling in reports to physicians or patients. They must report abnormalities immediately.

In some cases, specimens can be discarded after a test has been completed. These must be discarded according to safety regulations. Other specimens may be stored for future use.

Medical technologists working in smaller labs may perform a variety of tests. Individuals working in larger or specialty labs will handle specialized tests.

Medical technologists may work various shifts including days, evenings, nights, and weekends.

Salaries

Medical technologists may have annual earnings ranging from $26,000 to $49,000 or more. Variables include the experience, education, and responsibilities of the individual. Other factors affecting earnings include the specific job and geographic location.

Employment Prospects

Employment prospects are good for medical technologists. Individuals may find openings throughout the country in a variety of settings. These include hospitals, medical centers, independent labs, clinics, health maintenance organizations (HMOs), commercial labs, larger surgi-centers, urgi-centers, public health agencies, and private physicians' offices.

Advancement Prospects

Medical technologists can advance their careers by obtaining more education and experience. Some medical technologists become chief medical technologists or lab managers. Others find similar positions in other institutions which afford them more responsibility and increased earnings.

Education and Training

Generally, medical technologists must have a bachelor's degree with a major in medical technology or one of the other life sciences. Individuals might also go through a university or hospital medical technology program. There are some facilities that accept applicants who have a combination of on-the-job and specialized training.

Medical technology programs include courses in chemistry, biological sciences, microbiology, math, and clinical lab skills and practices.

Some states require all lab personnel to be licensed or registered. Voluntary certification is also available

Experience/Skills/Personality Traits

Medical technologists should have an investigative nature, an analytical mind, and problem solving skills. The ability to work under pressure is needed.

Computer skills are necessary. Individuals need to be detail oriented and organized. Manual dexterity is necessary. Communication skills are essential.

Unions/Associations

Medical Technologists may be members of the American Medical Technologists (AMT).

Tips for Entry

1. Graduate degrees are often needed for advancement. Consider continuing your education.
2. Get certified. It will give you the edge over other applicants.
3. Positions may be advertised in the classified section of newspapers under heading classifications including "Medical Technologist," "Technologist," "Labs," "Lab Technologist," "Health Care," and "Hospitals."
4. Send your resume and a cover letter to the personnel directors at hospitals, clinics, and labs. Remember to ask that your resume be kept on file if there are no current openings.
5. Jobs are often available in veterans' hospitals are medical centers. Information about employment is available from the Department of Veterans Affairs, Title 38 Employment Division (054D), 810 Vermont Avenue NW, Washington, DC 20420.
6. Part-time positions are often offered in hospitals and labs.

PHLEBOTOMIST

CAREER PROFILE

Duties: Collecting specimens; drawing blood; labeling specimens; delivering specimens to lab

Alternate Title(s): Lab Technician

Salary Range: $20,000 to $30,000+

Employment Prospects: Good

Advancement Prospects: Good

Best Geographical Location(s) for Position: Positions may be located throughout the country

Prerequisites:

Education or Training—Completion of a specific phlebotomy program, most of which are fairly short

Experience—No experience necessary

Special Skills and Personality Traits—Manual dexterity; ability to work under pressure; computer skills; attention to detail; interpersonal skills; communication skills

CAREER LADDER

```
┌─────────────────────────────────────────┐
│  Medical Technician or Technologist       │
└─────────────────────────────────────────┘

┌─────────────────────────────────────────┐
│             Phlebotomist                  │
└─────────────────────────────────────────┘

┌─────────────────────────────────────────┐
│        Lab Assistant or Student           │
└─────────────────────────────────────────┘
```

Position Description

A phlebotomist is a member of the pathology-laboratory staff. He or she is responsible for collecting specimens from patients at the request of physicians.

After the phlebotomist is notified that a specimen is needed from a patient, he or she prepares the patient for the procedure. This may include cleaning the area with an antiseptic. The individual will then draw blood from the patient, and label each specimen.

The phlebotomist may perform a variety of procedures to draw blood including venipunctures, heel sticks, and finger sticks. While doing these procedures, the individual must ensure that each test is done properly. He or she is responsible for labeling specimens, entering pertinent information into a computer, and distributing specimens to the proper lab area in a timely fashion.

The phlebotomist may be asked to perform duties in other locations including clinics and health fairs. In these cases, he or she may also be expected to transport specimens to the lab as soon as possible.

Patients are often frightened when having tests and other procedures performed. The phlebotomist must explain the procedure to the patient in order to make him or her as comfortable as possible.

The phlebotomist is expected to maintain strict confidentiality of all patient information. This is essential in all areas of health care. Other functions of the phlebotomist may include cleaning and stocking the phlebotomy tray and other work areas.

Phlebotomists may work various hours including evenings, nights, and weekends. Individuals may also be on call for emergencies.

Salaries

Phlebotomists may have annual earnings ranging from $20,000 to $30,000 or more. Variables include the experience, education, and responsibilities of the individual. Other factors affecting earnings include the specific job and geographic location.

Employment Prospects

Employment prospects are good for phlebotomists. Individuals may find positions throughout the country in a variety of settings. These include hospitals, medical centers, independent labs, clinics, health maintenance organizations (HMOs), commercial labs, public health agencies, and private physician's offices.

Advancement Prospects

Phlebotomists can obtain experience and education in order to advance. Individuals may locate similar jobs in larger facilities resulting in increased responsibilities and earnings. Others may climb the career ladder by becoming lab technicians or technologists, depending on the amount of additional education they obtain.

Education and Training

Generally, phlebotomists must have a minimum of a high school degree or its equivalent. Individuals must then complete a program in phlebotomy. These may be taught in community colleges, junior colleges, vocational-technical schools, or in hospitals. Sometimes phlebotomists are trained on the job. Training can be completed in a short time.

Some states may require lab workers to be licensed, registered, or certified.

Experience/Skills/Personality Traits

Phlebotomists should have excellent interpersonal skills with the ability to make others feel comfortable. They should be detail oriented and have the ability to work well under pressure. Manual dexterity is necessary.

Unions/Associations

Phlebotomists may be members of the local chapter of a health care union.

Tips for Entry

1. Job openings are often advertised in the classified section of newspapers under headings such as "Phlebotomist," "Labs," "Lab Technician," "Hospitals," and "Health Care."
2. Send your resume and a cover letter to personnel directors at hospitals, clinics, and labs. Remember to ask that your resume be kept on file if there are no current openings.
3. Many schools, hospitals, and colleges have career fairs. Find out when one is scheduled and speak to people in the field to see if this is a good career choice for you.

THERAPY

PHYSICAL THERAPIST

CAREER PROFILE

Duties: Assessing physical therapy needs; performing initial evaluations for patients; performing physical therapy procedures on patients

Alternate Title(s): P.T.

Salary Range: $28,000 to $65,000+

Employment Prospects: Excellent

Advancement Prospects: Good

Best Geographical Location(s) for Position: Positions may be located throughout the country

Prerequisites:

    Education or Training—Bachelor's degree in physical therapy or completion of a certificate program; some positions may require master's degree

    Experience—Experience in physical therapy setting helpful for most positions

    Special Skills and Personality Traits—Patience; compassion; empathy; enthusiasm; personableness; articulateness; physical and mechanical ability to use equipment relative to job

CAREER LADDER

```
┌─────────────────────────────────────┐
│  Physical Therapist at Larger or     │
│  More Prestigious Facility or        │
│  Physical Therapist Supervisor       │
└─────────────────────────────────────┘

┌─────────────────────────────────────┐
│        Physical Therapist            │
└─────────────────────────────────────┘

┌─────────────────────────────────────┐
│   College Student or Physical        │
│        Therapy Assistant             │
└─────────────────────────────────────┘
```

Position Description

Physical therapists develop therapies and exercise modalities to help patients ease pain, recover from injuries or illness, or regain use of body parts. Many people require physical therapy as a result of accidents or injuries. Others are born with physical disabilities or become disabled through an illness such as a stroke, heart attack, polio, or other diseases.

Physical therapy is very important to athletes who have been injured whether or not they are professionals. Almost any type of athlete from an amateur runner to a professional football player may become a physical therapy patient. Physical therapy may also be used by handicapped individuals who would like to excel or just participate in some type of physical activity.

The physical therapist works with a variety of rehabilitative personnel including physiatrists and physical therapy assistants. Specific duties depend on the situation and the specific job.

One of the first things a physical therapist does with a new patient is to evaluate the individual and develop a rehabilitation plan. The therapist may put the patient through a battery of tests to determine the extent of his or her injuries. It is often necessary for the physical therapist to be knowledgeable about all aspects of a patient's medical care.

The therapist must know which type of procedures and treatments will help ease a patient's pain. He or she will be required to set realistic rehabilitation goals for all patients.

The physical therapist may be responsible for instructing and supervising physical therapy assistants in all phases of their work. He or she will be required to instruct the assistant on how to run tests and how to keep proper documentation on each patient.

The physical therapist reevaluates patients after a series of treatments have been completed. After the reevaluation, the patient's therapy must be updated accordingly.

Records and documentation are extremely important in this field. In some situations, the physical therapist may be responsible for all paperwork and documentation of patient's progress, therapy, reactions, etc. In other situations, the individual will pass this responsibility on to an assistant.

Depending on the situation, the physical therapist may be required to participate in patient care conferences with individuals in the nursing or social services department or with the families of patients. The therapist is also responsible for instructing family members, coaches, trainers, etc. in the patient's physical therapy program.

Depending on the requirements of the job, the physical therapist may be required to perform additional duties including ordering equipment, scheduling daily work loads, assessing departmental needs, and assisting in the maintenance of the physical environment of the therapy department.

The physical therapist may be responsible to any number of people depending on the institution in which he or she works. The individual may report directly to the head physical therapist, physical therapist supervisor, physiatrist, or director of rehabilitative services.

He or she will usually work normal or fairly normal hours. While most hospitals and health care facilities usually schedule physical therapy sessions during the day, some facilities keep physical therapists on staff during all hours. During an emergency, physical therapists may be called in and asked to work beyond normal working hours.

Salaries

Salaries for physical therapists vary greatly depending on a number of variables, including the geographical location of the facility where the individual works as well as its size and prestige. Earnings also depend on the individual's education, experience, and responsibilities. The physical therapist's annual earnings can range from $28,000 to $65,000 plus. In addition, compensation is also usually augmented by liberal fringe benefit packages.

Employment Prospects

Employment prospects for physical therapists are excellent. Positions may be located throughout the country in independent physical therapy centers, hospitals, rehabilitation centers, nursing homes, and sports medicine clinics.

Advancement Prospects

Advancement prospects are good for physical therapist. Individuals can advance their careers by becoming supervisors or by locating positions in larger, more prestigious facilities.

Education and Training

A physical therapist is required to be a graduate of an approved school of physical therapy. The individual may be required to hold a bachelor of science degree, a certificate, or a master's degree.

Some states also require that physical therapists be licensed by the state.

Experience/Skills/Personality Traits

Physical therapists should genuinely like to help others. Compassion and empathy are traits that will help individuals excel in this career.

Therapists should be articulate because they must explain procedures and therapies to patients and their families, coaches, trainers, etc. They should be able to give directions to others in a way that is easily understood. Physical therapists must often have the ability to supervise assistants and aides.

Physical therapists should be positive, personable, and enthusiastic so that they can motivate patients to help themselves.

Therapists must also have both the physical and the mechanical ability to use equipment relevant to the job, such as wheelchairs, stretchers, lifts, geriatric chairs, whirlpools, and traction equipment.

Unions/Associations

Physical therapists working in health care facilities may belong to a variety of health care unions which represent workers in hospital or health care facilities. They may also belong to trade associations including the American Physical Therapy Association (APTA). This organization provides educational guidance and support for those working in the physical therapy field.

Tips for Entry

1. Positions are often advertised in the classified section of newspapers. Look under headings such as "Physical Therapy," "Health Care," "Hospitals," "Physical Therapist," "Sports Medicine," or "Therapist."
2. Send your resume to hospitals or health care facilities with a short cover letter. Ask that your resume be kept on file if a position is not currently available.
3. Call the personnel director of hospitals and health care facilities in the areas you want to work and try to set up an appointment for an interview.
4. There are employment agencies located throughout the country specializing in jobs in the health care industry. Check to see who pays the fee (you or the employer) before getting involved.
5. If you are still in school or taking part in an accredited training program, contact the job placement office for job possibilities.
6. Check out the American Physical Therapy Society website for career help and possible openings. The web address is in Appendix II.

PHYSICAL THERAPY ASSISTANT

CAREER PROFILE

Duties: Assisting physical therapist in treating patients; administering physical therapy treatments such as hydrotherapy, massage, heat treatments, etc.; doing paperwork

Alternate Title(s): Assistant Physical Therapist; Physical Therapist Assistant; P.T.A.

Salary Range: $19,000 to $34,000+

Employment Prospects: Excellent

Advancement Prospects: Excellent

Best Geographical Location(s) for Position: Positions may be located throughout the country

Prerequisites:

    Education or Training—Two-year associate's degree from college offering physical therapy or physical therapy assistant program

    Experience—No experience required; experience in health care facility may be preferred

    Special Skills and Personality Traits—Patience; compassion; empathy; enthusiasm; articulateness; strength; ability to follow instructions

CAREER LADDER

```
┌─────────────────────────────┐
│     Physical Therapist      │
└─────────────────────────────┘

┌─────────────────────────────┐
│ Physical Therapy Assistant  │
└─────────────────────────────┘

┌─────────────────────────────┐
│      College Student        │
└─────────────────────────────┘
```

Position Description

Physical therapy assistants are paraprofessionals who are responsible for providing direct patient care under immediate direction and supervision. They may also be required to assist physical therapists, physiatrists, and/or other rehabilitation specialists in certain procedures and functions not related to direct patient care.

Physical therapy assistants provide patients with various therapies and exercise modalities developed by the physical therapist. These therapies help the patient ease pain, recover from an injury or illness, or regain use of a body part.

Duties will depend on the situation and the specific job. Physical therapy assistants may work with physical therapists or physiatrists in evaluating new patients and implementing care or rehabilitation plans. They may be instructed about which particular tests to perform on the patient. It is important in physical therapy treatment to know the extent of injuries. Assistants may be asked to measure the amount of weight an athlete can put on his or her leg or how far a joint can bend.

Assistants may help patients walk, climb stairs or inclines, or perform other exercises to regain mobility. They must make sure to carefully follow instructions when performing therapy or a patient may have a treatment that is too strenuous or not strenuous enough to help the individual.

In many cases, physical therapy assistants help a patient not only ease the pain, but also learn how to deal with pain. They may for example assist the patient by providing heat therapy, hydrotherapy, such as whirlpool baths or wet packs, or massages.

In some cases, assistants help physical therapists reevaluate patients after a series of treatments have been completed. It is often the responsibility of the physical therapy assistants to do a great deal of the documentation, creating records of a patient's problems and capabilities and updating the records to reflect current capabilities and progress.

Physical therapy assistants are responsible directly to the head physical therapist, psychiatrist, or rehabilitation specialist, depending on the institution in which they are working. They usually work normal or fairly normal hours. While most hospitals and health care facilities usually schedule physical therapy sessions during the day, some facilities keep both physical therapist and assistants on staff during all hours.

Salaries

Salaries for physical therapy assistants vary greatly depending on a number of variables, including the geographical location of the facility where the individual works as well as its size and prestige. Earnings will also depend on the individual's education, experience, and responsibilities. The physical therapy assistant's annual earnings can range from $19,000 to $34,000 or more. In addition, compensation is also usually augmented by liberal fringe benefit packages.

Employment Prospects

Employment prospects are excellent for physical therapy assistants as there is currently a nationwide shortage of qualified individuals. There are many opportunities in hospitals, rehabilitation centers, nursing homes, and other health care facilities. Physical therapy assistants may also work in sports medicine clinics which are springing up throughout the country or in independent physical therapy centers. One of the important things about this position is that jobs may be located in almost any geographical location.

While some institutions only have one or two people in this position, many hire a number of physical therapy assistants to be on staff. There are also opportunities to work on a part-time basis.

Advancement Prospects

Advancement prospects are excellent for physical therapy assistants. Individuals can advance their career by becoming full-fledged physical therapists. In order to climb the career ladder, however, the physical therapy assistant must take additional training. This usually includes at least another two years of schooling in an institution that has an accredited program in physical therapy.

Education and Training

Physical therapy assistants are usually required to hold an associate's degree from a two-year college that offers a physical therapy or physical therapy assistants program.

Experience/Skills/Personality Traits

The physical therapy assistant should have a great deal of patience. This is important because the individual will often be working with patients who can't do very much. A small step by a patient may be a major accomplishment and it may take a long time to achieve.

The assistant should be a giving person and genuinely like to help others. Compassion and empathy are traits that will help the individual excel in his or her career.

The physical therapy assistant should be articulate. He or she should be able to follow directions and to explain them to others in a way they understand. The assistant should additionally be positive, personable, and enthusiastic so that he or she can motivate patients to help themselves. Many of the patients who work with the assistant will be under severe emotional and physical strain. A smiling face at a therapy session can sometimes make the difference between success and failure. It is imperative that the individual has the physical and emotional strength to work with injured and disabled patients.

Unions/Associations

Some physical therapy assistants belong to a variety of health care unions that represent workers in hospitals or health care facilities. They may also belong to trade associations including the American Physical Therapy Association (APTA). This organization provides educational guidance and support for those working in the physical therapy field.

Tips for Entry

1. Positions can often be located in the classified section of the newspaper. Look under headings such as "Health Care," "Hospitals," "Physical Therapy," "Sports Medicine," or "Therapists."
2. Send your resume with a cover letter to hospitals or health care facilities. Ask that your resume be kept on file if a position is not currently available.
3. Consider calling the personnel director of hospitals and health care facilities in the areas you want to work and trying to set up an appointment for an interview.
4. If you are still in school or taking part in an accredited training program, contact the job placement office for job possibilities.

RECREATIONAL THERAPIST

Duties: Rehabilitating patients through activities; developing activities; monitoring progress

Alternate Title(s): None

Salary Range: $25,000 to $58,000+

Employment Prospects: Excellent

Advancement Prospects: Fair

Best Geographical Location(s) for Position: Positions may be located throughout the country

Prerequisites:

Education or Training:—Bachelor's degree in therapeutic recreation

Experience—Internship required

Special Skills and Personality Traits—Sensitivity; tact; imagination; creativity; patience

```
┌─────────────────────────────────┐
│   Recreational Therapist        │
│   Supervisor or Administrator   │
└─────────────────────────────────┘

┌─────────────────────────────────┐
│     Recreational Therapist      │
└─────────────────────────────────┘

┌─────────────────────────────────┐
│        College Student          │
└─────────────────────────────────┘
```

Position Description

Recreational therapists try to rehabilitate patients with mental, physical, and/or emotional disabilities through the use of a variety of activities. They also help patients develop activities that will provide them with exercise, fun, mental stimulation, and creative outlets.

Patients may need a recreational therapist for a number of reasons. They may have suffered a stroke and become paralyzed. Some patients may be mentally disturbed or recovering alcoholics or drug abusers. Other patients may be older individuals living in nursing homes. Recreational therapists also work with people in community-based park and recreation departments or those participating in special education programs.

An array of activities may be used to treat patients and improve their physical, mental, and emotional well-being. These can include arts and crafts, games, dancing, music, singing, exercising, performing skits, and playing sports. Other activities may include field trips to zoos, museums, ball games, or shopping centers. The type of activities chosen will depend on the interests and capabilities of the patient.

Recreational therapists may work in clinical settings including hospitals or rehabilitation centers. In these settings the goal of the recreational therapist is mainly to treat and rehabilitate patients with medical problems.

Recreational therapists working in long-term car facilities, nursing homes, residential facilities, or community recreation departments work to improve the general health and well-being of patients. They may however, also be called upon to treat specific medical problems as well.

Recreational therapists work closely with other medical professionals including social workers, physicians, nurses, psychologists, and physical and occupational therapists. Part of their job is to assess patients. This may be accomplished in a number of ways. They may talk to the patients and their families. They may also utilize information from medical record and the medical staff.

After assessing patients, recreational therapists develop and implement a therapeutic activity program based on their individual needs and interests. The course of action must be dependent on the patients' emotional status as well as their physical and mental condition.

Recreational therapists monitor and keep accurate records of patients' progress. They must observe patients' reactions to activities and determine if they are helping. If they are not, recreational therapists are responsible for developing a new course of action.

Recreational therapists may work various shifts depending on the specific work situation.

Salaries

Earnings for recreational therapists can range from approximately $25,000 to $58,000 or more annually depending on a number of variables. These include the experience, responsibilities, and education of the individual as well as the specific employment setting and its geographic location.

Employment Prospects

Employment prospects for recreational therapists are excellent. Positions may be located throughout the country in a variety of settings including hospitals, rehabilitation centers, long-term care facilities, adult day care programs, community mental health centers, schools, residential facilities for the mentally retarded, and residential facilities for substance abusers.

Advancement Prospects

Advancement prospects are fair for recreational therapists who obtain additional experience and training. Recreational therapists may climb the career ladder by locating similar jobs in more prestigious facilities. Others may become supervisors or move into other administrative or management positions.

Education and Training

While educational requirements vary, most positions for recreational therapists require a bachelor's degree in either therapeutic recreation or recreation with an emphasis in therapeutic recreation.

Courses in these programs include therapeutic recreation, clinical practice and helping skills, program design, management, professional issues, human anatomy, physiology, abnormal psychology, medical and psychiatric terminology, and the characteristics of illnesses and disabilities. A 360-hour internship is required.

There are some positions, such as that of activity director in nursing homes, that may accept an associate's degree in recreational therapy or training in either art, drama, or music

therapy. Some jobs do not require a degree if the applicant has work experience.

Positions may either prefer or require certification. This is obtained through the National Council for Therapeutic Recreation Certification. Individuals must obtain a bachelor's degree in therapeutic recreation and pass a certification examination.

Experience/Skills/Personality Traits

Recreation therapists should genuinely enjoy helping others. The ability to work with those who have disabilities is imperative. Recreational therapists must be creative people with a great deal of imagination and ingenuity. Sensitivity, tact, and patience are essential to success in this field.

Unions/Associations

Recreational therapists working in various health care facilities may belong to a variety of health care unions that represent workers in hospital or health care facilities. They may also become members of the American Therapeutic Recreation Association (ATRA) or the National Therapeutic Recreation Society (NTRS). Both trade associations provide career guidance.

Tips for Entry

1. Jobs are often listed in trade association journals.
2. Job openings may be advertised in the classified section of the newspaper. Look under headings including "Recreational Therapist," "Nursing Home," "Long Term Care Facility," "Health Care," "Therapist," "Gerontology," or "Activities Director."
3. Get certified. While it is not always mandatory, it is usually preferred.
4. Check with your college placement office regarding job possibilities.
5. Volunteer in a nursing home or extended care facility to gain experience working in the field and make important contacts.

ART THERAPIST

CAREER PROFILE

Duties: Using art skills to treat physical, mental, and/or emotional disabilities in patients; developing course of action; monitoring progress

Alternate Title(s): None

Salary Range: $22,000 to $52,000+

Employment Prospects: Fair

Advancement Prospects: Fair

Best Geographical Location(s) for Position: Positions may be located throughout the country

Prerequisites:

Education or Training—Minimum requirement is a bachelor's degree in art therapy; some positions may require a master's degree

Experience—Apprenticeship in art therapy usually required

Special Skills and Personality Traits—Art skills; creativity; emotional stability; ability to work with handicapped and/or disabled people; patience

CAREER LADDER

```
┌─────────────────────────────┐
│   Art Therapy Supervisor    │
└─────────────────────────────┘

┌─────────────────────────────┐
│       Art Therapist         │
└─────────────────────────────┘

┌─────────────────────────────┐
│      College Student        │
└─────────────────────────────┘
```

Position Description

Art therapists use art and craft activities to treat physical, mental, and/or emotional disabilities in patients. They work with a number of other professionals in attempting to restore an individual's health, including physicians, nurses, teachers, physical therapists, music therapists, dance therapists, psychologists, and psychiatrists.

Art therapists assess patients' needs and then develop a course of action involving various art skills. Depending on the situation, art therapists may be able to make a breakthrough in a patient's therapy when all else has failed.

Art therapists may have varied duties depending on the specific job and patient. They may be responsible for choosing the type of art that decorates a facility. Decorations may be used either to soothe patients or to evoke various reactions.

Art therapists are trained to use art skills and techniques to help patients feel better or communicate feelings. They may also use various psychological forms of therapy to reach patients.

Art therapists may use painting, drawing, coloring, sculpting, crafting, or any other art skills to help patients. They may, for example, bring together a group of patients for an art class or to make scenery for a skit or play. Art therapists may work with a group of patients creating holiday decorations for the rest of the facility. This type of therapy may help patients build self-confidence or remember events from their past.

Art therapy may also be used to help handicapped patients feel a sense of accomplishment which they may not otherwise have. Painting or drawing a picture, modeling clay into a sculpture, or expressing any type of creativity may help patients feel better about themselves.

Art therapists may work with patients on a one-on-one basis or in a group, depending on the patients and their needs. Conferences are often held with other members of the professional team and with patients' families. At this time, therapists are able to discuss the individuals' needs and progress.

Other responsibilities of art therapists may include ordering materials and maintaining and repairing equipment. Art therapists may work a variety of hours depending on shifts.

Salaries

Salaries for art therapists vary depending on the experience, responsibilties, and education of the individual, the specific job setting, and the geographic location, size, and prestige of the facility.

Individuals just entering the field can earn from $22,000 to $30,000 plus annually. Those working at larger facilities and who have more experience may have yearly salaries ranging from $28,000 to $52,000 or more.

Employment Prospects

Employment prospects for art therapists are fair. Art therapists can work in a variety of settings including hospitals and other health care facilities, rehabilitation centers, nursing homes, extended care facilities, schools, and independent expressive arts therapy centers. Opportunities may be located throughout the country. Individuals may also work in private practice.

Advancement Prospects

Advancement prospects are fair for art therapists. With experience, individuals can climb the career ladder by locating similar positions at more prestigious facilities. Art therapists who obtain additional training can move into supervisory positions or private practice.

Education and Training

The minimum educational requirement for an art therapist is a bachelor's degree in art therapy. The program includes classes in fine arts, theory and practice of art therapy, and behavioral and social sciences. An apprenticeship is also included in the program.

Many positions may require a master's degree.

Experience/Skills/Personality Traits

Art therapists must be sensitive, creative, compassionate, and understanding. They should have a great deal of patience. The ability to work with people with physical, mental, or emotional disabilities is essential. Emotional stability is mandatory.

A basic knowledge of a variety of art skills is needed. People in this line of work must enjoy working with and helping others.

Unions/Associations

Art therapists working in hospitals or other health care facilities or schools may belong to unions specific to those settings. Individuals may belong to the American Art Therapy Association (AATA), the major organization for those in the field. This organization provides career guidance and professional support to members.

Tips for Entry

1. Jobs may be advertised in the classified section of newspapers. Look under headings such as "Art Therapist," "Therapist," "Health Care," "Schools," and "Education."
2. Be sure to check with your college placement office. They are often contacted regarding job possibilities and openings.
3. Gain experience and make contacts by volunteering to give art classes to schoolchildren or at senior citizen homes.
4. Send your resume and a short cover letter to hospitals, long-term care facilities, schools, etc. Remember to request that your resume be kept on file if there are no current openings.
5. Jobs may be located online. Check out hospital and health care facility websites as well as some of the more popular job sites.

MUSIC THERAPIST

CAREER PROFILE

Duties: Using music or musical activities to treat physical, mental, and/or emotional disabilities in patients

Alternate Title(s): None

Salary Range: $20,000 to $52,000+

Employment Prospects: Excellent

Advancement Prospects: Good

Best Geographical Location(s) for Position: Positions may be located throughout the country

Prerequisites:

Education or Training—Minimum requirement is a bachelor's degree in music therapy; some positions may require master's degree

Experience—Internship in music therapy usually required; experience working with handicapped or disabled individuals helpful

Special Skills and Personality Traits—Ability to play piano and/or guitar; ability to sing in front of others; emotional stability; ability to work with handicapped and/or disabled people; compassion; patience; empathy

CAREER LADDER

```
┌─────────────────────────────────┐
│  Music Therapy Consultant or     │
│  Music Therapy Supervisor        │
└─────────────────────────────────┘

┌─────────────────────────────────┐
│  Music Therapist                 │
└─────────────────────────────────┘

┌─────────────────────────────────┐
│  College Student                 │
└─────────────────────────────────┘
```

Position Description

Music therapists use music and musical activities to treat physical, mental, and/or emotional disabilities in patients. They work with a number of other professionals in attempting to restore an individual's health, including physicians, nurses, teachers, physical therapists, dance therapists, psychologists, and psychiatrists. Music therapists can often make a breakthrough in a patient's therapy when all else has failed.

Music therapists have varied duties depending on their specific job and patients. They may be responsible for choosing pieces of music to be used as background in certain rooms in a facility. Background music may be used either to soothe patients or to evoke various reactions.

Music therapists who work in hospitals, nursing homes, or extended care facilities may be responsible for bringing together a group of patients to sing or play instruments for the facility staff and other patients. This type of therapy may be used to bring people out of their shells, to build self-confidence, and for a variety of other reasons.

Many music therapists work with older patients. This type of therapy often helps withdrawn patients become more social. Therapists may, for example, teach a group of patients in a nursing home a new tune or play a recording of songs that were popular when they were younger.

Some music therapists work with handicapped children. For example, they might teach a blind child how to play a musical instrument. This generally gives the child a tremendous sense of accomplishment that he or she might not have had before.

Through the use of all these therapies, music therapists can often accomplish a degree of healing. It may help an aging patient remember the good old days or just make patients feel more secure.

Therapists may work with patients on a one-on-one basis or in a group, depending on each patient's needs. Conferences are often held with other members of the professional team and with the patients' families. At this time, the therapist is able to discuss the individuals' needs and progress.

It should be noted that the object of music therapy is not to make a patient an accomplished musician or vocalist. Rather, through the medium of music, therapists hope to improve the emotional, mental and/or physical stability of patients. As in most therapy, music therapists realize that progress may be slow. The slightest amount of progress can mean a great deal to the patient.

Salaries

Salaries for music therapists vary depending on experience, responsibilities, and education of the individual, as well as the specific job and the size, prestige, and geographic location of the facility.

Individuals just entering the field can earn between $20,000 and $29,000 annually. Those working at larger facilities and who have more experience may have yearly salaries ranging from $26,000 to $36,000 plus. Supervisory positions in the field of music therapy may offer annual earnings of $52,000 and up.

Employment Prospects

Employment prospects for music therapists are excellent. There are currently more positions than there are qualified individuals. Music therapists can work in a variety of situations including hospitals and other health care facilities, rehabilitation centers, nursing homes, extended care facilities, schools, and independent expressive arts therapy centers. Opportunities may be located throughout the country.

Advancement Prospects

Advancement prospects are good for music therapists who have the education, drive, and determination. Individuals may climb the career ladder by obtaining a similar position in a more prestigious facility. This will usually result in increased responsibilities and earnings.

Another method of career advancement is moving up to a supervisory or administrative position. One of the drawbacks of this career path is that it limits the contact that the therapist has with patients.

Music therapists can also find positions in research or teaching at a university. Some individuals advance their career by going into private practice and/or consulting.

Education and Training

The minimum educational requirement for a music therapist is a bachelor's degree in music therapy. Courses usually include music theory, voice studies, instrument lessons, psychology, sociology, and biology. Music therapists who aspire to work in the public school system must also have a teaching degree.

Many positions require a master's degree. There are a great many colleges throughout the country offering both an undergraduate and a graduate degree program in music therapy.

Music therapists must be licensed in order to obtain employment in most states and most facilities.

Experience/Skills/Personality Traits

Music therapists obtain experience in a number of ways. In order to be licensed, individuals go through a six-month internship program. Many music therapists also have worked at health facilities or schools in part-time time jobs or in voluntary positions to gain additional experience.

One of the most important personality traits a good music therapist must have is the ability to work with handicapped and disabled people. He or she must also have a great deal of patience. As noted previously, it often takes the music therapist a long time to see results. The music therapist must be compassionate, emphathetic, and emotionally stable. Liking people is essential in this job.

Music therapists must have the ability to play the piano and/or a guitar. Knowing how to play other instruments is a plus, as is the ability to sing in front of others. The individual must be able to teach others either to play an instrument or sing. Knowledge of all forms of music is essential.

Unions/Associations

There are two main associations that music therapists may belong to. These are the National Association for Music Therapy, Inc. (NAMT) and the American Association for Music Therapy (AAMT). Both of these organizations provide valuable help to those in the field. They help place qualified music therapists, conduct research, and act as liaisons for colleges that offer music therapy programs.

Tips for Entry

1. Jobs may be advertised in the classified section of newspapers. Look under headings such as "Music Therapist," "Therapist," "Health Care," and "Expressive Arts Therapist."

2. College placement offices are often aware of openings for music therapists. Many facilities or schools looking for people to fill positions send a list of openings to colleges and universities that grant degrees in music therapy.

3. Both the National Association for Music Therapy, Inc. (NAMT) and the American Association for Music Therapy (AAMT) have registration and placement services for their members. In addition, their newsletters often list job openings.

4. Many positions of music therapists are available through the federal government. These civil service positions can be located through state employment services.

DANCE THERAPIST

CAREER PROFILE

Duties: Using dance and movement activities to treat physical, mental, and/or emotional disabilities in patients

Alternate Title(s): Dance/Movement Therapist

Salary Range: $22,000 to $65,000+

Employment Prospects: Excellent

Advancement Prospects: Good

Best Geographical Location(s) for Position: Positions can be located throughout the country

Prerequisites:

Education or Training—Master's degree required

Experience—Internship required

Special Skills and Personality Traits—Dancing and movement skills; research skills; emotional stability; ability to work with handicapped and/or disabled people; compassion; patience; empathy

CAREER LADDER

```
┌─────────────────────────────────────┐
│  Dance Therapist in Private Practice,│
│  Supervisory or Administrative       │
│  Position                            │
└─────────────────────────────────────┘

┌─────────────────────────────────────┐
│         Dance Therapist              │
└─────────────────────────────────────┘

┌─────────────────────────────────────┐
│         Intern or Dancer             │
└─────────────────────────────────────┘
```

Position Description

Dance therapy, along with other expressive arts therapies, can often make a breakthrough with a patient who can not be reached in any other manner. Dance therapists use various forms of dance and movement to help patients regain their health. Therapists must have a thorough knowledge and understanding of body movement.

Individuals may be referred to dance therapists for a variety of reasons. These include physical, mental, and emotional disabilities or illness. Victims of various diseases, accidents, and handicaps may be patients of dance therapists.

The dance therapist's main function is to help restore an individual's health. This is accomplished with the help of other professionals including doctors, nurses, teachers, physical therapists, music therapists, psychologists, and/or psychiatrists. Together this team determines what course of action to take for a patient's therapy.

Dance therapists are registered with the American Dance Therapy Association (ADTA) and must go through a program of training. There are two levels of dance therapists. The first is called DTR (Dance Therapist Registered). This level is for those individuals who have completed the training and education for the basic level of competency in the

job. Individuals who complete additional requirements may go on to the next level called ADTR (Academy of Dance Therapists Registered).

The responsibilities of the dance therapist vary depending on the specific job and the specific patient. He or she must observe, assess, and evaluate each patient before developing a course of action.

Dance therapists may work with one patient at a time or with a group. They may teach a variety of forms of dance to a patient or have the patient move freely to observe his or her movements, facial expressions, etc. It is important for the dance therapist to realize that what works for one patient will not always help another.

Dance therapy may be used to soothe patients who are angry or irritated. It may also be used to evoke various reactions. Sometimes when a patient uses a great deal of energy moving around, he or she will lose inhibitions or gain the ability to talk about a problem. Dance and movement may also make people feel less self-conscious. In some cases, patients are able to express emotions through movement.

This job can be very fulfilling. Seeing a patient with an unhealthy emotional or physical status change and become healthier through dance and movement is very rewarding.

Salaries

Earnings for dance therapists can vary greatly depending on a number of factors, including the specific facility for which an individual is working, and its size, prestige, and geographic location. Other factors affecting salary include the individual's experience, responsibilities, and educational level.

Dance therapists can earn between $22,000 and $65,000 or more annually.

Employment Prospects

Employment prospects are excellent for dance therapists. Individuals can work in a variety of health care situations including hospitals and other health care facilities, psychiatric hospitals, mental health centers, rehabilitation centers, nursing homes, extended care facilities, schools, correctional facilities, and independent expressive arts therapy centers. Opportunities may be located throughout the country. Individuals may work full or part time.

Advancement Prospects

Dance therapists have good advancement prospects. With drive and determination, they can move into supervisory positions such as the director of recreation therapy or expressive arts therapy.

An individual may also advance his or her career by locating a similar position at a more prestigious facility. This usually results in increased responsibilities and earnings.

Another way to climb the career ladder is to go into private practice. In order to go into private practice or teach, dance therapists may need to fulfill additional requirements.

Education and Training

Dance therapists must hold a master's degree. The American Dance Therapy Association (ADTA) has approved the programs of a number of colleges throughout the country offering graduate degrees in dance therapy. They also allow alternative education requirements for individuals who do not attend one of the schools participating in approved programs.

Dance therapists may have undergraduate degrees in any area including liberal arts, dance, psychology, or physical education. Other helpful undergraduate classes include those in kinesiology and dance education.

Experience/Skills/Personality Traits

In order to be registered by the American Dance Therapy Association, the registering agency for this profession, dance therapists must fulfill certain requirements. Individuals need experience and may obtain this through an internship program. Dance therapists must have the ability to work with ill, handicapped, and/or disabled patients. They must have a great deal of patience because it often takes a long time for a patient to make any progress. The dance therapist must be compassionate, empathetic, and emotionally stable. He or she must have training in a variety of forms of dance. The ability to do research is helpful.

Unions/Associations

Dance therapists may belong to the American Dance Therapy Association (ADTA). This organization offers education, professional support, and guidance to its members and brings together individuals interested in the field. It is also the registering agency for dance therapists.

Tips for Entry

1. The job placement office of schools offering degrees in dance therapy often have listings of job openings. Many facilities send employment listings to these schools in hope of locating qualified applicants.
2. Job openings are also advertised in the classified section of the newspaper. Look under headings such as "Dance Therapy," "Health Care," "Therapist," "Recreation Therapy," and "Expressive Arts Therapist."
3. Send your resume and a short cover letter to the personnel directors of hospitals, rehabilitation centers, nursing homes, extended care facilities, schools, or independent expressive arts therapy centers. Request that they keep your resume on file if there is not a current opening.
4. There are positions for dance therapists available through the state and federal government. These civil service positions can be located by contacting your state and/or federal employment service.
5. Contact the American Dance Therapy Association (ADTA) for information on the requirements for becoming a registered dance therapist.

OCCUPATIONAL THERAPIST

CAREER PROFILE

Duties: Helping patients perform daily living and working skills; evaluating patients; teaching patients to become more independent

Alternate Title(s): O.T.; Industrial Therapists

Salary Range: $34,000 to $65,000+

Employment Prospects: Excellent

Advancement Prospects: Good

Best Geographical Location(s) for Position: Positions may be located throughout the country

Prerequisites:

Education or Training—Minimum requirement is a bachelor's degree

Experience—Supervised clinical internship necessary; experience working in health care or with handicapped or disabled individuals helpful

Special Skills and Personality Traits—Imagination; creativity; patience; communication skills; enthusiasm

CAREER LADDER

```
┌─────────────────────────────────┐
│  Occupational Therapist Supervisor │
│   or Occupational Therapist      │
│       in Private Practice         │
└─────────────────────────────────┘

┌─────────────────────────────────┐
│     Occupational Therapist        │
└─────────────────────────────────┘

┌─────────────────────────────────┐
│        College Student            │
└─────────────────────────────────┘
```

Position Description

Occupational therapists work with individuals who have mental, physical, developmental, or emotional problems and assist them in achieving the maximum independence possible. They help patients learn how to perform simple daily living skills and to develop work skills. It is the responsibility of the occupational therapist to evaluate each patient and then assess his or her therapy requirements. Some occupational therapists are also called industrial therapists. These individuals usually specialize in helping patients find and keep jobs.

Occupational therapists help patients compensate for loss of functions. They may work with a patient to improve basic motor functions or assist a patient in developing basic reasoning abilities.

The activities an occupational therapist chooses to work on with a patient depend on the disability of that person and on whether the disability is temporary. The occupational therapist must develop a course of action suited to the particular person. A patient who has been in an auto accident, for example, may just need some help recovering motor functions. A patient with a spinal cord injury or one suffering from muscular dystrophy will have to learn how to permanently adapt to a different lifestyle.

Occupational therapists may work with patients on learning how to do practical, everyday activities such as dressing, cooking, eating, cleaning, etc. They may also work with patients on time management skills, budgeting money, and using public transportation.

Occupational therapists might also be expected to work with patients in problem solving and decision-making activities. This may be accomplished by using games, computer programs, or role-playing situations. No matter what the method, the end result must be to help the patient learn how to be more independent.

Occupational therapists often help patients with permanent disabilities to cope by providing adaptive equipment and showing its proper use. This might include wheelchairs, walkers, canes, and splints. Occupational therapists often design or develop equipment to help patients cope with everyday problems encountered at work or home. Occupational therapists, working with computer-aided adaptive equipment, can teach patients with major limitations how to control their environment. This equipment allows people to communicate, walk, and operate telephones, computers, and television sets, among other things.

Occupational therapists may assist patients in finding employment. In these cases, occupational therapists must determine the type of job the patient is capable of handling and then search for openings in the particular field. They may then help the patient to learn skills necessary to keep the job.

Occupational therapists may work with children, teenagers, adults, or senior citizens. No matter the age of the patient, the therapist must determine the specific disability and then evaluate the patient's abilities. He or she can then develop and recommend therapies.

Additional responsibilities of occupational therapists include the accurate recording of the progress and activities of each patient. Many in this field find it very rewarding to see patients move from a stage in their life where they are totally dependent on others to a stage where they begin to become independent of others.

Occupational therapists may work in health care facilities, schools, offices, or may go to patient's homes to provide services.

Salaries

Earnings for occupational therapists can range from approximately $34,000 to $65,000+ or more depending on the geographical location, shift, and specific type of facility where the individual works. Other factors affecting earnings include the responsibilities, education, and experience of the occupational therapist. Occupational therapists in private practice may earn more than those who are salaried.

Employment Prospects

Employment prospects for occupational therapists are excellent. Positions may be located throughout the country in a variety of settings including hospitals, schools, rehabilitation centers, long-term care facilities, home health care agencies, and private practice.

Advancement Prospects

Advancement prospects are good for occupational therapists. Those interested in climbing the career ladder can obtain additional experience or education and become supervisors. Others may advance their careers by locating positions in more prestigious facilities or entering private practice.

Education and Training

Individuals aspiring to become occupational therapists must hold a minimum of a bachelor's degree. Bachelor's degrees and graduate programs in occupational therapy are offered throughout the country.

Courses covered include physical, biological, and behavioral sciences as well as the application of occupational theory and skills. Programs also include a six-month supervised clinical internship.

Many states require occupational therapists to be licensed. In order to obtain a license, individuals must graduate from an accredited program and pass a national certification exam.

Experience/Skills/Personality Traits

Occupational therapists must enjoy working with people and like to help others. Warmth and kindness are necessary to success in this field. Individuals should be imaginative and creative and have the ability to find new ways to teach skills to others. Excellent communication skills are mandatory.

Patience is a must in this field. It is often difficult for patients to acquire new skills on the first try. Occupational therapists should also be positive, personable, and enthusiastic so they can motivate patients to help themselves.

Unions/Associations

Occupational therapists working in various health care facilities may belong to a variety of health care unions which represent workers in hospital or health care facilities. Those working in schools may similarly belong to teachers' unions.

Individuals may also belong to the American Occupational Therapy Assocation (AOTA). This organization provides educational guidance and professional support to those in the field.

Tips for Entry

1. Send your resume and a short cover letter to hospitals, health care facilities, schools, nursing homes, independent living centers, and home health agencies. Ask that your resume by kept on file if a position is not available at the current time.

2. Positions are often advertised in the classified section of newspapers. Look under headings such as "Occupational Therapy," "Health Care," "Hospitals," "Education," "Occupational Therapist," or "Therapist."

3. There are employment agencies located throughout the country specializing in jobs in the health care industry. Check to see who pays the fee if you do get a job (you or the employer) before getting involved.

4. The job placement office at your college may also offer job possibilities.

OCCUPATIONAL THERAPY ASSISTANT

CAREER PROFILE

Duties: Assisting occupational therapists in administering occupational programs to patients; helping teach patients to become more independent; assisting patients in learning living and job skills

Alternate Title(s): COTA; O.T.A.

Salary Range: $24,000 to $38,000+

Employment Prospects: Excellent

Advancement Prospects: Good

Best Geographical Location(s) for Position: Positions may be located throughout the country

Prerequisites:

Education or Training—Two-year associates degree or certificate from accredited program

Experience—Supervised clinical internship necessary; experience working in health care or with handicapped or disabled individuals helpful

Special Skills and Personality Traits—Patience; understanding; motivation; imagination; creativity; communication skills; enthusiasm

CAREER LADDER

Occupational Therapist

Occupational Therapy Assistant

College Student

Position Description

Occupational therapy assistants work with those who have mental, physical, developmental, or emotional problems. As a result of these conditions, patients may have difficulty living independently or performing day-to-day living or work skills. Occupational therapy assistants work with occupational therapists to assist patients in learning how to lead more independent, productive lives.

Occupational therapy assistants assist occupational therapists in administering a medically oriented occupational program to patients. Occupational therapy assistants work to promote the rehabilitation of patients in hospitals and other institutions. Their goal is to help patients achieve the maximum independence possible.

The assistants are expected to help the occupational therapist plan a therapeutic plan of action for each patient. After the occupational therapist evaluates and assesses a patient's therapy needs, the occupational therapy assistants may help the patient to learn or relearn how to do practical everyday activities such as dressing, cooking, eating, and cleaning.

They may also work with patients on time management skills, budgeting money, and using public transportation.

Assistants also work to develop patients' work skills. This is especially important in helping patients lead productive lives. Assistants may conduct training sessions for patients to teach them how to interview for jobs, fill in applications, or handle other vocational skills.

Occupational therapy assistants are expected to observe patients to see how they respond to therapy. They must report any improvements or changes to the occupational therapist. If occupational therapy assistants see any problems being created by either a patient's work or home setting, they may recommend the setting be changed.

Patients may often be stressed by normal situations that occur in daily life or work settings. Occupational therapy assistants are responsible for helping patients learn how to cope with these stresses.

This can be a very rewarding job for people who enjoy working with people and helping others have a better life. Occupational therapy assistants may help patients whose disability is temporary or permanent. Whichever the case, the assistants are responsible for helping patients learn how to adapt to their present lifestyle and make their life more productive.

Salaries

Earnings for occupational therapy assistants can range from approximately $24,000 to $38,000 or more depending on the geographical location, shift, and specific type of facility where the individual works. Other factors affecting earnings include the experience, responsibilities, and education of the occupational therapy assistant.

Employment Prospects

Employment prospects for occupational therapy assistants are excellent. Positions may be located throughout the country in a variety of settings including hospitals, schools, rehabilitation centers, nursing homes, mental health facilities, long-term care facilities, and home health care agencies.

Advancement Prospects

Advancement prospects are good for occupational therapy assistants. Individuals can obtain additional experience and increase responsibilities and earnings. Occupational therapy assistants who increase their education can become full-fledged occupational therapists.

Education and Training

In order to become an occupational therapy assistant an individual must go through an approved two-year associate's degree program. These are offered at junior and community colleges throughout the country. There are also a limited number of certificate programs accredited by the American Occupational Therapy Association, Inc. (AOTA).

Many states also require occupational therapy assistants to be licensed. In order to obtain a license, individuals must graduate from an accredited program and pass an exam administered by the American Occupational Therapy Certification Board. Individuals who meet the requirements become Certified Occupational Therapy Assistants (COTA).

Experience/Skills/Personality Traits

Occupational therapy assistants must go through a supervised clinical experience as part of their education. In order to be successful in this field, individuals should genuinely like working with and helping other people. Occupational therapy assistants must be patient, understanding, and compassionate. Individuals should be warm and enthusiastic and find ways to motivate others. They should also be creative and imaginative and be able to develop new, different ways to teach skills to patients. Communication skills are essential in this job.

Unions/Associations

Occupational therapy assistants working in various health care facilities may belong to a variety of health care unions that represent workers in hospital or health care facilities. Those working in schools may similarly belong to teachers unions.

Individuals may also belong to the American Occupational Therapy Association (AOTA). This organization provides educational guidance and professional support to those in the field.

Tips for Entry

1. Get experience by volunteering at facilities where you can work with people with disabilities.
2. If you are still in school take classes in biology, psychology, and sociology. They will be helpful when attending college for this type of job.
3. Send your resume and a short cover letter to hospitals, health care facilities, nursing homes, independent living centers, and home health agencies. Ask that your resume be kept on file if a position is not currently available.
4. Positions are often advertised in the classified section of newspapers. Look under headings such as "Occupational Therapy," "Occupational Therapy Assistant," "Health Care," "Hospitals," "Education," and "Therapist."
5. There are employment agencies located throughout the country specializing in jobs in the health care industry. Check to see who pays the fee if you do get a job (you or the employer) before getting involved.
6. The job placement office at your college may offer job possibilities.

RESPIRATORY THERAPIST

CAREER PROFILE

Duties: Evaluating, treating, and caring for patients with breathing disorders and problems; testing capacity of lungs

Alternate Title(s): Respiratory Care Practitioner

Salary Range: $26,000 to $58,000+

Employment Prospects: Excellent

Advancement Prospects: Good

Best Geographical Location(s) for Position: Positions may be located throughout the country

Prerequisites:

Education or Training—Formal training through accredited two- or four-year program

Experience—Supervised clinical experience

Special Skills and Personality Traits—Compassion; mechanical aptitude; manual dexterity; math skills; communication skills; ability to follow instruction

CAREER LADDER

```
┌─────────────────────────────────────┐
│   Respiratory Therapist Supervisor   │
└─────────────────────────────────────┘

┌─────────────────────────────────────┐
│       Respiratory Therapist          │
└─────────────────────────────────────┘

┌─────────────────────────────────────┐
│          College Student             │
└─────────────────────────────────────┘
```

Position Description

Patients with heart or lung difficulties often have problems breathing. Respiratory therapists work under the supervision of physicians administering respiratory care and life support to patients. Respiratory therapists are responsible for the evaluation, treatment, and care of patients with breathing disorders and problems.

Respiratory therapists work with an array of patients ranging from premature infants with underdeveloped lungs to elderly people suffering from lung disease. They may also treat patients suffering from chronic problems such as asthma or provide emergency care for victims of heart failure, stroke, or shock.

It is the responsibility of the respiratory therapist to evaluate patients to determine the capacity of their lungs using a special instrument into which a patient breathes. The reading shows the volume and flow of air that the patient inhales and exhales. The reading is then compared with the norm for a person who is of similar age, sex, weight, and height. This information is used to determine if a patient has a lung capacity deficiency. The respiratory therapist also will draw an arterial blood sample to analyze blood gases. Results of all tests are given to the patient's physician.

A number of different things are used to treat breathing disorders. These range from the use of oxygen, oxygen mixtures, aerosol medications, and chest physiotherapy.

Therapists may be expected to place oxygen masks on patients to increase the concentration of oxygen in their lungs. When doing this, the therapist will, under the supervision of a physician, set the oxygen flow level. Respiratory therapists may also be responsible for connecting patients to ventilators. This is done for patients who cannot breathe on their own. As part of this function, the therapist may be expected to insert tubes into a patient's trachea, or windpipe, and connect the tube to the ventilator. In other situations, the respiratory therapist may be responsible for performing chest physiotherapy on patients. This procedure removes mucus from the lungs, helping patients to breathe easier. This is often used on patients suffering from cystic fibrosis. Other procedures the respiratory therapist may perform include positioning the patient, and thumping and vibrating his or her rib cage to help drain mucus in the lungs.

It is the duty of the respiratory therapist to check on patients in their care at regular intervals and make sure equipment is working properly. If patients are still having problems breathing or if levels of oxygen, carbon dioxide, or other matter are abnormal, the respiratory therapist must report this fact to the physician and change equipment or settings according to his or her instructions.

Another function of many respiratory therapists is teaching patients and their families how to use ventilators. With this knowledge, patients can live at home. Respiratory therapists working in home care are responsible for visiting patients several times a month to check and clean equipment and make sure it is being used correctly.

Respiratory therapists in hospitals or other medical facilities may work various shifts.

Salaries

Earnings for respiratory therapists can range from $26,000 to $58,000 or more depending on the education, experience, and responsibilities of the individual in addition to the specific job setting and its geographic location. Generally, respiratory therapists with a bachelor's degree will earn more than those with an associate's degree.

Employment Prospects

Employment prospects for respiratory therapists are excellent. Positions may be located throughout the country in a variety of settings including hospitals, rehabilitation centers, long-term care facilities, home health care agencies, and medical equipment rental companies.

Advancement Prospects

Advancement prospects are good for respiratory therapists. Individuals can climb the career ladder by obtaining experience and training. Some respiratory therapists advance by moving into supervisory positions. Others find more satisfaction in caring for critically ill patients.

Education and Training

Individuals aspiring to become respiratory therapists must earn either an associate's degree or a bachelor's degree. There are also programs available for those who already hold a four-year degree in another field. Supervised clinical experience is necessary in these programs.

Training programs are offered in colleges, universities, hospitals, medical schools, trade, and vocational-technical schools and in the armed forces. In addition to learning about anatomy, physiology, chemistry, physics, and math, students learn about equipment, clinical tests, and procedures.

Many states require respiratory therapists to be licensed. Voluntary certification and registration may be obtained by graduates of accredited programs. Respiratory therapists can earn the designation of Registered Respiratory Therapist (R.R.T.) by taking an exam offered by the National Board for Respiratory Care, Inc.

Experience/Skills/Personality Traits

Respiratory therapists must enjoy working with and helping others. Compassion and sensitivity are essential in this line of work. Warmth and kindness are also helpful traits.

As a great deal of this job entails operating respiratory therapy equipment, a mechanical aptitude and manual dexterity are needed. Math skills are also necessary to compute medication dosages and calculate test results. Communication skills and the ability to follow orders are also needed.

Unions/Associations

Respiratory therapists working in various health care facilities may belong to a variety of health care unions that represent workers in hospital or health care facilities.

Respiratory therapists may also become members of the American Association for Respiratory Care (AARC). This organization provides guidance and support to those in the field.

Tips for Entry

1. Send your resume with a short cover letter to hospitals, health care facilities, nursing homes, and home health agencies. Ask that your resume be kept on file if a position is not available at the time.
2. Job openings are often advertised in the classified section of the newspaper under headings such as "Respiratory Therapist," "Therapist," "Health Care," "Hospitals," and "Respiratory Care Practitioner."
3. While certification is voluntary, most employers prefer applicants to be certified and registered.
4. Continue your education. Specialized courses will help make you more marketable. A bachelor's degree will assist in career advancement.
5. Do not forget to check the job placement office at your college or school for leads.

GERIATRICS AND
LONG-TERM CARE

GERIATRIC CARE MANAGER

CAREER PROFILE

Duties: Coordinating personal, medical, and financial activities of elderly clients; visiting clients; paying bills; making appointments

Alternate Title(s): None

Salary Range: $28,000 to $150,000+

Employment Prospects: Fair

Advancement Prospects: Good

Best Geographical Location(s) for Position: Positions may be located throughout the country; areas with high senior citizen populations, such as Florida and Arizona, will have more opportunities

Prerequisites:

Education or Training—Educational requirements vary; master's in social work, gerontology, psychology, or business administration

Experience—Experience dealing with elderly helpful

Special Skills and Personality Traits—Accounting and bookkeeping skills; attention to detail; organization; communication skills; compassion

CAREER LADDER

```
┌─────────────────────────────────┐
│ Geriatric Care Manager in Larger or │
│ More Prestigious  Organization   │
│ or Self-Employed Geriatric       │
│ Care Manager                     │
└─────────────────────────────────┘

┌─────────────────────────────────┐
│ Geriatric Care Manager           │
└─────────────────────────────────┘

┌─────────────────────────────────┐
│ Student, Social Worker, Geriatric │
│ Social Worker, Attorney,         │
│ Business Person, etc.            │
└─────────────────────────────────┘
```

Position Description

Years ago, people grew up in an area, found a job, had a family, and lived in that same place throughout their entire lives. Today, society is more transitional; people are always on the move. Adult children take jobs in other locations; seniors retire to warmer locations. As a result, older parents are not always in the same geographic location as their children. Geriatric care managers serve as stand-in providers when families can not be around to assist a geriatric relative.

Geriatric care managers have varied responsibilities depending on the specific type of job. Functions can include visiting clients on a regular, routine basis to make sure they are safe, doing well, eating properly, and taking needed medications. Geriatric care managers may also be expected to make necessary appointments for clients to see physicians, dentists, therapists, or other medical practitioners. They are usually also responsible for making sure clients get to appointments, in some instances transport them.

The geriatric care manager is responsible for determining which agencies and/or social services clients are eligible to use. The individual will also be expected to fill out forms and applications necessary to use these services. These may include medicaid or insurance forms and reimbursements.

Some geriatric care managers are responsible for paying clients' bills. This function may also encompass keeping clients' day-to-day finances in order. The geriatric care manager may, for example, write checks for a client's rent, utilities, medical and pharmacy bills, etc. The individual may additionally take the client shopping for food, clothing, or other necessities.

While there are geriatric care managers who do estate planning, living wills, and family trusts, individuals who handle these tasks must have special training. The geriatric care manager may, however, recommend specialists to handle these jobs.

Geriatric care managers may be hired by adult children or other relatives who live too far away to be of any assistance to their aging relatives. Geriatric care managers may work for an agency or firm or be self-employed.

This is an interesting job for individuals who like working with older people. Often close bonds are formed between the geriatric care manager and clients because of the nature of the work. Geriatric care managers often make the difference between an aging relative being able to live at home alone and having to change living accommodations. The service offers relatives living in other locations peace of mind which they might not otherwise have.

Salaries

Geriatric care managers can earn from $28,000 to $85,000 or more annually depending on the specific job as well as the individual's education, experience, responsibilities, and geographic location.

Those who are self-employed may be reimbursed in a number of ways. They may be paid a flat fee for a project, an hourly rate, or a monthly retainer. Fees can range from approximately $25 for handling a simple project to $250 or more per hour for more complex tasks. Earnings for self-employed geriatric care managers will depend on the number of clients they have. Individuals who are trained in estate planning, family trusts, or living wills can earn up to $150,000 or more annually.

Employment Prospects

Employment prospects for geriatric care managers are fair. Geriatric care managers may find full- or part-time employment in a variety of settings throughout the country. These include home care organizations, hospitals, and private geriatric care management firms. Individuals may also be self-employed or work on a consulting basis.

Advancement Prospects

Individuals may climb the career ladder by finding a similar position with a larger or more prestigious organization. Others advance their careers in this field by becoming self-employed and building a large client base.

Education and Training

Educational requirements vary for this type of job. Good choices for majors for individuals interested in pursuing a career in this field include social work, gerontology, business, or psychology. The more education the individual has, the better. Graduate degrees may be required by employers. Self-employed geriatric care managers often hold an MBA or law degree. Additional courses and seminars in accounting, business, social work, psychology, and sociology will be useful.

Experience/Skills/Personality Traits

Geriatric care managers may have experience in various fields prior to this career. These may include social work, geriatrics, law, or business. Experience working with the elderly is essential. This may be obtained in work situations or through volunteering.

Geriatric care managers need a variety of skills depending on the specific job. No matter what the job, they must be organized and detail-oriented with excellent interpersonal skills. A knowledge of bookkeeping and accounting may be necessary. Communication skills are essential.

Geriatric care managers should be compassionate, understanding people who enjoy working with the elderly.

Certain states may require licensing or certification for individuals working in private practice. Geriatric care managers working with clients' finances may also need to be bonded.

Unions/Associations

Geriatric care managers may be members of the National Association of Private Geriatric Care Managers (NAPGCM). This organization can provide additional career information and professional support.

Tips for Entry

1. Job openings may be advertised in the newspaper classified section under "Geriatric Care Manager" or "Geriatrics."
2. Join trade associations. Read their journals and attend conferences. Trade journals may advertise job openings. Conferences will help you network and make important contacts.
3. Potential employers may contact the job placement offices at colleges or universities offering majors in gerontology.
4. Individuals interested in being self-employed geriatric care managers may obtain clients and referrals by volunteering to speak to senior citizen and civic groups.
5. Get experience working with the elderly by volunteering in nursing homes, extended care facilities, skilled nursing units of hospitals, or senior citizen activity centers.

GERIATRIC ASSESSMENT COORDINATOR

Duties: Assessing needs of geriatric patients; developing plan of care; coordinating services of health care and social service professionals

Alternate Title(s): Geriatric Assessment Manager

Salary Range: $35,000 to $70,000+

Employment Prospects: Good

Advancement Prospects: Good

Best Geographical Location(s) for Position: Positions may be located throughout the country

Prerequisites:

Education or Training—Educational requirements vary from bachelor's degree to master's degree

Experience—Experience working with elderly required

Special Skills and Personality Traits—Ability to work with elderly; compassion; attention to detail; organization; interpersonal skills; communication skills

```
┌─────────────────────────────────┐
│   Geriatric Program Director      │
└─────────────────────────────────┘

┌─────────────────────────────────┐
│ Geriatric Assessment Coordinator  │
└─────────────────────────────────┘

┌─────────────────────────────────┐
│   Student, Social Worker, or      │
│   Geriatric Social Worker         │
└─────────────────────────────────┘
```

Position Description

Medical science has helped people live longer, but with the aging process, a variety of problems may develop. Sometimes people develop physical or mental problems or experience emotional changes. It is often difficult for family members to know what an aging parent, aunt, uncle, or spouse may need. A fairly new job called geriatric assessment coordinator has evolved in the geriatric health care field to help with this situation.

The geriatric assessment coordinator is responsible for assessing the physical, emotional, and mental conditions of geriatric patients. The individual is a member of a multidisciplinary team including physicians, nurses, physical therapists, recreational therapists, occupational therapists, and nurse practitioners.

To begin with, the geriatric assessment coordinator meets with the geriatric patient and conducts interviews with the patient and family members. The geriatric assessment coordinator arranges for a variety of medical tests and examinations to help determine the patients' needs.

After the assessment, the geriatric assessment coordinator develops a plan of care. Depending on the needs of the patient, the individual will coordinate the services of

physicians, nurses, physical, occupational and recreational therapists, social workers, psychologists, psychiatrists, etc.

In some cases the patient may require a variety of services from social service agencies such as hot meal programs, adult day care, senior transportation, and home care. In other situations, the patient may have to make major decisions regarding medical problems, living arrangements, etc. The geriatric assessment coordinator discusses all possible options with patients and their families so that they can make informed decisions to live the highest possible quality of life.

In many situations, the coordinator has continuing contact with a patient in order to insure that the plan of care is followed. Geriatric assessment coordinators may also be expected to reassess patients after a period of time.

A great deal of the job of a geriatric assessment coordinator is paperwork, as they assist patients with filling out and filing forms and keep accurate records regarding patients' assessments and plans of care.

Salaries

Earnings for geriatric assessment coordinators range from $35,000 to $70,000 plus depending on a number of variables. These include the education, training, and responsibilities of the individual as well as the location, prestige, and size of the specific facility in which he or she works. Beginning salaries range from $35,000 to $38,000. Earnings will be at the higher end of the scale for individuals with higher education working in large prestigious facilities.

Employment Prospects

Employment prospects for geriatric assessment coordinators are good. Individuals may find openings throughout the country in hospitals, nursing homes, health maintenance organizations (HMOs), hospices, and geriatric clinics.

Advancement Prospects

Geriatric assessment coordinators can take a number of different paths toward career advancement. Many individuals obtain additional education and experience and land jobs in larger or more prestigious facilities resulting in increased responsibilities and earnings. Others advance their careers by becoming a director or administrator of a geriatric program.

As this is a relatively new career in a growing field, some individuals advance by finding ways to expand the program they are working in to include specialities including the caring for Alzheimer's or stroke patients, respite, or adult day care.

Education and Training

Educational requirements vary from job to job ranging from a minimum of a bachelor's degree in social work with courses in gerontology to a master's or Ph.D. in gerontology or social work with an emphasis on gerontology. Any additional courses in geriatrics are helpful.

Experience/Skills/Personality Traits

Geriatric assessment coordinators should have experience working with older people. This may be obtained through work experience, internships in the field, or volunteer service.

Geriatric assessment coordinators should be compassionate people with excellent interpersonal skills and the ability to work well with the elderly. Individuals should be detail-oriented, organized, and have good verbal and written communication skills.

Unions/Associations

Geriatric assessment coordinators may belong to a number of organizations which provide career information and professional support. These include the National Association of Private Geriatric Care Managers (NAPGCM), the American Geriatrics Society (AGS), and the Association for Gerontology in Higher Education (AGHE).

Tips for Entry

1. Join trade associations. Read trade journals and attend conferences. Trade journals may advertise job openings. Attending conferences will help you network and make important contacts.

2. Send your resume and a cover letter to the personnel directors of nursing homes, hospitals, extended care facilities, geriatric clinics, hospices, etc. Remember to ask that your resume be kept on file if there are no current openings.

3. Job openings may be advertised in newspaper classified sections under headings such as "Geriatrics Assessment Coordinator," "Geriatrics," "Health Care," "Nursing Homes," "Geriatric Clinics," "Hospitals," and "Skilled Nursing Units."

4. Get experience working with the elderly by volunteering in nursing homes, extended care facilities, or skilled nursing units of hospitals.

5. Potential employers may contact the job placement office at colleges or universities offering majors in gerontology.

GERIATRIC SOCIAL WORKER

CAREER PROFILE

Duties: Counseling and assisting elderly clients cope with social, personal, psychological, and economic problems; coordinating services of agencies; investigating abuse or neglect of elderly clients

Alternate Title(s): Social Worker

Salary Range: $26,000 to $58,000+

Employment Prospects: Good

Advancement Prospects: Good

Best Geographical Location(s) for Position: Positions may be located throughout the country

Prerequisites:

Education or Training—Educational requirements vary from bachelor's degree to master's degree

Experience—Experience through internships or supervised field instruction

Special Skills and Personality Traits—Ability to work with elderly; compassion; emotional stability; communication skills

CAREER LADDER

```
┌─────────────────────────────┐
│   Administrative or          │
│   Supervisory Position       │
└─────────────────────────────┘

┌─────────────────────────────┐
│   Geriatric Social Worker    │
└─────────────────────────────┘

┌─────────────────────────────┐
│   Student or Social Worker in│
│   Different Field            │
└─────────────────────────────┘
```

Position Description

The number of people in their seventies and beyond is growing and is projected to rise substantially in the next few years. This age group is characterized by mounting health, social, personal, psychological, and economic problems requiring some type of assistance. Geriatric social workers help aging people and their families cope with these types of problems. They help people who often can not help themselves. Duties depend on the specific employment situation and the clients with which the individual works.

The elderly can have special problems including inadequate housing and serious illness and disabilities. Individuals may be ill themselves or have an aging spouse who is sick. Sometimes the elderly are abused by family members and have nowhere to turn for help. In other cases elderly individuals have no relatives and may not have the ability to handle things on their own. Senior citizens often need help with medical matters, finances, food, nutrition, or housing.

Clients may be referred to geriatric social workers by physicians, clinics, agencies, or private individuals. Geriatric social workers may deal with clients who are in nursing homes, hospitals, extended care facilities, or the client's own home.

Many aging people want to stay in their homes as long as possible. The geriatric social worker tries to find ways to make this goal possible. He or she may, for example, locate home health aides, live-in help, or companions.

The geriatric social worker may also advise family caregivers. It is often difficult for those who care for the aging to cope with the problems that arise. The geriatric social worker may run support groups for family caregivers or adult children of aging parents.

Geriatric social workers try to develop ways for the elderly to live more productive, fulfilling lives. They are responsible for evaluating clients' problems and assisting them in finding solutions. Individuals often advise the elderly and their families on choices in areas including transportation, housing, and long-term care. Geriatric social workers may visit clients at their homes or may meet in an office setting. Individuals must keep accurate records and prepare reports on clients' problems, situations, and solutions.

Geriatric social workers often coordinate different agencies and services to help handle and solve clients' problems. These might include, for example, the local office of the aging, home health aides, Meals on Wheels, adult day care facilities, therapists, clinics, and nurses. Geriatric social workers must monitor the situation to make sure all services are received.

Geriatric social workers may be responsible for investigating reported cases of abuse or neglect involving the elderly. Abuse or neglect may involve family members, nursing home staff, or others. Sometimes elderly clients do not get proper nutrition or medical care because they are not taking care of themselves and they need assistance.

Geriatric social workers usually work a standard 40-hour week. They may, however, be expected to work weekends or evenings to meet with clients or handle emergencies when necessary.

Salaries

Earnings for geriatric social workers can range from approximately $26,000 to $58,000 or more annually. Factors effecting earnings include the education, experience, and responsibilities of the geriatric social worker. Other factors include the geographic area and specific employment setting.

Employment Prospects

Employment prospects for geriatric social workers are good. Individuals may find employment throughout the country in a variety of employment settings including state, county, municipal, and federal government agencies, hospices, home health agencies, nursing homes, hospitals, social service agencies, and extended care facilities. Geriatric social workers can also work part time, consult, or go into private practice.

Advancement Prospects

Geriatric social workers can advance their careers by obtaining additional experience and/or education. Individuals may find similar positions in larger agencies or more prestigious facilities leading to increased earnings and responsibilities. Others move into managerial, administrative, or supervisory positions. Some geriatric social workers choose to teach in colleges, universities, or go into research. They may also choose to go into private practice or consulting.

Education and Training

Educational requirements vary from job to job for geriatric social workers. The minimum requirement is a bachelor's degree. Good choices for majors are social work, sociology, or psychology, with an emphasis in gerontology.

Many positions require a master's degree in social work. Ph.D.s are often required for teaching and research.

Individuals graduating with a BSW go through a 400-hour supervised field experience program preparing them to work right after graduation. Those graduating with an MSW go through 900 hours of supervised field instruction or an internship.

Certain states require social workers in any field to be licensed or registered. Voluntary certification is available through the National Association of Social Workers (NASW).

Experience/Skills/Personality Traits

Geriatric social workers must be emotionally stable people. While it can be very fulfilling, this type of job can be emotionally draining. Many geriatric social workers began their careers as social workers in other fields.

Individuals should work well with others. The ability to work with the elderly is essential. Geriatric social workers should be caring, compassionate people with good judgment. They must be objective and dependable. Communication skills are necessary. The ability to make others feel comfortable is helpful. Counseling skills are needed.

Unions/Associations

Geriatric social workers may be members of the Association for Gerontology in Higher Education (AGHE), the Council on Social Work Education (CSWE), and the National Association of Social Workers (NASW).

Tips for Entry

1. If you aspire to work in the social work field, try to get either a BSW or MSW. As noted above, these will prepare you for work right after college. Those who have degrees in other fields may have to get experience in other ways before entering the field.

2. Send your resume and a cover letter to the personnel directors of hospices; home health agencies; county, municipal, and federal government agencies; social service agencies; nursing homes; hospitals; and extended care facilities. Remember to ask that your resume be kept on file if there are no current openings.

3. Part-time positions may be available even if no full-time positions are open.

4. Jobs may be advertised in the classified section of newspapers under headings including "Geriatric Social Worker," "Social Worker," "Geriatrics," "Hospitals," "Health Care," and "Social Service Agencies."

5. Volunteer at senior citizen centers, nursing homes, extended care facilities, and/or hospitals. This is a good way to gain experience working with the elderly and to make important contacts.

6. Jobs in state, county, municipal, and federal government agencies may be civil service positions.

7. Attend classes, seminars, and workshops on all facets of gerontology.

NURSING HOME ACTIVITIES DIRECTOR

CAREER PROFILE

Duties: Developing and implementing recreational activities for nursing home patients

Alternate Title(s): Geriatric Recreation Director; Director of Nursing Home Activities

Salary Range: $26,000 to $55,000+

Employment Prospects: Good

Advancement Prospects: Good

Best Geographical Location(s) for Position: Positions may be located throughout the country

Prerequisites:

Education or Training—Educational requirements vary from high school diploma and two years' experience to associate's or bachelor's degree

Experience—Experience working in geriatrics helpful

Special Skills and Personality Traits—Creativity; arts and crafts skills; organization; interpersonal skills; communication skills

CAREER LADDER

```
┌─────────────────────────────────────┐
│ Nursing Home Activities Director in  │
│   Larger, More Prestigious Facility  │
└─────────────────────────────────────┘

┌─────────────────────────────────────┐
│   Nursing Home Activities Director   │
└─────────────────────────────────────┘

┌─────────────────────────────────────┐
│   Activities Staffer or Recreational │
│     Staffer in Non-Geriatric Field   │
└─────────────────────────────────────┘
```

Position Description

The growing aging population has resulted in an increase in nursing homes and similar facilities. It is imperative for patients in nursing homes to find things to do to keep their minds and bodies active and provide a good quality of life. Nursing home activities directors are responsible for developing and implementing daily recreational activities for patients in the facility.

The nursing home activities director works with other professionals in the facility to develop recreational activities that meet the needs of each patient or resident. These professionals may include physicians, social workers, occupational therapists, physical therapists, recreational therapists, nurses, and pharmacists. In addition, the director may meet with a patient's family to discuss the patient's interests, likes, etc.

Patients or residents in nursing homes often have different levels of skills and capabilities. Some patients may suffer from emotional problems, senility, Alzheimer's disease, or periodic memory loss. Others may be fully aware mentally but have physical disabilities. Activities must be developed based on each individual's skills and capabilities.

When patients first enter a nursing home or similar facility, it is the responsibility of the activities director to develop a personalized activity care plan. The individual must assess each patient and his or her skills, capabilities, and interests.

If patients are able, they tell the activities director what types of activities they would be interested in pursuing. In this manner, the activities director can develop activities that will be enjoyable and appropriate for each patient. The activities director is also expected to plan the activities of patients who are unable to plan their own.

Activities can range from group events to projects done individually. These might include craft classes, cooking lessons, art projects, games, dances, bingo, reading times, and exercise classes. Trips to shopping centers, malls, zoos, sporting events, parks, or concerts may also be planned. Additionally, activities directors usually develop activities to celebrate residents' birthdays, holidays, and other special days and events.

Activities are planned to help patients fill their days in a productive and fulfilling manner. Activities help keep patients' minds active and stimulated. Some activities are planned to help patients keep physically active or to give them opportunities to socialize with others.

Activities directors may find ways to bring others into the facility to help patients who may not be able to leave the premises on a regular basis. Many activities directors have people bring pets into the facility. Dogs and cats, for example, are often used to help patients who are not responsive to other activities. Sometimes patients who have not smiled or spoken will respond to petting a dog or having a cat to cuddle.

The activities director is responsible for writing progress reports on patients periodically. This is important to make sure that patients are adjusting to a facility, participating in activities, and socializing with others. If the activities director finds patients are having difficulties, he or she may refer them to others in the interdisciplinary care team.

Additional responsibilities of activities directors may include supervising others on the activities staff and coordinating the efforts of volunteers. They may also be expected to order supplies and prepare budgets and any other administrative and/or statistical reports necessary.

Salaries

Earnings for nursing home activities directors can have a wide range depending on the specific facility, and its size, prestige, and geographic location. Earnings will also be dependent on the individual's education, responsibilities, and experience level.

Nursing home activities directors can earn between $26,000 and $55,000 or more. Generally, individuals with the most education working in larger facilities earn salaries on the higher end of the scale.

Employment Prospects

Employment prospects for nursing home activities directors are good. Individuals may locate positions throughout the country in an array of settings including private or public nursing homes, skilled nursing units in hospitals, and extended care or long-term facilities.

Advancement Prospects

Nursing home activities directors can advance their careers by obtaining additional experience and education. The most common method of career advancement is finding a similar position in a larger, more prestigious facility.

Education and Training

There are varying educational requirements for activities directors depending on the facility. Some positions require just a high school diploma and two years of experience working in a geriatric setting. Other facilities prefer or require applicants to hold either an associate's or bachelor's degree. Majors for this type of position might include geriatrics, occupational therapy, recreational therapy, therapeutic recreation, rehabilitation therapy, or social work.

Voluntary credentialing is available through the National Council for Therapeutic Recreation Certification. Some states may require nursing home activities directors to be state approved.

Experience/Skills/Personality Traits

Many nursing home activities directors have worked in nursing homes or other facilities as activity staffers or in other areas of geriatric care. Others may have had experience in the recreation field outside of geriatrics prior to taking positions as nursing home activities directors.

To be successful in this job, activities directors should be creative, organized people. They should have varied skills in arts and crafts, music, etc. Interpersonal skills are mandatory, and good communication skills are a must. Individuals should like working with others and have the ability to work well with the elderly.

Unions/Associations

Nursing home activities directors may be members of the National Association of Activities Professionals (NAAP), the National Council for Therapeutic Recreation Certification (NCTRC), the American Therapeutic Recreation Association (ATRA), or the National Therapeutic Recreation Society (NTRS). These organizations provide guidance and professional support.

Tips for Entry

1. Many trade associations and organizations offer comprehensive training courses, seminars, and workshops for nursing home activities directors. These are valuable for the training and for making contacts.
2. Send your resume and a cover letter to the personnel directors of nursing homes, hospitals, extended care facilities, etc.
3. Trade journals often advertise job openings.
4. Other job possibilities may be advertised in the classified section of newspapers under headings including "Health Care," "Geriatrics," "Nursing Homes," "Nursing Home Activities Director," "Director of Activities," "Geriatric Recreation Director," "Adult Homes," or "Long-Term Care Facilities."
5. Volunteer at senior citizen centers, nursing homes, extended care facilities, and/or hospitals. This is a good way to gain experience and make contacts.

HOME HEALTH AIDE

CAREER PROFILE

Duties: Providing personal care services to elderly, ill, or disabled patients; keeping patients' homes neat; planning and cooking meals; providing emotional support to patients

Alternate Title(s): Homemaker-Home Health Aide; Home Care Aide; Personal Care Attendant

Salary Range: $8 to $55+ per hour

Employment Prospects: Excellent

Advancement Prospects: Poor

Best Geographical Location(s) for Position: Positions may be located throughout the country

Prerequisites:

Education or Training—Formal training program recommended

Experience—Experience taking care of children or elderly helpful, but not required

Special Skills and Personality Traits—Compassion; caring; personableness; physical stamina; responsibility

CAREER LADDER

```
┌─────────────────────────────┐
│   Licensed Practical Nurse   │
└─────────────────────────────┘

┌─────────────────────────────┐
│      Home Health Aide        │
└─────────────────────────────┘

┌─────────────────────────────┐
│        Entry Level           │
└─────────────────────────────┘
```

Position Description

Home health aides handle a wide array of home health care services for elderly, ill, disabled, or incapacitated people who are living at home instead of in hospitals or other health care facilities. Home health aides have duties similar to those of nurse's aides in facilities. They may also perform light housekeeping duties. Individuals will have varied responsibilities depending on the specific client.

Home health aides may be expected to visit clients daily or only once or twice a week. Some clients require extensive care, while others have short-term care needs.

Functions of home health aides run the gamut of nursing, personal, and housekeeping services. Individuals may be expected to assist patients in bathing, dressing, and grooming. They may help patients move from the bed to a chair or walker.

Nursing responsibilities may include taking patients' vital signs such as pulse, temperature, respiration, and blood pressure. Home health aides also change nonsterile dressings, make sure patients take medications, assist with pre-

scribed exercises, give massages and alcohol rubs, and help patients with braces or artificial limbs.

A major responsibility for many home health aides is in the area of meal planning. They may be expected to plan nutritious meals around special diets. Home health aides shop for groceries and prepare, cook, and serve meals. If patients need help eating, the aide will assist in feeding them.

Home health aides may be asked to do light housekeeping including cleaning, laundry, and changing bed linens. Many home health aides serve as a companion, accompanying clients outside the home to physician appointments, to grocery stores, or just for walks outside.

One of the most satisfying functions of many home health aides is providing psychological and emotional support to clients. In some situations, the home health aide is the only person that the client sees on a regular basis. Home health aides often keep clients company, talk to them, share a meal, and discuss problems. Sometimes the home health aide will work with a family as a unit. For example, a home health aide working with a client who has cancer will also work with the family on their emotional needs.

It may be the responsibility of the home health aide to file either verbal or written reports detailing services accomplished during visits and to report on the emotional, mental, and physical condition of the client.

Home health aides may have varied working hours depending on the specific employment setting.

Salaries

Earnings for home health aides can vary greatly depending on the specific job setting and geographic location. Compensation is also based on the responsibilities, duties, education, qualifications, and experience of the individual. Home health aides working for an agency generally are paid an hourly rate. While this rate can range from $8 to $55 per hour, most home health aides earn between $8 and $25 hourly. Some home health aides are compensated with a weekly salary instead of hourly rates.

Employment Prospects

Employment prospects for home health aides are excellent. Individuals may find employment throughout the country. Home health aides may work for public or private home health agencies, visiting nurse associations, public health or welfare departments, hospitals, hospices, or temporary help agencies. Individuals may also be self-employed.

Advancement Prospects

Advancement prospects are poor for home health aides. Many people are happy to remain home health aides and continue helping people in their current capacity. Those who wish to climb the career ladder must obtain additional education and training. They can then become nurse's aides, L.P.N.s, or R.N.s.

Education and Training

Governmental regulations specify that home health aides whose employers will be reimbursed by Medicare must go through a seventy-five-hour training program supervised by an experienced registered nurse. This program includes both classroom and practical training. Home health aides must also pass a competency exam. Subjects covered in the training program include communications skills; basic infection control procedures; observation, reporting, and documentation of patient status, and the care of services furnished; maintenance of a clean, safe, and healthy environment; and personal hygiene and grooming. Other subject matter includes reading and recording patients' vital signs; basic elements of body function and changes; recognition of and procedures for emergencies; the physical, emotional, and developmental characteristics of the patients served; safe transfer techniques; normal range of motion; and positioning and basic nutrition.

Recommended training programs must be approved by the Health Care Financing Administration. They are offered by employment agencies, the American Red Cross, hospitals, home health agencies, high schools, vocational-technical schools, community and junior colleges, and adult education programs. Additional training programs, seminars, and lectures are often offered on specialized topics such as caring for patients with Alzheimer's disease or AIDS.

States may have specific training regulations and laws. Voluntary certification is offered through the Foundation for Hospice and Home Care.

Experience/Skills/Personality Traits

Home health aides should enjoy working with and helping others. They must be compassionate and caring. Stamina and physical strength are necessary. The ability to follow directions is mandatory. Individuals should be cheerful, emotionally stable, and responsible people.

Many jobs do not require any experience at all in the health care field. Some may not even require the applicant to hold a high school diploma.

Unions/Associations

Individuals aspiring to become home health aides can contact the Foundation for Hospice and Home Care (FHHC) to obtain additional career information.

Tips for Entry

1. Job openings in this field are often advertised in newspaper classified sections under headings such as "Home Health Aide," "Home Health Care," "Homemaker Home Health Aide," and "Home Care."
2. Contact home health care agencies in your area to see if there are openings. Agencies may be located in the yellow pages.
3. Home health care agencies usually advertise their services in the newspaper.
4. Training programs are often offered by home health care agencies at no cost.

DIETETICS AND NUTRITION

DIETICIAN

Duties: Analyzing dietary needs and requirements; designing diets; promoting healthful eating habits

Alternate Title(s): Registered Dietician

Salary Range: $24,000 to $75,000+

Employment Prospects: Good

Advancement Prospects: Fair

Best Geographical Location(s) for Position: Positions may be located throughout the country

Prerequisites:
  Education or Training—Bachelor's degree in nutrition or food service administration
  Experience—Supervised experience necessary
  Special Skills and Personality Traits—Compassion; caring; personableness; physical stamina; responsibility

```
┌─────────────────────────────────┐
│  Director or Assistant Director of │
│      Dietary Department          │
└─────────────────────────────────┘

┌─────────────────────────────────┐
│           Dietician              │
└─────────────────────────────────┘

┌─────────────────────────────────┐
│           Student                │
└─────────────────────────────────┘
```

Position Description

Dieticians are concerned with the relationship between diet and health. They run food service systems in hospitals and other health care institutions and in schools and certain businesses. They are often responsible for promoting sound eating habits through education and research. Dieticians analyze people's dietary needs and requirements, design diets, and promote healthful eating habits.

Dieticians may work in a number of different areas. Clinical dieticians provide nutritional services for patients in hospitals, nursing homes, and other institutions. Clinical dieticians are often responsible for managing the food service department of facilities.

Dieticians in these settings are expected to assess patients' nutritional needs and then develop and implement appropriate nutritional programs. They must then evaluate the program and determine its results. Clinical dieticians may confer with a patient's physician to make sure that all medical and nutritional needs are met. Clinical dieticians may also specialize in specific areas, such as people who are overweight, underweight, anorexic, diabetic, or suffering from hypertension.

Other individuals specialize as community dieticians. These people counsel individuals and groups on nutritional practices. Community dieticians may work in public health clinics, home health agencies, and health maintenance organizations (HMOs). They evaluate the needs of individuals and then establish nutritional care plans. Community dieticians must also instruct individuals and their families on how and what to eat. In some cases this includes teaching individuals how to shop for groceries and prepare special meals.

Administrative dieticians oversee large-scale meal planning and preparation in health care facilities, prisons, schools, and company cafeterias. These individuals are also responsible for hiring, training, and directing other dieticians and food service workers in the facility. They are additionally expected to plan budgets for food, purchase food, equipment, and supplies, and make sure that sanitary regulations are adhered to by staff members.

Dieticians may work various shifts in hospitals or other health care facilities. Those working in other settings may have more normal working hours.

Salaries

Dieticians may earn between $24,000 and $75,000 or more annually, depending on the specific job, size, and type of facility, and geographic location as well as the experience, education, and responsibilities of the individual.

Employment Prospects

Employment prospects are good for dieticians. More people are beginning to recognize the relationship between diet and health. Individuals may find full- or part-time employment throughout the country in a variety of settings including hospitals, nursing homes, extended care facilities, schools, colleges, prisons, community agencies, hotels, medical clinics, private weight loss companies, health spas, and convalescent centers. Some dieticians are also self-employed.

Advancement Prospects

Dieticians can advance their careers by obtaining experience and/or education. Some individuals climb the career ladder by becoming the director or assistant director of a dietary department. Dieticians may also advance their careers by moving into a specialty such as pediatric or geriatric dietetics.

Education and Training

Dieticians must have a bachelor's degree with a major in dietetics, foods and nutrition, food service system management, or a related area. Courses include foods, nutrition, institution management, chemistry, biology, microbiology, business, economics, statistics, and computer science.

Certain states require dieticians to be either licensed, certified, or registered. Credentials may be obtained through the Commission on Dietetic Registration of the American Dietetic Association (ADA). Individuals who pass a certification examination after completing their education and obtaining supervised experience are awarded the Registered Dietician credential. Graduate education is available for those interested in advancing their careers.

Experience/Skills/Personality Traits

Dieticians should have good verbal communication skills. An interest in food and nutrition is helpful. Individuals should be personable, caring, compassionate people who enjoy helping others. Tact is often necessary when dealing with patients. Dieticians should be responsible people with good judgment and decision-making skills. They must be able to work independently. Teaching skills are needed to teach and explain nutrition to others.

Unions/Associations

Dieticians may be members of the American Dietetic Association (ADA). This organization can provide additional information on approved school programs and careers in this field.

Tips for Entry

1. If you are still in high school and considering becoming a dietician, take classes in biology, chemistry, math, health, and home economics.
2. Become a registered dietician even if your state does not require registration. This will give you an edge above other applicants.
3. Job openings are often advertised in the classified section of newspapers under headings including "Dieticians," "Registered Dietician," "Health Care Food Services," "Hospitals," and "Food Service."
4. Send your resume and a cover letter to the personnel directors at hospitals, nursing homes, extended care facilities, schools, colleges, etc. Remember to ask that your resume be kept on file if there are no current openings.
5. You might also consider sending your resume to companies that provide food services to businesses, colleges, universities, hotels, etc.
6. Check out job possibilities online. Start at some of the more popular sites such as www.monster.com and www.hotjobs.com.

DIETETIC TECHNICIAN

CAREER PROFILE

Duties: Assisting in nutritional care of patients; teaching patients about proper nutrition; designing diets; promoting healthful eating habits

Alternate Title(s): D.T.R.

Salary Range: $20,000 to $32,000+

Employment Prospects: Good

Advancement Prospects: Fair

Best Geographical Location(s) for Position: Positions may be located throughout the country

Prerequisites:
    Education or Training—Associate's degree from an ADA-approved program for dietetic technicians
    Experience—Supervised experience necessary
    Special Skills and Personality Traits—Interest in food and nutrition; teaching skills; communication skills; caring; personableness

CAREER LADDER

```
┌─────────────────────────────────┐
│   Dietetic Technician in Larger  │
│  Facility or Registered Dietician│
└─────────────────────────────────┘

┌─────────────────────────────────┐
│       Dietetic Technician        │
└─────────────────────────────────┘

┌─────────────────────────────────┐
│    Student or Dietetic Assistant │
└─────────────────────────────────┘
```

Position Description

Dietetic technicians work under the supervision of a registered dietician. They are responsible for assisting in the nutritional care of patients. Dietetic technicians may have varied duties and functions depending on the size and structure of the institution in which they work. As part of the health care team, dietetic technicians, like dieticians, are concerned with the relationship between diet and health.

Dietetic technicians, in the dietary department of institutions, help dieticians with many of their responsibilities. They may also assist individuals in learning about and improving their nutritional care.

Dietetic technicians are responsible for teaching patients about proper nutrition. They start by helping patients make proper menu selections. To accomplish this, they may interview patients to learn about their current eating habits, likes, dislikes, etc. They must also determine any medical reasons that patients should or should not eat certain foods. For example, patients with cardiovascular disease would be advised not to eat high-salt diets. Those with diabetes might need to be instructed on food exchanges.

Dietetic technicians in some situations are responsible for the day-to-day supervision of food production in the institution. They may also be expected to oversee others in the dietary department, including dietetic assistants and food service workers.

Many dietetic technicians also are expected to perform administrative duties for the dietician. They may be responsible for coordinating work schedules for others in the department as well as putting together job specifications and assisting in the training of workers. They may develop and implement budgets and cost control measures for the department. They may also be responsible for evaluating food programs.

Some dietetic technicians work on creating standardized recipes which can then be adapted to specialized diets of patients. Others work directly in the kitchen area supervising food production or overseeing preparation of specialized therapeutic meals.

Many dietetic technicians counsel patients and their families on correct eating habits and good nutrition. In addition to making suggestions regarding proper nutrition, dietetic technicians may actually plan menus and/or teach patients how to shop wisely and prepare foods to meet nutritional requirements.

Dietetic technicians may work various shifts in hospitals or other health care facilities. Those working in other settings may have more normal working hours.

Salaries

Dietetic technicians may earn between $20,000 and $32,000 or more annually depending on the specific job, size, and type of facility and its geographic location as well as the experience, education, and responsibilities of the individual.

Staring salaries are generally between $20,000 and $26,000 annually.

Employment Prospects

Employment prospects are good for dietetic technicians. This field will continue to expand as people see the relationship between proper nutrition and good health. Individuals may find full- and part-time employment throughout the country in a variety of settings including hospitals, nursing homes, extended care facilities, schools, colleges, prisons, community agencies, hotels, medical clinics, private weight loss companies, health spas, and convalescent centers. In large institutions there are often many dietetic technicians on staff.

Advancement Prospects

Dietetic technicians may take a number of different paths to career advancement. Those who obtain experience may locate similar jobs in larger facilities resulting in increased responsibilities and earnings. Individuals may also obtain additional education and become registered dieticians.

Education and Training

In order to become a dietetic technician an individual must attend and complete a two-year associate's degree program approved by the American Dietetic Association (ADA). These are offered at community colleges and junior colleges throughout the country. Programs include classroom study, practical instruction, and supervised experience. Courses include nutrition, menu planning, nutrition and disease, interviewing techniques, food science, sanitation, safety, and food management systems.

Dietetic technicians can become registered by completing the approved education and passing an examination offered by the Commission on Dietetic Registration. Individuals completing these requirements will be designated as Dietetic Technician, Registered or D.T.R.

Experience/Skills/Personality Traits

Dietetic technicians should enjoy working with and helping others. The ability to follow orders is necessary. Good communication skills, both verbal and written, are essential.

Dietetic technicians should have an interest in food and nutrition. Teaching skills are needed to teach and explain nutrition to others. The ability to make food both flavorful and visually attractive is necessary.

Unions/Associations

Dietetic technicians may obtain additional career information from the American Dietetic Association (ADA). This organization also provides professional support to its members.

Tips for Entry

1. If you are still in high school and considering becoming a dietetic technician, take classes in biology, chemistry, business math, health, home economics, and English.
2. Become registered even if it is not required. This designation will give you an edge over other applicants.
3. Job openings are often advertised in the classified section of newspapers under headings including "Dietetic Technician," "Dietary," "Health Care Food Services," "Hospitals," and "Food Service."
4. Send your resume and a cover letter to the personnel directors at hospitals, nursing homes, extended care facilities, schools, colleges, etc. Remember to ask that your resume be kept on file if there are no current openings.
5. You might also consider sending your resume to companies that provide food services to businesses, colleges, universities, hotels, etc.
6. Make contacts during your clinical experience and network.

NUTRITIONAL COUNSELOR

CAREER PROFILE

Duties: Analyzing nutritional needs of individuals; counseling them regarding eating habits and nutritional problems; planning nutritious, healthful meals

Alternate Title(s): Nutritionist

Salary Range: $21,000 to $85,000+

Employment Prospects: Good

Advancement Prospects: Fair

Best Geographical Location(s) for Position: Positions may be located throughout the country

Prerequisites:

Education or Training—Educational requirements vary from a one-year program through a master's degree in nutritional science

Experience—Experience in nutrition helpful

Special Skills and Personality Traits—Interest in and understanding of food and nutrition; teaching skills; communication skills; compassion; understanding

CAREER LADDER

```
┌─────────────────────────────────┐
│  Nutritional Counselor in Larger or │
│   More Prestigious Facility or   │
│          Self-Employed           │
└─────────────────────────────────┘

┌─────────────────────────────────┐
│      Nutritional Counselor       │
└─────────────────────────────────┘

┌─────────────────────────────────┐
│         College Student          │
└─────────────────────────────────┘
```

Position Description

Nutrition deals with the science of food and the way it affects the body. Studies have found that there is a major correlation between proper nutrition and better health. Nutritional counselors analyze nutrition programs for groups or individuals and conduct programs in order to control disease and promote good health.

Nutritional counselors may work with any individual interested in improving his or her diet and seeking good health and fitness. They may also work with professional, collegiate, or amateur athletes who are attempting to improve their performance. Nutritional counselors may work in hospitals, clinics, nursing homes, agencies, sports training camps, health clubs, or sports medicine clinics, or be self-employed.

One of the main functions of nutritional counselors is to plan nutritious, healthful meals and menus for their clients. In order to accomplish this, they must interview clients to determine the type of diet they are currently following, the specific physical activities they do routinely, and any medical problems. Counselors must also find out the likes and dislikes of clients.

Nutritional counselors analyze the nutritional requirements of clients based on this information as well as their height and weight. Counselors can then formulate a dietary plan of nutritious meals and snacks. They may also recommend dietary or nutritional supplements.

At times, nutritional counselors may be expected to find ways to motivate clients to eat properly. Planning a nutritious food program is useless unless someone can and will follow it. Counselors must explain the correlation between eating properly and good health and fitness.

Nutritional counselors may work on a one-on-one basis with clients or may plan menus for groups. They must help clients learn what specific foods or types of foods are most beneficial and may be expected to teach clients how to prepare foods in the most nutritious manner. They may teach clients ways to cut fat from their diet or explain why broiling food is better than frying.

Nutritional counselors may lecture to groups on nutrition and healthy eating patterns. They might also offer lessons on preparing food in healthy and tasty ways.

Nutritional counselors in hospitals or other health care facilities may work various shifts. Those who work in other types of businesses or are self-employed may have more normal working hours.

Salaries

Salaries of nutritional counselors can range from approximately $21,000 to $85,000 or more depending on the experience, education, responsibilities, and duties of the individual as well as the specific job. Another factor affecting earnings is the individual's reputation in the field. Generally, those with advanced education will earn more than individuals with lesser degrees. Those who work with well-known sports teams or athletes or in larger or more prestigious settings will earn more than their counterparts in other employment situations.

Employment Prospects

Employment prospects are good for nutritional counselors and getting better. Individuals may find employment throughout the country in hospitals, nursing homes, sports medicine clinics, schools, colleges, universities, professional sports teams, supermarket chains, health clubs, and food companies.

Advancement Prospects

Nutritional counselors can advance their careers by obtaining additional experience and/or education and locating a position in a more prestigious or larger facility. This will lead to increased responsibilities and earnings. Nutritional counselors may find jobs with sports teams, athletes, or celebrities. Some individuals climb the career ladder by becoming self-employed.

Education and Training

Educational requirements for nutritional counselors vary from job to job. Some positions require a minimum of a one-year program in nutrition. Others may prefer a two-year associates' degree in food and nutrition. A great many positions require a four-year college degree with a major in foods and nutrition. Some may even require a master's degree in nutrition.

Any continuing education in the form nars, and symposiums on nutrition and fo

Nutritional counselors may be requir members of the American Dietetic Association

Experience/Skills/Personality Traits

Nutritional counselors must have a keen interest in food and nutrition and should enjoy helping others. They should be personable, caring, compassionate people who know how to deal with and relate to individuals on a variety of levels.

Good verbal communication skills are needed. Teaching skills are needed to explain nutrition to others. Nutritional counselors should be healthy, fit people themselves with an understanding of exercise and fitness as well as nutrition.

Unions/Associations

While there are no specific trade associations for nutritional counselors, individuals may be members of the American Dietetic Association (ADA).

Tips for Entry

1. If you are still in high school and considering becoming a nutritional counselor take classes in biology, chemistry, math, health, counseling, and home economics.
2. Get registered by the American Dietetic Association (ADA) even if your job does not require it. This gives you a level of professional competence which others may not have.
3. Get as much education as you can in this field. The better your educational background, the better your chances of obtaining a job and advancing your career.
4. Contact health and fitness clubs and spas about openings. If they do not have a staff nutritional counselor, try to create a position for yourself. You may have to work part time at a couple of clubs in order to get your career started but it will be worth it.
5. Jobs may be advertised in newspapers' classified sections under headings such as "Nutritional Counselor," "Nutritionist," "Nutrition," "Health Clubs," "Spas," "Health Care," or "Dietary."

FOOD SERVICE WORKER

CAREER PROFILE

Duties: Assisting in the preparation and delivery of food trays to hospital patients

Alternate Title(s): Dietary Aide.

Salary Range: $16,000 to $24,000+

Employment Prospects: Good

Advancement Prospects: Poor

Best Geographical Location(s) for Position: Positions may be located throughout the country

Prerequisites:
Education or Training—On-the-job training
Experience—No experience necessary
Special Skills and Personality Traits—Ability to follow written and oral instructions; manual dexterity; communication skills

CAREER LADDER

```
┌─────────────────────────────┐
│   Food Service Supervisor   │
└─────────────────────────────┘

┌─────────────────────────────┐
│    Food Service Worker      │
└─────────────────────────────┘

┌─────────────────────────────┐
│        Entry Level          │
└─────────────────────────────┘
```

Position Description

Health care facilities such as hospitals, nursing homes, and long-term care facilities provide patients with meals and other nourishment. Food service workers are the individuals responsible for assisting in the preparation and delivery of food trays to these patients.

Food service workers may perform an array of routine functions in the kitchen, tray line, or dishwashing areas. Specific responsibilities depend on the size and structure of the dietary department.

Some food service workers may be responsible for stripping food carts and trays. They will have to sort and rinse dishes and/or silverware and prepare them for the dishwasher. Individuals may be responsible for loading and/or unloading the dishwasher. Food service workers may also be responsible for washing pots and pans or handling other cleaning duties.

Food service workers may be responsible for collecting trash and sorting cans, bottles, and other materials. They may then be expected to transport the trash and any recyclables to the proper areas.

Some food service workers assist in food preparation. They may, for example, prepare food in a blender for patients who are on soft or liquid diets.

Many food service workers work on a tray assembly line, serving food and beverages and stacking trays on carts. In order to accomplish this, food service workers are often given production orders so that they know what items are to go on each patient's tray. They must then check to be sure everything that is supposed to be on the tray is there.

Food service workers may be expected to bring tray carts to patients and serve each tray to the proper patient. After patients have eaten, food service workers are responsible for collecting and stacking dirty trays on the cart and returning the cart to the kitchen. Some also handle dishwashing and other clean-up duties.

Food service workers may work various shifts including mornings, days, evenings, or nights.

Salaries

Food service workers in hospitals or other health care facility settings can earn between $16,000 and $24,000 or more depending on the specific facility and its geographic location as well as the experience and responsibilities of the individual.

Employment Prospects

Employment prospects are good for food service workers in health care facilities. There are a variety of settings throughout the country in which individuals may find employment. These include hospitals, nursing homes, and long-term care facilities.

Advancement Prospects

Food service workers may advance their careers by obtaining training and/or experience. Some become head food service workers or food service supervisors, organizing and directing others in the area. With additional training a food service worker may become a hospital cook.

Education and Training

Generally, food service workers are trained on the job. Training may also be obtained in vocational-technical schools.

Experience/Skills/Personality Traits

Food service workers must have the ability to follow oral and written instructions. They should be able to stand on their feet for long periods of time. Good communication and interpersonal skills are helpful. Manual dexterity is needed.

Unions/Associations

Food service workers may be members of local health care unions. Additional information may be obtained by contacting the American Hospital Association (AHA).

Tips for Entry

1. Jobs are often advertised in the classified section of newspapers under headings such as "Food Service Worker," "Dietary Aide," "Health Care Food Services," and "Hospitals."

2. Send your resume and a cover letter to the personnel directors at hospitals, nursing homes, extended care facilities, etc. Remembers to ask that your resume be kept on file if there are no current openings.

3. You might also stop in at the personnel office of hospitals, nursing homes, extended care facilities, etc. to see if there are openings.

4. Many hospitals and schools hold career fairs. Visit one to see if this career is for you.

PHARMACEUTICALS

PHARMACIST

CAREER PROFILE

Duties: Dispensing drugs and medications; advising patients about side effects of drugs; compounding medications

Alternate Title(s): Registered Pharmacist; Community Pharmacist

Salary Range: $38,000 to $100,000+

Employment Prospects: Good

Advancement Prospects: Fair

Best Geographical Location(s) for Position: Positions may be located throughout the country

Prerequisites:

Education or Training—Five-year bachelor of science in pharmacy program

Experience—Supervised internship

Special Skills and Personality Traits—Understanding of drugs and interactions; good memory; computer skills; reliability; responsibility

CAREER LADDER

```
┌─────────────────────────────────┐
│  Director of Pharmacy Services   │
│      or Owner of Pharmacy        │
└─────────────────────────────────┘

┌─────────────────────────────────┐
│           Pharmacist             │
└─────────────────────────────────┘

┌─────────────────────────────────┐
│         College Student          │
└─────────────────────────────────┘
```

Position Description

Pharmacists are responsible for dispensing the drugs that physicians and other health practitioners prescribe for patients. They may mix preparations, deliver prescriptions, and package and label drugs and medications. They may advise physicians regarding the selection, dosage, and side effects of certain medications. Pharmacists may have a variety of other duties depending on the setting in which they are working.

Pharmacists are responsible for providing information to patients regarding medications and their use. They are expected to advise patients about any possible side effects of prescription drugs as well as interactions with other medications or foods. Individuals often answer customers' questions regarding possible adverse reactions from specific medications. They may also answer questions regarding over-the-counter medications.

Many pharmacies stock medical equipment and home health supplies, so pharmacists may offer advice on this type of merchandise. Depending on the type of pharmacy in which they work, individuals may also be expected to order other types of merchandise such as cosmetics, health and beauty aids, and other merchandise not related to medicine.

While most medications are produced by pharmaceutical companies, pharmacists are often called upon to compound ingredients to create actual medications. Compounding is the mixing of ingredients to form drugs including powders, tablets, capsules, ointments, and solutions.

Pharmacists working in hospitals or clinics may be expected to go on rounds with physicians. Other duties in this type of setting include making sterile solutions and monitoring drug regimens. Pharmacists often advise patients on how to use medications once they are discharged from the hospital or clinic. They may also be expected to order medical supplies.

It is essential to keep records of patients' drug therapies to make sure that dangerous drug interactions do not happen. Today, the majority of pharmacies are computerized. Pharmacists enter information into the computer for each customer. They may also print out information for patients on the side effects or interactions.

Depending on the specific employment situation, pharmacists may work regular hours or various work shifts. Those working in hospital or community pharmacies may work evenings, nights, weekends, or holidays.

Salaries

Earnings for pharmacists can vary greatly depending on a number of factors including the experience and responsibilities of the individual as well as the size, prestige, and geographic location of the specific pharmacy. Annual earnings may range from $38,000 to $100,000 or more. Those who own their own pharmacy may have higher earnings.

Employment Prospects

Employment prospects are good for pharmacists. Full- and part-time positions are available throughout the country. Individuals may find positions in any location housing a pharmacy. This includes hospitals, extended care facilities, medical centers, clinics, and health maintenance organizations (HMOs). There are also employment possibilities in retail pharmacies.

Advancement Prospects

Pharmacists may advance their careers by locating similar positions in larger or more pretigious pharmacies. Some individuals become store managers or pharmacy supervisors. Those working in hospitals or health care settings may land jobs as the director or assistant director of pharmacy services. Many individuals strive to climb the career ladder by opening up their own drug store.

Education and Training

In order to become a pharmacist an individual must go through a five-year pharmacy program at an accredited college. These programs lead to a bachelor of science in pharmacy degree. Those seeking a doctor of pharmacy degree must finish at least six years of school.

Requirements needed to enter a college of pharmacy vary. Some schools admit students directly after graduation from high school, while others require them to have one to two years of college-level pharmacy education. Some schools require applicants to pass the Pharmacy College Admission Test known as the P-CAT.

Pharmacists are required to be licensed to practice in the United States. In order to obtain a license, individuals must graduate from an accredited college of pharmacy, pass a state exam, and serve an internship under a licensed pharmacist.

Experience/Skills/Personality Traits

As noted previously, pharmacists obtain experience by serving an internship. Individuals must be responsible, reliable, and dependable. Successful pharmacists are personable people who enjoy helping others. Computer skills are essential to this job. Individuals must have a good memory.

Unions/Associations

Those aspiring to become pharmacists may contact the American Society of Hospital Pharmacists (ASHP), the American Association of Colleges of Pharmacy (AACP), or the National Association of Boards of Pharmacy (NABP) for additional career information.

Tips for Entry

1. Positions are often advertised in the classified section of newspapers under headings such as "Pharmacist," "Pharmacy," "Retail Pharmacy," "Health Care," "Hospitals," or "Community Pharmacist."
2. Send your resume and a short cover letter to the personnel directors at hospitals, nursing homes, extended care facilities, and health maintenance organizations (HMOs). Remember to ask that your resume be kept on file if there are no current openings.
3. Remember to register with your college placement office.
4. Contact retail pharmacies to inquire about job possibilities.
5. Every job has its positive and negative points. Decide whether you want to work in a small retail pharmacy, large chain store, or hospital.

PHARMACY TECHNICIAN

CAREER PROFILE

Duties: Assisting pharmacist in mixing preparations; delivering prescriptions; packaging and labeling drugs and medications

Alternate Title(s): Pharmacy Assistant

Salary Range: $22,000 to $30,000+

Employment Prospects: Fair

Advancement Prospects: Poor

Best Geographical Location(s) for Position: Positions may be located throughout the country

Prerequisites:

Education or Training—Five- to ten-month training program
Experience—No experience necessary
Special Skills and Personality Traits—Conscientiousness; attention to detail; math skills; reliability; organization

CAREER LADDER

```
┌─────────────────────────────────┐
│          Pharmacist             │
└─────────────────────────────────┘

┌─────────────────────────────────┐
│      Pharmacy Technician        │
└─────────────────────────────────┘

┌─────────────────────────────────┐
│      Student or Entry Level     │
└─────────────────────────────────┘
```

Position Description

Pharmacy technicians work under the direct supervision and direction of registered pharmacists. It is their responsibility to assist the pharmacist in a number of different areas. Specific duties will depend on the employment setting.

One of the main functions of the pharmacy technician is mixing preparations for prescriptions or filling routine orders for unit doses of pharmaceutical drugs. This is always done under the supervision of a pharmacist. Individuals may also be expected to deliver prescriptions. In some cases, the pharmacy technician will be asked to fill orders for nonprescription pharmaceuticals.

Individuals working in hospitals or other health care facilities are expected to deliver pharmaceutical orders to each nursing unit and to pick up pharmacy charge sheets from each department.

Another duty of the pharmacy technician is maintaining the pharmacy's stock. It is imperative that pharmacy technicians keep records of all drugs that are delivered to the pharmacy. They must read the instructions accompanying each drug that comes in to determine how it should be properly stored. Drugs and other pharmaceuticals must also be packaged and labeled when they arrive. If the pharmacy is short on items, pharmacy technicians are expected to advise supervisors and order supplies if requested. Pharmacy technicians are often responsible for figuring the cost and computing charges for different drugs.

Pharmacy technicians are expected to prepare and file reports and forms regarding activities in the pharmacy. They may also handle miscellaneous typing and filing and answer the phones.

Pharmacy technicians generally work a normal 40-hour week. Those working in hospitals or other health care facilities may work various shifts including nights, evenings, and weekends.

Pharmacy technicians are directly responsible to the registered pharmacist or pharmacist supervisor with whom they work.

Salaries

Pharmacy technicians can earn between approximately $22,000 and $30,000 or more annually depending on the education, experience, and responsibilities of the individual as well as the specific job setting and its geographic location.

In some facilities pharmacy technicians are unionized and have minimum earnings negotiated and set by the union.

Pharmacy technicians are often paid an hourly wage. This can start at approximately $9 per hour.

Employment Prospects

Employment prospects are fair for pharmacy technicians. Individuals may find positions in any location housing a pharmacy. These may include hospitals, extended care facilities, medical centers, clinics, and health maintenance organizations (HMOs). There are also employment possibilities in retail pharmacies.

Advancement Prospects

In order to advance their careers, pharmacy technicians must obtain additional training. Some individuals go back to school to become registered pharmacists.

Education and Training

Individuals interested in pursuing careers as pharmacy technicians must have a minimum of a high school diploma or its equivalent. They can then go on to a pharmacy technician program offered in a community or junior college. These programs last between five and ten months. There are also hospitals which offer similar training programs.

A small number of states require state licensing of pharmacy technicians.

Experience/Skills/Personality Traits

Pharmacy technicians must be able to follow orders. They should be detail-oriented, responsible, conscientious, and organized. Math skills are needed. An interest in science and technology is helpful.

Unions/Associations

Pharmacy technicians may become members of the American Association of Pharmacy Technicians (AAPT). This organization provides career information and professional guidance and support. Individuals interested in pursuing this career may also contact the American Council on Pharmaceutical Education (ACPE) to learn more about educational possibilities.

Tips for Entry

1. Positions are often advertised in the classified section of newspapers under headings such as "Pharmacy Technician," "Pharmacy Assistant," "Pharmacy," "Retail Pharmacy," "Health Care," or "Hospitals."
2. Send your resume and a short cover letter to the personnel directors at hospitals, nursing homes, extended care facilities, and health maintenance organizations (HMOs). Remember to ask that your resume be kept on file if there are no current openings.
3. Your college placement office may know of job openings.
4. Contact retail pharmacies to inquire about job possibilities.

MEDICAL RECORDS

MEDICAL RECORDS ADMINISTRATOR

CAREER PROFILE

Duties: Managing and overseeing medical records department; establishing policies, procedures, and standards; supervising employees in department

Alternate Title(s): Director of Medical Records

Salary Range: $40,000 to $80,000+

Employment Prospects: Good

Advancement Prospects: Good

Best Geographical Location(s) for Position: Positions may be located throughout the country

Prerequisites:

Education or Training—Bachelor's degree in medical record administration

Experience—Experience in medical records department helpful

Special Skills and Personality Traits—Conscientiousness; attention to detail; organization; communication skills, supervisory skills; analytical mind

CAREER LADDER

```
┌─────────────────────────────────────┐
│  Medical Records Administrator of    │
│  Larger or More Prestigious Facility │
└─────────────────────────────────────┘

┌─────────────────────────────────────┐
│  Medical Records Administrator       │
└─────────────────────────────────────┘

┌─────────────────────────────────────┐
│  Student or Medical Records          │
│  Technician                          │
└─────────────────────────────────────┘
```

Position Description

Medical records document patients' medical history, diagnosis, tests, treatment, and other pertinent information. The medical records department of a health care facility houses the records of all patients in one centralized location. Medical records technicians compile and record the data on each patient's medical history and retrieve it when necessary. The person in charge of the department is the medical records administrator.

The medical records administrator has a great deal of responsibility as the director of the department. He or she is expected not only to manage the department but to establish pertinent policies, procedures, and standards. The individual is responsible for supervising and overseeing all employees of the medical records department as well as the work they must complete.

In smaller facilities, the medical records administrator might also have the duties of the medical records technician. In larger facilities with numerous people on staff, the medical records administrator will be responsible for helping in the selection and hiring of staff employees. He or she will also oversee training of department members.

Depending on the specific job, the individual may be responsible for designing the information system to make sure that medical records can be input easily as well as stored, tracked, and retrieved efficiently. The medical records administrator is also responsible for ensuring that medical data and other medical records are kept confidential.

Information collected in medical records is used in a number of ways. In addition to being used for reimbursement from federal and state agencies, HMOs, and insurance companies, information may be utilized to diagnose and treat patients, to conduct research, and to study quality assurance issues. It is therefore imperative that the medical records administrator make sure that medical data is accurate. He or she is expected to monitor the quality of the work done by others in the department in areas including coding, transcription, analysis, filing, and statistics.

As the head of the department, the medical records administrator may be asked to attend administrative staff meetings. He or she is also expected to establish and maintain communications between the medical records department and the other departments within the facility and the medical staff.

Medical records administrators generally work a normal 40-hour week.

Salaries

Earnings for medical records administrators can range from $40,000 to $80,000+ or more depending on a number of variables. Generally, individuals working in larger facilities will have earnings at the higher end of the scale.

Employment Prospects

Employment prospects are good for medical records administrators. Individuals may find positions throughout the country in hospitals, medical centers, clinics, health maintenance organizations (HMOs), and group medical practices.

Advancement Prospects

Medical records administrators can advance their careers by obtaining additional experience and locating positions in larger or more prestigious facilities. This will result in increased responsibilities and earnings.

Education and Training

Medical records administrators must have a bachelor's degree in medical record administration. Courses include disease classification systems, statistics, computerized health information systems, legal issues regarding medical records, biology, and medical science and terminology.

Individuals who have a bachelor's degree in a different field may take a one-year post-baccalaureate certificate program in medical record administration.

Individuals must usually become a Registered Records Administrator (RRA) by passing a national accreditation exam.

Experience/Skills/Personality Traits

Medical records administrators should be detail-oriented, conscientious, organized individuals with good communication skills. They should possess supervisory skills and have aptitude for thinking analytically. An interest in data processing, statistics, and medical science is helpful in this career.

Unions/Associations

Medical records administrators may be members of the American Medical Records Association (AMRA). This group provides career information and offers professional support to members.

Tips for Entry

1. Most employers prefer or require individuals to be accredited.
2. Positions are often advertised in the classified section of newspapers under headings such as "Health Care," "Hospitals," "Medical Records," "Medical Records Administration," or "Medical Records Administrator."
3. Send your resume and a short cover letter to the personnel directors at hospitals, clinics, nursing homes, medical groups, and health maintenance organizations (HMOs). Remember to ask that your resume be kept on file if there are no current openings.
4. Smaller facilities may provide useful experience in handling the responsibilities of both medical records technician and administrator.
5. Make sure that the program you are planning on attending is accredited by the Committee on Allied Health Education and Accreditation (CAHEA) of the American Medical Association. The address is located in the appendix of this book.
6. College placement offices may know of job openings.
7. If you are still in high school, take courses in biology, chemistry, and math to help prepare you for education in this field.

MEDICAL RECORDS TRANSCRIPTIONIST

CAREER PROFILE

Duties: Inputting information into medical record system; transcribing letters, medical reports, and other medical data

Alternate Title(s): None

Salary Range: $23,000 to $36,000+

Employment Prospects: Fair

Advancement Prospects: Fair

Best Geographical Location(s) for Position: Positions may be located throughout the country

Prerequisites:
  Education or Training—On-the-job training or training program in community or junior college
  Experience—No experience necessary
  Special Skills and Personality Traits—Computer and typing skills; conscientiousness; attention to detail; organization

CAREER LADDER

```
┌─────────────────────────────────────┐
│   Medical Records Transcription      │
│   Coordinator or Supervisor or       │
│   Medical Records Technician         │
└─────────────────────────────────────┘


┌─────────────────────────────────────┐
│   Medical Records Transcriptionist   │
└─────────────────────────────────────┘


┌─────────────────────────────────────┐
│       Student or Entry Level         │
└─────────────────────────────────────┘
```

Position Description

Medical records transcriptionists work in the medical records department, taking information supplied by physicians and inputting it into the medical record information system. Medical records transcriptionists must know how to use a variety of office equipment, including transcribing equipment, photocopiers, typewriters, word processors, and computers.

The medical records transcriptionists may have varied duties depending on the size of their department or the medical facility. They may be asked to transcribe letters, medical reports, or other important medical data.

It is imperative that medical records transcriptionists make sure all information is accurate. They must not only proofread all work that is done but also check the accuracy of information provided, such as a patient's name, address, and hospital ID number. After information is transcribed and records are completed, medical records transcriptionists are expected to make copies and forward information to the proper people for approval and any necessary signatures.

In order to assure that records are done in a timely fashion, medical records transcriptionists often are expected to develop daily reports detailing names of reports that were done as well as the dates they were received and transcribed.

Depending on the specific situation, medical records transcriptionists may be expected to answer telephones, give messages, and assist others in the medical records department.

Medical records transcriptionists generally work a normal 40-hour week. When there is a heavy work load, they may be asked to work overtime.

Salaries

Medical records transcriptionists can earn between $23,000 and $36,000 or more depending on the education, experience, and responsibilities of the individual as well as the specific job setting, facility size, and its geographic location. In some facilities medical records transcriptionists are unionized, and their earnings are negotiated and set by the union.

Employment Prospects

Employment prospects are fair for medical records transcriptionists. Individuals may find positions throughout the country in hospitals, medical centers, clinics, health maintenance organizations (HMOs), and group medical practices.

Advancement Prospects

In order to advance their career, medical records transcriptionists must obtain additional experience and/or education. They may become transcription coordinators or supervisors. Individuals can also study to become a medical records technician.

Education and Training

Individuals interested in pursuing careers as medical records transcriptionists must have a minimum of a high school diploma or its equivalent. From there they can either take a course in a local community or junior college or receive on-the-job training.

Experience/Skills/Personality Traits

Medical records transcriptionists must be detail-oriented, conscientious, and organized. Individuals must be computer competent and have excellent typing skills. The ability to pick up medical terminology and an interest in medical science is helpful to success in this career.

Unions/Associations

Those interested in a career in this field may become members of the American Association of Medical Transcription (AAMT). This organization can provide additional career information and professional guidance and support.

Tips for Entry

1. Take typing classes in school to make sure you are a quick and accurate typist.
2. You should also try to take a couple of computer courses to become comfortable working on a computer.
3. Positions are often advertised in the classified section of newspapers under headings such as "Health Care," "Hospitals," "Medical Records," or "Medical Records Transcriptionist."
4. Send your resume and a short cover letter to the personnel directors at hospitals, clinics, nursing homes, medical groups, and health maintenance organizations (HMOs). Remember to ask that your resume be kept on file if there are no current openings.

MEDICAL RECORDS TECHNICIAN

CAREER PROFILE

Duties: Recording data on patients' medical history; assembling and storing medical records; coding procedures; retrieving data

Alternate Title(s): Health Information Technician; Medical Records Coder; Coder Specialist

Salary Range: $23,000 to $34,000

Employment Prospects: Good

Advancement Prospects: Good

Best Geographical Location(s) for Position: Positions may be located throughout the country

Prerequisites:

Education or Training—Two-year formal training program in medical records technology leading to an associate's degree

Experience—Experience as medical records clerk helpful, but not required

Special Skills and Personality Traits—Computer and typing skills; conscientiousness; attention to detail; organization; communication skills

CAREER LADDER

```
┌─────────────────────────────────┐
│   Medical Records Administrator   │
│        or Director of Medical     │
│         Records Department        │
└─────────────────────────────────┘

┌─────────────────────────────────┐
│    Medical Records Technician     │
└─────────────────────────────────┘

┌─────────────────────────────────┐
│             Student               │
└─────────────────────────────────┘
```

Position Description

Physicians, nurses, and other medical personnel require medical records on patients so they can easily find out what procedures, medications, and tests have been administered and what the results were. Medical records technicians are responsible for compiling and recording data on each patient's medical history and retrieving it when necessary.

Medical records technicians may have varied duties depending on the size of the facility in which they work. In larger facilities the medical records technician may have more specialized duties. In smaller facilities, he or she may be responsible for an entire department.

Medical records technicians may also be called health information technicians. Individuals in this field who specialize in coding information are referred to as medical records coders or coding specialists.

Medical records technicians record information on each patient. This may include the patient's symptoms, medical history, results of examinations, lab test reports, diagnoses,

and treatments. Individuals are responsible for making sure that each patient's medical chart is complete and that forms are identified and signed.

Medical records technicians must assign a classification code to each diagnosis and procedure that has been performed on a patient. This is often done by consulting a classification manual. Each symptom, disease, diagnosis, operation, and treatment has a code assigned to it. Using this method, each procedure will have a similar code no matter which facility it was performed in. This is important for reimbursement requirements. Codes are used for billing/payment to and from insurance companies and other reimbursement agencies.

Computer software programs are also utilized to assign patients to a diagnosis-related group commonly known as a DRG. The DRG is important in that it determines the amount of money the facility will be reimbursed by Medicare or other insurance programs.

Medical records technicians may be responsible for tabulating and analyzing data. This information may be used for a variety of reasons including improving patient care, research, and controlling costs.

The medical records technician is expected to input all compiled data and information into the computer system. This information is then stored until retrieval is necessary. It is essential this be done in a timely manner so that the health care facility can receive proper reimbursements.

Medical records technicians generally work a normal 40-hour week. However, some medical records departments are open 24 hours a day. In these cases, individuals may work various shifts including weekends or nights.

Salaries

Medical records technicians may have annual earnings ranging from $23,000 to $34,000 or more depending on the education, experience, and responsibilities of the individuals as well as the specific setting, size, and geographic location of the facility. Accredited individuals may have higher earnings. Some medical records technicians working in unionized settings will have minimum earnings set by the union.

Employment Prospects

Employment prospects are good for medical records technicians. Individuals may find positions throughout the country in hospitals, medical centers, clinics, health maintenance organizations (HMOs), and group medical practices.

Advancement Prospects

Advancement prospects are good for medical records technicians. Individuals can advance their careers by obtaining experience and/or education and locating administrative or management positions as section supervisors, directors of medical records departments, or medical records administrators.

Other medical records technicians advance their careers by specializing in various areas such as coding.

Education and Training

Recommended education for medical records technicians is a two-year formal training program leading to an associate's degree. These programs are offered at community and junior colleges throughout the country. Training includes courses in medical terminology and diseases, anatomy, physiology, legal issues relating to medical records, coding and abstraction of data, statistics, databases, quality assurance methods, and computers.

An optional method of training is offered by the American Medical Records Association (AMRA). This is an independent study program of 17 modules offered by mail. Individuals in this program must take approximately 30 semester hours of classes at a local college.

Accreditation is available through the American Health Information Management Association (AHIMA). In order to become accredited, individuals must graduate from a program accredited by the Committee on Allied Health Education and Accreditation (CAHEA) of the American Medical Association and pass a written examination.

Experience/Skills/Personality Traits

Medical records technicians must be detail-oriented, conscientious, organized individuals. Computer and typing skills are essential to this job. Communications skills are necessary. An interest in medical science is helpful.

Unions/Associations

Medical records technicians may belong to unions in health care settings. They may also be members of the American Medical Records Association (AMRA). This group provides career information and offers professional support to members.

Tips for Entry

1. Most employers prefer to hire individuals who are accredited.
2. Positions are often advertised in the classified section of newspapers under headings such as "Health Care," "Hospitals," "Medical Records," "Medical Records Technicians," or "Health Information Technicians."
3. Send your resume and a short cover letter to the personnel directors at hospitals, clinics, nursing homes, medical groups, and health maintenance organizations (HMOs). Remember to ask that your resume be kept on file if there are no current openings.
4. Make sure that the program you are planning to attend is accredited by the Committee on Allied Health Education and Accreditation (CAHEA) of the American Medical Association. The address is located in the appendix of this book.
5. College placement offices may know of job openings.
6. The most marketable individuals are those who are trained in specialties. Continue your education.

RADIOLOGY AND BIOTECHNOLOGY

RADIATION THERAPY TECHNOLOGIST

CAREER PROFILE

Duties: Preparing patients for radiation treatment; administering radiation

Alternate Title(s): Radiation Therapist

Salary Range: $30,000 to $60,000+

Employment Prospects: Excellent

Advancement Prospects: Good

Best Geographical Location(s) for Position: Positions may be located throughout the country

Prerequisites:

Education or Training—Two-year associate's degree program or hospital-based training program
Experience—Experience working with cancer patients helpful, but not required
Special Skills and Personality Traits—Compassion; emotional stability; mechanical abilities; ability to follow instructions

CAREER LADDER

```
┌─────────────────────────────────────┐
│   Radiation Therapy Supervisor       │
└─────────────────────────────────────┘

┌─────────────────────────────────────┐
│   Radiation Therapy Technologist     │
└─────────────────────────────────────┘

┌─────────────────────────────────────┐
│   Student, X-Ray Technician,         │
│   Nurse, Radiographer, etc.          │
└─────────────────────────────────────┘
```

Position Description

Radiation therapy technologists have an important job in the treatment of cancer. Their main functions are to prepare cancer patients for radiation treatment and to administer radiation in order to halt or slow the growth of cancer cells.

Radiation therapy technologists must administer prescribed doses of ionizing radiation to specific body parts. This is done with a variety of equipment, such as high-energy linear accelerators with electron capabilities. Radiation therapy technologists must accurately position patients under the equipment so that the affected body part is treated while the rest of the body is protected from radiation.

Patients are often frightened of both the disease and the treatment. Radiation therapy technologists help patients understand what will be occurring by explaining the treatment and possible side effects. They also try to make patients feel comfortable while easing as much of their anxiety as possible. In many situations, the individual is also responsible for reassuring patients' families regarding the procedures.

Radiation therapy technologists must carefully observe patients during each treatment to check for reactions and side effects to the radiation. These may include nausea, hair loss, and skin irritation. Radiation therapy technologists keep records on patients and perform follow-ups to chart their progress.

As patients must usually have more than one treatment, radiation therapy technologists generally see the same patient a number of times. They therefore may build a close relationship with certain patients. Psychologically, it is often difficult to treat extremely ill or dying people on a daily basis. However, many in this field feel that they are helping some patients live productive lives.

Salaries

Radiation therapy technologists may earn between $30,000 and $60,000 or more depending on the experience, education, and responsibilities of the individual as well as the specific employment setting, size, and its geographic location.

Employment Prospects

Employment prospects are excellent for radiation therapy technologists. With the increased occurrence of cancer in the country, more and more people are needed for this job.

Individuals may find employment throughout the country in hospitals, physicians' offices, HMOs, and clinics.

Advancement Prospects

Radiation therapy technologists may advance their careers by obtaining more experience and training. Individuals may locate similar positions in larger or more prestigious facilities leading to increased responsibilities and earnings. They may also find supervisory or administrative positions.

Education and Training

Radiation therapy technologists must go through a formal educational training program. Individuals may either go through a hospital-based program or community or junior college program leading to an associate's degree. It is important to make sure that the program is accredited through the Committee on Allied Health Education and Accreditation (CAHEA).

Courses include medical ethics, methods of patient care, oncology, pathology, anatomy and physiology, radiation physics, radiation techniques, and clinical dosimetry.

Individuals who have worked in health care such as nurses, medical technologists, or radiographers may be able to take one-year certificate programs in this field.

Radiation therapy technologists must be licensed. This is accomplished by graduating from an accredited program and passing a national certification examination given by the American Registry of Radiologic Technologists (ARRT).

Experience/Skills/Personality Traits

Radiation therapy technologists should be compassionate people who like to help others. Emotional stability is necessary. The ability to make patients feel comfortable and put them at ease is essential to success in this field.

Radiation therapy technologists should be mechanically inclined individuals. A familiarity with medical terminology is useful. Individuals must be able to follow instructions. Communication skills are imperative. The ability to work with patients who are very ill is essential.

Unions/Associations

Individuals interested in pursing a career in this field can obtain additional career information from the American Society of Radiologic Technologists (ASRT) or the American Registry of Radiologic Technologists (ARRT).

Tips for Entry

1. Volunteer in the oncology unit of a local hospital to see if you like working in this type of atmosphere.
2. A strong background in math and science is helpful in this field. If you are still in school, take classes in this area.
3. Continue your education. This will help make you more marketable and give you the opportunity to earn higher salaries.
4. Jobs in this field are often advertised in the classified section of newspapers under headings such as "Radiation Therapy," "Radiation Therapy Technologist," "Cancer Care," "Health Care," or "Health Care Professional."
5. Send your resume and a cover letter to hospitals with a cancer care unit. Remember to ask that your resume be kept on file if there are no current openings.
6. Many high schools, vocational-technology schools, junior or community colleges, and hospitals hold health fair career days. These are a good way to learn more about careers in this field and talk to people who are already in the profession.

NUCLEAR MEDICINE TECHNOLOGIST

CAREER PROFILE

Duties: Administering radiopharmaceuticals; operating diagnostic imaging equipment; preparing correct dosage of radiopharmaceuticals

Alternate Title(s): None

Salary Range: $27,000 to $51,000+

Employment Prospects: Good

Advancement Prospects: Good

Best Geographical Location(s) for Position: Positions may be located throughout the country

Prerequisites:

Education or Training—Nuclear Medicine Technology program ranging from one to four years

Experience—Experience in health care helpful, but not necessary

Special Skills and Personality Traits—Ability to put others at ease; communication skills; computer skills; personableness; compassion; emotional stability; physical stamina

CAREER LADDER

```
Nuclear Medicine Technology
Supervisor or Chief Technologist
```

```
Nuclear Medicine Technologist
```

```
Radiologic Technologist, Ultrasound
Technologist, or Student
```

Position Description

Nuclear medicine technologists work with advanced equipment to diagnose and treat disease. Nuclear medicine uses unstable atoms called radionuclides which emit radiation spontaneously. These radionuclides are purified and compounded like other drugs and form radiopharmaceuticals. Nuclear medicine may be used to assist doctors in the diagnosis and treatment of a number of diseases including cancer, heart disease, and Alzheimer's disease.

Nuclear medicine technologists are responsible for administering radiopharmaceuticals to patients. They must then monitor the characteristics and functions of tissues or organs in which they localize. Concentrations of radioactivity that are higher or lower than normal indicate abnormalities.

One of the functions of nuclear medicine technologists is to operate cameras that detect and map the radioactive drug in a patient's body. This creates an image on photographic film. Nuclear medicine technologists also operate diagnostic imaging equipment, which creates an image by projecting an X ray through the patient.

Nuclear medicine technologists are responsible for preparing the correct dosage of the radiopharmaceuticals. They may administer them by mouth, injection, or other means. It is imperative to adhere to safety standards when preparing radiopharmaceuticals in order to keep the dose of radiation, which can affect both the patient and the workers, as low as possible.

Nuclear medicine technologists are expected to explain test procedures to patients, and often to their families. This is usually a scary time for both, so the individual must be patient and show a great deal of compassion. Often, a small amount of reassurance from the technologist can make the patient feel more comfortable and less frightened.

Before a treatment, the nuclear medicine technologist must position the patient and make sure that the patient has been properly prepared for the treatment. The individual then turns on a gama scintillation camera or scanner. This will create the images of the distribution of the radiopharmaceutical as it passes through or localizes in the patient's body. Images are produced on a computer screen or film and a physician will interpret them later.

The nuclear medicine technologist must monitor each patient's condition during the procedure and record the patient's condition.

Other functions of the nuclear medicine technologist may include keeping patient records and recording the amount and type of radionuclides each patients receives and the amount that is disposed of. He or she will prepare reports and give images, data analysis, and other pertinent patient information to the physician.

Nuclear medicine technologists usually work a normal 40-hour week. Depending on the shifts they are assigned, individuals may work days, evenings, nights, or weekends.

Salaries

Nuclear medicine technologists may earn between $27,000 and $51,000 or more depending on a number of factors. These include the experience, education, and responsibilities of the individual as well as the specific employment setting, size, and its geographic location.

Employment Prospects

Employment prospects are excellent for nuclear medicine technologists. Individuals may find employment throughout the country in hospitals, medical centers, nursing homes, public health agencies, and imaging centers.

Advancement Prospects

Nuclear medicine technologists may take a number of paths to career advancement. With additional experience and/or education individuals may become supervisors, chief technologists, or department administrators. Other individuals climb the career ladder by specializing in clinical areas. Some nuclear medicine technologists teach or take positions in research laboratories.

Education and Training

Individuals aspiring to become nuclear medicine technologists may go through nuclear medicine technology programs ranging from one to four years. Depending on the program, individuals may obtain a certificate, associate's degree, or bachelor's degree.

Certificate programs are often offered in hospitals. Accredited degree programs may be located in community or junior colleges, four-year colleges, and universities. In many situations, health professionals such as radiologic technologists and ultrasound technologists take a one-year certificate program so they may specialize in nuclear medicine.

Courses include physical sciences, biological effects of radiation exposure, radiation protection and procedure, imaging techniques, computer applications, and the use of radio-pharmaceuticals.

Certain states require nuclear medicine technologists to be licensed. Voluntary certification is also available through the American Registry of Radiologic Technologists (ARRT) and the Nuclear Medicine Technology Certification Board (NMTCB).

Experience/Skills/Personality Traits

Nuclear medicine technologists should be compassionate people who like to help others. Emotional stability is necessary. Physical stamina is essential as individuals must often be on their feet for long hours and may be required to lift or turn disabled patients. The ability to make patients feel comfortable and put them at ease is also necessary. Individuals should have good communication skills and interact well with others. Computer skills are needed.

Unions/Associations

Individuals interested in pursuing a career in this field can obtain additional career information from the Society of Nuclear Medicine Technologists Section (SNMTS), the American Society of Radiologic Technologists (ASRT), or the American Registry of Radiologic Technologists (ARRT).

Tips for Entry

1. It is important to make sure that the program you select is accredited through the Committee on Allied Health Education and Accreditation (CAHEA). Their address is located in the appendix in the back of this book.
2. Get certified and/or registered. Employers generally prefer to hire certified or registered people.
3. Part-time opportunities are often available in this field.
4. Jobs in this field are often advertised in the classified section of newspapers under headings such as "Nuclear Medicine," "Nuclear Medicine Technologist," "Health Care," or "Health Care Professional."
5. Send your resume and a cover letter to hospitals and imaging centers. Remember to ask that your resume be kept on file if there are no current openings.
6. Many high schools, vocational-technology schools, junior or community colleges, and hospitals hold health fair career days. These programs are a good way to learn more about careers in this field and talk to people who are already in the profession.

DIAGNOSTIC MEDICAL SONOGRAPHER

CAREER PROFILE

Duties: Operating ultrasound equipment; explaining procedure to patient; setting up machines; taking images

Alternate Title(s): Medical Sonographer; Sonographer

Salary Range: $31,000 to $48,000+

Employment Prospects: Excellent

Advancement Prospects: Fair

Best Geographical Location(s) for Position: Positions may be located throughout the country

Prerequisites:
   Education or Training—Formal training program in diagnostic medical sonography
   Experience—Experience working in health care helpful
   Special Skills and Personality Traits—Mechanical abilities; communication skills; personableness; ability to put others at ease

CAREER LADDER

```
┌─────────────────────────────────┐
│  Diagnostic Medical Sonographer  │
│      in Specialized Area or      │
│      Department Supervisor       │
└─────────────────────────────────┘

┌─────────────────────────────────┐
│  Diagnostic Medical Sonographer  │
└─────────────────────────────────┘

┌─────────────────────────────────┐
│  Student or Health Professional  │
│     from Other Health Fields     │
└─────────────────────────────────┘
```

Position Description

Ultrasound is a procedure that uses non-ionizing, high-frequency sound waves. These are aimed into areas of a patient's body, and with the proper equipment, doctors can visualize internal parts of the body. Ultrasound procedures are used to aid physicians in diagnosing disease and injuries. Diagnostic medical sonographers are the individuals who work with this equipment and run procedures.

Diagnostic medical sonographers are responsible for working the equipment that collects the reflected echoes of sound waves. These echoes form an image which can be viewed on a screen. The diagnostic medical sonographer can then record the image on a printout strip or photograph it for interpretation and diagnosis by a doctor.

The sonographer takes the patient's medical history, explains the procedure to the patient, and answers any questions that may arise. The individual must make sure that the patient is as comfortable as possible. The sonographer then sets up the machines to take the best possible picture of the area that needs testing. After that the sonographer will position the patient for the procedure.

The sonographer must view the screen as the scans are occurring. In this way, he or she can look for small differences between healthy and pathological areas. The individual must make sure that images are satisfactory for diagnostic purposes.

Some sonographers specialize in specific areas. These can include vascular, neurosonography, echocardiography, abdominal, obstetrics/gynocology, or ophthalmology.

Diagnostic medical sonographers may work full or part time. They can work varied shifts including days, evenings, nights, and weekends.

Salaries

Diagnostic medical sonographers may earn between $31,000 and $48,000 or more depending on the experience, education, and responsibilities of the individual as well as the specific employment setting, size, and its geographic location.

Employment Prospects

Employment prospects are excellent for diagnostic medical sonographers. Individuals may find employment throughout the country in hospitals, physicians' offices, clinics, and imaging centers. Part-time opportunities are available.

Advancement Prospects

Diagnostic medical sonographers may advance their careers by obtaining more experience and training. Individuals may locate similar positions in larger or more prestigious facilities leading to increased responsibilities and earnings. They may also find supervisory or administrative positions. Some sonographers specialize in specific areas. Others go into teaching or research.

Education and Training

Diagnostic medical sonographers must go through a formal educational training program in diagnostic medical sonography. Individual education may range in length from one to four years and lead to either a certificate, associate's degree, or bachelor's degree.

One-year programs are usually designed for people who have worked in other health care occupations and want to change their field or specialize in sonography. It is important to make sure that programs are accredited through the Committee on Allied Health Education and Accreditation (CAHEA).

Some states may require licensing. Voluntary certification is available through the American Registry of Diagnostic Medical Sonographers (ARDMS).

Experience/Skills/Personality Traits

Diagnostic medical sonographers should be able to make patients feel comfortable and put them at ease. Communication skills are needed. Individuals must be compassionate and deal well with others.

Sonographers should be mechanically inclined individuals who like operating high-tech equipment. An interest in anatomy and physiology is helpful. A familiarity with medical terminology is most useful.

Unions/Associations

Individuals interested in pursuing a career in this field can obtain additional career information from the Society of Diagnostic Medical Sonographers (SDMS) and the American Registry of Diagnostic Medical Sonographers (ARDMS).

Tips for Entry

1. Diagnostic medical sonographer programs often prefer applicants who have a background in science and math.
2. Most employers prefer to hire individuals who are registered. Make sure you get your certification.
3. Continue your education. This will make you more marketable and enable you to earn higher salaries.
4. Jobs in this field are often advertised in the classified section of newspapers under headings such as "Diagnostic Medical Sonographer," "Medical Sonographer," "Sonographer," "Health Care," or "Health Care Professional."
5. Send your resume and a cover letter to hospitals, clinics, and diagnostic imaging centers. Remember to ask that your resume be kept on file if there are no current openings.

TECHNICIANS AND TECHNOLOGISTS

SURGICAL TECHNOLOGIST

CAREER PROFILE

Duties: Preparing and setting up operating room; prepping patients for surgery; assisting surgeons during surgery

Alternate Title(s): Operating Room Technician; Private Scrub

Salary Range: $24,000 to $35,000+

Employment Prospects: Good

Advancement Prospects: Good

Best Geographical Location(s) for Position: Positions may be located throughout the country

Prerequisites:

Education or Training—Formal training program lasting from nine to 24 months

Experience—No experience necessary

Special Skills and Personality Traits—Manual dexterity; ability to follow instructions; emotional stability; responsibility; ability to respond quickly

CAREER LADDER

```
┌─────────────────────────────────┐
│  Surgical Technologist First    │
│  Assistant or Surgical Assistant│
│  in Specialized Field of Surgery│
└─────────────────────────────────┘

┌─────────────────────────────────┐
│      Surgical Technologist       │
└─────────────────────────────────┘

┌─────────────────────────────────┐
│            Student               │
└─────────────────────────────────┘
```

Position Description

Surgical technologists work in operating rooms of hospitals, clinics, and surgi-centers. They have a wide array of responsibilities before, during, and after operations. Individuals work under the supervision of surgeons and registered nurses. Duties will be dependent on the training individuals have gone through.

Surgical technologists are responsible for helping set up the operating room. This can include making sure there are surgical instruments, equipment, sterile linens, and necessary fluids in the room. Surgical technologists also assemble nonsterile equipment and make sure it is working properly.

Other responsibilities of surgical technologists include preparing patients for operating procedures. This might entail washing, shaving, and disinfecting incision sites.

Surgical technologists should make patients feel more at ease. To do this, they may talk to the patients and help calm them as much as possible.

Surgical technologists transport patients to the correct operating room. They must then position patients on the operating table and cover them with sterile surgical drapes.

Before the operation, the surgical technologists help the surgical team scrub and assist them in putting on the sterile gloves, gowns, and masks that are necessary to keep the environment sterile.

During surgery surgical technologists pass instruments and other sterile supplies to surgeons or surgeon assistants. They may also hold retractors, cut sutures, and count sponges, needles, supplies, and other instruments. During some procedures, surgical technologists may be responsible for operating certain equipment such as sterilizers, lights, or suction machines. In some cases, surgical technologists prepare specimens and bring them to the lab for analysis. They might also help apply dressings.

After an operation is completed, surgical technologists are responsible for bringing the patient back to the recovery room. They may also be expected to restock the operating room and prepare it for the next operation.

Surgical technologists may work various hours including evenings, nights, and weekends. Individuals may also be on call for emergencies.

Salaries

Surgical technologists can have annual earnings ranging from $24,000 to $35,000 or more. Variables affecting earnings include the training, experience, and responsibilities of the individual as well as the specific job setting. Generally, the more training the surgical technologist has, the higher his or her earnings.

Employment Prospects

Employment prospects are good for surgical technologists. Individuals may work in various employment settings including hospitals, surgi-centers, clinics, and offices of physicians practicing outpatient surgery.

Advancement Prospects

Advancement prospects are good for surgical technologists. Individuals may advance their careers by obtaining additional training. There are a number of different paths for surgical technologists to pursue. Some individuals specialize in a particular area of surgery. Others climb the career ladder by becoming first assistants.

Education and Training

Surgical technologists must go through formal accredited programs. These are offered in junior colleges, community colleges, vocational schools, universities, hospitals, and the military.

Programs may be between nine and 24 months in duration and may lead to either a certificate, diploma, or associate's degree. Programs include classroom study and supervised clinical experience.

Voluntary certification is offered through the Liaison Council on Certification for the Surgical Technologist. In order to become certified, individuals must graduate from a formal accredited program and pass a national certification exam. To maintain certification, surgical technologists must continue their education or take another exam.

Experience/Skills/Personality Traits

Surgical technologists should be emotionally stable, responsible, and conscientious individuals. They should have manual dexterity and a familiarity with medical terminology is needed. Individuals need to be able to follow instructions and respond quickly.

Unions/Associations

Surgical technologists may be members of the Association of Surgical Technologists (AST). This organization provides professional guidance to members.

Tips for Entry

1. Jobs in this field are often advertised in the classified section of newspapers under headings such as "Surgical Technologist," "Health Care," "Operating Room Technician," or "Private Scrub."
2. Send your resume and a cover letter to the personnel directors at hospitals and surgi-centers. Remember to ask that your resume be kept on file if there are no current openings.
3. The key to success in this field is to continue your education. Specialization will help make you more marketable and give you the opportunity to earn a high salary.
4. While certification is voluntary, it does give one applicant an edge over another.

CARDIOLOGY TECHNOLOGIST

CAREER PROFILE

Duties: Preparing patients for procedures; assisting physicians in cardiac catheterizations, balloon angioplasty, and other procedures; monitoring blood gasses

Alternate Title(s): Cardiovascular Technologist

Salary Range: $26,000 to $39,000+

Employment Prospects: Good

Advancement Prospects: Fair

Best Geographical Location(s) for Position: Positions may be located throughout the country

Prerequisites:

Education or Training—Two-year college program

Experience—Experience working or volunteering in health care helpful

Special Skills and Personality Traits—Mechanical aptitude; communication skills; personableness; reliability; ability to put others at ease

CAREER LADDER

```
┌─────────────────────────────────┐
│  Cardiology Technologist in Larger │
│    or More Prestigious Facility    │
│      or in Specialized Field       │
└─────────────────────────────────┘

┌─────────────────────────────────┐
│      Cardiology Technologist      │
└─────────────────────────────────┘

┌─────────────────────────────────┐
│  Nurse's Aide, EKG Technician,    │
│       or College Student          │
└─────────────────────────────────┘
```

Position Description

As some people age, their blood vessels become blocked. This blockage can lead to heart and blood vessel diseases. Physicians utilize specialized procedures to determine if blockages exist in patients' blood vessels. One of these procedures is called cardiac catheterization. Cardiology technologists specialize in helping physicians perform cardiac catheterizations. The procedure is invasive and is done by winding a small tube called a catheter through a blood vessel in the patient's leg to his or her heart.

When blockages are found, cardiology technologists may also assist the physician in performing balloon angioplasty. In this procedure, technologists assist the doctor by inserting a catheter with a balloon on the end to the point of the obstruction.

Cardiology technologists have a number of responsibilities. The first is to position patients on the examination table and make them as comfortable as possible. In order to perform this procedure correctly, the technologist must clean and shave the patient's leg and administer a local anesthesia to the leg near the groin.

Cardiology technologists are expected to monitor patients' blood gases as well as their heart rate. This is done with special EKG equipment. If the technologist notices changes, he or she must notify the physician.

The cardiology technologist often assists physicians in other cardiovascular procedures. These may include preparing and monitoring patients during open heart surgery or the implantation of pacemakers. Some cardiology technologists with special training assist physicians in noninvasive peripheral vascular tests using ultrasound equipment. This equipment transmits sound waves to form images on a screen.

Cardiology technologists may be responsible for clerical duties such as scheduling appointments, maintaining patients' files, caring for equipment, and typing physicians' interpretations of procedure results.

Salaries

Cardiology technologists can earn between $26,000 and $39,000 or more annually, depending on the education, experience, and responsibilities of the individual. Other variables include the specific facility and its location.

Employment Prospects

Employment prospects are good for cardiology technologists because of the increased numbers of older people with heart disease in the population. Individuals may find employment in a number of settings including hospitals, medical centers, cardiologists' offices, health maintenance organizations (HMOs), cardiac rehabilitation centers, clinics, and nursing homes.

Advancement Prospects

With additional training and/or experience cardiology technologists can move into specialized positions or find similar positions in larger facilities. These will lead to increased earnings and responsibilities.

Education and Training

Cardiology technologists need to complete a two-year college program. These are offered at both junior and community colleges. One year of this program includes core courses. The second year includes specialized instruction in either invasive, noninvasive, or noninvasive peripheral cardiology.

Individuals who have experience in an allied health profession may have the first year of core courses waived.

Experience/Skills/Personality Traits

Some individuals enter this field from other positions in health care, such as nurse's aides or EKG technicians. Some people have had no experience in health care prior to going to school to pursue this career.

Cardiology technologists must have the ability to put others at ease. Interpersonal and communication skills are necessary. Individuals should be personable, reliable people with a mechanical aptitude. The ability to follow instructions is essential.

Unions/Associations

Individuals interested in becoming cardiology technologists should contact the American Society for Cardiovascular Professionals (ASCP), the Society of Vascular Technology (SVT), and the American College of Cardiology.

Tips for Entry

1. Jobs in this field are often advertised in the classified section of newspapers under headings such as "Cardiologist Technologist," "Cardiac Rehabilitation," "Cardiac Clinic," "Health Care," "Health Care Professional," or "Cardiovascular Technologist."
2. Send your resume and a cover letter to cardiologists' offices, cardiac rehabilitation centers, cardiac clinics, and hospitals. Remember to ask that your resume be kept on file if there are no current openings.
3. Talk to a cardiology technologist at a hospital or nursing home to learn more about career opportunities.
4. Volunteer at a hospital or nursing home while you are still in school to make sure you like working in this type of setting.
5. Remember to check with the placement office at your college to see if they are aware of any job openings.
6. Continue your education. This will help make you more marketable and give you the opportunity to earn a higher salary.
7. If you are hooked into one of the Internet services, locate and log onto the section dealing with careers. Seek out the job classification in which you have an interest.

EEG TECHNOLOGIST

CAREER PROFILE

Duties: Operating EEG machines; applying electrodes to patient's body; reading and reviewing EEG charts

Alternate Title(s): Electroneurodiagnostic Technologist; Neurophysologic Technologist

Salary Range: $23,000 to $37,000+

Employment Prospects: Good

Advancement Prospects: Good

Best Geographical Location(s) for Position: Positions may be located throughout the country

Prerequisites:

Education or Training—On-the-job training or formal program in EEG technology

Experience—No prior health care experience necessary

Special Skills and Personality Traits—Manual dexterity; good vision; aptitude for working with electronic equipment; communication skills; ability to put others at ease

CAREER LADDER

```
┌─────────────────────────────────┐
│   Chief EEG Technologist or      │
│      EEG Lab Supervisor          │
└─────────────────────────────────┘

┌─────────────────────────────────┐
│        EEG Technologist          │
└─────────────────────────────────┘

┌─────────────────────────────────┐
│           Student                │
└─────────────────────────────────┘
```

Position Description

Brain waves are electrical impulses which may be recorded by electroencephalograph (EEG) machines. EEG technologists operate the EEG machines to assist neurologists in diagnosing and treating diseases and other illnesses.

Neurologists may use EEGs to diagnose brain tumors, strokes, toxic or metabolic disorders, and epilepsy. EEGs may also determine whether there is any brain activity in a patient. When there is no brain activity, patients are considered clinically dead. EEGs are also utilized to determine if patients have organic diseases such as Alzheimer's and to check into the possibility of a patient recovering from a coma.

EEG technologists have a number of responsibilities. They take a patient's medical history and attempt to make the patient feel comfortable and at ease. Technologists then apply electrodes to designated spots on a patient's head. They are responsible for determining the appropriate combination of instrument controls and electrodes to assure the best possible results.

EEG technologists may apply electrodes to other parts of the body as well. These may include the chest, arms, legs, and spinal column. This will help record activity from the central and peripheral nervous system in a patient.

EEG procedures may be performed when a patient is resting, sleeping, or doing various activities. For example, the EEG technologist may be expected to monitor the brain and the heart of a patient who is carrying out normal everyday activities over a 24-hour period of time. To do this the technologist must attach a special EEG machine recorder called a Halter Monitor to the patient. After the correct time period, the technologist will take the readings from the recorder that the patient has been carrying around. The technologist reviews the information and determines which parts the physician should see.

EEG technologists may work in labs or in operating rooms. Depending on their position, they may have supervisory or administrative duties such as managing the EEG lab, arranging schedules, keeping records, and keeping the equipment in working order.

Salaries

EEG technologists can earn between $23,000 and $37,000 or more annually, depending on the experience, education, and responsibilities of the individual. Other factors include the specific employment setting and its geographic location.

Generally, individuals handling more complicated tests and working in larger facilities in metropolitan areas will receive the highest earnings.

Employment Prospects

Employment prospects are good for EEG technologists. Individuals may find employment in a number of settings including hospitals, medical centers, health maintenance organizations (HMOs), clinics, and nursing homes.

Advancement Prospects

Advancement prospects are good for EEG technologists who obtain additional training and experience. They can go on to do more sophisticated testing or become EEG lab supervisors or chief EEG technologists.

Education and Training

EEG technologists may be trained on the job or may complete a formal training program in EEG technology. These programs are offered throughout the country in junior and community colleges, four-year colleges, universities, vocational-technology schools, medical centers, and hospitals. Programs last from one to two years and include lab experience and classroom instruction. Courses encompass human anatomy, physiology, neurology, neuroanatomy, neurophysiology, medical terminology, computer technology, electronics, and instrumentation. Graduates of these programs receive an associate's (AA) degree or certificate.

Voluntary registration is available through the American Board of Registration of Electroencephalgraphic Technologists.

Experience/Skills/Personality Traits

EEG technologists are not required to have any prior experience in health care. A desire to learn these skills is generally enough. EEG Technologists should have manual dexterity and good vision. An aptitude for working with electronic equipment is needed. The ability to make patients feel comfortable and put them at ease is helpful in this type of career.

A familiarity with medical terminology is useful. Individuals should have the ability to follow instructions. Communication skills are imperative.

Unions/Associations

Individuals interested in pursuing a career in this field can obtain additional career information from the American Society of Electroneurodiagnostic Technologists (ASET) and the American Board of Registration for Electroencephalgraphic Technologists (ABRET).

Tips for Entry

1. If you are still in school take courses in health, biology, and math.
2. While registration is voluntary, it will give you an edge over other job applicants. It will also help you advance your career.
3. Jobs in this field are often advertised in the classified section of newspapers under headings such as "EEG Technologist," "Electroneurodiagnostic Technologist," "Neurophysiologic Technologist," "Health Care," or "Health Care Professional."
4. Send your resume and a cover letter to hospitals in the area. Remember to ask that your resume be kept on file if there are no current openings.
5. Many vocational-technology schools, junior or community colleges, and hospitals hold health fair career days. These are a good way to learn more about careers in this field and talk to people who are already in the profession.
6. Continue your education. This will help make you more marketable and give you the opportunity to earn a higher salary.

EKG TECHNICIAN

CAREER PROFILE

Duties: Operating the electrocardiograph machine; preparing patients for EKG; performing stress tests

Alternate Title(s): Cardiovascular Technician

Salary Range: $18,000 to $32,000+

Employment Prospects: Fair

Advancement Prospects: Fair

Best Geographical Location(s) for Position: Positions may be located throughout the country

Prerequisites:

Education or Training—On-the-job training

Experience—Experience working or volunteering in health care helpful, but not necessary

Special Skills and Personality Traits—Mechanical abilities; ability to follow instructions; communication skills; ability to put others at ease

CAREER LADDER

```
┌─────────────────────────────┐
│   Cardiology Technologist   │
│     or EKG Supervisor       │
└─────────────────────────────┘

┌─────────────────────────────┐
│       EKG Technician        │
└─────────────────────────────┘

┌─────────────────────────────┐
│        Entry Level          │
└─────────────────────────────┘
```

Position Description

Electrocardiograph (EKG) technicians operate equipment that helps physicians diagnose and treat patients. The electrocardiograph is one of these machines. It records and transmits electrical impulses of a patient's heartbeats.

EKGs are used for an array of reasons. Most importantly, they are utilized to diagnose and treat heart or circulatory ailments in patients. EKGs are given routinely before surgery. They also may be performed during physical exams.

It is the responsibility of the EKG technician to operate the electrocardiograph machine. Within the scope of this responsibility, the EKG technician may have a variety of functions depending on the extent of his or her training and experience.

When performing an EKG, the EKG technician applies a special cream to the patient's skin. Electrodes are then attached to various parts of the patient's body, including the arms, legs, and chest. The individual will then turn on the electrocardiograph machine so that a reading can be obtained. It is imperative that the EKG technician recognize problems caused by technical errors such as crossed leads or electrical interference. Otherwise readings can be marred. After the test is done, the EKG technician is responsible for removing the electrodes from the patient's body.

EKG technicians who have had additional training may be expected to perform other tests. These might include a Halter Monitor. For this test, the EKG technician places electrodes on the patient's chest. The individual is then attached to a portable EKG for a 24- to 48-hour period. The patient is expected to go about his or her normal daily routine. After this time, the tape from the monitor is placed into a scanner, read, and sent to the patient's physician.

EKG technicians may also perform treadmill stress tests on patients. Before this is done, the EKG technician must explain the procedure to the patient, take a medical history, and connect him or her to the EKG monitor. The EKG technician must take a reading before the patient begins the stress test. He or she must then monitor the patient's heart while on the treadmill.

EKG technicians may be expected to prepare the EKG results for the patient's physician. They may be required to enter the results into a computer. They may also make sure that the reading shows no major deviations from the norm before giving the information to the physician.

EKG technicians may work various shifts depending on their specific employment setting.

Salaries

EKG technicians can earn between $18,000 and $32,000 or more, depending on the experience and responsibilities of the individual. Other factors include the specific employment setting and its geographic location.

Generally individuals handling more complicated tests and working in larger facilities in metropolitan areas will earn the highest salaries.

Employment Prospects

Employment prospects are fair for EKG technicians. Individuals may find employment in a number of settings including hospitals, medical centers, cardiologists' offices, health maintenance organizations (HMOs), cardiac rehabilitation centers, clinics, and nursing homes.

Some positions will be filled by nurses trained to perform basic EKG procedures.

Advancement Prospects

Advancement prospects are good for EKG technicians who obtain additional training and experience. Individuals can go on to do more sophisticated testing or become EKG supervisors or cardiology technologists.

Education and Training

EKG technicians may be trained on the job or go through certificate programs. On-the-job programs usually last approximately two to four months. Applicants must be high school graduates. These programs are taught by EKG supervisors or cardiologists. Certificate programs are usually one year in length.

Basic training prepares individuals to perform basic EKG procedures. Additional training teaches individuals to handle ill patients, interpret graphs, and write reports for physicians. More specialized tests such as Halter monitoring and stress testing require more specialized training.

While licensing is not mandatory, voluntary credentialling may give one person an edge over another. This is available through the Cardiovascular Credentialling International and National Board of Cardiovascular Testing.

Experience/Skills/Personality Traits

EKG technicians are not required to have any prior experience in health care. A desire to learn these skills is generally enough. EKG technicians should be mechanically inclined. The ability to make patients feel comfortable and put them at ease is helpful in this type of career.

A familiarity with medical terminology is useful. Individuals should have the ability to follow instructions. Communication skills are imperative.

Unions/Associations

Individuals interested in pursuing a career in this field can obtain additional career information from the Cardiovascular Credentialling International and National Board of Cardiovascular Testing (CCI/NBCT) and the American Society for Cardiovascular Professionals (ASCP).

Tips for Entry

1. Jobs in this field are often advertised in the classified section of newspapers under headings such as "EKG Technician," "Cardiac Rehabilitation," "Cardiac Clinic," "Health Care," "Health Care Professional," or "Cardiovascular Technician."

2. Send your resume and a cover letter to cardiologists' offices, cardiac rehabilitation centers, cardiac clinics, and hospitals. Remember to ask that your resume be kept on file if there are no current openings.

3. Many vocational-technology schools, junior or community colleges, and hospitals hold health fair career days. These are a good way to learn more about careers in this field and talk to people who are already in the profession.

4. Continue your education. This will help make you more marketable and enable you to earn a higher salary.

COUNSELING

MENTAL HEALTH COUNSELOR

CAREER PROFILE

Duties: Helping patients obtain optimum mental health; counseling patients; monitoring progress

Alternate Title(s): Counselor

Salary Range: $28,000 to $55,000+

Employment Prospects: Good

Advancement Prospects: Fair

Best Geographical Location(s) for Position: Positions may be located throughout the country

Prerequisites:

Education or Training—Master's degree in counseling, social work, or psychology

Experience—Supervised clinical experience

Special Skills and Personality Traits—Desire to work with others; ability to work independently and as part of team; sensitivity; communication skills; emotional stability

CAREER LADDER

```
┌─────────────────────────────┐
│   Mental Health Agency      │
│ Supervisor or Administrator │
└─────────────────────────────┘

┌─────────────────────────────┐
│  Mental Health Counselor    │
└─────────────────────────────┘

┌─────────────────────────────┐
│          Student            │
└─────────────────────────────┘
```

Position Description

Every person deals with their emotions in different ways. Some people let things slide off their back; others develop stress-related illness or mental, physical, or emotional problems. Mental health counselors work with patients in their quest to attain better mental health. They often work with other mental health specialists to attain this goal.

Patients may have a variety of problems for which mental health counselors may be expected to provide help. Patients may have addictions; family, marital, or parenting problems; or job and career concerns. Patients may also suffer from stress or low self-esteem. Some may even be suicidal. Problems may be emotional or mental. In many cases these problems lead to physical illnesses.

It is the responsibility of the mental health counselor to help patients learn how to cope with their situations in a positive and up-beat manner. Mental health counselors may work with patients on a one-to-one basis or in groups.

Sometimes patients are referred to mental health counselors by physicians. In other situations they may be referred by psychologists, social workers, nurses, school counselors, or psychiatrists. In some cases, a court may order someone to seek counseling.

Part of the responsibility of mental health counselors is to help patients understand their problems. Counselors must then work with patients to determine possible solutions. They may assist patients in developing a course of action for solving problems or find ways to approach the problems so that they are less worrisome and stressful.

Mental health counselors are responsible for evaluating their patients both before and during counseling. They are expected to keep accurate records documenting patient progress.

Salaries

Earnings for mental health counselors can range from $28,000 to $55,000 or more depending on the education, experience, and responsibilities an individual has, in addition to the specific job setting and its geographic location.

Employment Prospects

Employment prospects for mental health counselors are good. Positions may be located throughout the country in a variety of settings including hospitals, rehabilitation centers, long-term care facilities, home health care agencies, private or community mental health agencies, or schools. Some mental health counselors are self-employed.

Advancement Prospects

Advancement prospects are fair for mental health counselors who obtain experience and continue their training. Individuals may climb the career ladder by finding supervisory or administrative positions or going into private practice. Other practitioners go into research, consulting, or teaching.

Education and Training

Individuals aspiring to become mental health counselors must have a master's degree in mental health counseling, psychology, social work, gerontological counseling, substance abuse counseling, agency or community counseling, or counseling psychology.

Voluntary certification is available through the National Board of Certified Clinical Mental Health Counselors (NBCCMHC). In order to obtain certification individuals must hold a master's degree in counseling, have a minimum of two years of professional counseling experience, go through a supervised clinical experience, and pass a written exam.

Experience/Skills/Personality Traits

Successful mental health counselors should have a genuine interest in working with and helping others. The ability to work both independently and as part of a team is essential. Sensitivity, warmth, and kindness are also useful in this career.

Mental health counselors require the ability to gain a patient's trust and confidence. Communication skills are necessary, as are listening skills.

Unions/Associations

Mental health counselors working in various health care facilities, schools, or agencies may belong to a variety of unions which represent workers in those specific facilities.

Individuals may contact the American Mental Health Counselors Association (AMHC) and the National Board for Certified Counselors (NBCC) for additional career and certification information.

Tips for Entry

1. Send your resume with a short cover letter to hospitals, health care facilities, nursing homes, and private and community agencies. Ask that your resume be kept on file if a position is not available at the current time.
2. Job openings are often advertised in the classified section of the newspaper under headings including "Mental Health Counselor," "Counselor," "Mental Health," "Agencies," "Mental Health Agency," etc.
3. Job openings can often be located through the job placement office at your college.
4. Get certified. While certification is voluntary, most employers prefer their counselors to be certified.
5. Continue your education. Specialized courses will make you more marketable.
6. Psychiatrists, psychologists, and clinical social workers in private practice often utilize the services of mental health counselors. Contact them for possible employment.

SUBSTANCE ABUSE COUNSELOR

CAREER PROFILE

Duties: Counseling patients who abuse or are addicted to drugs or alcohol; facilitating therapy sessions; monitoring progress

Alternate Title(s): Counselor; Drug and Alcohol Abuse Counselor; Alcohol and Drug Abuse Counselor

Salary Range: $18,000 to $48,000+

Employment Prospects: Excellent

Advancement Prospects: Fair

Best Geographical Location(s) for Position: Positions may be located throughout the country; metropolitan areas may have more jobs

Prerequisites:

Education or Training—Educational requirements vary; programs include one-year certificate program, associate's degree and bachelor's degree in alcohol and drug technology

Experience—Supervised clinical experience

Special Skills and Personality Traits—Communication skills; sensitivity; objectivity; ability to work independently or as part of a team; good interpersonal skills; emotional stability

CAREER LADDER

```
┌─────────────────────────────────┐
│   Administrative or Supervisory  │
│   Job in Substance Abuse Facility│
└─────────────────────────────────┘

┌─────────────────────────────────┐
│    Substance Abuse Counselor     │
└─────────────────────────────────┘

┌─────────────────────────────────┐
│   Student or Worker in Substance │
│          Abuse Facility          │
└─────────────────────────────────┘
```

Position Description

Substance abuse is a growing problem in our country. Substance abuse counselors work with people who are addicted to drugs or alcohol.

Substance abuse counselors have a difficult job. In order for a patient to overcome an addiction, he or she must admit that there is a problem. Until this occurs, the substance abuse counselor may feel very frustrated, as it is hard to help someone who does not feel they need help or want to be helped. Even when patients want to be helped, addictions are difficult and time consuming to break. Substance abuse counselors develop motivational techniques designed to move patients through the stages of therapy necessary to break the addiction.

Substance abuse counselors may have an array of responsibilities depending on the specific situation in which they are employed. They may counsel anyone who has an addiction problem or may specialize in working with specific groups of people. These may include children, teenagers, pregnant women, business executives, athletes, etc. Sometimes counselors also work with the families of addicts.

Some substance abuse counselors specialize in helping people using certain drugs. Individuals may, for example, work with heroin addicts, cocaine addicts, amphetamine addicts, or alcoholics.

Substance abuse counselors usually do not work alone. Instead they are part of a team of health professionals which may include psychologists, psychiatrists, physicians, social workers, and psychiatric nurses.

Counselors are responsible for assessing and evaluating the extent and pattern of each patient's abuse problem. This is accomplished by asking probing questions that will evoke emotions in patients, breaking down psychological walls. Listening is as important as asking questions in this job. Substance abuse counselors are then expected to develop treatment plans with the multidisciplinary team. Individuals will counsel patients either on a one-on-one basis, in group counseling, or a combination of the two. The substance abuse counselor must keep accurate records and prepare reports on each patient and his or her progress.

Substance abuse counselors may work varied hours depending on the specific employment setting. They may work during the day, in the evenings, or on weekends.

Salaries

Earnings for substance abuse counselors can range from approximately $18,000 to $48,000 or more, depending on the specific employment setting, prestige, and geographic location as well as the education, experience, responsibilities, and expertise of the individuals.

Substance abuse counselors working in prestigious private facilities will usually earn more than their counterparts working in public or governmental agencies.

Employment Prospects

Employment prospects are excellent for substance abuse counselors. Individuals have the opportunity to work full or part time in this profession. Positions may be located throughout the country in a wide array of employment settings including hospitals, schools, colleges, universities, prisons, private or public substance abuse centers, health maintenance organizations (HMOs), mental health facilities, community service organizations, and federal, state, county, or local governmental agencies. There also are opportunities in many large corporations.

Advancement Prospects

There are a number of paths toward career advancement for substance abuse counselors. Individuals with additional experience and/or education can often find similar positions in more prestigious facilities. Others are promoted to supervisory or administrative jobs.

Education and Training

Educational requirements vary for substance abuse counselors. There are a number of options for education including one-year certificate programs, associate's degrees, bachelor's degrees, and graduate degrees in alcohol and drug technology. The most marketable people will be those who have a minimum of an associate's degree in alcohol and drug technology from an accredited school.

Many states require substance abuse counselors to be certified. This is accomplished through either state certification or certification by the National Association of Alcoholism and Drug Abuse Counselors (NAADAC). Certification requirements usually include graduation from an accredited educational program, passing written and oral exams, participation in supervised clinical experience, and taped samples of clinical work.

Experience/Skills/Personality Traits

As noted previously, substance abuse counselors usually participate in supervised clinical experience. There are often many entry-level and volunteer positions in which individuals can obtain experience. Many substance abuse counselors were former abusers themselves, making it easier to empathize with patients. It is imperative for people working in this area to be non-judgmental. Individuals should also be emotionally stable, empathetic people. Counseling, communication, and interpersonal skills are necessary.

Unions/Associations

Substance abuse counselors may be members of the National Association of Alcoholism and Drug Abuse Counselors (NAADAC), the National Academy of Certified Clinical Mental Health Counselors (NACCMHC), the National Board for Certified Counselors (NBCC), or the National Association of Substance Abuse Trainers and Educators (NASATE).

Tips for Entry

1. Jobs in this field are often advertised in the classified section of newspapers under headings such as "Substance Abuse Counselor," "Alcohol and Drug Counselor," "Drug and Alcohol Counselor," "Mental Health Counseling," and "Detox Clinics."
2. Send your resume and a cover letter to the personnel directors of detox clinics, hospitals, social service agencies, etc. Remember to ask that your resume be kept on file if there are no current openings.
3. Part-time positions may be available even if no full-time positions are open.
4. Remember to check with the placement office at your college to see if they are aware of any job openings.
5. Continue to attend classes, seminars, and workshops in various facets of substance abuse counseling. These will not only make you more marketable but will help you make important contacts as well.

REHABILITATION COUNSELOR

CAREER PROFILE

Duties: Assisting patients in dealing with disabilities; counseling patients on a personal and vocational level; developing and implementing rehabilitation programs

Alternate Title(s): None

Salary Range: $26,000 to $57,000+

Employment Prospects: Good

Advancement Prospects: Fair

Best Geographical Location(s) for Position: Positions may be located throughout the country

Prerequisites:
  Education or Training—Master's degree in rehabilitation counseling, counseling and guidance, or counseling psychology
  Experience—Supervised clinical experience
  Special Skills and Personality Traits—Tact; sensitivity; patience; creativity; emotional stability

CAREER LADDER

```
┌─────────────────────────────┐
│   Rehabilitation Supervisor  │
│   or Agency Administrator    │
└─────────────────────────────┘

┌─────────────────────────────┐
│   Rehabilitation Counselor   │
└─────────────────────────────┘

┌─────────────────────────────┐
│      College Student         │
└─────────────────────────────┘
```

Position Description

Rehabilitation counselors assist patients in dealing with their disabilities. To accomplish this, they help patients learn how to handle the personal, social, and vocational impact of their specific disabilities through guidance and counseling or both a personal and vocational level.

Patients may have emotional, mental, or physical disabilities. Some may have suffered strokes or are living with disabling diseases. Others are recovering from accidents or from substance abuse or addictions. Patients might also be mentally challenged. Some patients have personal or social problems dealing with others. It is the responsibility of rehabilitation counselors to find ways for patients to work around their disabilities while highlighting their assets. The rehabilitation counselor can then help patients overcome the barriers to employment or independent living.

The rehabilitation counselor begins by assessing the patient. When doing this, he or she must determine not only the disabilities of the patient but the abilities as well. The rehabilitation counselor evaluates the strengths of the patient and then looks at the limitations.

The rehabilitation counselor confers with the patient in developing and implementing a rehabilitation program. In planning this program, the rehabilitation counselor will emphasize activities that focus on the patient's strengths. The goal is to help the patient lead a more independent and satisfying life.

A major function of rehabilitation counselors is to help patients find work that will be suitable for them. They must take into account patients' physical and mental abilities as well as their interests, personality traits, aptitude, and skills. In many situations rehabilitation counselors help patients train for jobs or assist them in locating training.

Rehabilitation counselors work not only with the patients but often with their families as well. They may also work with an array of other medical and health care professionals including physicians, psychologists, and occupational therapists. Individuals may also meet with employers or potential employers, teachers, etc. to determine what types of activities will help the patient overcome handicaps.

Rehabilitation counselors are responsible for keeping accurate records on patients' progress. They may also coordinate additional services to assist patients in their goal of becoming independent.

Salaries

Earnings for rehabilitation counselors can range from $26,000 to $57,000 or more, depending on the education, experience, and responsibilities of the individual in addition to the specific job setting and its geographic location.

Employment Prospects

Employment prospects for rehabilitation counselors are good. Positions may be located throughout the country in a variety of settings. These include federal, state, or local vocational rehabilitation agencies; private for-profit facilities; schools; hospitals; industry; and nonprofit rehabilitation programs.

Advancement Prospects

Rehabilitation counselors may advance their careers by obtaining additional experience and education. Individuals may climb the career ladder in this field by becoming supervisors or agency administrators. Others go into research, consulting, or private practice.

Education and Training

Rehabilitation counselors are required to hold a master's degree in rehabilitation counseling, counseling and guidance, or counseling psychology. Graduate programs are accredited through the Council on Rehabilitation Education (CORE). A supervised clinical experience is required.

Many jobs prefer or require applicants to be certified. The Commission on Rehabilitation Counselor Certification certifies people who have graduated from an accredited education program, gone through an internship, and passed a written exam.

Experience/Skills/Personality Traits

Rehabilitation counselors must have a genuine interest in working with and helping others. They must also have the ability to work independently and as part of a team.

Rehabilitation counselors must be creative people with ingenuity. Tact, sensitivity, and warmth are helpful in this career. Communication skills are essential.

Unions/Associations

Rehabilitation counselors working in various health care facilities, schools, or agencies may belong to a variety of unions which represent workers in those specific facilities.

Individuals may contact the American Counseling Association (ACA), the National Rehabilitation Counseling Association (NRCA), and the National Council on Rehabilitation Education for additional career and certification information.

Tips for Entry

1. Send your resume with a short cover letter to hospitals, health care facilities, nursing homes, and private and community agencies. Ask that your resume be kept on file if a position is not available at the current time.
2. Job openings are often advertised in the classified section of the newspaper under headings including "Rehabilitation Counselor," "Counselor," "Mental Health," "Agencies," and "Mental Health Agency."
3. Job openings can often be located through the job placement office at your college.
4. Get certified. While certification is voluntary, most employers prefer their counselors to be certified.
5. Continue your education. Specialized courses will help make you more marketable.
6. Psychiatrists, psychologists, and clinical social workers in private practice often utilize the services of rehabilitation counselors. Contact them for possible employment.

SPEECH AND HEARING

SPEECH-LANGUAGE PATHOLOGIST

CAREER PROFILE

Duties: Diagnosing and treating individuals with speech and language problems

Alternate Title(s): None

Salary Range: $33,000 to $68,000+

Employment Prospects: Good

Advancement Prospects: Good

Best Geographical Location(s) for Position: Positions may be located throughout the country

Prerequisites:

Education or Training—Master's degree in speech-language pathology

Experience—Supervised clinical experience

Special Skills and Personality Traits—Communication skills; patience; tact; sensitivity; ability to deal with problems objectively

CAREER LADDER

```
┌─────────────────────────────────┐
│   Speech-Language Pathologist in│
│   Supervisory or Administrative │
│   Position or in Private Practice│
└─────────────────────────────────┘

┌─────────────────────────────────┐
│   Speech-Language Pathologist   │
└─────────────────────────────────┘

┌─────────────────────────────────┐
│        College Student          │
└─────────────────────────────────┘
```

Position Description

Speech-language pathologists specialize in the prevention, diagnosis, and treatment of speech and language problems.

Speech and language problems have a variety of causes. Patients may have a brain injury or deterioration. They may suffer from cerebral palsy, mental retardation, or the effects of a stroke. Others have hearing loss, cleft palates, voice pathology, or a variety of emotional problems.

Speech-language pathologists work with patients who cannot make speech sounds. Sometimes patients can make the sounds, but do so in an unclear fashion. An example would be a patient who has a lisp. Speech-language pathologists may also work with patients with speech rhythm and fluency disorders such as stuttering.

Speech-language pathologists often also help patients who have problems with speech quality. This might involve harsh voices or inappropriate pitch. Depending on the situation, speech-language pathologists may assist patients with oral motor difficulties that cause eating or swallowing problems. Other patients have problems understanding or producing language.

Speech-language pathologists are responsible for determining the nature and extent of a speech impairment. This is accomplished through the use of special instruments and written or oral tests. Pathologists may also record a patient's speech to analyze irregularities.

Speech-language pathologists may work with patients who have little or no speech. In these situations, they may suggest alternative means of communication. These may include using sign language or an automated device such as a computer.

Other functions of speech-language pathologists may include teaching patients how to improve their voices, make certain sounds, or increase language skills.

The speech-language pathologist may work with a patient's family or teachers in order to explain methods of dealing with speech problems. They may also work in conjunction with audiologists, social workers, and physicians in treating the patient.

Salaries

Earnings for speech-language pathologists can range from approximately $33,000 to $68,000 or more annually depending on the specific setting and geographical area they are working in as well as their experience and responsibilities. Individuals working in private practice will usually have earnings on the higher end of the scale.

Employment Prospects

Employment prospects for speech-language pathologists are good. Individuals may locate positions throughout the country in an array of settings including schools, hospitals, health clinics, hearing centers, home health care agencies, nursing homes, long-term care facilities, and physicians' offices. Speech-language pathologists also can go into private practice or consulting.

Advancement Prospects

Speech-language pathologists can advance their careers by locating similar positions in larger or more prestigious facilities. Many individuals climb the career ladder by moving into supervisory or administrative positions. There are also speech-language pathologists who go into private practice or consulting.

Education and Training

Speech-language pathologists are required to have a master's degree in speech-language pathology.

Most states regulate speech-language pathologists, requiring them to be licensed or certified. Licensing is obtained by graduating from an accredited master's program, participating in 375 hours of supervised clinical experience, passing a national examination, and having nine months or postgraduate professional experience. Some states require continuing education to renew licenses.

Individuals interested in obtaining a Certificate of Clinical Competence (CCC) from the American Speech-Language-Hearing Association must complete the above requirements.

Experience/Skills/Personality Traits

Speech-language pathologists need good communication skills. This is important in explaining test results, diagnoses, and treatments to clients in an understandable manner.

Speech-language pathologists should enjoy working with and helping others. Sensitivity, tact, and patience are imperative. Individuals must also have the ability to deal with problems in an objective manner.

Unions/Associations

Speech-language pathologists may belong to the American Speech-Language-Hearing Association (ASLHA). This organization offers career information and professional support.

Tips for Entry

1. Send your resume and a short cover letter to the superintendent of schools in a number of districts. Even if the system does not need a fulltime speech-language pathologist, it may contract out this position.
2. Send your resume and a cover letter to the personnel directors of hospitals, nursing homes, extended care facilities, and clinics.
3. Job openings may be advertised in the classified section of newspapers. Look under headings such as "Speech-Language Pathologist," "School Speech-Language Pathologist," "Health Care," "Schools," or "Clinics."
4. College placement offices are often advised of job openings.
5. Consider volunteering your services at health fairs and clinics. These are excellent ways to make contacts and get experience.

AUDIOLOGIST

CAREER PROFILE

Duties: Assessing and treating individuals with hearing disorders

Alternate Title(s): None

Salary Range: $30,000 to $75,000+

Employment Prospects: Good

Advancement Prospects: Fair

Best Geographical Location(s) for Position: Positions may be located throughout the country

Prerequisites:
  Education or Training—Master's degree in audiology
  Experience—Supervised clinical experience
  Special Skills and Personality Traits—Patience; compassion; sensitivity; emotional stability; communication skills

CAREER LADDER

```
┌─────────────────────────────────┐
│ Audiologist in Supervisory or   │
│ Administrative Position or       │
│ in Private Practice              │
└─────────────────────────────────┘

┌─────────────────────────────────┐
│          Audiologist             │
└─────────────────────────────────┘

┌─────────────────────────────────┐
│        College Student           │
└─────────────────────────────────┘
```

Position Description

Audiologists specialize in assessing and treating people with hearing and hearing-related disorders. This is accomplished in a number of ways.

The audiologist must first determine the range, nature, and degree of a patient's hearing. This is done with the help of a number of electroaccoustic instruments such as puretone, audiometers, and acoustic impedent equipment. Some instruments test the loudness at which people start to hear sounds. Other instruments are used to test the ability to distinguish between sounds as well as the nature and extent of hearing loss. The audiologist may coordinate his or her test results with medical, educational, or psychological information provided by other professionals.

After the audiologist makes the diagnosis, a course of treatment must be determined and implemented. Treatment ranges from simple procedures such as cleaning wax out of a patient's ear canals to the fitting of a hearing aid, or training in auditory, speech, or lip reading. Audiologists often recommend the use of amplifiers for patients who need the sound level boosted.

Depending on the situation, audiologists may work with a patient's family or teachers, explaining methods of dealing with a hearing disorder or loss.

Audiologists may work in conjunction with speech-language pathologists, social workers, and physicians in treating the patient.

Salaries

Earnings for audiologists have a wide range. Individuals can earn between $30,000 to $75,000 or more annually, depending on the specific setting and geographical area they are working in as well as their experience and responsibilities. Individuals working in private practice will usually have earnings on the higher end of the scale.

Employment Prospects

Employment prospects for audiologists are good. Individuals may locate positions throughout the country in an array of settings including health clinics, hospitals, hearing centers, home health care agencies, nursing homes, long-term care facilities, physician's offices, or schools. Audiologists can also consult or go into private practice.

Advancement Prospects

Audiologists can take a number of paths to career advancement. Many people seek out similar positions in larger or more prestigious facilities. Others locate supervisory or administrative positions. Many go into private practice and build successful businesses with large patient bases.

Education and Training

Audiologists are required to have a master's degree in audiology. The program covers classes in the anatomy and physiology of areas involved with hearing, the development of hearing and hearing disorders, acoustics, and the treatment of hearing disorders. The program also includes supervised clinical training.

Most states regulate audiologists, requiring them to be licensed or certified. Licensing requires graduation from an accredited master's program, participation in 375 hours of supervised clinical experience, passing a national examination, and having nine months of postgraduate professional experience. Some states require continuing education to renew licenses.

Individuals interested in obtaining a Certificate of Clinical Competence (CCC) from the American Speech-Language-Hearing Association must complete the above requirements.

Experience/Skills/Personality Traits

Audiologists must be personable people who enjoy working with others. Sensitivity, compassion, and patience are essential.

Communication skills are a must. Audiologists must also have the ability to deal with problems in an objective manner. Individuals must have the ability to concentrate when performing tests. They must also be detail-oriented.

Unions/Associations

Audiologists may belong to the American Speech-Language-Hearing Association (ASLHS). This organization offers career information and professional support.

Tips for Entry

1. Send your resume and a cover letter to the personnel directors of nursing homes, hospitals, extended care facilities, and clinics.
2. You might also consider sending your resume to the superintendent of schools in various districts.
3. Job openings may be advertised in the classified section of newspapers. Look under headings such as "Audiologist," "Health Care," "Schools," "School Audiologist," or "Clinics."
4. Your college placement office may also know of openings.
5. Consider volunteering your services at health fairs and clinics. It is a good way for people to get to know you.

MISCELLANEOUS CAREER OPPORTUNITIES

PROSTHETIST

CAREER PROFILE

Duties: Designing and creating artificial limbs; measuring limbs and stumps; maintaining prosthesis

Alternate Title(s): C.P.; Certified Prosthetist

Salary Range: $27,000 to $65,000+

Employment Prospects: Good

Advancement Prospects: Fair

Best Geographical Location(s) for Position: Positions may be located throughout the country

Prerequisites:
Education or Training—Bachelor's degree in prosthetics
Experience—Supervised clinical lab experience
Special Skills and Personality Traits—Ability to work independently, skillfully, and accurately; patience; compassion; aptitude for science and engineering

CAREER LADDER

```
┌─────────────────────────────────┐
│   Prosthetist Supervisor or     │
│  Owner of Prosthesis Business   │
└─────────────────────────────────┘

┌─────────────────────────────────┐
│         Prosthetist             │
└─────────────────────────────────┘

┌─────────────────────────────────┐
│        College Student          │
└─────────────────────────────────┘
```

Position Description

Prosthetists design and create devices called prostheses, which are used to replace limbs that have been lost as a result of birth defects, accidents, amputation, or other physical handicaps. Prosthetists may create artificial arms, hands, legs, and feet, among other body parts. The artificial limbs help patients be more self-sufficient and help them feel better about themselves.

Prosthetists are extremely skilled individuals. They use prescriptions from doctors to design prostheses. Usually they must also examine the patient to measure limbs and stumps. As each patient's body is different, it is imperative that accurate measurements be taken so that the device will fit perfectly.

After taking measurements, the prosthetist must make a plaster cast of the limb to determine the correct type of limb to be made. The plaster cast makes it easier to correct any problems or irregularities before the actual prosthesis is made.

The prosthetist must then determine what material is best suited for the prosthesis. Devises may be made out of wood, leather, metal, or new lightweight plastics. The most important consideration when making the limb is creating one that will best fit the patient's needs.

The prosthesis may be made by either the prosthetist or his assistants. They are created using hand and power tools. Each design must be followed specifically in order to assure proper fit and comfort.

After the device or appliance, as it may be referred to, is made it is up to the prosthetist to fit it to the patient. During this period, the individual can make any necessary adjustments to make sure the limb is comfortable and aligned correctly.

The prosthetist counsels patients on the correct usage of the device. He or she may work with others in the health care field such as physical therapists, physicians, and other specialists to assist patients in getting used to their prosthesis. Prosthetists may additionally provide routine maintenance of the device and repair it when necessary.

Salaries

Annual earnings for prosthetists can range from $27,000 to $65,000 or more, depending on the education, training, talent, experience, and certification of the individual in addition to the specific job setting and its geographic location.

Employment Prospects

Employment prospects for prosthetists are good. The increase in the elderly population in this country as well as advancements in this field are creating many new opportunities. Individuals may work in prosthetic businesses, private offices, or institutional settings. Other positions may be located throughout the country in federal, state, or local agencies; hospitals; clinics or rehabilitation centers. Opportunities also exist in the military.

Advancement Prospects

Prosthetists may advance their careers by obtaining additional experience, education, and/or certification and opening up their own business. Individuals may also become supervisors in hospitals, clinics, or rehabilitation centers. Some prosthetists climb the career ladder by going into research or teaching.

Education and Training

Prosthetists must have a bachelor's degree in prosthetics. Courses include biology, anatomy, physics, and engineering. In addition to classroom study, individuals work in labs learning how to make and fit designs. Some individuals who have degrees in areas other than prosthetics must take additional courses to get certified.

Certification is necessary for many positions and for advancement. This is available from the American Board for Certification in Orthotics and Prosthetics (ABCOP). To obtain certification, individuals must go through an approved educational program, pass a certifying examination, and have one year of clinical experience.

Experience/Skills/Personality Traits

Prosthetists must have a genuine interest in working with and helping others. They must also have the ability to work independently, as they usually work with a minimum of supervision. Individuals should enjoy working with their hands. Prosthetists must also have the ability to work accurately and skillfully.

Prosthetists must be patient, compassionate, caring people. Tact, sensitivity, and warmth are helpful in this career because patients often have difficulty accepting the loss of a limb or the need for a prosthesis. Individuals should also have an aptitude and understanding of science and engineering.

Unions/Associations

Prosthetists may be members of the American Academy of Orthotists and Prosthetists (AAOP). This organization provides professional support for its members.

Tips for Entry

1. While certification is not always required, it is needed for career advancement. It is also useful to illustrate professional competence. Get certified as soon as possible.
2. Send your resume with a short cover letter to hospitals, clinics, and rehabilitation centers. Ask that your resume be kept on file if a position is not available at the current time.
3. Job openings are often advertised in the classified section of the newspaper under headings such as "Prosthetist," "Prosthetist/Orthotic Rehabilitation," Clinic," or "Health Care."
4. Job openings can often be located through the job placement office at your college.
5. Continue your education. Advances in this field are always occurring. More education will make you more marketable.

MEDICAL ILLUSTRATOR

CAREER PROFILE

Duties: Drawing illustrations of human anatomy and surgical procedures for reference, training, publication, research, etc.

Alternate Title(s): Medical Artist; Illustrator

Salary Range: $24,000 to $100,000+

Employment Prospects: Poor

Advancement Prospects: Fair

Best Geographical Location(s) for Position: Positions may be located throughout the country; more possibilities will exist in metropolitan areas hosting large teaching hospitals

Prerequisites:

Education or Training—Master's degree in medical illustration

Experience—Portfolio usually required

Special Skills and Personality Traits—Artistic ability; detailed knowledge of living organisms, surgical and medical procedures, and human and animal anatomy

CAREER LADDER

```
┌─────────────────────────────────┐
│   Successful Freelance Medical   │
│  Illustrator or Medical Illustrator │
│   With More Prestigious Company  │
└─────────────────────────────────┘

┌─────────────────────────────────┐
│       Medical Illustrator        │
└─────────────────────────────────┘

┌─────────────────────────────────┐
│         College Student          │
└─────────────────────────────────┘
```

Position Description

Medical illustrators combine artistic skills with knowledge of the biological sciences. They may be expected to draw illustrations of human anatomy or of surgical procedures.

Medical illustrations may be used for medical publications, journals, and textbooks. They may also be utilized in audiovisual presentations for teaching purposes. Some medical illustrations are used in court to visually demonstrate various exhibits.

Medical illustrators may be expected to do line drawings or develop full-color renderings. In many cases, individuals are required to do research to properly illustrate assignments. Sometimes, medical illustrators work with physicians or collaborate with others to do this research. In other situations, medical illustrators may be required to observe medical procedures so that they can properly illustrate them.

With today's technology, medical illustrators may work with computers as well as with more traditional illustrating mediums. The most marketable medical illustrators can work in more than one medium.

Medical illustrators may work normal hours if they are employed by a hospital or firm. Those who freelance have more varied hours and may work nights, evenings, or weekends as well as days.

Salaries

Earnings for medical illustrators can vary greatly. Individuals who are employed full time may earn between $24,000 and $100,000 or more depending on the type of work they are doing and their specific employer. Medical illustrators who freelance may be paid by the project or the hour.

Employment Prospects

Employment prospects are poor for medical illustrators. Positions may be located in larger teaching hospitals or teaching institutions or with publishers of medical books or texts. Individuals may also work for attorneys producing exhibits for court cases or for doctors. Many people in this field freelance.

Advancement Prospects

Advancement prospects for this type of position are based to a great extent on talent, skill, and luck. Individuals who are good at what they do can find positions at larger or more prestigious facilities. Medical illustrators may also advance their careers by locating freelance work illustrating medical books or texts.

Education and Training

Educational requirements vary for medical illustrators depending on the job. Some positions require a bachelor's degree combining art and pre-medical courses. More often than not, however, positions require a master's degree in medical illustration. It should be noted that there are only a small number of schools in the United States offering this type of degree.

Experience/Skills/Personality Traits

It is essential that medical illustrators have not only artistic ability but also a detailed knowledge of living organisms, surgical and medical procedures, and human and animal anatomy.

Individuals in this field are usually required to have a portfolio illustrating abilities in various styles of medical illustration.

Unions/Associations

Medical illustrators may be members of the Association of Medical Illustrators (AMI). This organization provides career guidance and support to its members.

Tips for Entry

1. Positions are often advertised in the classified section of newspapers under headings such as "Medical Illustrator," "Illustrator," or "Technical Illustrator."
2. The college placement office may know of job possibilities. Since there are so few schools offering a degree in this area, many employers seeking this specialty will go directly to the appropriate colleges or universities.
3. Send your resume and a short cover letter to larger teaching hospitals requesting an interview.
4. Put together a portfolio of your best work. You will usually need to show one prior to being hired for any position.
5. Contact publishers of medical books. They often are looking for freelancers to handle projects.

MEDICAL WRITER

CAREER PROFILE

Duties: Developing and writing material for medical reports, manuals, and related medical and technical publications; writing medical, technical, and health information in understandable language for consumers

Alternate Titles: Writer; Technical Writer

Salary Range: $25,000 to $150,000+

Employment Prospects: Good

Advancement Prospects: Fair

Best Geographical Location(s) for Position: Positions may be located throughout the country

Prerequisites:

Education or Training—Bachelor's degree; advanced degree may be required

Experience—Writing experience required

Special Skills and Personality Traits—Excellent writing skills; good command of the English language; ability to translate medical and technical information into understandable language; understanding of scientific, pharmaceutical, medical, and/or technical areas

CAREER LADDER

```
┌─────────────────────────────┐
│  Senior Medical Writer or   │
│      Project Manager        │
└─────────────────────────────┘

┌─────────────────────────────┐
│       Medical Writer        │
└─────────────────────────────┘

┌─────────────────────────────┐
│           Writer            │
└─────────────────────────────┘
```

Position Description

Medical writers write and edit a variety of medical and biomedical communications. Some individuals may write for the medical profession. Others may write for consumers.

The duties of the medical writer will vary depending on the specific type of employment. Generally, however, individuals are expected to write articles, reports, and documentation, etc. There are a number of different types of medical writing. Some are more scientific and technical than others.

Regulatory medical writing is very scientific. Individuals who do this type of work are expected to write documents such as reports for new drug applications. These are generally geared towards governmental regulatory agencies such as the U.S. Food and Drug Administration (FDA). For example, a medical writer working for a pharmaceutical company may be responsible for preparing clinical documentation for the FDA on a new drug the company has developed.

Medical writers might also do scientific writing. Responsibilities for this type of job might include developing journal articles for clinical trials of drugs or clinical study reports.

Some medical writers handle promotional writing. This may be less scientific, but technical just the same. For example, pharmaceutical firms often have medical writers develop journal articles, sales sheets, direct mail, and brochures for the pharmaceuticals they want to introduce to physicians.

Many medical writers write educational material. This may be geared towards physicians, sales reps, or consumers. The brochures and posters seen in the doctor's office are often developed and written by medical writers. These informational pieces help educate patients and the general public on a medical or health issue or product. Another example of this type of writing might be preparing copy for the direction sheets found in medications.

As part of the job, medical writers may also be expected to review or provide feedback on documents prepared by a company's internal personnel. Medical writers may author articles for trade magazines or may write medical pieces for consumer publications and newspapers.

One of the most important functions of a medical writer is the ability to take medical, scientific, and technical information and put it into easy-to-understand language. These individuals make complex information easier to read and follow.

Salaries

Earnings for medical writers vary greatly depending on the experience, education, and reputation of the individual. Other factors include the specific employment situation and geographic location. There are some medical writers who have annual salaries of $25,000. Others may earn $150,000 or more.

Employment Prospects

Employment prospects for medical writers are good. Individuals may work full or part time or on a freelance basis. Medical writers may work for a variety of companies, including those involved in pharmaceuticals, medical communications, and biotechnology. Individuals might also be employed by hospitals, medical schools, publications, and nonprofit organizations in the health care field.

Advancement Prospects

Advancement prospects for medical writers are based to a large extent on their career aspirations. Some individuals advance their career by obtaining a large number of high-paying freelance assignments. Others may become project managers or senior medical writers.

Education and Training

Requirements vary from job to job. Generally, the minimum requirement is a bachelor's degree. Some positions require or prefer advanced degrees or training in specific areas of science, pharmaceuticals, medicine, or health care. The more technical your education in this field, the more marketable you will be.

Experience/Skills/Personality Traits

Medical writers need excellent communication skills. A good command of the English language is essential, as is the ability to translate complex information into easy-to-understand language.

Depending on the specific job, employers may require individuals to have experience in medical, pharmaceutical, or biotechnology writing.

Unions/Associations

The best-known association for those in the medical writing field is the American Medical Writers Association (AMWA). This educational organization promotes and advances biomedical communications.

Tips for Entry

1. If you are interested in getting into a career in this field and are still in school, consider a student membership in the American Medical Writers Association.
2. Get experience in all facets of writing.
3. Look for a job online. Start with some of the better-known sites such as www.monster.com and www.hotjobs.com. You might then look for specialty sites.
4. Consider sending your resume to pharmaceutical companies.
5. If you're interested in medical writing for consumers, you might also want to send your resume and some writing samples to consumer magazines and consumer medical or health-oriented websites.

BIOMEDICAL EQUIPMENT TECHNICIAN

CAREER PROFILE

Duties: Inspecting, maintaining, calibrating, and repairing electrical, electronic, mechanical, hydraulic, and pneumatic equipment

Alternate Title(s): None

Salary Range: $18,000 to $85,000+

Employment Prospects: Good

Advancement Prospects: Good

Best Geographical Location(s) for Position: Positions may be located throughout the country

Prerequisites:

Education or Training—Two-year associate's degree program

Experience—Practical experience through educational program

Special Skills and Personality Traits—Mechanical abilities; dexterity; accuracy; ability to work under pressure; communication skills

CAREER LADDER

```
┌─────────────────────────────┐
│   Biomedical Equipment       │
│   Technician Supervisor      │
└─────────────────────────────┘

┌─────────────────────────────┐
│ Biomedical Equipment Technician │
└─────────────────────────────┘

┌─────────────────────────────┐
│      College Student         │
└─────────────────────────────┘
```

Position Description

There is a great deal of equipment used in medical technology today. It is essential that equipment be working properly in order to get accurate results. The people who keep this equipment working are called biomedical equipment technicians. Individuals may specialize in the repair and maintenance of specific types of equipment or may work on a variety of different equipment.

Biomedical equipment may include electronic, electrical, mechanical, pneumatic, or hydraulic paraphernalia and instruments. These items are used in medical diagnosis, research, and therapy. Examples of equipment might be artificial kidney machines, patient monitors, chemical analyzers, X-ray machines, radiation monitors, ultrasound machines, etc.

Biomedical equipment technicians install equipment when needed and are responsible for inspecting, testing, and calibrating each piece of equipment to make sure it is functioning correctly. This may be done utilizing special test equipment, written specifications, or other means. Sometimes the individual must take the equipment apart to find a malfunction. When there are problems, the biomedical

equipment technician is expected to repair or replace the defective parts. In some cases, the biomedical equipment technician will not actually fix the equipment but notify the manufacturer to repair it instead.

An important function of the biomedical equipment engineer is performing safety checks on radiation and electrical equipment. Individuals may be required to change components of equipment to meet various diagnostic or therapeutic needs. They may be expected to teach others how to use equipment properly and safely. Additional duties include keeping accurate records of equipment checks, ordering parts and supplies, and evaluating new equipment.

Biomedical equipment technicians usually work a standard 40-hour week.

Salaries

Annual earnings for biomedical equipment technicians can vary greatly, ranging from approximately $18,000 to $85,000 or more, depending on the experience, education, and training of the individual as well as the specific job and its geographic area.

Individuals working for biomedical equipment manufacturers usually have higher earnings than their counterparts in other industries. Certified biomedical equipment technicians earn more than individuals holding no certification. Individuals handling supervisory jobs will have earnings at the higher end of the pay scale.

Employment Prospects

Employment prospects are good for biomedical equipment technicians. Individuals may find work in a variety of settings including biomedical equipment manufacturers, medical centers, medical schools, and hospitals.

Advancement Prospects

Biomedical equipment technicians may find career advancement in a number of ways. One path is to obtain certification, which can result in increased earnings. Some climb the career ladder by obtaining additional training and experience. These individuals may become supervisors or lead workers. Those working for biomedical equipment manufacturers can locate similar positions in larger or more prestigious companies.

Education and Training

Biomedical equipment technicians must go through at least a two-year program leading to an associate's degree. Programs may be called biomedical equipment technology, medical electronics technology, or biomedical engineering technology. Courses include anatomy, physiology, chemistry, physics, electrical and electronic fundamentals, biomedical equipment construction, and design and medical equipment troubleshooting. Practical experience is included in the program.

Voluntary certification is offered through the International Certification Commission for Clinical Engineering and Biomedical Technology (ICCCEBT). To obtain certification individuals must pass a written exam.

Experience/Skills/Personality Traits

Individuals interested in pursuing a career in this field should have a great deal of mechanical ability and dexterity. They should enjoy working with their hands and must be able to work skillfully and precisely. The ability to work under pressure is essential. Communication skills are also needed.

Unions/Associations

Biomedical equipment technicians may be members of the Association for the Advancement of Medical Instrumentation (AAMI). This organization provides professional support and guidance to its members.

Tips for Entry

1. If you aspire to work in this field and you are still in school take classes in chemistry, physics, biology, electronics, shop, and drafting.
2. Jobs may be advertised in the classified section of newspapers under headings including "Biomedical Equipment Technician," "Biomedical Equipment Manufacturers," and "Health Care."
3. Send your resume and a cover letter to the personnel directors of biomedical equipment manufacturers, hospitals, and medical centers. Remember to ask that your resume be kept on file if there are no current openings.
4. Be sure to register with the placement office at your college. They often know of openings in the field.
5. Get certified even if it is not required. This may give you an edge over other applicants and will usually help you earn more money.
6. Continue your education. Technology in this field is always changing.

APPENDIXES

APPENDIX I
DEGREE AND NON-DEGREE PROGRAMS

A. COLLEGES AND UNIVERSITIES OFFERING PROGRAMS IN HEALTH SERVICES ADMINISTRATION

The following is a listing of programs, grouped by state, offering degrees in health services administration. More colleges are beginning to grant degrees in this area every year.

Check the newest copy of *Lovejoy's* (found in the reference section of libraries or in guidance counseling centers) for additional school programs in this field.

ALABAMA

Auburn University
202 Martin Hall
Auburn University, AL 36849
Phone: (334) 844-4000
E-mail: admissions@auburn.edu
www.auburn.edu

Birmingham-Southern College
900 Arkadelphia Road
Birmingham, AL 35254
Phone: (205) 226-4600
E-mail: admission@bsc.edu
www.bsc.edu

University of Alabama
Box 870132
Tuscaloosa, AL 35487
Phone: (205) 348-6010
E-mail: admissions@ua.edu
www.ua.edu

ARIZONA

Harding University
900 East Center
Searcy, AR 72149
Phone: (501) 279-4000
E-mail: admissions@harding.edu
www.harding.edu

University of Arizona
PO Box 210066
Tucson, AZ 85721
Phone: (520) 621-2211
E-mail: appinfo@arizona.edu
www.arizona.edu

CALIFORNIA

California State University—Long Beach
1250 Bellflower Boulevard
Long Beach, CA 90840

Phone: (562) 985-5471
www.csulb.edu

California State University— San Marcos
333 South Twin Oaks Valley Road
San Marcos, CA 92096
Phone: (760) 750-4000
E-mail: apply@csusm.edu
www.csusm.edu

National University
11255 North Torrey Pines Road
La Jolla, CA 92037
Phone: (619) 563-7100
E-mail: admissions@nu.edu
www.nu.edu

San Jose State University
One Washington Square
San Jose, CA 95192
Phone: (408) 924-1000
E-mail: info@soar.sjsu.edu
www.sjsu.edu

University of La Verne
1950 Third Street
La Verne, CA 91750
Phone: (909) 593-3511
E-mail: admissions@ulv.edu
www.ulv.edu

COLORADO

Metropolitan State College of Denver
PO Box 173362-CB-16
Denver, CO 80217-3362
Phone: (303) 556-3058
www.mscd.edu

CONNECTICUT

Albertus Magnus College
700 Prospect Street
New Haven, CT 06511
Phone: (203) 773-8550
E-mail: admissions@albertus.edu
www.albertus.edu

Quinnipiac University
Mount Carmel Avenue
Hamden, CT 06518
Phone: (203) 582-8200
E-mail: admissions@quinnipiac.edu
www.quinnipiac.edu

University of Connecticut
2131 Hillside Road, Unit 3088
Storrs, CT 06268-3088
Phone: (860) 486-2000
E-mail: beahusky@uconn.edu
www.uconn.edu

DISTRICT OF COLUMBIA

Southeastern University
501 I Street, SW
Washington, DC 20024
E-mail: admissions@admin.seu.edu
www.seu.edu

FLORIDA

Barry University
11300 Northeast Second Avenue
Miami Shores, FL 33161-6695
Phone: (305) 899-3000
E-mail: admissions@mail.barry.edu
www.barry.edu

Florida A&M University
Tallahassee, FL 32307
E-mail: admissions@famu.edu
www.famu.edu

Florida Atlantic University
PO Box 3091
Boca Raton, FL 33431
Phone: (561) 297-3000
E-mail: admisweb@fau.edu
www.fau.edu

Florida International University
University Park
Miami, FL 33199
Phone: (305) 348-2000
E-mail: admiss@fiu.edu
www.fiu.edu

Lynn University
3601 North Military Trail
Boca Raton, FL 33431
Phone: (561) 237-7000
E-mail: admission@lynn.edu
www.lynn.edu

Saint Leo University
PO Box 6665
Saint Leo, FL 33574-6665
Phone: (352) 588-8200
E-mail: admission@saintleo.edu
www.saintleo.edu

University of Central Florida
4000 Central Florida Boulevard
Orlando, FL 32816
Phone: (407) 823-2000
E-mail: admission@mail.ucf.edu
www.ucf.edu

GEORGIA

Clayton College and State University
5900 North Lee Street
Morrow, GA 30260
E-mail: ccsu-info@mail.clayton.edu
www.clayton.edu

IDAHO

Idaho State University
741 South Seventh Avenue
Pocatello, ID 83209
Phone: (208) 282-0211
E-mail: info@isu.edu
www.isu.edu

ILLINOIS

Benedictine University
5700 College Road
Lisle, IL 60532
Phone: (630) 829-6000
E-mail: admissions@ben.edu
www.ben.edu

Roosevelt University
430 South Michigan Avenue
Chicago, IL 60605
Phone: (312) 341-3500
E-mail: applyRU@roosevelt.edu
www.roosevelt.edu

**Southern Illinois University—
    Carbondale**
Mail Code 4512
Carbondale, IL 62901
E-mail: admrec@siu.edu
www.siu.edu/cwis

**University of Illinois—
    Urbana-Champaign**
901 West Illinois
Urbana, IL 61801
Phone: (217) 333-1000
E-mail: undergraduate@admissions.
    uiuc.edu
www.uiuc.edu

INDIANA

Calumet College of St. Joseph
2400 New York Avenue
Whiting, IN 46394
Phone: (219) 473-7770
E-mail: admissions@ccsj.edu
www.ccsj.edu

Indiana University Northwest
3400 Broadway
Gary, IN 46408
Phone: (219) 980-6500
E-mail: jdix@iunhaw1.iun.indiana.edu
www.indiana.edu

Indiana University—South Bend
1700 Mishawaka Avenue
PO Box 7111
South Bend, IN 46634-7111
Phone: (219) 237-4599
E-mail: admissions@iusb.edu
www.indiana.edu

**Indiana University-Purdue
    University—Fort Wayne**
2101 East Coliseum Boulevard
Fort Wayne, IN 46805
Phone: (219) 481-6100
E-mail: ipfwadms@ipfw.edu
www.ipfw.edu

**Indiana University-Purdue
    University—Indianapolis**
425 North University Boulevard
Indianapolis, IN 46202-5143
Phone: (317) 274-5555
E-mail: apply@iupui.edu
www.indiana.edu

University of Evansville
1800 Lincoln Avenue
Evansville, IN 47722
Phone: (812) 479-2000
E-mail: admission@evansville.edu
www.evansville.edu

University of Southern Indiana
8600 University Boulevard
Evansville, IN 47712
Phone: (812) 464-8600
E-mail: enroll@usi.edu
www.usi.edu

IOWA

Mount St. Clare College
400 North Bluff Boulevard
PO Box 2967
Clinton, IA 52733-2967
E-mail: admissns@clare.edu
www.clare.edu

KANSAS

Friends University
2100 West University Street
Wichita, KS 67213
Phone: (316) 295-5000
E-mail: learn@friends.edu
www.friends.edu

Wichita State University
1845 Fairmount
Wichita, KS 67260
Phone: (316) 978-3456
E-mail: admissions@wichita.edu
www.wichita.edu

KENTUCKY

Eastern Kentucky University
521 Lancaster Avenue
Richmond, KY 40475
Phone: (859) 622-1000
E-mail: admissions@eku.edu
www.eku.edu

University of Kentucky
206 Administration Building
Lexington, KY 40506
Phone: (859) 257-9000
E-mail: admissio@pop.uky.edu
www.uky.edu

Western Kentucky University
One Big Red Way
Bowling Green, KY 42101-3576
Phone: (270) 745-0111
E-mail: admission@wku.edu
www.wku.edu

LOUISIANA

Nicholls State University
PO Box 2004
University Station
Thibodaux, LA 70310
Phone: (877) 642-4655
E-mail: nichweb@mail.nich.edu
www.nicholls.edu

MAINE

University of New England
Hills Beach Road
Biddeford, ME 04005
Phone: (207) 283-0171
E-mail: admissions@mailbox.une.edu
www.une.edu

MARYLAND

Columbia Union College
7600 Flower Avenue
Takoma Park, MD 20912
Phone: (301) 891-4000
E-mail: enroll@cuc.edu
www.cuc.edu

Towson University
8000 York Road
Towson, MD 21252-0001
Phone: (410) 704-2000
E-mail: admissions@towson.edu
www.towson.edu

MASSACHUSETTS

Elms College
291 Springfield Street
Chicopee, MA 01013
Phone: (413) 594-2761
E-mail: admissions@elms.edu
www.elms.edu

Lasell College
1844 Commonwealth Avenue
Newton, MA 02466
Phone: (617) 243-2000
E-mail: info@lasell.edu
www.lasell.edu

Springfield College
263 Alden Street
Springfield, MA 01109
Phone: (413) 748-3000
E-mail: admissions@spfldcol.edu
www.spfldcol.edu

Stonehill College
320 Washington Street
Easton, MA 02357
Phone: (508) 565-1000
E-mail: admissions@stonehill.edu
www.stonehill.edu

MICHIGAN

Baker College of Flint
1050 West Bristol Road
Flint, MI 48507
Phone: (810) 767-7600
E-mail: crowe_t@fafl.baker.edu
www.baker.edu

Cleary College
3750 Cleary College Drive
Howell, MI 48843
Phone: (517) 548-3670
E-mail: admissions@cleary.edu
www.cleary.edu

Concordia College
4090 Geddes Road
Ann Arbor, MI 48105
Phone: (734) 995-7300
E-mail: admissions@ccaa.edu
www.ccaa.edu

**Davenport University—Eastern
  Regions**
4801 Oakman Boulevard
Dearborn, MI 48126
www.davenport.edu

Eastern Michigan University
Ypsilanti, MI 48197
Phone: (734) 487-1849
E-mail: undergraduate.admissions
        @emich.edu
www.emich.edu

Ferris State University
901 State Street
Big Rapids, MI 49307
Phone: (231) 591-2000
E-mail: admissions@ferris.edu
www.ferris.edu

Madonna University
36600 Schoolcraft Road
Livonia, MI 48150
www.munet.edu

University of Detroit Mercy
PO Box 19900
Detroit, MI 48219
Phone: (313) 993-1000
E-mail: admissions@udmercy.edu
www.udmercy.edu

University of Michigan—Dearborn
4901 Evergreen
Dearborn, MI 48128
Phone: (313) 593-5000
E-mail: admissions@umd.umich.edu
www.umd.umich.edu

MINNESOTA

Concordia College—Moorhead
901 South Eighth Street
Moorhead, MN 56562
Phone: (218) 299-4000
E-mail: admissions@cord.edu
www.cord.edu

University of Minnesota—Crookston
2900 University Avenue
Crookston, MN 56716
Phone: (218) 281-6510
E-mail: info@mail.crk.umn.edu
www.crk.umn.edu

MISSISSIPPI

Jackson State University
1400 J. R. Lynch Street
Jackson, MS 39217
Phone: (601) 979-2121
E-mail: admappl@ccaix.jsums.edu
www.jsums.edu

MISSOURI

Lindenwood University
209 South Kingshighway
St. Charles, MO 63301
Phone: (636) 949-2000
E-mail: admissions@lindenwood.edu
www.lindenwood.edu

Maryville University of St. Louis
13550 Conway Road
St. Louis, MO 63141-7299
Phone: (800) 627-9855
E-mail: admissions@maryville.edu
www.maryville.edu

Southeast Missouri State University
One University Plaza
Cape Girardeau, MO 63701
Phone: (573) 651-2000
E-mail: admissions@semovm.semo.edu
www.semo.edu

MONTANA

Montana State University—Billings
1500 North 30th Street
Billings, MT 59101

Phone: (406) 657-2011
E-mail: admissions@msubillings.edu
www.msubillings.edu

University of Great Falls
1301 20th Street, S
Great Falls, MT 59405
Phone: (406) 761-8210
E-mail: adminrec@ugf.edu
www.ugf.edu

NEBRASKA

Bellevue University
1000 Galvin Road, S
Bellevue, NE 68005
Phone: (402) 291-8100
E-mail: bellevue_u@scholars.
  bellevue.edu
www.bellevue.edu

Hastings College
800 North Turner Avenue
Hastings, NE 68901-7696
Phone: (402) 463-2402
E-mail: admissions@hastings.edu
www.hastings.edu

NEVADA

University of Nevada—Las Vegas
4505 South Maryland Parkway
Las Vegas, NV 89154
Phone: (702) 895-3011
E-mail: undrgradadmision@ccmail.
  nevada.edu
www.unlv.edu

NEW HAMPSHIRE

University of New Hampshire
Thompson Hall
Durham, NH 03824
Phone: (603) 862-1234
E-mail: admissions@unh.edu
www.unh.edu

NEW JERSEY

St. Peter's College
2641 Kennedy Boulevard
Jersey City, NJ 07306-5997
Phone: (201) 915-9000
E-mail: admissions@spc.edu
www.spc.edu

Thomas Edison State College
101 West State Street
Trenton, NJ 08608-1176
E-mail: admissions@tesc.edu
www.tesc.edu

NEW YORK

**City University of New York—
  Lehman College**
250 Bedford Park Boulevard, W
Bronx, NY 10468
Phone: (718) 960-8000
E-mail: enroll@lehman.cuny.edu
www.lehman.cuny.edu

Daemen College
4380 Main Street
Amherst, NY 14226-3592
Phone: (716) 839-3600
E-mail: admissions@daemen.edu
www.daemen.edu

Dominican College of Blauvelt
470 Western Highway
Orangeburg, NY 10962
E-mail: admissions@dc.edu
www.dc.edu

Ithaca College
100 Job Hall
Ithaca, NY 14850-7020
Phone: (607) 274-3124
E-mail: admission@ithaca.edu
www.ithaca.edu

**Long Island University—C. W. Post
  Campus**
720 Northern Boulevard
Brookville, NY 11548-1300
Phone: (516) 299-2000
E-mail: enroll@cwpost.liu.edu
www.liu.edu

Medaille College
18 Agassiz Circle
Buffalo, NY 14214
Phone: (716) 884–3281
E-mail: jmatheny@medaille.edu
www.medaille.edu

Molloy College
1000 Hempstead Avenue
Rockville Centre, NY 11571
E-mail: lalbanese@molloy.edu
www.molloy.edu

St. Francis College
180 Remsen Street
Brooklyn, NY 11201
E-mail: admissions@stfranciscollege.edu
www.stfranciscollege.edu

St. John's University
8000 Utopia Parkway
Jamaica, NY 11439
Phone: (718) 990-6161
E-mail: admissions@stjohns.edu
www.stjohns.edu

St. Joseph's College, New York
245 Clinton Avenue
Brooklyn, NY 11205-3688
Phone: (718) 636-6800
E-mail: asinfob@sjcny.edu
www.sjcny.edu

SUNY—Fredonia
Fredonia, NY 14063-1136
Phone: (716) 673-3111
E-mail: admissionsinq@fredonia.edu
www.fredonia.edu

SUNY—Empire State College
2 Union Avenue
Saratoga Springs, NY 12866
Phone: (518) 587-2100
E-mail: admissions@esc.edu
www.esc.edu

NORTH CAROLINA

Appalachian State University
Boone, NC 28608
Phone: (828) 262-2000
E-mail: admissions@appstate.edu
www.appstate.edu

Gardner-Webb University
PO Box 997
Boiling Springs, NC 28017
Phone: (704) 406-2361
E-mail: admissions@gardner-webb.edu
www.gardner-webb.edu

**University of North Carolina—
  Chapel Hill**
South Building, CB # 9100
Chapel Hill, NC 27599
Phone: (919) 962-2211
E-mail: uadm@email.unc.edu
www.unc.edu

Western Carolina University
Cullowhee, NC 28723
Phone: (828) 227-7211
E-mail: admiss@wcu.edu
www.wcu.edu

OHIO

Bowling Green State University
110 McFall Center
Bowling Green, OH 43403
Phone: (419) 372-2531
E-mail: admissions@bgnet.bgsu.edu
www.bgsu.edu

David N. Myers College
112 Prospect Avenue
Cleveland, OH 44115
Phone: (216) 696-9000

E-mail: admissions@dnmyers.edu
www.dnmyers.edu

Heidelberg College
310 East Market Street
Tiffin, OH 44883
E-mail: admission@heidelberg.edu
www.heidelberg.edu

Miami University—Oxford
Oxford, OH 45056
Phone: (513) 529-1809
E-mail: admission@muohio.edu
www.muohio.edu

Ohio State University—Columbus
190 North Oval Mall
Columbus, OH 43210
Phone: (614) 292-6446
E-mail: askabuckeye@osu.edu
www.osu.edu

Ohio University
Athens, OH 45701
Phone: (740) 593-1000
E-mail: admissions.freshman@ohiou.edu
www.ohiou.edu

Union Institute
440 East McMillan Street
Cincinnati, OH 45206
E-mail: admissions@tui.edu
www.tui.edu

University of Cincinnati
PO Box 210063
Cincinnati, OH 45221-0063
Phone: (513) 556-6000
E-mail: admissions@uc.edu
www.uc.edu

Ursuline College
2550 Lander Road
Pepper Pike, OH 44124
Phone: (440) 449-4200
E-mail: admission@ursuline.edu
www.ursuline.edu

Wilberforce University
PO Box 1001
Wilberforce, OH 45384
Phone: (937) 376-2911
E-mail: kchristm@wilberforce.edu
www.wilberforce.edu

OKLAHOMA

Langston University
PO Box 907
Langston, OK 73050
E-mail: admission@speedy.lunet.edu
www.lunet.edu

Northeastern State University
600 North Grand
Tahlequah, OK 74464
E-mail: nsuinfo@nsuok.edu
www.nsuok.edu

Southwestern Oklahoma State University
100 Campus Drive
Weatherford, OK 73096-3098
Phone: (580) 772-6611
E-mail: swosuinfo@swosu.edu
www.swosu.edu

OREGON

Concordia University
2811 Northeast Holman
Portland, OR 97211
Phone: (800) 321-9371
E-mail: admissions@cu-portland.edu
www.cu-portland.edu

Oregon State University
104 Kerr Administration Building
Corvallis, OR 97331
Phone: (541) 737-1000
E-mail: osuadmit@orst.edu
www.oregonstate.edu

PENNSYLVANIA

Arcadia University
450 South Easton Road
Glenside, PA 19038-3295
Phone: (215) 572-2900
E-mail: admiss@arcadia.edu
www.arcadia.edu

Arcadia University
450 South Easton Road
Glenside, PA 19038-3295
Phone: (215) 572-2900
E-mail: admiss@arcadia.edu
www.arcadia.edu

Chestnut Hill College
9601 Germantown Avenue
Philadelphia, PA 19118-2693
Phone: (215) 248-7000
E-mail: chcapply@chc.edu
www.chc.edu

Duquesne University
600 Forbes Avenue
Pittsburgh, PA 15282
Phone: (412) 396-6000
E-mail: admissions@duq.edu
www.duq.edu

Eastern College
1300 Eagle Road
St. Davids, PA 19087-3696
Phone: (610) 341-5800
E-mail: ugadm@eastern.edu
www.eastern.edu

Juniata College
1700 Moore Street
Huntingdon, PA 16652
Phone: (814) 641-3000
E-mail: admissions@juanita.edu
www.juniata.edu

King's College
133 North River Street
Wilkes-Barre, PA 18711
Phone: (570) 208-5900
E-mail: admssns@kings.edu
www.kings.edu

Lebanon Valley College
101 North College Avenue
Annville, PA 17003
Phone: (717) 867-6100
E-mail: admission@lvc.edu
www.lvc.edu

Marywood University
2300 Adams Avenue
Scranton, PA 18509-1598
Phone: (570) 348-6211
E-mail: ugadm@ac.marywood.edu
www.marywood.edu

Pennsylvania State University— University Park
University Park Campus
University Park, PA 16802
E-mail: admissions@psu.edu
www.psu.edu

Point Park College
201 Wood Street
Pittsburgh, PA 15222
Phone: (800) 321-0129
E-mail: enroll@ppc.edu
www.ppc.edu

Robert Morris College
881 Narrows Run Road
Moon Township, PA 15108
Phone: (412) 262-8200
E-mail: enrollmentoffice@robert-morris.edu
www.robert-morris.edu

Seton Hill College
Seton Hill Drive
Greensburg, PA 15601
Phone: (724) 834-2200
E-mail: admit@setonhill.edu
www.setonhill.edu

St. Joseph's University
5600 City Avenue
Philadelphia, PA 19131
Phone: (610) 660-1000
E-mail: admissions@sju.edu
www.sju.edu

University of Pittsburgh
4200 Fifth Avenue
Pittsburgh, PA 15260
Phone: (412) 624-4141
E-mail: oafa+@pitt.edu
www.pitt.edu/~oafa

University of Scranton
800 Linden Street
Scranton, PA 18510-4694
Phone: (570) 941-7400
E-mail: admissions@scranton.edu
www.scranton.edu

Waynesburg College
51 West College Street
Waynesburg, PA 15370
Phone: (724) 627-8191
E-mail: admissions@waynesburg.edu
www.waynesburg.edu

York College of Pennsylvania
Country Club Road
York, PA 17405-7199
Phone: (717) 846-7788
E-mail: admissions@ycp.edu
www.ycp.edu

RHODE ISLAND

Providence College
Eaton Street and River Avenues
Providence, RI 02918
Phone: (401) 865-1000
E-mail: pcadmiss@providence.edu
www.providence.edu

SOUTH CAROLINA

Lander University
320 Stanley Avenue
Greenwood, SC 29649
Phone: (864) 388-8000
E-mail: admissions@lander.edu
www.lander.edu

SOUTH DAKOTA

Black Hills State University
1200 University Street, Unit 9500
Spearfish, SD 57799-9500
Phone: (800) 255-2478
E-mail: admissions@bhsu.edu
www.bhsu.edu

University of South Dakota
414 East Clark Street
Vermillion, SD 57069
Phone: (877) 269-6837
E-mail: admiss@usd.edu
www.usd.edu

TENNESSEE

Belmont University
1900 Belmont Boulevard
Nashville, TN 37212
Phone: (615) 460-6000
E-mail: buadmission@mail.belmont.edu
www.belmont.edu

Martin Methodist College
433 West Madison Street
Pulaski, TN 38478
Phone: (931) 363-9804
E-mail: admissions@martinmethodist.edu
www.martinmethodist.edu

Southern Adventist University
PO Box 370
Collegedale, TN 37315
Phone: (423) 238-2111
E-mail: admissions@southern.edu
www.southern.edu

Tennessee State University
3500 John Merritt Boulevard
Nashville, TN 37209
Phone: (615) 963-5000
E-mail: jcade@tnstate.edu
www.tnstate.edu

TEXAS

Dallas Baptist University
3000 Mountain Creek Parkway
Dallas, TX 75211
Phone: (214) 333-7100
E-mail: admiss@dbu.edu
www.dbu.edu

McMurry University
South 14th and Sayles Boulevard
Abilene, TX 79697
Phone: (915) 793-3800
E-mail: admissions@mcm.edu
www.mcm.edu

Southwest Texas State University
601 University Drive
San Marcos, TX 78666
Phone: (512) 245-2111
E-mail: admissions@swt.edu
www.swt.edu

Texas Southern University
3100 Cleburne
Houston, TX 77004
Phone: (713) 313-7011
www.tsu.edu

University of North Texas
PO Box 311277
Denton, TX 76203
Phone: (940) 565-2000
E-mail: undergrad@unt.edu
www.unt.edu

UTAH

Weber State University
1103 University Circle
Ogden, UT 84408-1103
Phone: (801) 626-6000
E-mail: admissions@weber.edu
www.weber.edu

VIRGINIA

Mary Baldwin College
New and Frederick Streets
Staunton, VA 24401
Phone: (540) 887-7000
E-mail: admit@mbc.edu
www.mbc.edu

Norfolk State University
700 Park Avenue
Norfolk, VA 23504
Phone: (757) 823-8600
E-mail: admissions@nsu.edu
www.nsu.edu

Virginia Wesleyan College
1584 Wesleyan Drive
Norfolk/Virginia Beach, VA 23502-5599
Phone: (757) 455-3200
E-mail: admissions@vwc.edu
www.vwc.edu

WASHINGTON

Eastern Washington University
MS 148
Cheney, WA 99004
Phone: (509) 359-6200
E-mail: admissions@mail.ewu.edu
www.ewu.edu

University of Washington
Seattle, WA 98195
Phone: (206) 543-2100
E-mail: askuwadm@u.washington.edu
www.washington.edu

WEST VIRGINIA

College of West Virginia
PO Box 9003
Beckley, WV 25802-9003
Phone: (304) 253-7351
E-mail: gocwv@cwv.edu
www.cwv.edu

Fairmont State College
1201 Locust Avenue
Fairmont, WV 26554
Phone: (304) 367-4000
E-mail: admit@mail.fscwv.edu
www.fscwv.edu

West Virginia University Institute of Technology
405 Fayette Pike
Montgomery, WV 25136
Phone: (304) 442-3071
E-mail: admissions@wvutech.edu
www.wvutech.edu

WISCONSIN

University of Wisconsin—Eau Claire
105 Garfield Avenue
Eau Claire, WI 54701
Phone: (715) 836-2637
E-mail: ask-uwec@uwec.edu
www.uwec.edu

Viterbo University
815 South Ninth Street
La Crosse, WI 54601
Phone: (608) 796-3000
E-mail: admission@viterbo.edu
www.viterbo.edu

B. COLLEGES AND UNIVERSITIES OFFERING PRE-MED PROGRAMS

The following is a state-by-state listing of colleges and universities offering pre-med. Check the newest copy of *Lovejoy's* (found in the reference section of libraries or in guidance counseling centers) for additional programs in this field.

ALABAMA

Spring Hill College
4000 Dauphin Street
Mobile, AL 36608
Phone: (334) 380-4000
E-mail: admit@shc.edu
www.shc.edu

ARIZONA

John Brown University
2000 West University Street
Siloam Springs, AR 72761
Phone: (501) 524-3131
E-mail: jbuinfo@jbu.edu
www.jbu.edu

CALIFORNIA

Mount St. Mary's College
12001 Chalon Road
Los Angeles, CA 90049
Phone: (310) 954-4000
E-mail: admissions@msmc.la.edu
www.msmc.la.edu

University of Redlands
PO Box 3080
1200 East Colton Avenue
Redlands, CA 92373
Phone: (909) 793-2121
E-mail: admissions@uor.edu
www.redlands.edu

COLORADO

Regis University
3333 Regis Boulevard
Denver, CO 80221
Phone: (800) 388-2366
E-mail: regisadm@regis.edu
www.regis.edu

FLORIDA

Florida Institute of Technology
150 West University Boulevard
Melbourne, FL 32901
Phone: (321) 674-8000
E-mail: admissions@fit.edu
www.fit.edu

Stetson University
421 North Woodland Boulevard
Deland, FL 32720
Phone: (386) 822-7000
E-mail: admissions@stetson.edu
www.stetson.edu

HAWAII

Hawaii Pacific University
1164 Bishop Street
Honolulu, HI 96813
Phone: (808) 544-0200
E-mail: admissions@hpu.edu
www.hpu.edu

IDAHO

Boise State University
1910 University Drive
Boise, ID 83725
Phone: (208) 426-1011
E-mail: bsuinfo@boisestate.edu
www.boisestate.edu

University of Idaho
PO Box 442282
Moscow, ID 83844-2282
Phone: (208) 885-6111
E-mail: admappl@uidaho.edu
www.its.uidaho.edu/uihomee

ILLINOIS

Augustana College
639 38th Street
Rock Island, IL 61201-2296
Phone: (309) 794-7000
E-mail: admissions@augustana.edu
www.augustana.edu

St. Xavier University
3700 West 103rd Street
Chicago, IL 60655
Phone: (773) 298-3000
E-mail: admission@sxu.edu
www.sxu.edu

INDIANA

Bethel College
1001 West McKinley Avenue
Mishawaka, IN 46545
Phone: (219) 259-8511
E-mail: admissions@bethelcollege.edu
www.bethelcollege.edu

Tri-State University
One University Avenue
Angola, IN 46703
Phone: (219) 665-4100
E-mail: admit@tristate.edu
www.tristate.edu

University of Indianapolis
1400 East Hanna Avenue
Indianapolis, IN 46227-3697
Phone: (317) 788-3368
E-mail: admissions@uindy.edu
www.uindy.edu

IOWA

Maharishi University of Management
Fairfield, IA 52557
Phone: (515) 472-7000
E-mail: admissions@mum.edu
www.mum.edu

Marycrest International University
1607 West 12th Street
Davenport, IA 52804
E-mail: mfarber@mcrest.edu
www.mcrest.edu

KANSAS

Pittsburg State University
1701 South Broadway
Pittsburg, KS 66762
Phone: (620) 231-7000
E-mail: psuadmit@pittstate.edu
www.pittstate.edu

KENTUCKY

Murray State University
15th and Main Streets
Murray, KY 42071
Phone: (270) 762-3011
E-mail: admissions@murraystate.edu
www.murraystate.edu

LOUISIANA

Louisiana College
Pineville, LA 71359
Phone: (318) 487-7011
E-mail: admissions@lacollege.edu
www.lacollege.edu

University of Louisiana—Lafayette
PO Drawer 41008
Lafayette, LA 70504-1008
Phone: (337) 482-1000
E-mail: enroll@louisiana.edu
www.usl.edu

MASSACHUSETTS

Hampshire College
893 West Street
Amherst, MA 01002
Phone: (413) 549-4600
E-mail: admissions@hampshire.edu
www.hampshire.edu

Harvard University
Undergraduate Office
Byerly Hall
8 Garden Street
Cambridge, MA 02138
E-mail: college@fas.harvard.edu
www.college.harvard.edu

Simmons College
300 The Fenway
Boston, MA 02115
Phone: (617) 521-2000
E-mail: ugadm@simmons.edu
www.simmons.edu

University of Massachusetts—Amherst
University Center
37 Mather Drive
Amherst, MA 01003-9291
Phone: (413) 545-0111
E-mail: mail@admissions.umass.edu
www.umass.edu

MICHIGAN

Cornerstone University
1001 East Beltline, NE
Grand Rapids, MI 49525
Phone: (616) 949-5300
E-mail: admissions@cornerstone.edu
www.cornerstone.edu

Olivet College
320 South Main Street
Olivet, MI 49076
E-mail: admissions@olivetnet.edu
www.olivetnet.edu

University of Detroit Mercy
PO Box 19900
Detroit, MI 48219-0900
Phone: (313) 993-1000
E-mail: admissions@udmercy.edu
www.udmercy.edu

MINNESOTA

St. Mary's University of Minnesota
700 Terrace Heights
Winona, MN 55987
Phone: (507) 452-4430
E-mail: admissions@smumn.edu
www.smumn.edu

MISSOURI

Avila College
11901 Wornall Road
Kansas City, MO 64145
Phone: (816) 942-8400
E-mail: admissions@mail.avila.edu
www.avila.edu

NEVADA

University of Nevada—Reno
Reno, NV 89557
Phone: (775) 784-1110
E-mail: asknevada@unr.edu
www.unr.edu

NEW YORK

Le Moyne College
1419 Salt Springs Road
Syracuse, NY 13214-1399
Phone: (315) 445-4100
E-mail: admission@mail.lemoyne.edu
www.lemoyne.edu

Long Island University—C. W. Post Campus
720 Northern Boulevard
Brookville, NY 11548-1300
Phone: (516) 299-2000
E-mail: enroll@cwpost.liu.edu
www.liu.edu

Mount St. Mary College
330 Powell Avenue
Newburgh, NY 12550
Phone: (845) 561-0800
E-mail: mtstmary@msmc.edu
www.msmc.edu

Rochester Institute of Technology
One Lomb Memorial Drive
Rochester, NY 14623
Phone: (716) 475-2411
E-mail: admissions@rit.edu
www.rit.edu

Touro College
844 Avenue of the Americas
New York, NY 10001
www.touro.edu

NORTH CAROLINA

Barton College
Box 5000
Wilson, NC 27893
Phone: (252) 399-6300
E-mail: enroll@barton.edu
www.barton.edu

Catawba College
2300 West Innes Street
Salisbury, NC 28144
Phone: (704) 637-4111
E-mail: admission@catawba.edu
www.catawba.edu

**North Carolina State University—
   Raleigh**
Box 7001
Raleigh, NC 27695
Phone: (919) 515-2191
E-mail: undergrad_admissions@ncsu.edu
www.ncsu.edu

North Carolina Wesleyan College
3400 North Wesleyan Boulevard
Rocky Mount, NC 27804
Phone: (252) 985-5100
E-mail: adm@ncwc.edu
www.ncwc.edu

Pfeiffer University
PO Box 960
Misenheimer, NC 28109
Phone: (704) 463-1360
E-mail: admiss@pfeiffer.edu
www.pfeiffer.edu

St. Augustine's College
1315 Oakwood Avenue
Raleigh, NC 27610-2298
Phone: (919) 516-4000
E-mail: admissions@es.st-aug.edu
www.st-aug.edu

OHIO

Antioch College
795 Livermore Street
Yellow Springs, OH 45387

Phone: (937) 767-7331
E-mail: admissions@antioch-college.edu
www.antioch-college.edu

Bluffton College
280 West College Avenue
Suite 1
Bluffton, OH 45817
Phone: (419) 358-3000
E-mail: admissions@bluffton.edu
www.bluffton.edu

Kent State University
PO Box 5190
Kent, OH 44242-0001
Phone: (330) 672-2121
E-mail: KENTADM@Admissions.
   Kent.edu
www.kent.edu

Ohio University
Athens, OH 45701
Phone: (740) 593-1000
E-mail: admissions.freshman@ohiou.edu
www.ohiou.edu

Ohio Wesleyan University
61 South Sandusky Street
Delaware, OH 43015
Phone: (740) 368-2000
E-mail: owuadmit@cc.owu.edu
www.owu.edu

University of Findlay
1000 North Main Street
Findlay, OH 45840
Phone: (419) 422-8313
E-mail: admissions@findlay.edu
www.findlay.edu

University of Toledo
2801 West Bancroft
Toledo, OH 43606
Phone: (419) 530-4636
E-mail: enroll@utnet.utoledo.edu
www.utoledo.edu

OKLAHOMA

St. Gregory's University
1900 West MacArthur Drive
Shawnee, OK 74804
Phone: (405) 878-5100
E-mail: admissions@sgc.edu
www.sgc.edu

OREGON

Pacific University
2043 College Way
Forest Grove, OR 97116

Phone: (877) 722-8648
E-mail: admissions@pacificu.edu
www.pacificu.edu

PENNSYLVANIA

Cabrini College
610 King of Prussia Road
Radnor, PA 19087-3698
Phone: (610) 902-8100
E-mail: admit@cabrini.edu
www.cabrini.edu

Carlow College
3333 Fifth Avenue
Pittsburgh, PA 15213
E-mail: admissions@carlow.edu
www.carlow.edu

Edinboro University of Pennsylvania
Edinboro, PA 16444
Phone: (888) 846-2676
E-mail: eup_admissions@edinboro.edu
www.edinboro.edu

Indiana University of Pennsylvania
216 Pratt Hall
Indiana, PA 15705
Phone: (724) 357-2100
E-mail: admissions-inquiry@grove.
   iup.edu
www.iup.edu

Lehigh University
27 Memorial Drive, W
Bethlehem, PA 18015
Phone: (610) 758-3000
E-mail: admissions@lehigh.edu
www.lehigh.edu

Mansfield University of Pennsylvania
Alumni Hall
Mansfield, PA 16933
Phone: (570) 662-4000
E-mail: admissns@mnsfld.edu
www.mansfield.edu

Marywood University
2300 Adams Avenue
Scranton, PA 18509-1598
Phone: (570) 348-6211
E-mail: ugadm@ac.marywood.edu
www.marywood.edu

**Pennsylvania State University—
   University Park**
University Park Campus
University Park, PA 16802
E-mail: admissions@psu.edu
www.psu.edu

Philadelphia University
School House Lane and Henry Avenue
Philadelphia, PA 19144
Phone: (215) 951-2700
E-mail: admissions@philau.edu
www.philau.ed

Seton Hill College
Seton Hill Drive
Greensburg, PA 15601
Phone: (724) 834-2200
E-mail: admit@setonhill.edu
www.setonhill.edu

St. Francis University
PO Box 600
Loretto, PA 15940
Phone: (814) 472-3000
E-mail: admissions@francis.edu
www.francis.edu

Waynesburg College
51 West College Street
Waynesburg, PA 15370
Phone: (724) 627-8191
E-mail: admissions@waynesburg.edu
www.waynesburg.edu

SOUTH CAROLINA

Charleston Southern University
PO Box 118087
9200 University Boulevard
Charleston, SC 29423
Phone: (843) 863-7000
E-mail: enroll@csuniv.edu
www.csuniv.edu

TENNESSEE

David Lipscomb University
3901-4001 Granny White Pike
Nashville, TN 37204-3951
Phone: (800) 333-4358

E-mail: admissions@lipscomb.edu
www.lipscomb.edu

Freed-Hardeman University
158 East Main Street
Henderson, TN 38340-2399
E-mail: admissions@fhu.edu
www.fhu.edu

Tusculum College
PO Box 5035
Greeneville, TN 37743
Phone: (423) 636-7300
E-mail: admissions@tusculum.edu
www.tusculum.edu

University of Tennessee—Martin
200 Hall-Moody Administration Building
Martin, TN 38238
Phone: (731) 587-7000
E-mail: admitme@utm.edu
www.utm.edu

TEXAS

Midwestern State University
3410 Taft Boulevard
Wichita Falls, TX 76308
E-mail: school.relations@nexus.
      mwsu.edu
www.mwsu.edu

University of Houston
4800 Calhoun Road
Houston, TX 77204
Phone: (713) 743-1000
E-mail: admissions@uh.edu
www.uh.edu

West Texas A&M University
PO Box 60999
Canyon, TX 79016
Phone: (806) 651-2000
E-mail: lvars@mail.wtamu.edu
www.wtamu.edu

UTAH

Westminster College
1840 South 1300, E
Salt Lake City, UT 84105-3697
Phone: (801) 484-7651
E-mail: admispub@wcslc.edu
www.wcslc.edu

VIRGINIA

Virginia Union University
1500 North Lombardy Street
Richmond, VA 23220
www.vuu.edu

VERMONT

Bennington College
One College Drive
Bennington, VT 05201
Phone: (802) 442-5401
E-mail: admissions@bennington.edu
www.bennington.edu

WASHINGTON

Evergreen State College
2700 Evergreen Parkway, NW
Olympia, WA 98505
Phone: (360) 866-6000
E-mail: admissions@evergreen.edu
www.evergreen.edu

Evergreen State College
2700 Evergreen Parkway, NW
Olympia, WA 98505
Phone: (360) 866-6000
E-mail: admissions@evergreen.edu
www.evergreen.edu

Washington State University
French Administration Building
Pullman, WA 99164
E-mail: admiss@wsu.edu
www.wsu.edu

C. COLLEGES AND UNIVERSITIES OFFERING DEGREES IN MUSIC THERAPY

The following, provided by the American Music Therapy Association, is a listing of programs offering degrees in music therapy. Asterisks (*) following a college name indicates that graduate program approval is pending. Schools are grouped by state. More colleges are beginning to grant degrees in this area every year. Check the newest copy of *Lovejoy's* (found in the reference section of libraries or in guidance counseling centers) for additional school programs in this field.

ALABAMA

University of Alabama
Box 870132
Tuscaloosa, AL 35487
Phone: (205) 348-6010
E-mail: admissions@ua.edu
http://www.ua.edu

ARIZONA

Arizona State University*
Tempe, AZ 85287
Phone: (480) 965-9011
E-mail: information@asu.edu
http://www.asu.edu

CALIFORNIA

**California State University—
    Northridge**
18111 Nordhoff Street
Northridge, CA 91330
Phone: (818) 677-1200
E-mail: admissions.records@csun.edu
http://www.csun.edu

Chapman University
One University Drive
Orange, CA 92866
Phone: (714) 997-6815
E-mail: admit@chapman.edu
http://www.chapman.edu

University of the Pacific*
3601 Pacific Avenue
Stockton, CA 95211
Phone: (209) 946-2011
E-mail: admissions@uop.edu
http://www.uop.edu

COLORADO

Colorado State University*
Fort Collins, CO 80523
Phone: (970) 491-1101
E-mail: admissions@colostate.edu
http://www.colostate.edu

NAROPA University*
2130 Arapahoe Avenue
Boulder, CO 80301
www.naropa.edu

DISTRICT OF COLUMBIA

Howard University
2400 Sixth Street, NW
Washington, DC 20059
Phone: (202) 806-6100
E-mail: admission@howard.edu
http://www.howard.edu

FLORIDA

Florida State University*
Tallahassee, FL 32306
Phone: (850) 644-2525
E-mail: admissions@admin.fsu.edu
http://www.fsu.edu

University of Miami*
PO Box 248025
Coral Gables, FL 33124
Phone: (305) 284-2211
E-mail: admission@miami.edu
http://www.miami.edu

GEORGIA

Georgia College and State University
Campus PO Box 52
Milledgeville, GA 31061
Phone: (478) 445-5004
E-mail: info@gcsu.edu
http://www.gcsu.edu

University of Georgia*
212 Terrell Hall
Athens, GA 30602
Phone: (706) 542-3000
E-mail: undergrad@admissions.uga.edu
http://www.uga.edu

ILLINOIS

Illinois State University*
Campus Box 2200
Normal, IL 61790-2200
Phone: (309) 438-2111

E-mail: ugradadm@ilstu.edu
http://www.ilstu.edu

Western Illinois University
One University Circle
Macomb, IL 61455
Phone: (309) 295-1414
E-mail: admissions@wiu.edu
http://www.wiu.edu

**Indiana University-Purdue
    University—Fort Wayne**
2101 Coliseum Boulevard East
Fort Wayne, IN 46805
Phone: (219) 481-6714

St. Mary of the Woods College
St. Mary of the Woods, IN 47876

University of Evansville
1800 Lincoln Avenue
Evansville, IN 47722
Phone: (812) 479-2000
E-mail: admission@evansville.edu
http://www.evansville.edu

IOWA

University of Iowa*
107 Calvin Hall
Iowa City, IA 52242-1396
Phone: (319) 335-3500
E-mail: admissions@uiowa.edu
http://www.uiowa.edu

Warttburg College
2229 9th Street
Waverly, IA 50677

KANSAS

University of Kansas*
1502 Iowa
Lawrence, KS 66045
Phone: (785) 864-2700
E-mail: adm@ku.edu
http://www.ku.edu

KENTUCKY

University of Louisville
2301 South Third Street
Louisville, KY 40292

Phone: (502) 852-5555
E-mail: admitme@gwise.louisville.edu
http://www.louisville.edu

LOUISIANA

Loyola University New Orleans*
6363 St. Charles Avenue
New Orleans, LA 70118
Phone: (504) 865-2011
E-mail: admit@loyno.edu
http://www.loyno.edu

MASSACHUSETTS

Anna Maria College
Sunset Lane
Paxton, MA 01612
Phone: (508) 849-3300
E-mail: admission@annamaria.edu
http://www.annamaria.edu

Berklee College of Music
1140 Boylston Street
Boston, MA 02215
Phone: (617) 266-1400
E-mail: admissions@berklee.edu
http://www.berklee.edu

Lesley University*
29 Everett Street
Cambridge, MA 02138

MICHIGAN

Eastern Michigan University
Ypsilanti, MI 48197
Phone: (734) 487-1849
E-mail: undergraduate.admissions
          @emich.edu
http://www.emich.edu

Michigan State University*
East Lansing, MI 48824
Phone: (517) 355-1855
E-mail: admis@msu.edu
http://www.admis.msu.edu

Western Michigan University*
1903 West Michigan Avenue
Kalamazoo, MI 49008
Phone: (616) 387-1000
E-mail: ask-wmu@wmich.edu
http://www.wmich.edu

MINNESOTA

Augsburg College
2211 Riverside Avenue, S
Minneapolis, MN 55454

Phone: (612) 330-1000
E-mail: admissions@augsburg.edu
http://www.augsburg.edu

University of Minnesota*
School of Music
2106 4th Street S
Minneapolis, MN 55403

MISSISSIPPI

William Carey College
498 Tuscan Avenue
Hattiesburg, MS 39401-5499
Phone: (601) 582-5051
E-mail: admiss@wmcarey.edu
http://www.wmcarey.edu

MISSOURI

Maryville University of St. Louis
13550 Conway Road
St. Louis, MO 63141-7299
Phone: (800) 627-9855
E-mail: admissions@maryville.edu
http://www.maryville.edu

University of Missouri—Kansas City*
5100 Rockhill Road
Kansas City, MO 64110
Phone: (816) 235-1000
E-mail: admit@umkc.edu
http://www.umkc.edu

NEW JERSEY

Montclair State University*
One Normal Avenue
Upper Montclair, NJ 07043
Phone: (973) 655-4000
E-mail: undergraduate.admissions@
          montclair.edu
http://www.montclair.edu

NEW YORK

Molloy College
1000 Hempstead Avenue
Rockville Centre, NY 11571
E-mail: lalbanese@molloy.edu
http://www.molloy.edu

Nazareth College of Rochester
4245 East Avenue
Rochester, NY 14618-3790
Phone: (716) 389-2525
E-mail: admissions@naz.edu
http://www.naz.edu

New York University*
70 Washington Square S
New York, NY 10012
Phone: (212) 998-1212
E-mail: admissions@nyu.edu
http://www.nyu.edu

**State University of New York—
    Fredonia**
Fredonia, NY 14063-1136
Phone: (716) 673-3111
E-mail: admissionsinq@fredonia.edu
http://www.fredonia.edu

**State University of New York College of
    Arts and Sciences—New Paltz**
75 South Manheim Boulevard
New Paltz, NY 12561
Phone: (845) 257-2121
E-mail: admissions@newpaltz.edu
http://www.newpaltz.edu

NORTH CAROLINA

Appalachian State University
Boone, NC 28608
Phone: (828) 262-2000
E-mail: admissions@appstate.edu
http://www.appstate.edu

East Carolina University*
East Fifth Street
Greenville, NC 27858-4353
Phone: (252) 328-6131
E-mail: admis@mail.ecu.edu
http://www.ecu.edu

Queens College
1900 Selwyn Avenue
Charlotte, NC 28274
Phone: (704) 337-2200
E-mail: cas@queens.edu
http://www.queens.edu

NORTH DAKOTA

University of North Dakota
Grand Forks, ND 58202
Phone: (800) 225-5863
E-mail: enrolser@sage.und.nodak.edu
http://www.und.edu

OHIO

Baldwin-Wallace College
275 Eastland Road
Berea, OH 44017
Phone: (440) 826-2900
E-mail: admission@bw.edu
http://www.bw.edu

College of Wooster
Galpin Hall
Wooster, OH 44691
Phone: (330) 263-2000
E-mail: admissions@wooster.edu
http://www.wooster.edu

Ohio University*
Athens, OH 45701
Phone: (740) 593-1000
E-mail: admissions.freshman@ohiou.edu
http://www.ohiou.edu

University of Dayton
300 College Park
Dayton, OH 45469
Phone: (937) 229-1000
E-mail: admission@udayton.edu
http://www.udayton.edu

OKLAHOMA

**Southwestern Oklahoma State
    University**
100 Campus Drive
Weatherford OK 73096-3098
Phone: (580) 772-6611
E-mail: swosuinfo@swosu.edu
http://www.swosu.edu

OREGON

Marylhurst University
17600 Pacific Highway (Highway 43)
PO Box 261
Marylhurst, OR 97036
Phone: (800) 634-9982
E-mail: admissions@marylhurst.edu
http://www.marylhurst.edu

PENNSYLVANIA

Duquesne University
600 Forbes Avenue
Pittsburgh, PA 15282
Phone: (412) 396-6000
E-mail: admissions@duq.edu
http://www.duq.edu

Elizabethtown College
One Alpha Drive
Elizabethtown, PA 17022
Phone: (717) 361-1000
E-mail: admissions@etown.edu
http://www.etown.edu

Immaculata College*
1145 King Road
Immaculata, PA 19345
Phone: (610) 647-4400
E-mail: admiss@immaculata.edu
http://www.immaculata.edu

Mansfield University of Pennsylvania
Alumni Hall
Mansfield, PA 16933
Phone: (570) 662-4000
E-mail: admissns@mnsfld.edu
http://www.mansfield.edu

Marywood University
2300 Adams Avenue
Scranton, PA 18509-1598
Phone: (570) 348-6211
E-mail: ugadm@ac.marywood.edu
http://www.marywood.edu

MCP Hahnemann University*
245 North 15th Street
MS 905
Philadelphia, PA 19102

**Slippery Rock University of
    Pennsylvania**
Old Main – 308
Slippery Rock, PA 16057
Phone: (724) 738-9000
E-mail: apply@sru.edu
http://www.sru.edu

Temple University*
1801 North Broad Street
Philadelphia, PA 19122-6096
Phone: (215) 204-7000
E-mail: tuadm@mail.temple.edu
http://www.temple.edu

SOUTH CAROLINA

Charleston Southern University
PO Box 118087
9200 University Boulevard
Charleston, SC 29423
Phone: (843) 863-7000
E-mail: enroll@csuniv.edu
http://www.csuniv.edu

TENNESSEE

Tennessee Technological University
Campus Box 5006 USPS 077-460
Cookeville, TN 38505
Phone: (931) 372-3101
E-mail: u_admissions@tntech.edu
http://www.tntech.edu

TEXAS

Sam Houston State University
PO Box 2208
Huntsville, TX 77341

Southern Methodist University*
PO Box 750296
Dallas, TX 75275-0296
Phone: (214) 768-2000

E-mail: enrol_serv@mail.smu.edu
http://www.smu.edu

Texas Woman's University*
Box 425587
Denton, TX 76204-5587
Phone: (940) 898-2000
E-mail: admissions@twu.edu
http://www.twu.edu

West Texas A&M University
WTAMU
Box 60879
Canyon, TX 79016

UTAH

Utah State University
Old Main Hill
Logan, UT 84322
Phone: (435) 797-1000
E-mail: admit@cc.usu.edu
http://www.usu.edu

VIRGINIA

Radford University*
PO Box 6890
RU Station
Radford, VA 24142
Phone: (540) 831-5000
E-mail: ruadmiss@radford.edu
http://www.radford.edu

Shenandoah University
1460 University Drive
Winchester, VA 22601
Phone: (540) 665-4500
E-mail: admit@su.edu
http://www.su.edu

WISCONSIN

Alverno College
3400 South 43rd Street
PO Box 343922
Milwaukee, WI 53234-3922
Phone: (414) 382-6000
E-mail: admissions@alverno.edu
http://www.alverno.edu

University of Wisconsin—Eau Claire
105 Garfield Avenue
Eau Claire, WI 54701
Phone: (715) 836-2637
E-mail: ask-uwec@uwec.edu
http://www.uwec.edu

University of Wisconsin—Oshkosh
800 Algoma Boulevard
Oshkosh, WI 54901
E-mail: oshadmuw@uwosh.edu
http://www.uwosh.edu

D. COLLEGES AND UNIVERSITIES OFFERING PROGRAMS FOR PHYSICIAN ASSISTANTS

The following is a listing of Physician Assistant programs provided by the American Academy of Physician Assistants. They are grouped by state. More colleges are beginning to grant degrees in this area every year. Check the newest copy of *Lovejoy's* (found in the reference section of libraries or in guidance counseling centers) for additional schools offering programs in this field.

Refer to the following key for credentials offered in each school.

C—Certificate of Completion
A—Associate's Degree
B—Bachelor's Degree
M—Master's Degree

ALABAMA

University of Alabama at Birmingham—C, B
Surgical Physician Assistant Program
School of Health Related Professions
SHR2 Annex
1530 3rd Avenue South
Birmingham, AL 35294
Phone: (205) 934-4407
E-mail: wilsonc@shrp.uab.edu
http://www.uab.edu

University of South Alabama—M
Department of Physician Assistant Studies
1504 Springhill Avenue, Suite 4410
Mobile, AL 36604
Phone: (334) 434-3641
E-mail: pastudies@usamail.usouthal.edu
http://www.southalabama.edu

ARIZONA

Arizona School of Health Sciences—M
Physician Assistant Program
3210 West Camelback Road
Phoenix, AZ 85017
Phone: (602) 589-1016
E-mail: paprogram@ashs.edu
http://www.ashs.edudiscpl_pa.htm

Midwestern University—B, M
Office of Admissions
Physician Assistant Program
19555 North 59th Avenue
Glendale, AZ 85308
Phone: (623) 572-3215
http://www.midwestern.edu

CALIFORNIA

Charles R. Drew University of Medicine and Science—C, B
Physician Assistant Program
College of Health Sciences
1731 East 120th Street
Los Angeles, CA 90059

Phone: (323) 563-5879
E-mail: belassit@cdrewu.edu
http://www.cdrewu.edu

Loma Linda University—M
Physician Assistant Program
School of Allied Health Professions
Loma Linda, CA 92350
Phone: (909) 558-7295
http://www.llu.edullu-sahp-pa

Riverside County Regional Medical Center/Riverside Community College—C
Primary Care PA Program
16130 Lasselle Street
Moreno Valley, CA 92551
Phone: (909) 485-6100

Samuel Merritt College—M
Physician Assistant Program
370 Hawthorne Avenue
Oakland, CA 94609
Phone: (510) 869-6576
E-mail: admission@samuelmerritt.edu

Stanford University School of Medicine—A, C
Primary Care Associate Program
School of Medicine
703 Welch Road, Suite F-1
Palo Alto, CA 94304
Phone: (650) 723-7043
E-mail: pcap-information@lists.stanford.edu
http://www.stanford.edu

University of California at Davis—C
Physician Assistant Program Family Nurse Practitioner Program
Department of Family and Community Medicine
2516 Stockton Boulevard
Suite 254
Sacramento, CA 95817
Phone: (916) 734-3551
E-mail: patty.frank@ucdmc.ucdavis.edu
http://www.ucdavis.edu

University of Southern California Keck School of Medicine—M
Primary Care Physician Assistant Program
1975 Zonal Avenue
Los Angeles, CA 90089
Phone: (323) 442-1328
http://www.usc.edu

Western University of Health Sciences—M
Primary Care Physician Assistant Program
College Plaza
Pomona, CA 91766
Phone: (909) 469-5378
E-mail: admissions@westernu.edu
http://www.westernu.edu

COLORADO

Red Rocks Community College—C, M
Physician Assistant Program
13300 West 6th Avenue
Campus Box 38
Lakewood, CO 80228
Phone: (303) 914-6386
E-mail: arlene.duran@rrr.ccoes.edu
http://www.rrcc.cccoes.edu

University of Colorado School of Medicine—C, M
Child Health Associate PA Program
School of Medicine
Box C-219
4200 East Ninth Avenue
Denver, CO 80262
Phone: (303) 315-4614
E-mail: chapa-info@uchsc.edu
http://www.uchsc.edu

CONNECTICUT

Quinnipiac University—C, M
Physician Assistant Program
Office of Graduate Admission
Hamden, CT 06518
Phone: (203) 582-8672

E-mail: graduate@quinnipiac.edu
http://www.quinnipiac.edu

Yale University School of Medicine—M
Physician Associate Program
School of Medicine
47 College Street
New Haven, CT 06510
Phone: (203) 785-4252
E-mail: janet.liscio@yale.edu
http://www.med.yale.edu

DISTRICT OF COLUMBIA

George Washington University—
  M, MPH
Physician Assistant Program
2175 K Street, NW
Suite 820
Washington, DC 20037
Phone: (202) 530-2390
E-mail: npamag@gwumc.edu
http://gwis.circ.gwu.edu

Howard University—C, B
Physician Assistant Program
College of Pharmacy, Nursing, and Allied
Health Sciences
6th and Bryant Streets, NW
Annex I
Washington, DC 20059
Phone: (202) 806-7536
E-mail: mbarnard@howard.edu
http://www.howard.edu

FLORIDA

Barry University School of Graduate
  Medical Sciences—C, M
Physician Assistant Program
11300 Northeast Second Avenue
Miami Shores, FL 33161
Phone: (305) 899-3964
E-mail: mweiner@mail.barry.edu
http://www.barry.edu

Miami-Dade Community College—A
Physician Assistant Program
Medical Center Campus
950 Northwest 20th Street
Miami, FL 33127
Phone: (305) 237-4051
E-mail: taylow@mdcc.edu
http://www.mdcc.edu

Nova Southeastern University—B, M
Physician Assistant Program
3200 South University Drive
Fort Lauderdale, FL 33328

Phone: (954) 262-1250
E-mail: redavis@nova.edu
http://www.nova.edu

University of Florida—C, M
Physician Assistant Program
PO Box 100176
Gainesville, FL 32610
Phone: (352) 265-7955
E-mail: ops@pap.ufl.edu
http://www.ufl.edu

GEORGIA

Emory University School of
  Medicine—M
Physician Assistant Program
1462 Clifton Road
Suite 280
Atlanta, GA 30322
Phone: (404) 727-7825
E-mail: ljohn07@learnlink.emory.edu
http://www.emory.edu

Medical College of Georgia—B
Physician Assistant Program
Augusta, GA 30912
Phone: (706) 721-2725
E-mail: underadm@mail.mcg.edu
http://www.mcg.edu

South University—B, M
Physician Assistant Program
9 Mall Court
Savannah, GA 31406
Phone: (912) 691-6023
E-mail: southcollege@southcollege.edu

IDAHO

Idaho State University—C, B
Physician Assistant Program
Campus Box 8253
Pocatello, ID 83209
Phone: (208) 282-4726
E-mail: ruchanit@isu.edu
http://www.isu.edu

ILLINOIS

Cook County Hospital Malcolm X
  College—C, A
Physician Assistant Program
1900 West Van Buren Street
Number 3241
Chicago, IL 60612
Phone: (312) 850-7255
http://www.ccc.edumalcolmx

Finch University of Health Sciences
  The Chicago Medical School—M
3333 Green Bay Road, Building 51
North Chicago, IL 60064
Phone: (847) 578-3312
http://www.finchcms.edu

Midwestern University—C, B, M
Physician Assistant Program
555 31st Street
Downers Grove, IL 60515
Phone: (800) 458-6253
E-mail: admissil@midwestern.edu
http://www.midwestern.eduPages/
PAPG.html

Southern Illinois University at
  Carbondale—C, B
Physician Assistant Program
Lindegren Hall, Room 129
Mail Code 6516
Carbondale, IL 62901
Phone: (618) 453-5527
http://www.siu.edu

INDIANA

Butler University Clarian Health—C, B
Physician Assistant Program
College of Pharmacy and Health Sciences
4600 Sunset Avenue
Indianapolis, IN 46208
Phone: (317) 940-9969
E-mail: tepp@butler.edu
http://www.butler.edu

University of Saint Francis—M
Physician Assistant Program
2701 Spring Street
Fort Wayne, IN 46808
Phone: (219) 434-3100
E-mail: jroth@sc.edu
http://www.sfc.edu

IOWA

Des Moines University Osteopathic
  Medical Center—C, M
Physician Assistant Program
3200 Grand Avenue
Des Moines, IA 50312
Phone: (515) 271-1603
E-mail: pam.chambers@dmu.edu
http://www.uomhs.edu

University of Iowa—C, M
Physician Assistant Program
College of Medicine
5167 Westlawn
Iowa City, IA 52242

Phone: (319) 335-8922
E-mail: paprogram@uiowa.edu
http://www.uiowa.edu

KANSAS

Wichita State University—B
Physician Assistant Program
College of Health Professions
Campus Box 43
Wichita, KS 67260
Phone: (316) 978-3011
E-mail: biddle@chp.twsu.edu
http://www.wichita.edu

KENTUCKY

University of Kentucky—C, M
Physician Assistant Program
121 Washington Avenue
Lexington, KY 40536
Phone: (606) 323-1100, extension 273
E-mail: mspas-dgs@lsv.uky.edu
http://www.uky.edu

LOUISIANA

**Louisiana State University Health
Sciences Center—B**
Physician Assistant Program
School of Allied Health Professions
1501 Kings Highway
PO Box 33932
Shreveport, LA 71130
Phone: (318) 675-7317
E-mail: kwilli6@lsuhsc.edu
http://www.lsumc.edu

MAINE

**The University of New England—
C, M**
Physician Assistant Program
11 Hills Beach Road
Biddeford, ME 04005
Phone: (207) 283-0171, extension 2608
E-mail: dfarrell@mailbox.une.edu
http://www.une.edu

MARYLAND

**Anne Arundel Community
College—C**
School of Health Professions, Wellness,
and Physical Education
Physician Assistant Program
101 College Parkway
Arnold, MD 21012

Phone: (410) 315-7310
E-mail: pdfalkenstein@mail.aacc.cc.md.us
http://www.aacc.cc.md.us/

**Community College of Baltimore at
Essex—C, M**
Physician Assistant Program
7201 Rossville Boulevard
Baltimore, MD 21237
Phone: (410) 780-6579
E-mail: sshaw@ccbc.cc.md.us
http://www.ccbc.cc.md.us/campuses/
essex/essex.htm

**University of Maryland, Eastern
Shore—B**
Physician Assistant Program
Modular 934-5 Backbone Drive
Princess Anne, MD 21853
Phone: (410) 651-7584
http://www.umes.edu

MASSACHUSETTS

**Massachusetts College of Pharmacy
and Health Sciences—M**
Physician Assistant Program
179 Longwood Avenue, WB01
Boston, MA 02115
Phone: (617) 732-2140
E-mail: cfasser@mcp.edu
http://www.mcp.edu

Northeastern University—M
Physician Assistant Program
202 Robinson Hall
Boston, MA 02115
Phone: (617) 373-3195
http://www.northeastern.edu

**Springfield College Baystate Health
System—C, B**
Physician Assistant Program
263 Alden Street
Springfield, MA 01109
Phone: (800) 343-1257
http://www.springfieldcollege.edu

MICHIGAN

Central Michigan University—M
Physician Assistant Program
Foust Hall
Mount Pleasant, MI 48859
Phone: (989) 774-1237
E-mail: chpadmit@cmich.edu
http://www.cmich.edu

Grand Valley State University—M
Physician Assistant Studies Program
Medical Education and Research Center
1000 Monroe NW
Grand Rapids, MI 49503
Phone: (616) 233-6500
E-mail: pas@gvsu.edu
http://www.gvsu.edu

University of Detroit Mercy—M
Physician Assistant Program
8200 Outer Drive
PO Box 19900
Detroit, MI 48219
Phone: (313) 993-6177
E-mail: vitalel@udmercy.edu
http://www.udmercy.edu

Wayne State University—M
Department of Physician Assistant
Studies
Detroit, MI 48202
Phone: (313) 577-1368
E-mail: ab4754@wayne.edu
http://www.wayne.edu

Western Michigan University—M
Physician Assistant Program
Kalamazoo, MI 49008
Phone: (616) 387-5314
http://www.wmich.edu

MINNESOTA

Augsburg College—C, M
Physician Assistant Program
2211 Riverside Avenue
Minneapolis, MN 55454
Phone: (612) 330-1039
E-mail: paprog@augsburg.edu
http://www.augsburg.edu

MISSOURI

Saint Louis University—C, B, M
Physician Assistant Program
3437 Caroline Street
St. Louis, MO 63104
Phone: (314) 577-8521
E-mail: mayj@slu.edu
http://www.slu.edu

**Southwest Missouri State
University—M**
Department of Physician Assistant Studies
901 South National Avenue
Springfield, MO 65804
Phone: (417) 836-6151
E-mail: physicianasststudies@smsu.edu
http://www.smsu.edu

MONTANA

Rocky Mountain College—B
Physician Assistant Program
1511 Poly Drive
Billings, MT 59102
Phone: (406) 657-1190
E-mail: bentss@rocky.edu
http://www.rocky.edu

NEBRASKA

Union College—B, C
Physician Assistant Program
3800 South 4th Street
Lincoln, NE 68506
Phone: (402) 486-2527
E-mail: paprog@ucollege.edu
http://www.ucollege.edu

**University of Nebraska Medical
    Center—M**
Physician Assistant Program
Box 984300
Omaha, NE 68198
Phone: (402) 559-5266
E-mail: dklandon@unmc.edu
http://www.unmc.edu

NEW HAMPSHIRE

Notre Dame College—M
Physician Assistant Studies
2321 Elm Street
Manchester, NH 03104
Phone: (603) 222-7210
E-mail: ce-gradmissions@notredame.edu

NEW JERSEY

Seton Hall University—M
Physician Assistant Program
400 South Orange Avenue
South Orange, NJ 07079
Phone: (973) 761-7145
http://www.shu.edu

**The University of Medicine and
    Dentistry of New Jersey—M**
Physician Assistant Program
65 Bergen Street
Newark, NJ 07107
Phone: (973) 972-5954
http://www.umdnj.edu~gsbs/homepage.
    html

**University of Medicine and Dentistry
    of New Jersey and Rutgers
    University—B, M**
Physician Assistant Program
675 Hoes Lane
Piscataway, NJ 08854

Phone: (732) 235-4444
http://www.umdnj.edu

NEW MEXICO

**The University of New Mexico School
    of Medicine—B, C**
Department of Family and Community
Medicine
Physician Assistant Program
2400 Tucker NE
Albuquerque, NM 87131
Phone: (505) 272-9678
E-mail: paprogram@salud.unm.edu
http://hsc.unm.edusom

University of St. Francis—M
Physician Assistant Program
4401 Silver Avenue, SE
Suite B
Albuquerque, NM 87108
Phone: (505) 266-5565
E-mail: pa@stfrancis.edu
http://www.stfrancis.edu

NEW YORK

Albany Medical College—C, B, A
Physician Assistant Program
47 New Scotland Avenue
Mail Code 4
Albany, NY 12208
Phone: (518) 262-5251
E-mail: daisr@mail.amc.edu

Bronx Lebanon Hospital Center—C
Physician Assistant Program
1650 Selwyn Avenue
Suite 11D
Bronx, NY 10457
Phone: (718) 960-1255
http://www.bronx-leb.org

D'Youville College—B
Physician Assistant Program
320 Porter Avenue
Buffalo, NY 14201
Phone: (716) 881-7713
http://www.dyc.edu

Daemen College—B, M
Physician Assistant Program
4380 Main Street
Amherst, NY 14226
Phone: (800) 462-7652
E-mail: admissions@daemen.edu
http://www.daemen.edu

Le Moyne College—C, B
1419 Salt Springs Road
Syracuse, NY 13214

Phone: (315) 445-4745
E-mail: simonpa@mail.lemoyne.edu
http://www.lemoyne.edu

Mercy College—B, M
Graduate Program in Physician
    Assistant Studies
555 Broadway
Dobbs Ferry, NY 10522
Phone: (914) 674-7635
E-mail: paprogram@mercynet.edu
http://www.mercynet.edu

New York Institute of Technology—B
Physician Assistant Program
PO Box 8000
Old Westbury, NY 11568
Phone: (516) 686-3881
E-mail: sbarese@nyit.edu
http://www.nyit.edu

**Pace University Lenox Hill
    Hospital—C**
Physician Assistant Program
One Pace Plaza, Room Y-31
New York, NY 10038
Phone: (212) 346-1357
E-mail: paprogram@pace.edu
http://www.pace.edu

Rochester Institute of Technology—B
Physician Assistant Program
85 Lomb Memorial Drive
Rochester, NY 14623
Phone: (716) 475-2978
E-mail: hbmscl@rit.edu
http://www.rit.edu

**State University of New York at Stony
    Brook—C, B**
Physician Assistant Program
School of Health Technology
and Management
HSC, L2-052
Stony Brook, NY 11794
Phone: (631) 444-3190
E-mail: paprogram@sunysb.edu
http://www.sunysb.edu

**State University of New York
    Downstate Medical Center—B**
Physician Assistant Program
Health Science Center
450 Clarkson Avenue, Box 1222
Brooklyn, NY 11234
Phone: (718) 270-2324-5
E-mail: admissions@downstate.edu

**St. Vincent Catholic Medical Centers of
    New York—C, B**
Physician Assistant Program
Staten Island Region
75 Vanderbilt Avenue

Staten Island, NY 10304
Phone: (718) 354-5570

St. Vincent Catholic Medical Centers of New York—C, B
Physician Assistant Program
Brooklyn and Queens Region
175-05 Horace Harding Expressway
Fresh Meadows, NY 11365
Phone: (718) 357-0500
E-mail: tsimone@cmcny.com

The Brooklyn Hospital Center Long Island University—C, B
Physician Assistant Program
121 DeKalb Avenue
Brooklyn, NY 11201
Phone: (718) 260-2780
E-mail: tbhcpap@aol.com

The St. Vincent Catholic Medical Centers of New York
CUNY Medical School Harlem Hospital Center—C, B
506 Malcolm X Boulevard (Lenox Avenue), WP-Room 619
New York, NY 10037
Phone: (212) 939-2525
E-mail: shrcc@cunyvm.cuny.edu

Touro College—B
Physician Assistant Program
School of Health Sciences
1700 Union Boulevard
Bay Shore, NY 11706
Phone: (631) 665-1600
http://www.touro.edu

Touro College, Manhattan Campus—B
Physician Assistant Program
School of Health Sciences
27-33 West 23rd Street
New York, NY 10010
Phone: (212) 463-0400, extension 792
E-mail: ngraff@touro.edu
http://www.touro.edu

Wagner College Staten Island University Hospital—C, B
Physician Assistant Program
74 Melville Street
Staten Island, NY 10309-4035
Phone: (718) 226-2928
E-mail: nlowy@siuh.edu
http://www.siuh.edupa/pa.html

Weill Cornell Medical College—C
Physician Assistant Program (A Surgical Focus)
1300 York Avenue, F-1919
New York, NY 10021
Phone: (212) 746-5133 or 5134
E-mail: jdrawls@mail.med.cornell.edu
http://www.med.cornell.edu

NORTH CAROLINA

Duke University Medical Center—C, M
DUMC 3848
Physician Assistant Program
Durham, NC 27710
Phone: (919) 681-3155
E-mail: paadmission@mc.duke.edu
http://www.mc.duke.edu

East Carolina University—B, M
West Research Campus
1157 VOA Site "C" Road
Greenville, NC 27834
Phone: (252) 744-1100
E-mail: trubeg@mail.ecu.edu
http://www.ecu.edu

Methodist College—M
5107B College Centre Drive
Fayetteville, NC 28311
Phone: (910) 630-7495
E-mail: paprog@methodist.edu
http://www.methodist.edu

Wake Forest University School of Medicine—C
Medical Center Boulevard
Winston-Salem, NC 27157
Phone: (336) 716-4356
E-mail: shfoster@wfubmc.edu
http://isnet.is.wfu.edu

NORTH DAKOTA

University of North Dakota School of Medicine and Health Sciences—C
Department of Community Medicine and Rural Health
PO Box 9037
Grand Forks, ND 58202
Phone: (701) 777-2344
E-mail: mcdaniel@medicine.nodak.edu
http://www.med.und.nodak.edu

OHIO

Cuyahoga Community College—A
Surgical Physician Assistant Program
11000 Pleasant Valley Road
Parma, OH 44130
Phone: (216) 987-5363
E-mail: joyce.janicek@tri-c.cc.oh.us
http://www.tri-c.cc.oh.us/

Kettering College of Medical Arts—C, B
Physician Assistant Program
3737 Southern Boulevard
Kettering, OH 45429
Phone: (937) 296-7238
E-mail: neida.rowland@kmcnetwork.org
http://www.kcma.edu

Medical College of Ohio—M
Physician Assistant Program
School of Allied Health
3015 Arlington Avenue
Toledo, OH 43614
Phone: (419) 383-5408
E-mail: tlangenderfe@mco.edu
http://www.mco.edu

University of Findlay—B
Physician Assistant Program
1000 North Main Street
Findlay, OH 45840
Phone: (419) 424-4529
E-mail: davis@mail.findlay.edu
http://www.findlay.edu

OKLAHOMA

University of Oklahoma—M
Physician Associate Program
Health Sciences Center
PO Box 26901
Oklahoma City, OK 73190
Phone: (405) 271-2058
http://www.ou.edu

OREGON

Oregon Health Sciences University—M
Physician Assistant Program
3181 Southwest Sam Jackson Park Road GH219
Portland, OR 97201
Phone: (503) 494-1484
E-mail: paprgm@ohsu.edu
http://www.ohsu.edu

Pacific University—C, M
Physician Assistant Program
School of Physician Assistant Studies
2043 College Way
Forest Grove, OR 97116
Phone: (503) 359-2900
E-mail: pa@pacificu.edu
http://www.pacificu.edu

PENNSYLVANIA

Arcadia University—M
Physician Assistant Program
Brubaker Hall
Health Science Center
450 South Easton Road
Glenside, PA 19038
Phone: (215) 572-2082
E-mail: paruchg@camelot.beaver.edu
http://www.arcadia.edu

Chatham College—M
Physician Assistant Program
Woodland Road
Pittsburgh, PA 15232
Phone: (412) 365-1412
E-mail: admissions@chatham.edu
http://www.chatham.edu

DeSales University—B, M
Physician Assistant Program
2755 Station Avenue
Center Valley, PA 18034
Phone: (610) 282-1100, extension 1415

Duquesne University—M
Physician Assistant Program
John G. Rangos Sr. School of Health
Sciences
323 Health Sciences Building
Pittsburgh, PA 15282
Phone: (800) 456-0590
E-mail: pinevich@duq.edu
http://www.duq.edu

Gannon University—M
Physician Assistant Program
109 University Square
Erie, PA 16541
Phone: (814) 871-7420
http://www.gannon.edu

King's College—C, M
Physician Assistant Program
133 North River Street
Wilkes-Barre, PA 18711
Phone: (570)-208-5853
E-mail: sesedon@kings.edu
http://www.kings.edu

**Lock Haven University of
    Pennsylvania—C, M**
Physician Assistant Program in Rural
Primary Care
Lock Haven, PA 17745
Phone: (570) 893-2541
http://www.lhup.edu

MCP Hahnemann University—M
Physician Assistant Program
College of Nursing and Health Professions

245 North 15th Street
Mail Stop 504
Philadelphia, PA 19102
Phone: (215) 762-7135
E-mail: enroll@mcphu.edu
http://www.auhs.edu

Marywood University—B
Physician Assistant Program
2300 Adams Avenue
Scranton, PA 18509
Phone: (717) 348-6298
E-mail: ugadm@ac.marywood.edu
http://www.marywood.edu

Pennsylvania College of Technology—B
Physician Assistant Program
DIF #123
One College Avenue
Williamsport, PA 17701-5799
Phone: (570) 327-4779
E-mail: kmayer@pct.edu
http://www.pct.edu

**Philadelphia College of Osteopathic
    Medicine—C, M**
4170 City Avenue, Suite 005
Evans Hall
Philadelphia, PA 19131
Phone: (215) 871-6772
E-mail: kennethha@pcom.edu
http://www.pcom.edu

Philadelphia University—B, M
School House Lane and Henry Avenue
Philadelphia, PA 19144
Phone: (215) 951-2908
E-mail: mccombs@philau.edu
http://www.philau.edu

Saint Francis University—M
Department of Physician Assistant
Sciences
PO Box 600
Loretto, PA 15940
Phone: (814) 472-3020
E-mail: admissions@francis.edu

Seton Hill College—C, B
Physician Assistant Program
College Avenue
Greensburg, PA 15601
Phone: (800) 826-6234
E-mail: admit@setonhill.edu
http://www.setonhill.edu

SOUTH CAROLINA

**Medical University of South
    Carolina—B, M**
Physician Assistant Program
College of Health Professions

PO Box 250856
Charleston, SC 29425
Phone: (843) 792-0376
E-mail: jonesmo@musc.edu
http://www.musc.edu

SOUTH DAKOTA

University of South Dakota—C, B
Physician Assistant Studies Program
School of Medicine
414 East Clark Street
Vermillion, SD 57069
Phone: (605) 677-5128
E-mail: usdpa@usd.edu
http://www.usd.edu

TENNESSEE

Bethel College—M
Physician Assistant Program
325 Cherry Avenue
McKenzie, TN 38201
Phone: (901) 352-4004
http://www.bethel.edu

Trevecca Nazarene University—M
Physician Assistant Program
333 Murfreesboro Road
Nashville, TN 37210
Phone: (615) 248-1225
http://www.trevecca.edu

TEXAS

Academy of Health Sciences—C, B
Interservice Physician Assistant Program
Attn: MCCS HMP
3151 Scott Road, Suite 1202
Fort Sam Houston, TX 78234
Phone: (210) 221-8004

Baylor College of Medicine—C, M
Physician Assistant Program
Room 633E
One Baylor Plaza
Houston, TX 77030
Phone: (713) 798-4619
http://www.bcm.tmc.edu

**Texas Tech University Health Sciences
    Center—M**
School of Allied Health
Department of Diagnostic and Primary Care
Physician Assistant Program
3600 North Garfield
Midland, TX 79705
Phone: (915) 686-4213
E-mail: jrunyan@midland.cc.tx.us
http://www.ttuhsc.edu

The University of Texas Pan American—B
Physician Assistant Program
1201 West University Drive
Edinburg, TX 78539
Phone: (956) 381-2292
http://www.panam.edu

The University of Texas Medical Branch—M
Physician Assistant Program
School of Allied Health Services
301 University Boulevard
Galveston, TX 77555
Phone: (409) 772-3046
E-mail: rrahr@utmb.edu
http://www.utmbhealthcare.org/

University of North Texas—M
Physician Assistant Studies
Health Science Center at Fort Worth
3500 Camp Bowie Boulevard
Fort Worth, TX 76107
Phone: (817) 735-2301
E-mail: pa_program@hsc.unt.edu
http://www.unt.edu

University of Texas Health Science Center at San Antonio—B
Physician Assistant Program
Department of Physician Assistant Studies
7703 Floyd Curl Drive, MC 6249
San Antonio, TX 78229
Phone: (210) 567-8811
E-mail: blessing@uthscsa.edu
http://rmstewart.uthscsa.edu

University of Texas, Southwestern Medical Center at Dallas—M
Physician Assistant Program
6011 Harry Hines Boulevard
Dallas, TX 75390
Phone: (214) 648-1701
E-mail: isela.perez@utsouthwestern.edu
http://www.swmed.edu

UTAH

University of Utah—C, M
Physician Assistant Program
375 Chipeta Way
Salt Lake City, UT 84108
Phone: (801) 581-7764
E-mail: drobinson@upap.utah.edu
http://www.utah.edu

VIRGINIA

College of Health Sciences—B
Physician Assistant Program
920 South Jefferson Street
Roanoke, VA 24016
Phone: (540) 985-4016
E-mail: pa@health.chs.edu
http://www.chs.edu

Eastern Virginia Medical School—M
Physician Assistant Program
700 West Olney Road
PO Box 1980
Norfolk, VA 23501
Phone: (757) 446-7158
E-mail: paprog@evmsmail.evms.edu
http://www.evms.edu

James Madison University—C, B
Physician Assistant Program
Department of Health Sciences,
MSC 4301
Harrisonburg, VA 22807
Phone: (540) 568-2395
E-mail: paprogram@jmu.edu
http://www.jmu.edu

Shenandoah University—M
Division of Physician Assistant Studies
1460 University Drive
Winchester, VA 22601
Phone: (540) 545-7381
http://www.su.edu

WASHINGTON

University of Washington—C, B
MEDEX Northwest
Physician Assistant Program
4245 Roosevelt Way NE
Seattle, WA 98105
Phone: (206) 598-2600
http://www.washington.edu

WEST VIRGINIA

Alderson Broaddus College—B
Physician Assistant Department
PO Box 2036
Philippi, WV 26416
Phone: (304) 457-6283
E-mail: holt_m@ab.edu

Mountain State University—C, B
Physician Assistant Program
PO Box AG
Beckley, WV 25802
Phone: (304) 253-7351

WISCONSIN

Marquette University—M
Department of Physician Assistant Studies
College of Health Sciences
1700 Building
PO Box 1881
Milwaukee, WI 53201
Phone: (414) 288-5688
http://www.mu.edu

University of Wisconsin-La Crosse Gunderson Lutheran Medical Foundation Mayo School of Health-Related Sciences—C, B
Physician Assistant Program
1725 State Street
4031 Health Science Center
La Crosse, WI 54601
Phone: (608) 785-6620
E-mail: paprogram@uwlax.edu

University of Wisconsin-Madison—B
Physician Assistant Program
Room 1050, Medical Sciences Center
1300 University Avenue
Madison, WI 53706
Phone: (608) 263-5620
http://jumpgate.acadsvcs.wisc.eduadmissions/

E. COLLEGES AND UNIVERSITIES OFFERING MAJORS IN PUBLIC RELATIONS

The following is a listing of selected four-year schools granting degrees with majors in public relations. They are grouped by state.

The author does not endorse any one school over another. Use this list as a beginning. More colleges are beginning to grant degrees in this area every year. Check the newest copy of *Lovejoy's* (found in the reference section of libraries or in guidance counseling centers) for additional schools offering degrees in this field.

ALABAMA

Auburn University
202 Martin Hall
Auburn University, AL 36849
Phone: (334) 844-4000
E-mail: admissions@auburn.edu
http://www.auburn.edu

Spring Hill College
4000 Dauphin Street
Mobile, AL 36608
Phone: (334) 380-4000
E-mail: admit@shc.edu
http://www.shc.edu

University of Alabama
Box 870132
Tuscaloosa, AL 35487
Phone: (205) 348-6010
E-mail: uaadmit@enroll.ua.edu
http://www.ua.edu

University of North Alabama
Box 5121
Florence, AL 35632
Phone: (256) 765-4100
E-mail: admis1@unanov.una.edu
http://www.una.edu

ALASKA

University of Alaska—Anchorage
3211 Providence Drive
Anchorage, AK 99508
Phone: (907) 786-1800
E-mail: ayenrol@uaa.alaska.edu
http://www.uaa.alaska.edu

ARIZONA

Northern Arizona University
PO Box 4084
Flagstaff, AZ 86011
Phone: (520) 523-9011
E-mail: undergraduate.admissions
        @nau.edu
http://www.nau.edu

ARKANSAS

Harding University
900 East Center
Searcy, AR 72149
E-mail: admissions@harding.edu
http://www.harding.edu

John Brown University
2000 West University Street
Siloam Springs, AR 72761
Phone: (501) 524-3131
E-mail: jbuinfo@acc.jbu.edu
http://www.jbu.edu

CALIFORNIA

California State University—Stanislaus
801 West Monte Vista Avenue
Turlock, CA 95382
Phone: (209) 667-3122
E-mail: Outreach_Help_Desk@stan.
        csustan.edu
http://www.csustan.edu

Pacific Union College
One Angwin Avenue
Angwin, CA 94508
Phone: (707) 965-6336
E-mail: enroll@puc.edu
http://www.puc.edu

Pepperdine University
24255 Pacific Coast Highway
Malibu, CA 90263
Phone: (310) 456-4000
E-mail: admission-seaver
        @pepperdine.edu
http://www.pepperdine.edu

Point Loma Nazarene University
3900 Lomaland Drive
San Diego, CA 92106
Phone: (619) 849-2200
E-mail: admissions@ptloma.edu
http://www.ptloma.edu

San Jose State University
One Washington Square
San Jose, CA 95192
Phone: (408) 924-1000
E-mail: info@soar.sjsu.edu
http://www.sjsu.edu

University of Southern California
University Park
Los Angeles, CA 90089
Phone: (213) 740-2311
E-mail: admapp@enroll1.usc.edu
http://www.usc.edu

COLORADO

Colorado State University
Fort Collins, CO 80523
Phone: (970) 491-1101
E-mail: admissions@colostate.edu
http://www.colostate.edu

CONNECTICUT

Quinnipiac University
Mount Carmel Avenue
Hamden, CT 06518
Phone: (203) 582-8200
E-mail: admissions@quinnipiac.edu
http://www.quinnipiac.edu

DELAWARE

Delaware State University
1200 North Dupont Highway
Dover, DE 19901
Phone: (302) 857-6060
E-mail: dadmiss@dsc.edu
http://www.dsc.edu

DISTRICT OF COLUMBIA

American University
4400 Massachusetts Avenue, NW
Washington, DC 20016
Phone: (202) 885-1000
E-mail: afa@american.edu
http://www.american.edu

FLORIDA

Barry University
11300 Northeast Second Avenue
Miami Shores, FL 33161
Phone: (305) 899-3000

E-mail: admissions@mail.barry.edu
http://www.barry.edu

Florida A&M University
Tallahassee, FL 32307
E-mail: bcox2@famu.edu
http://www.famu.edu

Florida State University
Tallahassee, FL 32306
Phone: (850) 644-2525
E-mail: admissions@admin.fsu.edu
http://www.fsu.edu

University of Central Florida
4000 Central Florida Boulevard
Orlando, FL 32816
Phone: (407) 823-2000
E-mail: admission@mail.ucf.edu
http://www.ucf.edu

University of Florida
201 Criser Hall
Gainesville, FL 32611
Phone: (352) 392-3261
E-mail: freshman@ufl.edu
http://www.ufl.edu

University of Miami
PO Box 248025
Coral Gables, FL 33124
Phone: (305) 284-2211
E-mail: admission@miami.edu
http://www.miami.edu

GEORGIA

Augusta State University
2500 Walton Way
Augusta, GA 30904-2200
Phone: (706) 737-1400
E-mail: admissio@aug.edu
http://www.aug.edu

Columbus State University
4225 University Avenue
Columbus, GA 31907
Phone: (706) 568-2001
E-mail: admissions@colstate.edu
http://www.colstate.edu

Georgia Southern University
PO Box 8033
Statesboro, GA 30460
Phone: (912) 681-5611
E-mail: admissions@gasou.edu
http://www.gasou.edu

Shorter College
315 Shorter Avenue
Rome, GA 30165
Phone: (706) 291-2121

E-mail: admissions@shorter.edu
http://www.shorter.edu

Toccoa Falls College
PO Box 800-899
Toccoa Falls, GA 30598
Phone: (706) 886-6831
E-mail: admissions@toccoafalls.edu
http://www.toccoafalls.edu

University of Georgia
212 Terrell Hall
Athens, GA 30602
Phone: (706) 542-3000
E-mail: undergrad@admissions.uga.edu
http://www.uga.edu

HAWAII

Hawaii Pacific University
1164 Bishop Street
Honolulu, HI 96813
Phone: (808) 544-0200
E-mail: admissions@hpu.edu
http://www.hpu.edu

IDAHO

Northwest Nazarene University
623 Holly Street
Nampa, ID 83686
Phone: (208) 467-8011
E-mail: Admissions@nnu.edu

University of Idaho
PO Box 443151
Moscow, ID 83844-3151
Phone: (208) 885-6111
E-mail: admappl@uidaho.edu
http://www.uidaho.edu/index-ext.shtml

ILLINOIS

Bradley University
1501 West Bradley Avenue
Peoria, IL 61625
Phone: (309) 676-7611
E-mail: admissions@bradley.edu
http://www.bradley.edu

Columbia College
600 South Michigan Avenue
Chicago, IL 60605-1996
Phone: (312) 344-1600
E-mail: admissions@popmail.colum.edu
http://www.colum.edu

Illinois State University
Campus Box 2200
Normal, IL 61790-2200
Phone: (309) 438-2111

E-mail: ugradadm@ilstu.edu
http://www.ilstu.edu

McKendree College
701 College Road
Lebanon, IL 62254-1299
Phone: (618) 537-4481
E-mail: scordon@atlas.mckendree.edu
http://www.mckendree.edu

Monmouth College
700 East Broadway
Monmouth, IL 61462
Phone: (309) 457-2131
E-mail: admit@monm.edu
http://www.monm.edu

North Central College
30 North Brainard Street
PO Box 3063
Naperville, IL 60566
Phone: (630) 637-5100
E-mail: ncadm@noctrl.edu
http://www.noctrl.edu

Roosevelt University
430 South Michigan Avenue
Chicago, IL 60605
Phone: (312) 341-3500
E-mail: applyRU@roosevelt.edu
http://www.roosevelt.edu

INDIANA

Ball State University
2000 University Avenue
Muncie, IN 47306
E-mail: askus@wp.bsu.edu
http://www.bsu.edu

**Indiana University-Purdue
    University—Fort Wayne**
2101 East Coliseum Boulevard
Fort Wayne, IN 46805
Phone: (219) 481-6100
E-mail: ipfwadms@ipfw.edu
http://www.ipfw.edu

University of Southern Indiana
8600 University Boulevard
Evansville, IN 47712
Phone: (812) 464-8600
E-mail: enroll@usi.edu
http://www.usi.edu

IOWA

Drake University
2507 University Avenue
Des Moines, IA 50311
Phone: (515) 271-2011
E-mail: admitinfo@acad.drake.edu
http://www.drake.edu

Loras College
1450 Alta Vista
Dubuque, IA 52001
Phone: (319) 588-7100
E-mail: adms@loras.edu
http://www.loras.edu

Mount Mercy College
1330 Elmhurst Drive, NE
Cedar Rapids, IA 52402
Phone: (319) 363-8213
E-mail: admission@mmc.mtmercy.edu
http://www.mtmercy.edu

University of Northern Iowa
1227 West 27th Street
Cedar Falls, IA 50614
Phone: (319) 273-2311
E-mail: admissions@uni.edu
http://www.uni.edu/index.html

KENTUCKY

Eastern Kentucky University
521 Lancaster Avenue
Richmond, KY 40475
Phone: (859) 622-1000
E-mail: admissions@eku.edu
http://www.eku.edu

Murray State University
15th and Main Streets
Murray, KY 42071
E-mail: phil.bryan@murraystate.edu
http://www.murraystate.edu

Western Kentucky University
One Big Red Way
Bowling Green, KY 42101
Phone: (270) 745-0111
E-mail: admission@wku.edu
http://www.wku.edu

LOUISIANA

Louisiana State University—
   Shreveport
One University Place
Shreveport, LA 71115
Phone: (318) 797-5000
E-mail: admissions@pilot.lsus.edu
http://www.lsus.edu

University of Louisiana—Lafayette
PO Drawer 41008
Lafayette, LA 70504
Phone: (337) 482-1000
E-mail: enroll@louisiana.edu
http://www.usl.edu

MASSACHUSETTS

Boston University
121 Bay State Road
Boston, MA 02215
Phone: (617) 353-2000
E-mail: admissions@bu.edu
http://www.bu.edu

Emerson College
120 Boylston Street
Boston, MA 02116
Phone: (617) 824-8500
E-mail: admission@emerson.edu
http://www.emerson.edu

Northeastern University
360 Huntington Avenue
Boston, MA 02115
Phone: (617) 373-2000
E-mail: admissions@neu.edu
http://www.neu.edu

Simmons College
300 The Fenway
Boston, MA 02115
E-mail: ugadm@simmons.edu
http://www.simmons.edu

Suffolk University
Eight Ashburton Place
Beacon Hill
Boston, MA 02108
Phone: (617) 573-8000
E-mail: admission@admin.suffolk.edu
http://www.suffolk.edu

MICHIGAN

Andrews University
Berrien Springs, MI 49104
Phone: (800) 253-2874
E-mail: enroll@andrews.edu
http://www.andrews.edu

Central Michigan University
105 Warriner
Mount Pleasant, MI 48859
Phone: (517) 774-4000
E-mail: cmuadmit@cmich.edu
http://www.cmich.edu

Eastern Michigan University
Ypsilanti, MI 48197
Phone: (734) 487-1849
E-mail: undergraduate.admissions@
   emich.edu
http://www.emich.edu

Ferris State University
901 State Street
Big Rapids, MI 49307

Phone: (231) 591-2000
E-mail: admissions@ferris.edu
http://www.ferris.edu

Grand Valley State University
One Campus Drive
Allendale, MI 49401
Phone: (616) 895-6611
E-mail: go2gvsu@gvsu.edu
http://www.gvsu.edu

Madonna University
36600 Schoolcraft Road
Livonia, MI 48150
http://www.munet.edu

Northern Michigan University
1401 Presque Isle Avenue
Marquette, MI 49855
Phone: (906) 227-1000
E-mail: admiss@nmu.edu
http://www.nmu.edu

Wayne State University
656 West Kirby
Detroit, MI 48202
Phone: (313) 577-2424
E-mail: admissions@wayne.edu
http://www.wayne.edu

Western Michigan University
1201 Oliver Street
Kalamazoo, MI 49008
Phone: (616) 387-1000
E-mail: ask-wmu@wmich.edu
http://www.wmich.edu

MINNESOTA

Concordia College—Moorhead
901 South Eighth Street
Moorhead, MN 56562
Phone: (218) 299-4000
E-mail: admissions@cord.edu
http://www.cord.edu

Metropolitan State University
700 East Seventh Street
St. Paul, MN 55106
Phone: (651) 772-7779
E-mail: admission@metrostate.edu
http://www.metrostate.edu

St. Cloud State University
720 South Fourth Avenue
St. Cloud, MN 56301
Phone: (320) 255-2244
E-mail: scsu4u@stcloudstate.edu
http://www.stcloudstate.edu

St. Mary's University of Minnesota
700 Terrace Heights
Winona, MN 55987

Phone: (507) 452-4430
E-mail: admissions@smumn.edu
http://www.smumn.edu

Winona State University
PO Box 5838
Winona, MN 55987
Phone: (800) 342-5978
E-mail: admissions@vax2.winona.msus.
edu
http://www.winona.msus.edu

MISSISSIPPI

Mississippi University for Women
W Box 1600
Columbus, MS 39701
Phone: (662) 329-4750
E-mail: admissions@muw.edu
http://www.muw.edu

MISSOURI

Central Missouri State University
Administration Building
Warrensburg, MO 64093
Phone: (660) 543-4111
E-mail: admit@cmsul.cmsu.edu
http://www.cmsu.edu

Fontbonne College
6800 Wydown Boulevard
St. Louis, MO 63105
E-mail: pmusen@fontbonne.edu
http://www.fontbonne.edu

Northwest Missouri State University
800 University Drive
Maryville, MO 64468
E-mail: admissions@mail.nwmissouri.edu
http://www.nwmissouri.edu

Rockhurst University
1100 Rockhurst Road
Kansas City, MO 64110-2561
Phone: (816) 501-4000
E-mail: admission@rockhurst.edu
http://www.rockhurst.edu

St. Louis University
221 North Grand Boulevard
St. Louis, MO 63103
Phone: (314) 977-2222
E-mail: admitme@slu.edu
http://www.slu.edu

Stephens College
1200 East Broadway
Box 2121
Columbia, MO 65215
Phone: (573) 442-2211

E-mail: apply@sc.stephens.edu
http://www.stephens.edu

Webster University
470 East Lockwood Avenue
St. Louis, MO 63119
E-mail: admit@webster.edu
http://www.webster.edu

MONTANA

Carroll College
1601 North Benton Avenue
Helena, MT 59625
E-mail: enroll@carroll. edu
http://www.carroll.edu

Montana State University—Billings
1500 North 30th Street
Billings, MT 59101
Phone: (406) 657-2011
E-mail: admissions@msubillings.edu
http://www.msubillings.edu

NEBRASKA

Bellevue University
1000 Galvin Road, South
Bellevue, NE 68005
Phone: (402) 291-8100
E-mail: bellevue_u@scholars.
bellevue.edu
http://www.bellevue.edu

College of St. Mary
1901 South 72nd Street
Omaha, NE 68124
Phone: (402) 399-2400
E-mail: enroll@csm.edu
http://www.csm.edu

Creighton University
2500 California Plaza
Omaha, NE 68178
E-mail: admissions@creighton.edu
http://www.creighton.edu

Doane College
1014 Boswell Avenue
Crete, NE 68333
Phone: (402) 826-2161
E-mail: admissions@doane.edu
http://www.doane.edu

University of Nebraska—Kearney
905 West 25th Street
Kearney, NE 68849
Phone: (308) 865-8441
E-mail: admissionsug@unk.edu
http://www.unk.edu

NEW HAMPSHIRE

Rivier College
420 Main Street
Nashua, NH 03060
E-mail: rivadmit@rivier.edu
http://www.rivier.edu

NEW YORK

Buffalo State College
1300 Elmwood Avenue
Buffalo, NY 14222
E-mail: admissio@buffalostate.edu
http://www.buffalostate.edu

College of New Rochelle
Castle Place
New Rochelle, NY 10805
Phone: (914) 654-5000
E-mail: admission@cnr.edu
http://www.cnr.edu

College of St. Rose
432 Western Avenue
Albany, NY 12203
Phone: (800) 637-8556
E-mail: admit@rosnet.strose.edu
http://www.strose.edu

**City University of New York—Lehman
College**
250 Bedford Park Boulevard, West
Bronx, NY 10468
Phone: (718) 960-8000
E-mail: enroll@lehman.cuny.edu
http://www.lehman.cuny.edu

Ithaca College
100 Job Hall
Ithaca, NY 14850-7020
Phone: (607) 274-3124
E-mail: admission@ithaca.edu
http://www.ithaca.edu

Keuka College
Keuka Park, NY 14478
Phone: (315) 536-4411
E-mail: admissions@mail.keuka.edu
http://www.keuka.edu

**Long Island University—C. W. Post
Campus**
720 Northern Boulevard
Brookville, NY 11548-1300
Phone: (516) 299-2000
E-mail: enroll@cwpost.liu.edu
http://www.liu.edu

Mount St. Mary College
330 Powell Avenue
Newburgh, NY 12550

Phone: (914) 561-0800
E-mail: mtstmary@msmc.edu
http://www.msmc.edu

State University of New York—Oswego
7060 State Route 104
Oswego, NY 13126
E-mail: admiss@oswego.edu
http://www.oswego.edu

Syracuse University
201 Tolley Administration Building
Syracuse, NY 13244
Phone: (315) 443-1870
E-mail: orange@syr.edu
http://www.syracuse.edu

Utica College of Syracuse University
1600 Burrstone Road
Utica, NY 13502
E-mail: admiss@utica.ucsu.edu
http://www.utica.edu

NORTH CAROLINA

Appalachian State University
Boone, NC 28608
Phone: (828) 262-2000
E-mail: admissions@appstate.edu
http://www.appstate.edu

East Carolina University
Fifth Street
Greenville, NC 27858
E-mail: admis@mail.ecu.edu
http://www.ecu.edu

Elon College
2700 Campus Box
Elon College, NC 27244
Phone: (336) 584-9711
E-mail: admissions@elon.edu
http://www.elon.edu

Mars Hill College
100 Athletic Street
Mars Hill, NC 28754
E-mail: admissions@mhc.edu
http://www.mhc.edu

North Carolina A&T State University
1601 East Market Street
Greensboro, NC 27411
Phone: (336) 334-7500
E-mail: uadmit@ncat.edu
http://www.ncat.edu

**University of North Carolina—
   Greensboro**
1000 Spring Garden Street
Greensboro, NC 27412
Phone: (336) 334-5243

E-mail: undergrad_admissions
@uncg.edu
http://www.uncg.edu/adm

OHIO

Ashland University
401 College Avenue
Ashland, OH 44805
Phone: (419) 289-4142
E-mail: auadmsn@ashland.edu
http://www.ashland.edu

Bowling Green State University
110 McFall Center
Bowling Green, OH 43403
Phone: (419) 372-2531
E-mail: admissions@bgnet.bgsu.edu
http://www.bgsu.edu

Capital University
2199 East Main Street
Columbus, OH 43209
Phone: (614) 236-6011
E-mail: admissions@capital.edu
http://www.capital.edu

David N. Myers College
112 Prospect Avenue
Cleveland, OH 44115
Phone: (216) 696-9000
E-mail: admissions@dnmyers.edu
http://www.dnmyers.edu

Heidelberg College
310 East Market Street
Tiffin, OH 44883
E-mail: admission@heidelberg.edu
http://www.heidelberg.edu

Kent State University
PO Box 5190
Kent, OH 44242
Phone: (330) 672-2121
E-mail: KENTADM@admissions.
   kent.edu
http://www.kent.edu

Marietta College
215 Fifth Street
Marietta, OH 45750
Phone: (740) 376-4643
E-mail: admit@marietta.edu
http://www.marietta.edu

Ohio University
Athens, OH 45701
Phone: (740) 593-1000
E-mail: FRSHINFO@ohiou.edu
http://www.ohiou.edu

Otterbein College
College Avenue and Grove Street
Westerville, OH 43081
Phone: (614) 890-3000
E-mail: UOtterB@Otterbein.edu
http://www.otterbein.edu

Ursuline College
2550 Lander Road
Pepper Pike, OH 44124
Phone: (440) 449-4200
E-mail: joakley@ursuline.edu
http://www.ursuline.edu

Wright State University
3640 Colonel Glenn Highway
Dayton, OH 45435
Phone: (937) 775-3300
E-mail: admissions@wright.edu
http://www.wright.edu

Youngstown State University
One University Plaza
Youngstown, OH 44555
Phone: (330) 742-3000
E-mail: enroll@ysu.edu
http://www.ysu.edu

OKLAHOMA

Oklahoma Baptist University
500 West University
Shawnee, OK 74804
Phone: (405) 275-2850
E-mail: admissions@mail.okbu.edu
http://www.okbu.edu

Oklahoma Christian University
Box 11000
Oklahoma City, OK 73136
Phone: (405) 425-5000
E-mail: Kyle.Wray@oc.edu
http://www.oc.edu

Oral Roberts University
7777 South Lewis
Tulsa, OK 74171
Phone: (918) 495-6161
E-mail: admissions@oru.edu
http://www.oru.edu

University of Oklahoma
660 Parrington Oval
Norman, OK 73019
Phone: (405) 325-0311
E-mail: admrec@ouwww.ou.edu
http://www.ou.edu

OREGON

Marylhurst University
17600 Pacific Highway and Highway 43
PO Box 261
Marylhurst, OR 97036-0261

Phone: (800) 634-9982
E-mail: admissions@marylhurst.edu
http://www.marylhurst.edu

University of Oregon
1217 University of Oregon
Eugene, OR 97403
E-mail: uoadmit@oregon.uoregon.edu
http://www.uoregon.edu

University of Portland
5000 North Willamette Boulevard
Portland, OR 97203
Phone: (503) 943-7911
E-mail: admissions@up.edu
http://www.up.edu

Western Baptist College
5000 Deer Park Drive, SE
Salem, OR 97301
Phone: (503) 581-8600
E-mail: admissio@wbc.edu
http://www.wbc.edu

PENNSYLVANIA

Duquesne University
600 Forbes Avenue
Pittsburgh, PA 15282
Phone: (412) 396-6000
E-mail: admissions@duq.edu
http://www.duq.edu

Mansfield University of Pennsylvania
Alumni Hall
Mansfield, PA 16933
Phone: (570) 662-4000
E-mail: admissns@mnsfld.edu
http://www.mansfield.edu

**Pennsylvania State University—
 University Park**
University Park Campus
University Park, PA 16802
E-mail: admissions@psu.edu
http://www.psu.edu

Marywood University
2300 Adams Avenue
Scranton, PA 18509
Phone: (570) 348-6211
E-mail: ugadm@ac.marywood.edu
http://www.marywood.edu

Point Park College
201 Wood Street
Pittsburgh, PA 15222
Phone: (800) 321-0129
E-mail: enroll@ppc.edu
http://www.ppc.edu

University of Pittsburgh—Bradford
300 Campus Drive
Bradford, PA 16701
Phone: (800) 872-1787
E-mail: admissions@www.upb.pitt.edu
http://www.upb.pitt.edu

Westminster College
South Market Street
New Wilmington, PA 16172
Phone: (724) 946-8761
E-mail: admis@westminster.edu
http://www.westminster.edu

York College of Pennsylvania
Country Club Road
York, PA 17405-7199
Phone: (717) 846-7788
E-mail: admissions@ycp.edu
http://www.ycp.edu

RHODE ISLAND

University of Rhode Island
Green Hall
Kingston, RI 02881
Phone: (401) 874-1000
E-mail: uriadmit@uri.edu
http://www.uri.edu

SOUTH CAROLINA

**University of South Carolina—
 Columbia**
Columbia, SC 29208
Phone: (803) 777-7000
E-mail: admissions-ugrad@sc.edu
http://www.sc.edu

TENNESSEE

David Lipscomb University
3901-4001 Granny White Pike
Nashville, TN 37204
Phone: (800) 333-4358
E-mail: admissions@lipscomb.edu
http://www.lipscomb.edu

Middle Tennessee State University
1301 East Main Street
CAB Room 205
Murfreesboro, TN 37132
Phone: (615) 898-2300
E-mail: admissions@mtsu.edu
http://www.mtsu.edu

Southern Adventist University
PO Box 370
Collegedale, TN 37315
Phone: (423) 238-2111

E-mail: admissions@southern.edu
http://www.southern.edu

TEXAS

Southern Methodist University
PO Box 750296
Dallas, TX 75275
Phone: (214) 768-2000
E-mail: ugadmission@smu.edu
http://www.smu.edu

Texas Christian University
2800 South University Drive
Fort Worth, TX 76129
E-mail: frogmail@tcu.edu
http://www.tcu.edu

Texas Tech University
Box 42013
Lubbock, TX 79409
Phone: (806) 742-2011
E-mail: nsr@ttu.edu
http://www.texastech.edu

University of Houston
4800 Calhoun Road
Houston, TX 77004
Phone: (713) 743-1000
E-mail: admissions@uh.edu
http://www.uh.edu

West Texas A&M University
PO Box 60999
Canyon, TX 79016
Phone: (806) 651-2000
E-mail: apifer@mail.wtamu.edu
http://www.wtamu.edu

VIRGINIA

Hampton University
Tyler Street
Hampton, VA 23668
E-mail: admissions@hamptonu.edu
http://www.hamptonu.edu

Virginia Commonwealth University
821 West Franklin Street
Richmond, VA 23284
Phone: (804) 828-0100
E-mail: ugrad@vcu.edu
http://www.vcu.edu

WASHINGTON

Central Washington University
400 East Eighth Avenue
Ellensburg, WA 98926
Phone: (509) 963-1111

E-mail: cwuadmis@cwu.edu
http://www.cwu.edu

Eastern Washington University
MS 148
Cheney, WA 99004
Phone: (509) 359-6200
E-mail: admissions@mail.ewu.edu
http://www.ewu.edu

Gonzaga University
502 East Boone Avenue
Spokane, WA 99258
Phone: (509) 328-4220
E-mail: Ballinger@gu.gonzaga.edu
http://www.gonzaga.edu

Washington State University
French Administration Building
Pullman, WA 99164
E-mail: admiss@wsu.edu
http://www.wsu.edu

WEST VIRGINIA

West Virginia Wesleyan College
59 College Avenue
Buckhannon, WV 26201
Phone: (304) 473-8000
E-mail: admissions@wvwc.edu
http://www.wvwc.edu

WISCONSIN

Cardinal Stritch University
6801 North Yates Road
Milwaukee, WI 53217
Phone: (414) 410-4000
E-mail: admityou@stritch.edu
http://www.stritch.edu

Concordia University Wisconsin
12800 North Lake Shore Drive
Mequon, WI 53097

E-mail: admission@cuw.edu
http://www.cuw.edu

Marquette University
PO Box 1881
Milwaukee, WI 53201
Phone: (414) 288-7250
E-mail: admissions@marquette.edu
http://www.marquette.edu

Mount Mary College
2900 North Menomonee River Parkway
Milwaukee, WI 53222
Phone: (414) 258-4810
E-mail: admiss@mtmary.edu
http://www.mtmary.edu

APPENDIX II
ASSOCIATIONS AND UNIONS

The following is a listing of associations and unions discussed in this book as well as other associations that might be useful to you. Many of the organizations have branch offices located throughout the country that can provide you with the phone number and address of the closest local branch.

Academy of Dentistry for Persons with Disabilities
211 East Chicago Avenue
Chicago, IL 60611
Phone: (312) 440-2660
Fax: (312) 440-2824
E-mail: stein@uic.edu

Academy of Dispensing Audiologists (ADA)
3008 Millwood Avenue
Columbia, SC 29205
Phone: (803) 252-5646
Fax: (803) 765-0860
Toll-Free: (800) 445-8629
E-mail: info@audiologist.org
www.audiologist.org

Academy of Hospital Public Relations (AHPR)
33 Irving Place
New York, NY 10003
Phone: (212) 460-1480

Academy of Surgical Research (ASR)
13355 10th Avenue N Suite 108
Minneapolis, MN 55441
Phone: (763) 765-2300
Fax: (763) 765-2329
E-mail: manager@surgicalresearch.org
www.surgicalresearch.org

Accreditation Review Committee on Education for Physician Assistants (ARC-PA)
1000 North Oak Avenue
Marshfield, WI 54449-5788
Phone: (715) 389-3785
Fax: (715) 387-5163
E-mail: mccartyj@mfldclin.edu

Accreditation Review Committee on Education in Surgical Technology (ARC-ST)
c/o William J. Teutsch
7108-C South Alton Way
Englewood, CO 80112-2106

Phone: (303) 694-9262
Fax: (303) 694-3655

Accrediting Bureau of Health Education Schools (ABHES)
803 W. Broad Street
Suite 730
Falls Church, VA 22046
Phone: (703) 533-2082
Fax: (703) 998-2550
E-mail: abhes@erols.com
www.abhes.org

Alliance of Cardiovascular Professionals
910 Charles Street
Fredericksburg, VA 22401
Phone: (540) 370-0102
Fax: (540) 370-0015
E-mail: seanmce@aol.com

American Academy of Ambulatory Care Nursing (AAACN)
East Holly Avenue
Box 56
Pitman, NJ 08071-0056
Phone: (856) 256-2350
Fax: (856) 589-7463
Toll-Free: (800) 262-6877
E-mail: aaacn@ajj.com
www.aaacn.org

American Academy of Anesthesiologist Assistants (AAAA)
PO Box 81362
Wellesley, MA 02481
Phone: (800) 757-5858
Fax: (781) 239-3259
www.anesthetist.org

American Academy of Cosmetic Surgery (AACS)
737 North Michigan Avenue
Suite 820
Chicago, IL 60611
Phone: (312) 981-6760
E-mail: aacs@sba.com
www.cosmeticsurgery.org

American Academy of Nurse Practitioners (AANP)
National Administrative Office
PO Box 12846
Austin, TX 78711
Phone: (512) 442-4262
Fax: (512) 442-6469
E-mail: admin@aanp.org
www.aanp.org

American Academy of Pediatrics (AAP)
141 Northwest Point Boulevard
Elk Grove Village, IL 60007
Phone: (847) 228-5005
Fax: (847) 228-5097
Toll-Free (800) 433-9016
E-mail: Aapnews@aap.org

American Academy of Physician Assistants (AAPA)
950 North Washington Street
Alexandria, VA 22314-1552
Phone: (703) 836-2272
Fax: (703) 684-1924
E-mail: aapa@aapa.org
www.aapa.org

American Academy of Podiatric Practice Management
10918 Kingston Pike
Knoxville, TN 37922
Phone: (423) 966-5775
Fax: (423) 966-5743

American Art Therapy Association (AATA)
1202 Allanson Road
Mundelein, IL 60060
Phone: (847) 949-6064
Fax: (847) 566-4580
Toll-Free (888) 290-0878
www.arttherapy.org

American Association for Clinical Chemistry (AACC)
2101 L Street NW
Suite 202
Washington, DC 20037

Phone: (202) 857-0717
Fax: (202) 887-5093
Toll-Free: (800) 892-1400
E-mail: info@aacc.org
www.aacc.org

American Association for International Aging (AAIA)
1900 L Street, NW
Suite 510
Washington, DC 20036-5002
Phone: (202) 833-8893
Fax: (202) 833-8762

American Association for Medical Transcription (AAMT)
3460 Oakdale Road
Suite M
Modesto, CA 95355-9690
Phone: (209) 551-0883
Fax: (209) 551-9317
Toll-Free: (800) 982-2182
E-mail: aamt@sna.com
www.aamt.org

American Association for Respiratory Care (AARC)
11030 Ables Lane
Dallas, TX 75229
Phone: (972) 243-2272
Fax: (972) 484-2720
E-mail: info@aarc.org
www.aarc.org

American Association for Thoracic Surgery (AATS)
13 Elm Street
Manchester, MA 01944
Phone: (978) 526-8330
Fax: (978) 526-4018
E-mail: aats@prri.com
www.aats.org

American Association of Cardiovascular and Pulmonary Rehabilitation (AACVPR)
7600 Terrace Avenue
Middleton, WI 53562
Phone: (608) 831-6989
Fax: (608) 831-5122
E-mail: aacvpr@tmahq.com
http://www.aacvpr.org

American Association of Colleges of Pharmacy (AACP)
1426 Prince Street
Alexandria, VA 22314
Phone: (703) 739-2330
Fax: (703) 836-8982
E-mail: rpenna@aacp.org
www.aacp.org

American Association of Critical-Care Nurses (AACN)
101 Columbia
Aliso Viejo, CA 92656-1491
Phone: (949) 362-2000
Fax: (949) 362-2020
Toll-Free: (800) 899-AACN
E-mail: info@aacn.org
www.aacn.org

American Association of Homes and Services for the Aging (AAHSA)
901 E Street NW
Suite 500
Washington, DC 20004-2011
Phone: (202) 783-2242
Fax: (202) 783-2255
E-mail: info@aahsa.org
www.aahsa.org

American Association of Homes and Services for the Aging Research and Information Center
901 E Street NW
Suite 500
Washington, DC 20004-2037
Phone: (202) 508-9491
Fax: (202) 783-2255

American Association of Medical Assistants (AAMA)
20 North Wacker Drive
Suite 1575
Chicago, IL 60606-2963
Phone: (312) 899-1500
Fax: (312) 899-1259
Toll-Free: (800) 228-2262
www.aama-ntl.org

American Association of Pharmaceutical Scientists (AAPS)
2107 Wilson Boulevard
No. 700
Arlington, VA 22201
Phone: (703) 548-3000
Fax: (703) 684-7349
E-mail: aaps@aaps.org
www.pharmsci.org

American Association of Pharmacy Technicians (AAPT)
PO Box 1447
Greensboro, NC 27402
Phone: (336) 275-1700
Fax: (336) 275-7222

American Association of Spinal Cord Injury Nurses (AASCIN)
75-20 Astoria Boulevard
East Elmhurst, NY 11370
Phone: (718) 803-3782
Fax: (718) 803-0414
www.aascin.org

American College of Apothecaries (ACA)
PO Box 341266
Memphis, TN 38184-1266
Phone: (901) 383-8119
Fax: (901) 383-8882

American College of Cardiology (ACC)
9111 Old Georgetown Road
Bethesda, MD 20814
Phone: (301) 897-5400
Fax: (301) 897-9745
Toll-Free: (800) 253-4636
E-mail: exec@acc.org
www.acc.org

American College Health Association (ACHA)
PO Box 28937
Baltimore, MD 21240-8937
Phone: (410) 859-1500
Fax: (410) 859-1510
www.acha.org

American College of Cardiovascular Administrators (ACCA)
701 Lee Street
Suite 600
Des Plaines, IL 60016
Phone: (847) 759-8601 or (847) 759-8602
E-mail: info@aameda.org
www.aameda.org

American College of Chest Physicians
3300 Dundee Road
Northbrook, IL 60062-2348
Phone: (847) 498-1400
Fax: (847) 498-5460
Toll-Free: (800) 343-ACCP
E-mail: Accp@chestnet.org
www.chestnet.org
www.chestjournal.org

American College of Health Care Administrators (ACHCA)
1800 Diagonal Road 355
Alexandria, VA 22314
Phone: (703) 739-7900
Fax: (703) 739-7901
Toll-Free: (888) 88-ACHCA
E-mail: info@achca.org
www.achca.org

American College of Healthcare Executives (ACHE)
1 North Franklin
Suite 1700
Chicago, IL 60606-3491
Phone: (312) 424-2800
Fax: (312) 424-0023
E-mail: ache@ache.org
www.ache.org

American College of Healthcare Information Administrators (ACHIA)
701 Lee Street
Suite 600
Des Plaines, IL 60016
Phone: (847) 759-8601
Fax: (847) 759-8602
E-mail: info@aameda.org
www.aameda.org

American College of Nurse-Midwives (ACNM)
818 Connecticut Avenue
Suite 900
Washington, DC 20006
Phone: (202) 728-9860
Fax: (202) 289-9897
E-mail: info@acnm.org
www.midwife.org

American College of Obstetricians and Gynecologists (ACOG)
409 12th Street SW
PO Box 96920
Washington, DC 20090
Phone: (202) 638-5577
Fax: (202) 484-8107
E-mail: mgraves@acog.org
www.acog.org

American College of Osteopathic Obstetricians and Gynecologists (ACOOG)
900 Auburn Road
Pontiac, MI 48342
Phone: (248) 332-6360
Fax: (248) 332-4607
Toll-Free: (800) 875-6360
E-mail: acoog@mich.com
www.acoog.com

American College of Osteopathic Pediatricians (ACOP)
5550 Friendship Boulevard
Chevy Chase, MD 20815
Phone: (301) 968-4180
Fax: (301) 968-4199
E-mail: acop@osteohdq.org

American College of Physicians (ACP)
190 North Independence Mall West
Philadelphia, PA 19106
Phone: (215) 351-2600
Fax: (215) 351-2448
Toll-Free: (800) 523-1546
E-mail: interpub@mail.acponline.org
www.acponline.org

American College of Veterinary Internal Medicine (ACVIM)
1997 Wadsworth
Lakewood, CO 80215

Phone: (303) 231-9933
Fax: (303) 231-0880
Toll-Free: (800) 245-9081
E-mail: acvim@acvim.org
www.acvim.org

American Council on Pharmaceutical Education (ACPE)
311 West Superior Street
Suite 512
Chicago, IL 60610
Phone: (312) 664-3575
Fax: (312) 664-4652
www.acpe-accredit.org

American Dance Therapy Association (ADTA)
2000 Century Plaza
Suite 108
Columbia, MD 21044
Phone: (410) 997-4040
Fax: (410) 997-4048
E-mail: info@adta.org
www.adta.org

American Dental Assistants Association (ADAA)
203 North LaSalle Street
Suite 1320
Chicago, IL 60601-1225
Phone: (312) 541-1550
Fax: (312) 541-1496
Toll-Free: (800) SEE-ADAA
E-mail: adaa1@aol.com
www.dentalassistant.org

American Dental Association (ADA)
211 East Chicago Avenue
Chicago, IL 60611
Phone: (312) 440-2500
Fax: (312) 440-2800
E-mail: publicinfo@ada.org
www.ada.org

American Dental Hygienists' Association (ADHA)
444 North Michigan Avenue
Suite 3400
Chicago, IL 60611
Phone: (312) 440-8900
Fax: (312) 440-8929
Toll-Free: (800) 243-ADHA
E-mail: mail@adha.net
www.adha.org

American Diabetes Association (ADA)
1701 North Beauregard Street
Alexandria, VA 22311
Phone: (703) 549-1500
Fax: (703) 836-7439
Toll-Free: (800) DIABETES

E-mail: customerservice@diabetes.org
www.diabetes.org

American Dietetic Association (ADA)
216 West Jackson Boulevard
Chicago, IL 60606-6995
Phone: (312) 899-0040
Fax: (312) 899-1979
E-mail: membrshp@eatright.org
www.eatright.org

American Disabled for Attendant Program Today (ADAPT)
201 South Cherokee Street
Denver, CO 80223-1836
Phone: (303) 733-9324
Fax: (303) 733-6211
E-mail: adapt@adapt.org

American Federation of State, County and Municipal Employees (AFSCME)
1625 L Street NW
Washington, DC 20036
Phone: (202) 429-1000
Fax: (202) 429-1293
E-mail: education@afscme.org
www.afscme.org

American Foundation for Pharmaceutical Education (AFPE)
1 Church Street
Suite 202
Rockville, MD 20850-4158
Phone: (301) 738-2160
Fax: (301) 738-2161
E-mail: afpe@worldnet.att.net

American Geriatrics Society (AGS)
350 Fifth Avenue
Suite 801
New York, NY 10118
Phone: (212) 308-1414
Fax: (212) 832-8646
Toll-Free: (800) 247-4779
E-mail: info.amger
        @americangeriatrics.org
www.americangeriatrics.org

American Gynecological and Obstetrical Society (AGOS)
University of Utah
50 North Medical Drive
Salt Lake City, UT 84132
Phone: (801) 581-5501
Fax: (801) 581-7199

American Health Care Association (AHCA)
1201 L Street NW
Washington, DC 20005
Phone: (202) 842-4444
Fax: (202) 842-3860
www.ahca.org

American Heart Association (AHA)
7272 Greenville Avenue
Dallas, TX 75231
Phone: (214) 373-6300
Fax: (214) 987-4334
Toll-Free: (800) 242-1793
www.americanheart.org

American Hospital Association (AHA)
AHA Resource Center
One North Franklin
Chicago, IL 60606
Phone: (312) 422-2050
Fax: (312) 422-4700
E-mail: rc@aha.org
www.aha.org/resource

**American Health Information
Management Association (AMRA)**
233 North Michigan Avenue
Suite 2150
Chicago, IL 60601
Phone: (312) 233-1100
Fax: (312) 233-1090
E-mail: info@ahima.org
www.ahima.org

**American Institute of Chemical
Engineers (AICHE)**
3 Park Avenue
New York, NY 10016
Fax: (212) 591-8897
Toll-Free: (800) 242-4363
E-mail: xpress@aiche.org
www.aiche.org

American Institute of Homeopathy (AIH)
801 North Fairfax Street
Suite 306
Alexandria, VA 22314
Phone: (703) 246-9501
www.homeopathyusa.org

**American Laryngeal Papilloma
Foundation (ALPF)**
PO Box 6108
Spring Hill, FL 34611
Phone: (352) 686-8583
Fax: (352) 684-7191
E-mail: carrie@atlantic.net
www.alpf.org

American Lung Association (ALA)
1740 Broadway
New York, NY 10019-4374
Phone: (212) 315-8700
Fax: (212) 265-5642
Toll-Free: (800) LUNG
E-mail: info@lung.org
www.lung.org

American Marketing Association (AMA)
311 South Wacker Drive
Suite 5800
Chicago, IL 60606

Phone: (312) 542-9000
Fax: (312) 542-9001
Toll-Free: (800) 262-1150
E-mail: info@ama.org
www.ama.org

**American Medical Directors
Association (AMDA)**
10480 Little Patuxent Parkway
Suite 760
Columbia, MD 21044
Phone: (410) 740-9743
Fax: (410) 740-4572
Toll-Free: (800) 876-AMDA
E-mail: patdrews@amda.com
www.amda.com

**American Medical Technologists
(AMT)**
710 Higgins Road
Park Ridge, IL 60068
Phone: (847) 823-5169
Fax: (847) 823-0458
Toll-Free: (800) 275-1268
E-mail: amtmail@aol.com
www.amt1.com

American Music Therapy Association
8455 Colesville Road
Suite 1000
Silver Spring, MD 20910
Phone: (301) 589-3300
Fax: (301) 589-5175
E-mail: info@musictherapy.org
www.musictherapy.org

**American Neurological Association
(ANA)**
5841 Cedar Lake Road S
Minneapolis, MN 55416
Phone: (612) 545-6284
Fax: (612) 545-6073
www.aneuroa.org

**American Neuropsychiatric
Association (ANA)**
7701 East Kellog Drive
Suite 625
Wichita, KS 67207

American Nurses Association (ANA)
600 Maryland Avenue SW
Suite 100 West
Washington, DC 20024
Phone: (202) 651-7000
Fax: (202) 651-7001
Toll-Free: (800) 274-4262
www.nursingworld.org

**American Occupational Therapy
Association (AOTA)**
4720 Montgomery Lane
PO Box 31220
Bethesda, MD 20824

Phone: (301) 652-2682
Fax: (301) 652-7711
Toll-Free: (800) 377-8555
E-mail: praota@aota.org

**American Osteopathic Academy of
Sports Medicine (AOASM)**
7600 Terrace Avenue
Suite 203
Middleton, WI 53562-3174
Phone: (608) 831-4400
Fax: (608) 831-5122
E-mail: aoasm@tmahq.com

**American Pediatric Surgical
Association (APSA)**
c/o The Sherwood Group
60 Revere Drive
Suite 500
Northbrook, IL 60062
Phone: (847) 480-9576
Fax: (847) 480-9282
E-mail: apsa@apsa.org
www.eapsa.org

American Pharmaceutical Association
2215 Constitution Avenue, NW
Washington, DC 20037
Phone: (202) 429-7557
Fax: (202) 628-5425
Toll-Free: (800) 237-2742
www.aphanet.org

**American Physical Therapy
Association (APTA)**
1111 North Fairfax Street
Alexandria, VA 22314
Phone: (703) 684-2782
Fax: (703) 684-7343
Toll-Free: (800) 999-2782
E-mail: membership@apta.org
www.apta.org

American Physiological Society (APS)
9650 Rockville Pike
Bethesda, MD 20814-3991
Phone: (301) 530-7164
Fax: (301) 571-8305
Email: info@aps.faseb.org
www.faseb.org/aps/

**American Registry of Diagnostic
Medical Sonographers (ARDMS)**
600 Jefferson Plaza
Suite 360
Rockville, MD 20852
Phone: (301) 738-8401
Fax: (301) 738-0312
Toll-Free: (800) 541-9754
Email: administration@ardms.org

American Registry of Radiologic Technologists (ARRT)
1255 Northland Drive
St. Paul, MN 55120
Phone: (651) 687-0048
www.arrt.org

American Society for Clinical Laboratory Science (ASCLS)
7910 Woodmont Avenue
Bethesda, MD 20814
Phone: (301) 657-2768
Fax: (301) 657-2909
E-mail: ascls@ascls.org
www.ascls.org

American Society of Clinical Pathologists (ASCP)
2100 West Harrison
Chicago, IL 60612
Phone: (312) 738-1336
Fax: (312) 738-1619
Toll-Free: (800) 621-4142
E-mail: info@ascp.org
www.ascp.org

American Society of Electroneurodiagnostic Technologists (ASET)
204 West 7th Street
Carroll, IA 51401
Phone: (712) 792-2978
Fax: (712) 792-6962
E-mail: aset@netins.net
www.aset.org

American Society of Health System Pharmacists (ASHP)
7272 Wisconsin Avenue
Bethesda, MD 20814
Phone: (301) 657-3000
Fax: (301) 664-8867
E-mail: pdiso@ashp.org
www.ashp.org

American Society of Hospital Pharmacists (ASHP Foundation)
7272 Wisconsin Avenue
Bethesda, MD 20814
Phone: (301) 657-3000
Fax: (301) 664-8872
www.ashpfoundation.org

American Society of Psychopathology of Expression (ASPE)
c/o Dr. Irene Jakab
74 Lawton Street
Brookline, MA 02446
Phone: (617) 738-9821
Fax: (617) 975-0411

American Society of Radiologic Technologists (ASRT)
15000 Central Avenue SE
Albuquerque, NM 87123
Phone: (505) 298-4500
Fax: (505) 298-5063
Toll-Free: (800) 444-2778
E-mail: customerservices@asrt.org
www.asrt.org

American Speech-Language-Hearing Association
10801 Rockville Pike
Rockville, MD 20852
Fax: (301) 897-7355
Toll-Free: (800) 638-8255
E-mail: actioncenter@asha.org
www.asha.org

American Surgical Association (ASA)
c/o Robert P. Jones Jr., Ed.D.
13 Elm Street
Manchester, MA 01944
Phone: (978) 526-8330
Fax: (978) 526-7521
E-mail: asa@prri.com

American Therapeutic Recreation Association (ATRA)
1414 Prince Street
Suite 204
Alexandria, VA 22314
Phone: (703) 683-9420
Fax: (703) 683-9431
E-mail: membership@atra-tr.org
www.atra-tr.org

American Thoracic Society (ATS)
1740 Broadway
15th Floor
New York, NY 10019-4374
Phone: (212) 315-8700
Fax: (212) 315-6498
www.thoracic.org

Association for Gerontology in Higher Education (AGHE)
1030 15th Street, NW
Suite 240
Washington, DC 20005
Phone: (202) 289-9806
Fax: (202) 289-9824
E-mail: ctompkins@aghe.org
www.aghe.org

Association for Surgical Education (ASE)
SIU School of Medicine
Department of Surgery
PO Box 19655
Springfield, IL 62794
Phone: (217) 785-3835
Fax: (217) 524-2431

E-mail: ase@fgi.net
www.surgicaleducation.com

Association for the Advancement of Medical Instrumentation (AAMI)
1110 North Glebe Road
Number 220
Arlington, VA 22201-4795
Phone: (703) 525-4890
Fax: (703) 276-0793
Toll-Free: (800) 332-2264

Association of Clinical Research Professionals (ACRP)
1012 14th Street, NW
Suite 807
Washington, DC 20005
Phone: (202) 737-8100
Fax: (202) 737-8101
E-mail: office@acrpnet.org
www.acrpnet.org

Association of Clinical Scientists
PO Box 1287
Middlebury, VT 05753
Phone: (802) 462-2507
Fax: (802) 462-2673
E-mail: clinsci@sover.net
www.clinicalscience.org

Association of Jewish Aging Services (AJAS)
316 Pennsylvania Avenue, SE
Suite 402
Washington, DC 20003
Phone: (202) 543-7500
Fax: (202) 543-4090
E-mail: ajas@ajas.org
ajas.org

Association of Medical Illustrators (AMI)
2965 Flowers Road South
Suite 105
Atlanta, GA 30341
Phone: (404) 350-7900
Fax: (404) 351-3348

Association of Physician Assistants in Cardiovascular Surgery (APACVS)
PO Box 4834
Englewood, CO 80155
Phone: (303) 221-5651
Fax: (303) 771-2550
Toll-Free: (877) 221-5651
www.apacvs.org

Association of Reproductive Health Professionals (ARHP)
2401 Pennsylvania Avenue NW
Washington, DC 20037
Phone: (202) 466-3825

Fax: (202) 466-3826
E-mail: arhp@arhp.org
www.arhp.org

**Association of Physician Assistant
    Programs (APAP)**
950 North Washington Street
Alexandria, VA 22314
Phone: (703) 548-5538
Fax: (703) 684-1924
www.apap.org

**Association of Professors of
    Gynecology and Obstetrics (APGO)**
409 12th Street SW
Washington, DC 20024
Phone: (202) 863-2507
Fax: (202) 863-2514
Toll-Free: (800) 673-8444
E-mail: djohnson@acog.org
www.apgo.org

**Association of Surgical Technologists
    (AST)**
7108-C South Alton Way
Englewood, CO 80112-2106
Phone: (303) 694-9130
Fax: (303) 694-9169
E-mail: ast@ast.org
www.ast.org

**Association of University Programs in
    Health Administration (AUPHA)**
730 11th Street NW 4th Floor
Washington, DC 20001
Phone: (202) 638-1448
Fax: (202) 638-3429
E-mail: aupha@aupha.org
www.aupha.org

**Anxiety Disorders Association of
    America (ADAA)**
11900 Parklawn Drive
Suite 100
Rockville, MD 20852-2624
Phone: (301) 231-9350
Fax: (301) 231-7392
E-mail: anxdis@adaa.org
www.adaa.org

**Benign Essential Blepharospasm
    Research Foundation (BEBRF)**
PO Box 12468
Beaumont, TX 77726-2468
Phone: (409) 832-0788
Fax: (409) 832-0890
E-mail: bebrf@ih2000.net
www.blepharospasm.org

Cardiology Association
800 Peakwood Drive
Houston, TX 77090
Phone: (281) 444-1742

**Cardiovascular Credentialing
    International (CCI)**
4456 Corporation Lane
Virginia Beach, VA 23462
Phone: (757) 497-3380
Fax: (757) 497-3491
Toll-Free: (800) 326-0268
E-mail: ccircvt@nettek.net

**College of Osteopathic Healthcare
    Executives (COHE)**
5550 Friendship Boulevard
Suite 300
Chevy Chase, MD 20815-7201
Phone: (301) 968-2642
Fax: (301) 968-4195

**Commission on Opticianry
    Accreditation (COA)**
7023 Little River Turnpike
Number 207
Annandale, VA 22003
Phone: (703) 352-8028
Fax: (703) 691-3929
E-mail: coa@erols.com
www.coaccreditation.com

**Council for Advancement and Support
    of Education (CASE)**
1307 New York Avenue, NW
Washington, DC 20005
Phone: (202) 328-5900
Fax: (202) 387-4973
www.case.org

**Committee on Accreditation for
    Respiratory Care**
1248 Harwood Road
Bedford, TX 76021
Phone: (817) 283-2835
Fax: (817) 354-8519
Toll-Free: (800) 874-5615
E-mail: richwalker@coarc.com
www.coarc.com

**Council on Social Work Education
    (CSWE)**
1725 Duke Street
Suite 500
Alexandria, VA 22314
Phone: (703) 683-8080
Fax: (703) 683-8099
www.cswe.org

Cystic Fibrosis Foundation (CFF)
6931 Arlington Road
Bethesda, MD 20814
Phone: (301) 951-4422
Fax: (301) 951-6378
Toll-Free: (800) 344-4823
E-mail: info@cff.org
www.cff.org

**Dental Assisting National Board
    (DANB)**
676 North St. Clair
Suite 1880
Chicago, IL 60611
Phone: (312) 642-3368
Fax: (312) 642-8507
Toll-Free: (800) FOR-DANB
E-mail: danbmail@dentalassisting.com
www.danb.org

Direct Marketing Association (DMA)
1120 Avenue of the Americas
New York, NY 10036
Phone: (212) 768-7277
Fax: (212) 302-6714
E-mail: webmaster@the-dma.org
www.the-dma.org

**Direct Marketing Educational
    Foundation (DMEF)**
1120 Avenue of the Americas
New York, NY 10036
Phone: (212) 768-7277
Fax: (212) 302-6714
www.the-dma.org/dmef

Foundation for Blood Research
PO Box 190
Scarborough, ME 04070
Phone: (207) 883-4131
Fax: (207) 883-1527
Toll-Free: (800) 639-8605
E-mail: www.rritchie@fbr.org
www.fbr.org

Hospice Foundation of America (HFA)
777 17th Street
Number 401
Miami Beach, FL 33139
Fax: (305) 538-0092
Toll-Free: (800) 854-3402
E-mail: hfa@hospicefoundation.org
www.hospicefoundation.org

**International Society for
    Cardiovascular Surgery (ISCVS)**
13 Elm Street
Manchester, MA 01944
Phone: (978) 526-8330
Fax: (978) 526-7521
E-mail: iscvs@prri.com

**International Bronchoesophagological
    Society (IBES)**
c/o David R. Sanderson, M.D.
Mayo Clinic Scottsdale
13400 East Shea Boulevard
Scottsdale, AZ 85259
Phone: (602) 301-8000 or (602)
         301-8265
Fax: (602) 301-4869
E-mail: dsanderson@mayo.edu

Medical Group Management Association (MGMA)
104 Inverness Terrace East
Englewood, CO 80112-5306
Phone: (303) 799-1111
Fax: (303) 643-4439
Toll-Free: (877) 275-6462
www.mgma.com

National Academy of Opticianry (NAO)
8401 Corporate Drive
Number 605
Landover, MD 20785
Phone: (301) 577-4828
Fax: (301) 577-3880

National Alliance of Senior Citizens (NASC)
1700 18th Street NW
Suite 401
Washington, DC 20009
Phone: (202) 986-0118
Fax: (202) 986-2974

National Association for Practical Nurse Education and Service (NAPNES)
1400 Spring Street
Suite 330
Silver Spring, MD 20910
Phone: (301) 588-2491
Fax: (301) 588-2839
E-mail: napnes@bellatlantic.net

National Association for Practical Nurse Education and Service (NAPNES)
1400 Spring Street
Suite 330
Silver Spring, MD 20910
Phone: (301) 588-2491
Fax: (301) 588-2839
E-mail: napnes@bellatlantic.net

National Association of Alcoholism and Drug Abuse Counselors (NAADAC)
1911 Fort Myer Drive
Suite 900
Arlington, VA 22209
Phone: (703) 741-7686
Fax: (703) 741-7698
Toll-Free: (800) 548-0497
E-mail: naadac@naadac.org

National Association of Boards of Pharmacy (NABP)
700 Busse Highway
Park Ridge, IL 60068
Phone: (847) 698-6227
Fax: (847) 698-0124
E-mail: info@nabp.net
www.nabp.net

National Association of Emergency Medical Technicians (NAEMT)
408 Monroe Street
Clinton, MS 39056
Phone: (601) 924-7744
Fax: (601) 924-7325
Toll-Free: (800) 34-NAEMT
E-mail: naemthq@aol.com
www.naemt.org

National Association for Human Development (NAHD)
1424 16th Street NW
Suite 102
PO Box 100
Washington, DC 20036
Phone: (202) 328-2191
Fax: (202) 265-6682
E-mail: nahdcasa@worldnet.att.net

National Association of Health Services Executives (NAHSE)
8630 Fenton Street
Number 126
Silver Spring, MD 20910
Phone: (301) 588-2255
Fax: (301) 588-0011
E-mail: nahse_hq@compuserve.com

National Association of Professional Geriatric Care Managers (PGCM)
1604 North Country Club Road
Tucson, AZ 85716
Phone: (520) 881-8008
Fax: (520) 325-7925
E-mail: info@carmanager.org

National Association of Social Workers (NASW)
750 First Street NE
Suite 700
Washington, DC 20002
Phone: (202) 408-8600
Fax: (202) 336-8312
Toll-Free: (800) 638-8799
E-mail: info@naswdc.org
www.naswdc.org

National Association of Substance Abuse Trainers and Educators (NASATE)
1521 Hillary Street
New Orleans, LA 70118
Phone: (504) 286-5234

National Board for Certified Counselors (NBCC)
3 Terrace Way
Suite D
Greensboro, NC 27403
Phone: (336) 547-0607
Fax: (336) 547-0017

Toll-Free (800) 398-5389
E-mail: nbcc@nbcc.org
www.nbcc.org

National Board for Respiratory Care (NBRC)
8310 Nieman Road
Lenexa, KS 66214
Phone: (913) 599-4200
Fax: (913) 541-0156
E-mail: nbrc-info@nbrc.org
www.nbrc.org

National Center for Homeopathy (NCH)
801 North Fairfax Street
Suite 306
Alexandria, VA 22314
Phone: (703) 548-7790
Fax: (703) 548-7792
Toll-Free: (877) 624-0613
E-mail: info@homeopathic.org
www.homeopathic.org

National Coalition of Arts Therapy Associations (NCATA)
c/o ADTA
8455 Colesville Road
Suite 1000
Silver Spring, MD 20910
Phone: (714) 751-0103
www.ncata.com

National Council for Therapeutic Recreation Certification (NCTRC)
7 Elmwood Drive
New City, NY 10956
Phone: (914) 639-1439
Fax: (914) 639-1471
E-mail: nctrc@nctrc.org
www.nctrc.org

National Federation of Licensed Practical Nurses (NFLPN)
893 US Highway 70 W
Suite 202
Garner, NC 27529
Phone: (919) 779-0046
Fax: (919) 779-5642
Toll-Free: (800) 948-2511
E-mail: jbeal@mgmt4u.com
www.nflpn.org

National League for Nursing (NLN)
61 Broadway
33rd Floor
New York, NY 10006
Phone: (212) 363-5555
Fax: (212) 812-0393
Toll-Free: (800) 669-1656
www.nln.org

National Society of Fundraising Executives (NSFRE)
1101 King Street
Suite 700
Alexandria, VA 22314
Phone: (703) 684-0410
Fax: (703) 684-0540
Toll-Free: (800) 666-FUND
E-mail: nsfre@nsfre.org
www.nsfre.org

National Student Nurses' Association (NSNA)
555 West 57th Street
Suite 1327
New York, NY 10019
Phone: (212) 581-2211
Fax: (212) 581-2368
E-mail: nsna@nsna.org
www.nsna.org

National Therapeutic Recreation Society (NTRS)
22377 Belmont Ridge Road
Ashburn, VA 20148
Phone: (703) 858-0784
Fax: (703) 858-0794
Toll-Free: (800) 626-6772
E-mail: ntrsnrpa@aol.com
www.nrpa.org/branches/ntrs.htm

Opticians Association of America (OAA)
7023 Little River Turnpike
Number 207
Annandale, VA 22003
Phone: (703) 916-8856
Fax: (703) 916-7966
Toll-Free: (800) 443-8997
E-mail: oaa@opticians.org

Preventive Cardiovascular Nurses Association (LNTF)
7611 Elmwood Avenue
Suit 202
Middleton, WI 53562
Phone: (608) 831-5683
Fax: (608) 831-5122

E-mail: Intf@tmahq.com
www.Intf.org

Public Relations Society of America (PRSA)
33 Irving Place
New York, NY 10003
Phone: (212) 995-2230
E-mail: hq@prsa.org
www.prsa.org

Society for Cardiovascular Magnetic Resonance (SCMR)
c/o Tom Sims
19 Mantua Road
Mt. Royal, NJ 08061
Phone: (856) 423-7222
Fax: (856) 423-3420
E-mail: hq@scmr.org
www.scmr.org

Society of Air Force Physician Assistants
c/o Gina Ciolino
950 North Washington Street
Alexandria, VA 22314
Fax: (703) 684-1924
Toll-Free: (888) 903-2272
E-mail: safpa@aapa.org

Society of Cardiovascular Anesthesiologists (SCA)
1910 Byrd Avenue
Number 100
PO Box 11086
Richmond, VA 23230
Phone: (804) 282-0084
Fax: (804) 282-0090
E-mail: sca@societyhq.com
www.scahq.org

Society of Cardiovascular and Interventional Radiology (SCVIR)
10201 Lee Highway
Suite 500
Fairfax, VA 22030
Phone: (703) 691-1805
Fax: (703) 691-1855
Toll-Free: (800) 488-7284

Society of Critical Care Medicine (SCCM)
8101 East Kaiser Boulevard
3rd Floor
Anaheim, CA 92808-2259
Phone: (714) 282-6000
Fax: (714) 282-6050
E-mail: romi@sccm.org
www.sccm.org

Society of Diagnostic Medical Sonographers (SDMS)
12770 Coit Road
Suite 708
Dallas, TX 75251
Phone: (972) 239-7367
Fax: (972) 239-7378
Toll-Free: (800) 229-9506
E-mail: alysdale@sdms.org

Society of Invasive Cardiovascular Professionals (SICP)
c/o HMP Communications, LLC
950 West Valley Road
Suite 2800
Wayne, PA 19087
Phone: (610) 688-8220
Fax: (610) 688-8050
Toll-Free: (800) 237-7285
E-mail: sicphelp@voicnet.com
www.sicp.com

Society of Vascular Technology (SVT)
4601 Presidents Drive
Suite 260
Lanham, MD 20706
Phone: (301) 459-7550
Fax: (301) 459-5651
E-mail: info@svtnet.org
www.svtnet.org

Technologist Section of the Society of Nuclear Medicine (TSSNM)
1850 Samuel Morse Drive
Reston, VA 20190
Phone: (703) 708-9000
Fax: (703) 708-9015
www.snm.org

APPENDIX III
BIBLIOGRAPHY

A. BOOKS

There are thousands of books written on all aspects of health care and health care careers. The books listed below are separated into general categories. The subject matter in many of the books overlaps into other categories.

These books can be found in bookstores or libraries. If your local library does not have the books you want, you might ask your librarian to order them for you through the interlibrary loan system.

This list is meant as a beginning. For other books that might interest you, look in the career section of bookstores and libraries. You can also check *Books In Print* (found in the reference section or online in libraries) for other books on the subject.

CAREER PLANNING

Field, Shelly. *The Unofficial Guide to Hot Careers.* New York: Hungry Minds, 2000.

DENTISTRY

Anderson, Pauline C., and Pendleton, Alice E. *Dental Assisting Essentials.* Albany, N.Y.: Delmar Thomson Learning, 2000.

———. *The Dental Assistant.* Albany, N.Y.: Delmar Thomson Learning, 1994.

Kendall, Bonnie. *Dental Care Careers.* Lincolnwood, Ill.: NTC/Contemporary, 2000.

———. *Opportunities in Dental Care Careers.* Lincolnwood, Ill.: NTC/Contemporary Publishing, 2000.

DIETETICS, NUTRITION, AND FOOD SERVICE

Rodenstein, Judith. *Dietetic Career Recruitment Study.* Chicago: American Dietetic Association, 1990.

Sullivan, Catherine. *Health Care Food Service Systems Management.* Gaithersburg, Md.: Aspen Publishers, 1997.

Thomas, Paul R., and Robert Earl, eds. *Opportunities in the Nutrition and Food Sciences: Research Challenges and the Next Generation of Investigators.* Washington, D.C.: National Academy Press, 1994.

GENERAL HEALTH CARE CAREERS

Badasch, Shirley. *Introduction to Health Occupations.* Stanford, Conn.: Appleton & Lange, 1993.

———. *Introduction to Health Occupations: Today's Health Care Worker.* Old Tappan, N.J.: Prentice Hall, 1999.

Damp, Dennis Vet. *Health Care Job Explosion: High Growth Health Care Careers and Job Locator.* La Crosse, Wisc.: Brookhaven Press, 2001.

HEALTH CARE ADMINISTRATION

Cutler, David M. *The Changing Hospital Industry: Comparing Not-For-Profit and For-Profit Institutions (National Bureau of Economic Research Conference Report.)* Chicago: University of Chicago Press, 2000.

Kaluzny, Arnold, ed. *Health Care Management: Organization Design and Behavior.* Albany, N.Y.: Delmar Publishers, 1999.

Kastor, John. *Mergers of Teaching Hospitals in Boston, New York, and Northern California.* Ann Arbor: University of Michigan Press, 2001.

Salluzzo, Richard F., ed. *Emergency Department Management: Principles and Applications.* St. Louis, Mo.: Mosby-Year Book, 1997.

Wachter, Robert M., ed. *Hospital Medicine.* Hagerstown, Md.: Lippincott, Williams & Wilkins, 2000.

Weiss, Roberta. *Your Career in Administrative Medical Services.* Philadelphia: W. B. Saunders Company, 1996.

HEALTH CARE MARKETING, PUBLIC RELATIONS, PLANNING, AND DEVELOPMENT

Berkowitz, Erik N. *Essentials of Health Care Marketing.* Gaithersburg, Md.: Aspen Publishers, 1996.

Coile, Russell C., Jr. *Futurescan 2001: A Millennium Forecast of Healthcare Trends 2001–2005.* Chicago: Health Administration Press, 2001.

Field, Shelly. *Career Opportunities in Advertising and Public Relations.* New York: Facts On File, 2001.

Marlowe, David. *Healthcare Marketing Plans That Work.* Chicago: Society for Healthcare Strategy and Market Development, 1999.

Mutz, John, and Katherine Murray. *Fundraising for Dummies.* Chicago: Hungry Minds, 2000.

O'Malley, John. *Healthcare Marketing, Sales, and Service: An Executive's Companion.* Chicago: Health Administration Press, 2001.

Rynne, Terrence J. *Healthcare Marketing in Transition: Practical Answers to Pressing Questions.* Burr Ridge, Ill.: Probus Professional Publishers, 1995.

Semple Piggot, Carolyn. *Business Planning for Healthcare Management.* Houston, Tex.: Open University Press, 2000.

Sherman, Clayton. *Raising Standards in American Health Care: Best People, Best Practices, Best Results.* San Franciso: Jossey-Bass, 1999.

Snook, Donald, Jr. *Hospitals: What They Are and How They Work.* Frederick, Md.: Panel Publishers, 1992.

Sturm, Arthur. *The New Rules of Healthcare Marketing: 23 Strategies for Success.* Chicago: Health Administration Press, 1998.

Williamson, Stan, ed. *Fundamentals of Strategic Planning for Healthcare Organizations.* Binghamton, N.Y.: Haworth Press, 1997.

LABORATORY PERSONNEL

Varnadoe, Lionel A. *Medical Laboratory Management and Supervision: Operations, Review and Study Guide.* Philadelphia: F. A. Davis Co., 1996.

MEDICAL ASSISTING

Badasch, Shirley A. *Comprehensive Medical Assisting.* Stanford, Conn.: Appleton & Lange, 1995.

MEDICINE

Cavens, Travis. *Being a Pediatrician.* Belmont, Calif.: Lake Publishing, 2000.

Danek, Jennifer, and Marita Danek. *Becoming a Physician: A Practical and Creative Guide to Planning a Career in Medicine.* New York: John Wiley and Sons, 1997.

Goliszek, Andrew. *The Complete Medical School Preparation and Admissions Guide.* Winston-Salem, N.C.: Healthnet Press, 2000.

Kaufman, Daniel, Amy Burnham, and Chris Dowhan. *Essays That Will Get You into Medical School.* Hauppauge, N.Y.: Barrons Educational Series, 1998.

Oransky, Ivan, and Eric Poulsen, editors. *Insiders Guide to Medical Schools: Current Students Tell You What Their Medical School Is Really Like.* Princeton, N.J.: Peterson's Guides, 1999.

Peterson's 2000 U.S. and Canadian Medical Schools: A Comprehensive Guide to All 159 Accredited Medical Schools. Princeton, N.J.: Peterson's, 1999.

MEDICAL RECORDS AND HEALTH INFORMATION

Avila-Weil, Donna, and Mary Glaccum. *The Independent Medical Transcriptionist.* Windsor, Calif.: Rayve Productions, 1998.

Kinn, Mary E., and Maryann Woods. *The Medical Assistant: Administrative and Clinical.* Philadelphia: W.B. Saunders Co., 1999.

McMiller, Kathryn. *Being a Medical Records Clerk.* Old Tappan, N.J.: Prentice Hall, 1999.

Morrow, Norma Lee. *Being a Medical Transcriptionist.* Old Tappan, N.J.: Prentice Hall, 1991.

Rhodes, Sharon B., editor. *Dorland's Radiology Word Book for Medical Transcriptionists.* Philadelphia: Saunders Co., 2000.

NURSING

Bozell, Jeanna. *Anatomy of a Job Search—A Nurse's Guide to Finding and Landing the Job You Want.* Los Angeles: Springhouse Publishing Company, 1999.

Hannah, Kathryn J. *The Internet for Nurses and Allied Health Professionals.* New York: Springer-Verlag, 1997.

Katz, Janet R., and Carol Carter. *Majoring in Nursing: From Prerequisites to Postgraduate Study and Beyond.* New York: Noonday Press, 1999.

Vallano, Annette. *Kaplan Careers in Nursing: Manage Your Future in the Changing World of Healthcare.* Chicago: Kaplan, 1999.

NURSING ASSISTANTS

Badasch, Shirley. *Essentials for the Nursing Assistant in Long Term Care.* Albany, N.Y.: Delmar Thomson Learning, 1994.

PARAMEDICS, EMERGENCY MEDICAL TECHNICIANS

Kacen, Alex, and Terence J. Sacks. *Opportunities in Paramedical Careers.* Chicago: VGM Career Horizons, 2000.

Westfal, Richard, and John Filangeri. *EMT-Paramedic (P) PreTest Self Assessment and Review.* New York: McGraw-Hill Professional Publishing, 2000.

PHARMACOLOGY

VGM Career Horizons Staff. *VGM's Handbook of Health Care Careers.* Lincolnwood, Ill.: NTC/Contemporary Publishing Company, 1998.

Woodrow, Ruth. *Essentials of Pharmacology for Health Occupations.* 4th ed. Albany, N.Y.: Delmar Publishers, 2001.

Zubie, Metcalf. *Allied Health Professions Career Planning Guide.* Potomac, Md.: Betz Publishing Company, 1998.

PHYSICIAN ASSISTANTS

Hooker, Roderick S., and Cawley James. *Physician Assistants in American Medicine.* London: Churchill Livingstone, 1997.

Rodican, Andrew J. *Getting into the PA School of Your Choice.* New York: McGraw-Hill Professional Publishing, 1998.

Sacks, Terence J. *Opportunities in Physician Assistant Careers.* Lincolnwood, Ill.: McGraw Hill-NTC, 1994.

RADIOLOGY AND BIOTECHNOLOGY

Anderson, Anthony, editor. *The Radiology Technologist's Handbook to Surgical Procedures.* Boca Raton, Fla.: CRC Press, 1999.

Escamilla, Belinda, Lisa Ramfjord Elstun, and David W. Chang. *The Multiskilled Radiologic Technologist: A Competency-Based Approach.* Old Tappan, N.J.: Prentice Hall, 2001.

Rudman, Jack. *EKG Technician.* Lincolnwood, Ill.: National Learning Corporaton, 1997.

Selman, Joseph. *The Fundamentals of Imaging Physics and Radiobiology: For the Radiologic Technologist.* Springfield, Ill.: Charles C. Thomas, 2000.

Weiss, Roberta C. *The EKG Technician.* Old Tappan, N.J.: Prentice Hall, 1990.

———. *Your Career In Cardiovascular Technology.* Philadelphia: W. B. Saunders, 1996.

B. PERIODICALS

Magazines, newspapers, membership bulletins, and newsletters may be helpful for finding information about a specific job category, finding a job in a specific field, or giving you insight into what certain jobs entail.

As with the books in the previous section, this list should serve as a beginning. There are many periodicals that are not listed because of space limitations. The subject matter of some periodicals may overlap with others. Periodicals also tend to come and go. Look in your local library or in the newspaper/magazine shop for other periodicals that might interest you.

ADVERTISING

Advertising Age
Crain Communications, Inc. Chicago
740 Rush Street
Chicago, IL 60611
Subscription Address:
965 East Jefferson Avenue
Detroit, MI 48207
Phone: (312) 649-5417
Fax: (312) 280-3174
www.adage.com

Advertising Age's Creativity
Crain Communications, Inc. New York
220 East 42nd Street
New York, NY 10017
Subscription Address:
965 East Jefferson Avenue
Detroit, MI 48207
Phone: (212) 210-0100
Fax: (212) 210-0111

Journal of Advertising Research
641 Lexington Avenue
New York, NY 10022
Phone: (212) 751-5656
Fax: (212) 319-5265
www.arfsite.org/publish.html

ART THERAPY

American Journal of Art Therapy
Vermont College of Norwich University
Montpelier, VT 05602
Phone: (802) 828-8540
Fax: (802) 828-8585

AUDIOLOGY

Journal of the American Academy of Audiology
B. C. Decker Inc.
4 Hughson Street S
PO Box 620, LCDI
Hamilton, ON, Canada L8N 3K7
Phone: (905) 522-7017 or (800) 568-7281
Fax: (905) 522-7839
E-mail: info@bcdecker.com

CHIROPRACTORS

Sports Chiropractic and Rehabilitation
Lippincott, Williams & Wilkins
530 Walnut Street
Philadelphia, PA 19106
Phone: (215) 521-8300
Fax: (215) 521-8902
E-mail: Iww@Iww.com

CONSULTING

Consultants News
Kennedy Information
One Kennedy Place
Route 12 South
Fitzwilliam, NH 03447
Phone: (603) 585-6544
Fax: (603) 585-9555

COUNSELING/MENTAL HEALTH

Drug Abuse Update
National Families in Action
2957 Clairmont Road
Suite 150
Atlanta, GA 30329
Phone: (404) 248-9676
Fax: (404) 248-1312
E-mail: nfia@nationalfamilies.org, pkemp@mindspring.com
www.emory.edu/NFIA

Journal of Addiction and Mental Health
Addiction Research Foundation
33 Russell Street
Toronto, ON, Canada M5S 2S1
Phone: (416) 595-6059 or (800) 661-1111

Fax: (416) 593-4694
E-mail: MKTG@ARF.ORG

Journal of Mental Health and Aging
Springer Publishing Co.
c/o Donna Cohen, Ph.D., Editor
University of South Florida
Department of Aging and Mental Health
13301 Bruce B. Downs Boulevard
Tampa, FL 33612
Phone: (813) 974-4665 or
    (888) 822-4464
Fax: (813) 974-1968
E-mail: contactus@springerjournals.com

World Federation for Mental Health
    Annual Report
World Federation for Mental Health
Sheppard and Enoch Pratt Hospital
Box 6815
Baltimore, MD 21285
Phone: (410) 938-3180
Fax: (410) 938-3183
E-mail: wfmh@erols.com

DANCE THERAPY

American Journal of Dance Therapy
American Dance Therapy Association
2000 Century Plaza
Suite 108
10632 Little Patuxent Parkway
Columbia, MD 21044
Phone: (410) 997-4040
Fax: (410) 997-4048
E-mail: info@adta.org

DENTISTRY

Journal of the American College
    of Dentists
American College of Dentists
4403 Marlborough Avenue
San Diego, CA 92116
Phone: (619) 283-2203
Fax: (619) 283-2203

Oral Health
Southam Inc.
1450 Don Mills Road
Toronto, ON, Canada M3B 2X7
Phone: (416) 442-2052 or (800) 668-2374
Fax: (416) 442-2122

DIET AND NUTRITION

Health Diet and Nutrition
Publishing and Business Consultants
4427 West Slauson Avenue
Los Angeles, CA 90043-2717

International Journal of Sport Nutrition
    and Exercise Metabolism
Human Kinetics Publishers, Inc.
1607 North Market Street
PO Box 5076
Champaign, IL 61825-5076
Phone: (217) 351-5076 or (800) 747-4457
Fax: (217) 351-2674
E-mail: orders@hk.com

FUND-RAISING

Chronicle of Philanthropy
1255 23rd Street NW
Suite 700
Washington, DC 20037
Phone: (202) 466-1200
Fax: (202) 466-2078

Currents
Council for Advancement and Support of
Education (CASE)
1307 New York Avenue, NW
Suite 1000
Washington, DC 20005
Phone: (202) 328-5900 or (800) 554-8536
Fax: (202) 387-4973
E-mail: books@case.org

GERIATRICS

Journal of Aging and Ethnicity
Springer Publishing Co.
c/o Donald E. Gelfand, Ph. D., Editor
Department of Sociology
2228 F/AB
Wayne State University
Detroit, MI 48202
Phone: (313) 577-0774
Fax: (313) 577-2735
E-mail: contactus@springerjournals.com

Geriatric Nursing
Mosby, Inc.
11830 Westline Industrial Drive
St. Louis, MO 63146
Phone: (314) 872-8370 or (800) 325-4177
Fax: (314) 432-1380
E-mail: customer.support@mosby.com

Topics in Geriatric Rehabilitation
Aspen Publishers, Inc.
200 Orchard Ridge Drive
Gaithersburg, MD 20878
Phone: (301) 417-7500 or (800) 638-8437
Fax: (301) 417-7550
E-mail: customer.service@aspenpubl.com

GRANTS

Foundation Grants Index
Foundation Center
79 Fifth Avenue
New York, NY 10003
Phone: (212) 807-3690
Fax: (212) 807-3677
http://fdncenter.org

HEALTH CARE ADMINISTRATION

Health Care Management Review
Aspen Publishers, Inc.
200 Orchard Ridge Drive Number 200
Gaithersburg, MD 20878
Phone: (301) 417-7500 or (800) 638-8437
Fax: (301) 417-7650
E-mail: customer.service@aspenpubl.com

HMOs

Managed Healthcare
Advanstar Communications
7500 Old Oak Boulevard
Cleveland, OH 44130

LABORATORIES

Advance for Medical Laboratory
    Professionals
Merion Publications Inc.
2900 Horizon Drive
King of Prussia, PA 19406
Phone: (610) 278-1400 or
    (800) 355-5627
Fax: (610) 278-1425
E-mail: advance@merion.com
www.advanceweb.com

MARKETING

Direct Marketing
Hoke Communications
224 Seventh Street
Garden City, NY 11530
Phone: (516) 746-6700
Fax: (516) 294-8141

Health Marketing Quarterly
The Haworth Press, Inc.
10 Alice Street
Binghomton, NY 13904-1580
Phone: (800) 429-6784
E-mail: getinfo@haworthpressinc.com

Journal of Hospital Marketing
The Haworth Press, Inc.
10 Alice Street
Binghamton, NY 13904-1580
Phone: (800) 429-6784
E-mail: getinfo@haworthpressinc.com

Journal of Marketing
American Marketing Association
250 South Wacker Drive
Chicago, IL 60606
Phone: (312) 648-0536
Fax: (312) 993-7542
Subscription Address: Allen Press, Inc.
Box 1897
Lawrence, KS 66044
E-mail: subs@ama.org;
    orders@allenpress.com
http://www.ama.org/pubs/jminfo/index.html

Journal of Marketing Research
American Marketing Association
250 South Wacker Drive
Chicago, IL 60606
Phone: (312) 648-0536
Fax: (312) 993-7542
www.ama.org/pubs/jmr/index.html

Marketing News
American Marketing Association
311 South Wacker Drive
Suite 5800
Chicago, IL 60606
Phone: (312) 542-9000 or (800) 262-1150
Fax: (312) 542-9001
E-mail: info@ama.org, 458-1615@
    mcimail.com

Marketing Research
American Marketing Association
311 South Wacker Drive
Suite 5800
Chicago, IL 60606-2266
Phone: (312) 542-9000 or (800) 262-1150
Fax: (312) 542-9001
E-mail: info@ama.org

Medical Marketing and Media
CPS Communications, Inc.
7200 West Camino Real
Suite 215
Boca Raton, FL 33433
Phone: (561) 368-9301
Fax: (561) 368-7870
E-mail: webmaster@cpsnet.com

MEDICAL ADVERTISING

Med Ad News
Engel Publishing Partners
820 Bear Tavern Road
Suite 300
West Trenton, NJ 08628
Phone: (609) 530-0044
Fax: (609) 530-0207
E-mail: mwalsh@engelpub.com

Medical Advertising
Engel Publishing Partners
820 Bear Tavern Road
Suite 300
West Trenton, NJ 08628
Phone: (609) 530-0044
Fax: (609) 530-0207

NURSING

AANA Journal
AANA Publishing, Inc.
222 South Prospect Avenue
Park Ridge, IL 60068
Phone: (847) 692-7050
Fax: (847) 692-6968

American Journal of Critical Care
American Association of Critical Care
Nurses (AACN)
101 Columbia
Aliso Viejo, CA 92656
Phone: (949) 362-2000 or
    (800) 809-2273
Fax: (949) 362-2049
E-mail: aacninfo@aacn.org

Clinical Nurse Specialist
Lippincott, Williams & Wilkins
17128 Colima Road
Suite 544
Hacienda Heights, CA 91745
Phone: (626) 964-8465
Fax: (626) 913-8667
E-mail: lww@lww.com

Critical Care Nurse
101 Columbia
Aliso Viejo, CA 92656
Phone: (949) 362-2000 or (800) 899-1712
Fax: (949) 362-2049
E-mail: cntnurse@aol.com

Clinical Nurse Specialist
Lippincott, Williams & Wilkins
17128 Colima Road
Suite 544
Hacienda Heights, CA 91745
Phone: (626) 964-8465
Fax: (626) 913-8667
E-mail: lww@lww.com

Journal of Emergency Nursing
Mosby, Inc.
11830 Westline Industrial Drive
St. Louis, MO 63146
Phone: (314) 872-8370 or (800) 325-4177
Fax: (314) 432-1380
E-mail: customer.support@mosby.com

Journal of Gerontological Nursing
SLACK, Inc.
6900 Grove Rd.
Thorofare, NJ 08086
Phone: (856) 848-1000 or (800) 257-8290
Fax: (856) 853-5991
E-mail: slackinc@slackinc.com,
    jgn@slackinc.com

Journal of Nursing Administration
Lippincott, Williams & Wilkins
530 Walnut Street
Philadelphia, PA 19106
Phone: (215) 521-8300
Fax: (215) 521-8902
E-mail: lww@lww.com

Journal of Nursing Care Quality
Aspen Publishers, Inc.
200 Orchard Ridge Drive
Suite 200
Gaithersburg, MD 20878
Phone: (301) 417-7500
Fax: (301) 417-7550
E-mail: customer.service@aspenpubl.com

Nursing and Health Care Perspectives
National League for Nursing
61 Broadway
33rd Floor
New York, NY 10006
Phone: (212) 812-0383 or
(800) 669-1656
Fax: (212) 812-0393

OCCUPATIONAL THERAPY

*Occupational Therapy in Mental
    Health*
The Haworth Press, Inc.
10 Alice Street
Binghamton, NY 13904-1580
Phone: (607) 722-5857 or
    (800) 429-6784
Fax: (607) 722-6362
E-mail: getinfo@haworthpressinc.com

PHARMACY

*American Journal of Pharmaceutical
    Education*
American Association of Colleges of
Pharmacy
UNC School of Pharmacy
Chapel Hill, NC 27599-7360
Phone: (919) 962-0098
Fax: (919) 966-6919

Consultant Pharmacist
American Society of Consultant
  Pharmacists
1321 Duke Street
4th Floor
Alexandria, VA 22314
Phone: (703) 739-1300 or (800) 355-2727
Fax: (703) 739-1321

*Journal of the American
  Pharmaceutical Association*
American Pharmaceutical Association
2215 Constitution Avenue, NW
Washington, DC 20037
Phone: (202) 429-7557 or (800) 237-2742
Fax: (202) 628-5425
E-mail: japha@mail.aphanet.org

*Pharmacy Practice Management
  Quarterly*
Aspen Publishers, Inc.
200 Orchard Ridge Drive
Number 200
Gaithersburg, MD 20878
Phone: (301) 417-7500 or (800) 638-8437
Fax: (301) 417-7650

PHYSICAL THERAPY

*Advance for Physical Therapists and PT
  Assistants*
Merion Publications Inc.
2900 Horizon Drive
King of Prussia, PA 19406
Phone: (610) 278-1400 or (800) 355-5627
Fax: (610) 278-1425
E-mail: advance@merion.com

Physical Therapy
American Physical Therapy Association
1111 North Fairfax Street
Alexandria, VA 22314
Phone: (703) 684-2782 or (800) 999-2782
Fax: (703) 703-3169
E-mail: ptjourn@apta.org

Physical Therapy Case Reports
Lippincott, Williams & Wilkins
530 Walnut Street
Philadelphia, PA 19106
Phone: (215) 521-8300
Fax: (215) 521-8902
E-mail: lww@lww.com

Physical Therapy Products
Novicom, Inc.
4676 Admiralty Way
Suite 202
Marina del Rey, CA 90292
Phone: (310) 306-2206
Fax: (310) 306-5091

PT, Magazine of Physical Therapy
American Physical Therapy Association
1111 North Fairfax Street
Alexandria, VA 22314
Phone: (703) 684-2782 or (800) 999-2782
Fax: (703) 703-3169

PREVENTIVE MEDICINE

*American Journal of Preventive
  Medicine*
Elsevier Science Inc.
655 Avenue of the Americas
New York, NY 10010
Phone: (212) 989-5800 or (888) 437-4636
Fax: 212-633-3990
E-mail: usinfo@elsevier.com

PUBLIC RELATIONS
Public Relations Quarterly
Howard Penn Hudson Associates, Inc.
PO Box 311
Rhinebeck, NY 12572
Phone: (914) 876-2081 or
          (800) 572-3451
Fax: (914) 876-2561
E-mail: hphudson@aol.com

Public Relations Review
38091 Beach Road
PO Box 180
Coltons Point, MD 20626
Phone: (301) 769-3899
E-mail: 102062-2525@compuserve.com

Public Relations Strategist
33 Irving Place
New York, NY 10003
Phone: (212) 460-0360
Fax: (212) 995-0757

RADIOLOGY

*Advance for Radiologic Science
  Professionals*
Merion Publications Inc.
2900 Horizon Drive
King of Prussia, PA 19406
Phone: (610) 278-1400 or
          (800) 355-5627
Fax: (610) 278-1425
E-mail: advance@merion.com

RESPIRATORY CARE

*Advance for Respiratory Care
  Practitioners*
Merion Publications Inc.
2900 Horizon Drive
King of Prussia, PA 19406

Phone: (610) 278-1400 or (800) 355-5627
Fax: (610) 278-1425
E-mail: advance@merion.com

*Journal of Nuclear Medicine
  Technology*
Society of Nuclear Medicine, Inc.
1850 Samuel Morse Drive
Reston, VA 20190-5316
Phone: (703) 708-9000
Fax: (703) 708-9018

SOCIAL SERVICES

Clinical Supervisor
The Haworth Press, Inc.
10 Alice Street
Binghamton, NY 13904
Phone: (607) 722-5857 or (800) 429-6784
Fax: (607) 722-6362
E-mail: getinfo@haworthpressinc.com

Health and Social Work
National Association of Social Workers
750 1st Street, NE
Suite 700
Washington, DC 20002
Phone: (202) 408-8600
Fax: (202) 336-8312
E-mail: press@naswdc.org

New Social Worker
White Hat Communications
PO Box 5390
Harrisburg, PA 17110
Phone: (717) 238-3787
Fax: (717) 238-2090

Social Work with Groups
The Haworth Press, Inc.
10 Alice Street
Binghamton, NY 13904
Phone: (607) 722-5857 or (800) 429-6784
Fax: (607) 722-6362
E-mail: getinfo@haworthpressinc.com

VISION CARE

*Journal of Optometric Vision
  Development*
College of Optometrists in Vision
Development
243 North Lindbergh Boulevard
Suite 310
St. Louis, MO 63141
Phone: (314) 991-4007 or
          (888) 268-3770
Fax: (314) 991-1167

APPENDIX IV
GLOSSARY

The following is a list of abbreviations and terms that will prove helpful to individuals interested in the health care industry.

AA	Associate's degree
AACC	American Association for Clinical Chemistry
AACP	American Association of Colleges of Pharmacy
AAHA	American Association of Homes for the Aging
AAMA	American Association of Medical Assistants
AAMI	Association for the Advancement of Medical Instrumentation
AAMT	American Association for Music Therapy
AAMT	American Association of Medical Transcription
AANP	American Academy of Nurse Practitioners
AAOP	American Academy of Orthotists and Prosthetists
AAPA	American Academy of Physician Assistants
AAPT	American Association of Pharmacy Technicians, Inc.
AARC	American Association for Respiratory Care
AATA	American Art Therapy Association
ABHES	Accrediting Bureau of Health Education Schools
ABRET	American Board of Registration for Electroencephalographic Technologists
ACHA	American College of Healthcare Administrators
ACHE	American College of Healthcare Executives
ACLS	Advanced Cardiac Life Support
ACNM	American College of Nurse Midwives
ACPE	American Council on Pharmaceutical Education
ADA	American Dental Association
ADA	American Dietetic Association
ADAA	American Dental Assistant's Association
ADHA	American Dental Hygienists' Association
ADN	Associate's Degree in Nursing
ADTA	American Dance Therapy Association
ADTR	Academy of Dance Therapist Registered
AFSCME	American Federation of State, County and Municipal Employees
AGA	American Geriatrics Society
AGHE	Association for Gerontology in Higher Education
AHA	American Hospital Association
AHCA	American Health Care Association
AHPR	Academy of Hospital Public Relations
AMA	American Marketing Association
AMA	American Medical Association
AMI	Association of Medical Illustrators
AMRA	American Medical Records Association
AMT	American Medical Technologists
ANA	American Nurses' Association
AOTA	American Occupational Therapy Association
APAP	Association of Physician Assistant Programs
APTA	American Physical Therapy Association
ARDMS	American Registry of Diagnostic Medical Sonographers
ARRT	American Registry of Radiologic Technologists
ART	Accredited Records Technician
ASCP	American Society for Cardiovascular Professionals
ASCP	American Society of Clinical Pathologists
ASET	American Society of Electroneurodiagnostic Technologists
ASHP	American Society of Hospital Pharmacists
ASHPR	American Society for Hospital Public Relations
ASLHA	American Speech-Language-Hearing Association
ASMT	American Society for Medical Technologists
ASRT	American Society of Radiologic Technologists
AST	Association of Surgical Technologists
ATLS	Advanced Trauma Life Support
ATRA	American Therapeutic Recreation Association
AUPHA	Association of University Programs in Health Administration
BA	Bachelor of Arts Degree
BS	Bachelor of Science Degree
BSW	Bachelor's of Social Work
CAHEA	Committee on Allied Health Education and Accreditation
Calendar listing	Dated listings sent to the media by publicists regarding upcoming events and programs. They are designed to bring the events to the attention of the public, as well as news editors and others.
CASE	Council for the Advancement and Support of Education
CCC	Certificate of Clinical Competence
CCINBCT	Cardiovascular Credentialling International and National Board of Cardiovascular Testing
CCRN	Critical Care Registered Nurse
CCU	Coronary Care Unit or Critical Care Unit
CDA	Commission on Dental Accreditation
Circulation	The number of copies of a newspaper or magazine that are distributed.
CST	Certified Surgical Technologist
CSWE	Council on Social Work Education
DANB	Dental Assisting National Board, Inc.
Dateline	Information provided at the beginning of a news release indicating the specific town, city, etc. where the press or news release originated. In some instances the date may also be included.
DMMA	Direct Mail/Marketing Association, Inc.
DRG	Diagnostic Related Group

DTR	Dance Therapist Registered
E-Commerce	Electronic commerce
Electronic commerce	Buying and selling merchandise or services through the Internet
EMS	Emergency Medical Service
EMT	Emergency Medical Technician
EMT-A	Emergency Medical Technician-Ambulance
EMT-I	Emergency Medical Technician-Intermediate
EMT-P	Emergency Medical Technician-Paramedic
ER	Emergency Room
FHHC	Foundation for Hospice and Home Care
Five Ws	The "who, what, when, where, and why" on which publicists, those in public relations, reporters base their news stories and press releases.
FNP	Family Nurse Practitioner
HHA	Home Health Aide
HMO	Health Maintenance Organization
Home page	Main page of a website.
ICU	Intensive Care Unit
IPRA	International Public Relations Association
JCAH	Joint Commission on the Accreditation of Healthcare Organizations
Jingle	A musical tune in a commercial.
Lead	The opening lines of a news release or feature designed to attract reader interest.
Local	The local in a union is the local affiliation in a particular geographic area of a national or international union; may also refer to a local television or radio station in relation to a national station.
L.P.N	Licensed Practical Nurse
LTC	Long-Term Care
LVN	Licensed Vocational Nurse
MA	Master's of Arts Degree
M.D.	Medical Doctor
MGMA	Medical Group Management Association
MSW	Master's of Social Work
MT	Medical Technologist
NAADAC	National Association of Alcoholism and Drug Abuse Counselors
NAAP	National Association of Activities Professionals
NABP	National Association of Boards of Pharmacy
NACCMHC	National Academy of Certified Clinical Mental Health Counselors
NAEMT	National Association of Emergency Medical Technicians
NAHD	National Association of Hospital Development
NAHST	National Association of Human Services Technologists
NAMT	National Association for Music Therapy, Inc.
NAO	National Academy of Opticianry
NAPGCM	National Association of Private Geriatric Care Managers
NASATE	National Association of Substance Abuse Trainers and Educators
NASW	National Association of Social Workers
NBCC	National Board for Certified Counselors
NCCPA	National Commission on Certification of Physician Assistants, Inc.
NCTRC	National Council for Therapeutic Recreation Certification
Net	The Internet
NFLPN	National Federation of Licensed Practical Nurses, Inc.
NLN	National League for Nursing
NNSWM	National Network for Social Work Managers, Inc.
NSFRE	National Society of Fund Raising Executives
NSNA	National Student Nurses' Association
NTRS	National Therapeutic Recreation Society
OAA	Opticians Association of America
O.D.	Osteopathic Doctor
Online	Connected to the Internet
PA	Physician's Assistant
PC	Primary Care
Photo caption	The story line accompanying a photograph, identifying the people in the photo and/or telling the story about the photo.
Photo cropping	Trimming a photograph (manually or by electronic means) to reduce unnecessary and distracting elements; used to make a photo visually suitable to accompany a related story.
PRSA	Public Relations Society of America
Publicity peg	An interesting piece of information designed to grab the attention of a news editor.
RD	Registered Dietician
R.N.	Registered Nurse
RRT	Registered Respiratory Therapist
SDMS	Society of Diagnostic Medical Sonographers
Search the Net	Look for information on the Internet
SEIU	Service Employees International Union
Site	Website
SNMT	Society of Nuclear Medicine Technologists
Surf the Net	Going online to visit various sites on the Internet
Surgi-center	Medical office or clinic where minor outpatient surgeries are performed.
SVT	Society of Vascular Technology
Tearsheet	Copy of an advertisement from a newspaper or magazine; most companies will not pay for ads without a tearsheet.
Trades	Newspapers and magazines that are geared to a specific industry.
Union card	A card that is used to identify members of specific unions.
Urgi-center	Medical office or clinic where immediate medical care is dispensed.
Web	The World Wide Web
Website	A "place" on the World Wide Web
WWW	World Wide Web

INDEX

ABOUT THE AUTHOR

Shelly Field is a nationally recognized motivational speaker, career expert, stress specialist, and author of more than 25 best-selling books in the business and career fields.

Her books instruct people on how to obtain jobs in a wide array of areas including the hospitality, music, sports and communications industries, casinos and casino hotels, advertising, public relations, theater, the performing arts, entertainment, animal rights, health care, writing and art; and choosing the best career for the new century.

She is a frequent guest on local, regional, and national radio, cable, and television talk, information, and news shows and also does numerous print interviews and personal appearances.

Field is a featured speaker at conventions, expos, casinos, corporate functions, employee training and development sessions, career fairs, spouse programs, and events nationwide. She speaks on empowerment, motivation, careers, gaming, and human resources; attracting, retaining, and motivating employees; customer service; and stress reduction. Her popular seminars, "STRESS BUSTERS: Beating The Stress in Your Work and Your Life" and "The De-Stress Express" are favorites around the country.

President and CEO of The Shelly Field Organization, a public relations and management firm handling national clients, she also does corporate consulting and has represented celebrities in the sports, music, and entertainment industries as well as authors, businesses, and corporations.

For information about personal appearances or seminars contact The Shelly Field Organization at P.O. Box 711, Monticello, NY 12701, or log on to www.shellyfield.com.